The Beatitudes

The Beatitudes

An exposition of Matthew 5 : 1 – 12

THOMAS WATSON

THE BANNER OF TRUTH TRUST

THE BANNER OF TRUTH TRUST
3 Murrayfield Road, Edinburgh, EH12 6EL
P.O. Box 621, Carlisle, Pennsylvania 17013, USA

★

First published 1660
This edition revised in layout and
published by the Banner of Truth Trust 1971

Reprinted 1975
Reprinted 1980

★

ISBN 0 85151 035 3

★

Printed in Great Britain by
Hazell Watson & Viney Ltd,
Aylesbury, Bucks

To the Reader

Christian Reader,

I here present you with a subject full of sweet variety. This Sermon of Christ on the Mount is a piece of spiritual needlework, wrought about with divers colours; here is both usefulness and sweetness. In this portion of Holy Scripture you have a breviary of religion, the Bible epitomized. Here is a garden of delight, set with curious knots, where you may pluck those flowers which will deck the hidden man of your heart. Here is the golden key which will open the gate of Paradise. Here is the conduit of the Gospel, running wine to cherish such as are poor in spirit and pure in heart. Here is the rich cabinet wherein the Pearl of Blessedness is locked up. Here is the golden pot in which is that manna which will feed and refocillate (revive) the soul unto everlasting life. Here is a way chalked out to the Holy of Holies.

Reader, how happy were it if, while others take up their time and thoughts about secular things which perish in the using, you could mind eternity and be guided by this Scripture-clue which leads you to the Beatific Vision. If, after God has set life before you, you indulge your sensual appetite and still court your lusts, how inexcusable will be your neglect and how inexpressible your misery!

The Lord grant that while you have an opportunity, and the wind serves you, you may not lie idle at anchor, and when it is too late begin to hoist up sails for Heaven. Oh now, Christian, let your loins be girt, and your lamps burning, that when the Lord Jesus, your blessed Bridegroom, shall knock, you may be ready to go in with Him to the marriage-supper, which shall be the prayer of him who is

Yours in all true affection and devotion,

THOMAS WATSON

Contents

Contents

Contents

1 *Introduction*

And seeing the multitudes, he went up into a mountain: and when he was set, his disciples came unto him. And he opened his mouth, and taught them.

MATTHEW 5:1, 2

The blessed evangelist St Matthew, the penman of this sacred history, was at first by profession a publican or gatherer of toll; and Christ, having called him from the custom-house, made him a gatherer of souls. This holy man in the first chapter sets down Christ's birth and genealogy. In the second, his dignity – a star ushers in the wise men to him, and as a king he is presented with gold and frankincense and myrrh (*vv* 9–11). In the third chapter the evangelist records his baptism; in the fourth, his temptations; in the fifth, his preaching, which chapter is like a rich mine. Every vein has some gold in it.

There are four things in this chapter which offer themselves to our view,

1 The Preacher
2 The Pulpit
3 The Occasion
4 The Sermon

The preacher : Christ and his qualifications

1 The Preacher. *Jesus Christ.* The best of preachers. 'He went up.' He in whom there was a combination of virtues, a constellation of beauties. He whose lips were not only sweet as the honey-comb, but did drop as the honey-comb. His words, an oracle; his works, a miracle; his life, a pattern; his death, a sacrifice. 'He went up into a mountain and taught.' Jesus Christ was every way ennobled and qualified for the work of the ministry.

(i) Christ was an *intelligent* preacher. He had 'the Spirit without measure' (John 3:34) and knew how to speak a word in due season, when to humble, when to comfort. We cannot know all the faces of our hearers. Christ knew the hearts of his hearers. He understood what

[13]

doctrine would best suit them, as the husbandman can tell what sort of grain is proper for such-and-such a soil.

(ii) Christ was a *powerful* preacher. 'He spake with authority' (Matthew 7:29). He could set men's sins before them and show them their very hearts. 'Come, see a man which told me all things that ever I did' (John 4:29). That is the best glass, not which is most richly set with pearl, but which shows the truest face. Christ was a preacher to the conscience. He breathed as much zeal as eloquence. He often touched upon the heart-strings. What is said of Luther is more truly applicable to Christ. He spake 'as if he had been within a man'. He could drive the wedge of his doctrine in the most knotty piece. He was able with his two-edged sword to pierce an heart of stone. 'Never man spake like this man' (John 7:46).

(iii) Christ was a *successful* preacher. He had the art of converting souls. 'Many believed on him.' (John 10:42), yea, persons of rank and quality. 'Among the chief rulers many believed' (John 12:42). He who had 'grace poured into his lips' (Psalm 45:2), could pour grace into his hearers' hearts. He had the key of David in his hand, and when he pleased did open the hearts of men, and make way both for himself and his doctrine to enter. If he did blow the trumpet his very enemies would come under his banner. Upon his summons none dare but surrender.

(iv) Christ was a *lawful* preacher. As he had his unction from his Father, so his mission. 'The Father that sent me bears witness of me' (John 8:18). Christ, in whom were all perfections concentred, yet would be solemnly sealed and inaugurated into his ministerial as well as mediatory office. If Jesus Christ would not enter upon the work of the ministry without a commission, how absurdly impudent are they who without any warrant dare invade this holy function! There must be a lawful admission of men into the ministry. 'No man taketh this honour to himself, but he that is called of God, as was Aaron' (Hebrews 5:4). Our Lord Christ, as he gave apostles and prophets who were extraordinary ministers, so pastors and teachers who were initiated and made in an ordinary way (Ephesians 4:11); and he will have a ministry perpetuated; 'Lo I am with you alway, even unto the end of the world' (Matthew 28:20). Sure, there is as much need of ordination now as in Christ's time and in the time of the apostles, there being then extraordinary gifts in the church which are now ceased.

The ministry does not 'lie in common'

But why should not the ministry lie in common? 'Hath the Lord spoken only by Moses?' (Numbers 12:2). Why should not one preach as well as another? I answer – Because God (who is the God of order) has made the work of the ministry a select, distinct office from any other. As in the body natural the members have a distinct office, the eye is to see, the hand to work; you may as well say, why should not the hand see as well as the eye? Because God has made the distinction. He has put the seeing faculty into the one and not the other. So here, God has made a distinction between the work of the ministry and other work.

Where is this distinction? We find in Scripture a distinction between pastor and people. 'The elders (or ministers) I exhort . . . Feed the flock of God which is among you' (1 Peter 5:2). If anyone may preach, by the same rule all may, and then what will become of the apostle's distinction? Where will the flock of God be if all be pastors?

God has cut out the minister his work which is proper for him and does not belong to any other. 'Give attendance to reading, to exhortation, to doctrine . . . give thyself wholly to them', or, as it is in the Greek, 'Be thou wholly in them' (1 Timothy 4, 13–15). This charge is peculiar to the minister and does not concern any other. It is not spoken to the tradesman that he should give himself wholly to doctrine and exhortation. No, let him look to his shop. It is not spoken to the ploughman that he should give himself wholly to preaching. No, let him give himself to his plough. It is the minister's charge. The apostle speaks to Timothy and, in him, to the rest who had the hands of the presbytery laid on them. And 'Study to shew thyself approved . . ., a workman that needeth not to be ashamed, rightly dividing the word of truth' (2 Timothy 2:15). This is spoken peculiarly to the minister. Everyone that can read the word aright cannot divide the word aright. So that the work of the ministry does not lie in common; it is a select, peculiar work. As none might touch the ark but the priests, none may touch this temple-office but such as are called to it.

But if a man has gifts, is not this sufficient? I answer, No! As grace is not sufficient to make a minister, so neither are gifts. The Scripture puts a difference between gifting and sending. 'How shall they preach unless they be sent?' (Romans 10:15). If gifts were enough to constitute a minister, the apostle should have said, 'How shall they preach unless they be gifted?' but he says 'unless they be sent?' As in other callings, gifts do not make a magistrate. The attorney that pleads at the bar may have as good gifts as the judge that sits upon the bench, but he must have a commission before he sit as judge. If it be thus in matters civil, much more in ecclesiastical and sacred, which are, as Bucer [1] says, 'things of the highest importance'. Those therefore that usurp the ministerial work without any special designation and appointment discover more pride than zeal. They act out of their sphere and are guilty of theft. They steal upon a people, and, as they come without a call, so they stay without a blessing. 'I sent them not, therefore they shall not profit this people at all' (Jeremiah 23:32). And so much for the first, the preacher.

The pulpit

2 *The pulpit* where Christ preached. 'He went up into a mountain.'

The law was first given on the mount, and here Christ expounds it on the mount. This mount, as is supposed by Jerome [2] and others of the learned, was Mount Tabor. It was a convenient place to speak in, being seated above the people, and in regard of the great confluence of hearers.

3 *The Occasion* of Christ's ascending the mount: 'Seeing the multitude.'

The occasion

The people thronged to hear Christ, and he would not dismiss the congregation without a sermon, but 'seeing the multitude he went up'. Jesus Christ came from heaven as a factor [3] for souls. He lay leiger [4] here awhile; preaching was his business. The people could not be so desirous to hear as he was to preach. He who treated faint bodies with compassion (Matthew 15:32), much more pitied dead souls. It was his 'meat and drink' to do his Father's will (John 4:34). 'And seeing the multitude', he goes up into the mount and preaches. This he did not only for the consolation of his hearers, but for the imitation of his ministers.

[1] German theologian of the Reformation Period (d. 1551).
[2] One of the greatest scholars of the early Christian church (d. A.D. 420).
[3] Commissioned (by the Father) to perform a work.
[4] To take up residence (as an ambassador 'lies leiger' abroad for his country). The poet Richard Corbet wrote in 1635, 'He was Nature's factour here, And legier lay for every shire'.

Ministers should embrace opportunities of service

From whence observe that Christ's ministers according to Christ's pattern must embrace every opportunity of doing good to souls. Praying and preaching and studying must be our work. 'Preach the word; be instant in season, out of season' (2 Timothy 4:2). Peter, seeing the multitude, lets down the net and, at one draught, catches three thousand souls (Acts 2:41). How zealously industrious have God's champions been in former ages in fulfilling the work of their ministry, as we read of Chrysostom[1], Augustine[2], Basil the Great[3], Calvin, Bucer and others, who for the work of Christ 'were nigh unto death'. The reasons why the ministers of Christ (according to his pattern) should be ambitiously desirous of all opportunities for soul-service are:

(i) *Their commission*: God has entrusted them as ambassadors (2 Corinthians 5:20). Now you know an ambassador waits for a day of audience, and as soon as a day is granted, he faithfully and impartially delivers the mind of his prince. Thus Christ's ministers, having a commission delegated to them to negotiate for souls, should be glad when there is a day of audience, that they may impart the mind and will of Christ to his people.

(ii) *Their titles*: Ministers are called God's sowers (1 Corinthians 9:11). Therefore they must upon all occasions be scattering the blessed seed of the Word. The sower must go forth and sow; yea, though the seed fall upon stones, as usually it does, yet we must disseminate and scatter the seed of the Word upon stony hearts, because 'even of these stones God is able to raise up children' to himself.

Ministers are called stars. Therefore they must shine by word and doctrine in the firmament of the church. Thus our Lord Christ has set them a pattern in the text: 'Seeing the multitude, he went up into the mountain.' Here was a light set upon an hill, the bright morning star shining to all that were round about. Christ calls his ministers 'the light of the world' (Matthew 5:14). Therefore they must be always giving forth their lustre. Their light must not go out till it be in the socket,[4] or till violent death as an extinguisher put it out.

(iii) *Christ's ministers must catch at all occasions of doing good to others*, in regard of the work which they are about, and that is saving of souls. What a precious thing is a soul! Christ takes, as it were, a pair of

[1] Bishop of Constantinople (d. A.D. 407).
[2] Bishop of Hippo Regis (N. Africa) (d. A.D. 430).
[3] One of the three Cappadocian 'fathers'; Bishop of Caesarea (d. A.D. 379).
[4] That is, until life itself ends.

scales in his hands and he puts the world in one scale and the soul in the other, and the soul outweighs (Matthews 16:26). The soul is of a noble origin, of a quick operation; 'tis a flower of eternity; here, in the bud; in heaven, fully ripe and blown. The soul is one of the richest pieces of embroidery that ever God made, the understanding bespangled with light, the will invested with liberty, the affections like musical instruments tuned with the finger of the Holy Ghost. The soul is Christ's partner, the angels' familiar. Now if the souls of men are of so noble an extract and made capable of glory, oh how zealously industrious should Christ's ministers be to save these souls! If Christ spent his blood for souls, well may we spend our sweat. It was Augustine's prayer that Christ might find him at his coming either praying or preaching. What a sad sight is it to see precious souls as so many pearls and diamonds cast into the dead sea of hell!

(iv) The ministers of Christ, 'seeing the multitude', must *'ascend the mount'*, because there are so many emissaries of Satan who lie at the catch to subvert souls. How the old serpent casts out of his mouth floods of water after the woman to drown her! (Revelation 12:15). What floods of heresy have been poured out in city and country, which have overflowed the banks not only of religion but civility. Ignatius calls error 'the invention of the devil', and Bernard calls it 'a sweet poison'. Men's ears, like sponges, have sucked in this poison. Never were the devil's commodities more vendible in England than now. A fine tongue can put off bad wares. The Jesuit can silver over his lies, and dress error in truth's coat. A weak brain is soon intoxicated. When flattery and subtlety meet with the simple, they easily become a prey. The Romish whore entices many to drink down the poison of her idolatry and filthiness, because it is given in 'a golden cup' (Revelation 17:4). If all who have the plague of the head should die, it would much increase the bill of mortality. Now if there be so many emissaries of Satan abroad, who labour to make proselytes to the church of Rome, how it concerns them whom God has put into the work of the ministry to bestir themselves and lay hold on all opportunities, that by their spiritual antidotes they may 'convert sinners from the error of their way and save their souls from death!' (James 5:20). Ministers must not only be 'pastores', but 'proeliatores'.[1] In one hand they must hold the bread of life and 'feed the flock of God'; in the other hand, they must hold the sword of the Spirit and fight against those errors which carry damnation in their front.

[1] Fighters, warriors.

(v) *The ministers of Christ should wait for all opportunities of soul-service*, because the preaching of the Word meets so many adverse forces that hinder the progress and success of it. Never did a pilot meet with so many Euroclydons and cross-winds in a voyage, as the spiritual pilots of God's church do when they are transporting souls to heaven.

Some hearers have bad memories (James 1:25). Their memories are like leaking vessels. All the precious wine of holy doctrine that is poured in runs out immediately. Ministers cannot by study find a truth so fast as others can lose it. If the meat does not stay in the stomach, it can never breed good blood. If a truth delivered does not stay in the memory, we can never be, as the apostle says, 'nourished up in the words of faith' (1 Timothy 4:6). How often does the devil, that fowl of the air, pick up the good seed that is sown! If people suffer at the hands of thieves, they tell everyone and make their complaint they have been robbed; but there is a worse thief they are not aware of! How many sermons has the devil stolen from them! How many truths have they been robbed of, which might have been so many death-bed cordials! Now if the Word preached slides so fast out of the memory, ministers had need the oftener to go up the preaching mount, that at last some truth may abide and he as 'a nail fastened by the masters of assemblies'.

The ears of many of our hearers are stopped with earth. I mean the cares of the world, that the Word preached will not enter, according to that in the parable, 'Hearing they hear not' (Matthew 13:13). We read of Saul, his eyes were open, yet 'he saw no man' (Acts 9:8). A strange paradox! And is it not as strange that men's ears should be open, yet 'in hearing hear not'? They mind not what is said: 'They sit before thee as my people sitteth . . . but their heart goeth after their covetousness' (Ezekiel 33:31). Many sit and stare the minister in the face, yet scarce know a word he says. They are thinking of their wares and drugs and are often casting up accounts in the church. If a man be in a mill, though you speak never so loud to him, he does not hear you for the noise of the mill. We preach to men about matters of salvation, but the mill of worldly business makes such a noise that they cannot hear; 'in hearing they hear not'. It being thus, ministers who are called 'sons of thunder' had need often ascend the mount and 'lift up their voice like a trumpet' (Isaiah 58:1) that the deaf ear may be syringed and un-stopped, and may hear 'what the Spirit saith unto the churches' (Revelation 2:7).

Others, as they have earth in their ears, so they have a stone in their hearts. They make 'their hearts as an adamant stone, lest they should hear the law' (Zechariah 7:12). The ministers of Christ therefore must be frequently brandishing the sword of the Spirit and striking at men's sins, that, if possible, they may at last pierce the heart of stone. When the earth is scorched with the sun, it is so hard and crusted together, that a shower of rain will not soften it. There must be shower after shower before it will be either moist or fertile. Such an hardened piece is the heart of man naturally. It is so stiffened with the scorchings of lust, that there must be 'precept upon precept' (Isaiah 28:10). Our doctrine must 'distil as the dew, as the small rain on the tender herb, and as the showers upon the grass' (Deuteronomy 32:2).

(vi) *Christ's ministers, according to the example of their Lord and Master, should take all occasions of doing good,* not only in regard of God's glory, but their own comfort. What triumph is it, and cause of gladness, when a minister can say on his death-bed, 'Lord, I have done the work which thou gavest me to do,' I have been trading for souls! When a minister comes to the mount of glory, the heavenly mount, it will be a great comfort to him that he has been so often upon the preaching mount. Certainly if the angels in heaven rejoice at the conversion of a sinner (Luke 15:7, 10), how shall that minister rejoice in heaven over every soul that he has been instrumental to convert! As it shall add a member to Christ's body, so a jewel to a minister's crown. 'They that are wise', or as the original carries it, 'They that are teachers shall shine (not as lamps or tapers, but) as stars (Daniel 12:3); not as planets, but as fixed stars in the firmament of glory for ever.'

And though 'Israel be not gathered', yet shall God's ministers 'be glorious in the eyes of the Lord' (Isaiah 49:5). God will reward them not according to their success, but their diligence. When they are a 'savour of death' to men, yet they are a 'sweet savour' to God. In an orchard the labourer that fells a tree is rewarded as well as he that plants a tree. The surgeon's bill is paid though the patient die.

Exhortations to ministers

First, let me crave liberty to speak a word to the Elishas, my reverend and honoured brethren in the ministry. You are engaged in a glorious service. God has put great renown upon you. He has entrusted you with two most precious jewels, his *truths* and the *souls* of his people. Never was this honour conferred upon any angel to convert souls! What princely dignity can parallel this? The pulpit is higher than the throne, for a truly constituted minister represents no less than God himself. 'As though God did beseech you by us, we pray you in Christ's stead, be ye reconciled to God' (2 Corinthians 5:20). Give me leave to say as the apostle, 'I magnify my office' (Romans 11 : 13). Whatever our persons are, the office is sacred. The ministry is the most honourable employment in the world. Jesus Christ has graced this calling by his entering into it. Other men work in their trade; ministers work with God. 'We are labourers together with God' (1 Corinthians 3 : 9). O high honour! God and his ministers have one and the same work. They both negotiate about souls. Let the sons of the prophets wear this as their crown and diadem.

But while I tell you of your dignity, do not forget your duty. Imitate this blessed pattern in the text, 'the Lord Jesus who, seeing the multitudes, went up and taught'. He took all occasions of preaching. Sometimes he taught in the temple (Mark 14 : 49); sometimes in a ship (Mark 4 : 1), and here, upon the mount. His lips were a tree of life that fed many. How often did he neglect his food, that he might feast others with his doctrine! Let all the ministers of Christ tread in his steps! Make Christ not only your Saviour, but your example. Suffer no opportunities to slip wherein you may be helpful to the souls of others. Be not content to go to heaven yourselves, but be as the Primum Mobile,[1] which draws other orbs along with it. Be such shining lamps that you may light others to heaven with you. I will conclude with that of the apostle: 'Therefore, my beloved brethren, be ye steadfast, unmoveable, always abounding in the work of the Lord, forasmuch as ye know that your labour is not in vain in the Lord' (1 Corinthians 15 : 58).

Exhortations to the flock of God

Secondly, let me turn myself to the flock of God. If ministers must take all opportunities to preach, you must take all opportunities to hear. If there were twice or thrice a week a certain sum of money to be distributed to all comers, then people would resort thither. Now think thus with yourselves; when the Word of God is preached, the bread of life is distributed, which is more precious than 'thousands of gold and silver' (Psalm 119 : 72). In the Word preached, heaven and salvation is offered to you. In this field the pearl of price is hid. How should you 'flock like doves' to the windows of the sanctuary (Isaiah 60 : 8)! We read the gate of the temple was called 'beautiful' (Acts 3 : 2). The gate of God's house is the beautiful gate. Lie at 'these posts of wisdom's doors' (Proverbs 8 : 34).

Not only hear the Word preached, but encourage those ministers who do preach by liberal maintaining of them. Though I hope all who have

[1] Primary motive power.

God's Urim and Thummim written upon them can say, as the apostle, 'I seek not yours, but you' (2 Corinthians 12:14), yet that scripture is still canonical, 'So hath the Lord ordained, that they which preach the gospel should live of the gospel' (I Corinthians 9:14). Are not labourers in a vineyard maintained by their labours? says Peter Martyr. And the apostle puts the question, 'Who planteth a vineyard and eateth not the fruit of it? (1 Corinthians 9:7). Hypocrites love a cheap religion. They like a gospel that will put them to no charges. They are content so they may have golden bags, to have wooden priests. How many by saving their purses have lost their souls! Julian the Apostate robbed the ministers, pretending conscience. I need not tell you how vengeance pursued him. Is it not pity the fire on God's altar should go out for want of pouring on a little golden oil? David would not offer that to God which cost him nothing (2 Samuel 24:24).

Encourage God's ministers by your fruitfulness under their labours. When ministers are upon the 'mount', let them not be upon the rocks. What cost has God laid out upon this city![1] Never, I believe, since the apostles' times was there a more learned, orthodox, powerful ministry than now. God's ministers are called stars (Revelation 1:20). In this city every morning a star appears, besides the bright constellation on the Lord's Day. Oh you that feed in the green pastures of ordinances, be fat and fertile; you that are planted in the courts of God, flourish in the courts of God (Psalm 92:13). How sad will it be with a people that shall go laden to hell with Gospel blessings! The best way to encourage your ministers is to let them see the travail of their souls in your new birth. It is a great comfort when a minister not only woos souls, but wins souls. 'He that winneth souls is wise' (Proverbs 11:30). This is a minister's glory. 'For what is our joy, or crown of rejoicing? Are not even ye?' (1 Thessalonians 2:19). A successful preacher wears two crowns, a crown of righteousness in heaven, and a crown of rejoicing here upon earth. 'Are not ye our crown?'

Encourage your ministers by praying for them. Their work is great. It is a work that will take up their head and heart, and all little enough. It is a work fitter for angels than men. 'Who is sufficient for these things?' (2 Corinthians 2:16). Oh pray for them! Christ indeed, when he ascended the mount and was to preach, needed none of the people's prayers for him. He had a sufficient stock by him, the divine nature to supply him, but all his under-officers in the ministry need prayer. If Saint Paul, who abounded in the graces of the Spirit and supernatural revelations, begged prayer (1 Thessalonians 5:25), then surely other

[1] London.

[22]

ministers need prayer who do not pretend to any such revelations.

And pray for your ministers that God will direct them what to preach, that he will cut out their work for them. 'Go preach . . . the preaching that I bid thee' (Jonah 3:2). It is a great matter to preach suitable truths; there are 'acceptable words' (Ecclesiastes 12:10).

Pray that God will go forth with their labours, or else 'they toil and catch nothing'. God's Spirit must fill the sails of our ministry. It is not the hand that scatters the seed which makes it spring up, but the dews and influences of heaven. So it is not our preaching, but the divine influence of the Spirit that makes grace grow in men's hearts. We are but pipes and organs. It is God's Spirit blowing in us that makes the preaching of the Word by a divine enchantment allure souls to Christ. Ministers are but stars to light you to Christ. The Spirit is the loadstone to draw you. All the good done by our ministry is 'due to the Lord's excellent and effectual working' (Bucer). Oh then pray for us, that God will make his work prosper in our hands. This may be one reason why the Word preached does not profit more, because people do not pray more. Perhaps you complain the tool is dull, the minister is dead and cold. You should have whetted and sharpened him by your prayer. If you would have the door of a blessing opened to you through our ministry, you must unlock it by the key of prayer.

2 There is a blessedness in reversion

Blessed are the poor in spirit.
MATTHEW 5 : 3

Having done with the occasion, I come now to the sermon itself. 'Blessed are the poor in spirit'. Christ does not begin his Sermon on the Mount as the Law was delivered on the mount, with commands and threatenings, the trumpet sounding, the fire flaming, the earth quaking, and the hearts of the Israelites too for fear; but our Saviour (whose lips 'dropped as the honey-comb') begins with promises and blessings. So sweet and ravishing was the doctrine of this heavenly Orpheus that, like music, it was able to charm the most savage natures, yea, to draw hearts of stone to him.

To begin then with this first word, '*Blessed*'. If there be any blessedness in knowledge, it must needs be in the knowledge of blessedness. For the illustration of this, I shall lay down two aphorisms or conclusions.

[I] That there is a blessedness in reversion.[1]
[II] That the godly are in some sense already blessed.

[I] That there is a blessedness in reversion: The people of God meet with many knotty difficulties and sinking discouragements in the way of religion. Their march is not only tedious but dangerous, and their hearts are ready to despond. It will not be amiss therefore to set the crown of blessedness before them to animate their courage and to inflame their zeal. How many scriptures bring this olive-branch in their mouth, the tidings of blessedness to believers! 'Blessed is that servant whom his Lord, when he cometh, shall find so doing' (Matthew 24:46). 'Come, ye blessed of my Father' (Matthew 25:34). Blessedness is the perfection of a rational creature. It is the whetstone of a Christian's industry, the height of his ambition, the flower of his joy. Blessedness is the desire of all men. Aquinas calls it the 'ultimate end'. This is the 'white' every man aims to hit; to this centre all the lines are drawn.

[1] That is to say, the fulness of the blessedness lies in the future.

Wherein does blessedness consist? Millions of men mistake both the nature of blessedness and the way thither. Some of the learned have set down two-hundred-and-eighty-eight several opinions about blessedness, and all have shot wide of the mark. I shall show wherein it does not consist, and then wherein it does consist.

Wherein blessedness does not consist

(1) Wherein blessedness does not consist. It does not lie in the acquisition of worldly things. Happiness cannot by any art of chemistry be extracted here. Christ does not say, 'Blessed are the rich', or 'Blessed are the noble', yet too many idolize these things. Man, by the fall, has not only lost his crown, but his headpiece. How ready is he to terminate his happiness in externals! Which makes me call to mind that definition which some of the heathen philosophers give of blessedness, that it was to have a sufficiency of subsistence and to thrive well in the world. And are there not many who pass for Christians, that seem to be of this philosophical opinion? If they have but worldly accommodations, they are ready to sing a requiem to their souls and say with that brutish fool in the gospel, 'Soul, thou hast much goods laid up for many years, take thine ease . . .' (Luke 12:19). 'What is more shameful', says Seneca[1] 'than to equate the rational soul's good with that which is irrational.' Alas, the tree of blessedness does not grow in an earthly paradise. Has not God 'cursed the ground' for sin? (Genesis 3:17). Yet many are digging for felicity here, as if they would fetch a blessing out of a curse. A man may as well think to extract oil out of a flint, or fire out of water, as blessedness out of these terrestrial things.

King Solomon arrived at more than any man. He was the most magnificent prince that ever held the sceptre. *For his parentage:* he sprang from the royal line, not only that line from which many kings came, but of which Christ himself came. Jesus Christ was of Solomon's line and race, so that for heraldry and nobility none could show a fairer coat of arms. *For the situation of his palace:* it was in Jerusalem, the princess and paragon of the earth. Jerusalem, for its renown, was called 'the city of God'. It was the most famous metropolis in the world. 'Whither the tribes go up, the tribes of the Lord' (Psalms 122:4). *For wealth:* his crown was hung full of jewels. He had treasures of gold and of pearl and 'made silver to be as stones' (1 Kings 10:27). *For worldly joy:* he had the flower and quintessence of all delights – sumptuous fare, stately edifices, vineyards, fish-ponds, all sorts of music to

[1] Roman philosopher, tutor to Emperor Nero, A.D. 1st century.

enchant and ravish the senses with joy. If there were any rarity, it was a present for king Solomon's court. Thus did he bathe himself in the perfumed waters of pleasure.

For wisdom: he was the oracle of his time. When the queen of Sheba came to pose him with hard questions, he gave a solution to all her doubts (1 Kings 10:3). He had a key of knowledge to unlock nature's dark cabinet, so that if wisdom had been lost, it might have been found here, and the whole world might have lighted their understanding at Solomon's lamp. He was an earthly angel, so that a carnal eye surveying his glory would have been ready to imagine that Solomon had entered into that paradise out of which Adam was once driven, or that he had found another as good. Never did the world cast a more smiling aspect upon any man; yet when he comes to give in his impartial verdict, he tells us that the world has vanity written upon its frontispiece, and all those golden delights he enjoyed were but a painted felicity, a glorious misery. 'And behold all was vanity' (Ecclesiastes 2:8). Blessedness is too noble and delicate a plant to dwell in nature's soil.

Blessedness does not lie in externals

That blessedness does not lie in externals, I shall prove by these five demonstrations.

(i) Those things which are not commensurate to the desires of the soul can never make a man blessed; but transitory things are not commensurate to the desires of the soul; therefore they cannot render him blessed. Nothing on earth can satisfy.

'He that loveth silver shall not be satisfied with silver' (Ecclesiastes 5:10). Riches are unsatisfying:

Because they are not real. The world is called a 'fashion' (1 Corinthians 7:31). The word in the Greek signifies a mathematical figure, sometimes a show or apparition. Riches are but tinned over. They are like alchemy, which glisters a little in our eyes, but at death all this alchemy will be worn off. Riches are but sugared lies, pleasant impostures, like a gilded cover which has not one leaf of true comfort bound up in it.

Because they are not suitable. The soul is a spiritual thing; riches are of an earthly extract, and how can these fill a spiritual substance? A man may as well fill his treasure chest with grace, as his heart with gold. If a man were crowned with all the delights of the world, nay, if God should build him an house among the stars, yet the restless eye of his unsatisfied mind would be looking still higher. He would be prying

[26]

beyond the heavens for some hidden rarities which he thinks he has not yet attained to; so unquenchable is the thirst of the soul till it come to bathe in the river of life and to centre upon true blessedness.

(ii) That which cannot quiet the heart in a storm cannot entitle a man to blessedness; but earthly things accumulated cannot rock the troubled heart quiet; therefore they cannot make one blessed. If the spirit be wounded, can the creature pour wine and oil into these wounds? If God sets conscience to work, and it flies in a man's face, can worldly comforts take off this angry fury? Is there any harp to drive away the 'evil spirit'? Outward things can no more cure the agony of conscience than a silken stocking can cure a gouty leg. When Saul was sore distressed (1 Samuel 28:15), could all the jewels of his crown comfort him? If God be angry, whose 'fury is poured out like fire, and the rocks are thrown down by him' (Nahum 1:6), can a wedge of gold be a screen to keep off this fire? 'They shall cast their silver in the streets; their silver and their gold shall not be able to deliver them in the day of the wrath of the Lord' (Ezekiel 7:19). King Belshazzar was carousing and ranting it. 'He drank wine in the golden vessels of the temple' (Daniel 5:3), but when the fingers of a man's hand appeared, 'his countenance was changed' (verse 6), his wine grew sour, his feast was spoiled with that dish which was served in upon the wall. The things of the world will no more keep out trouble of spirit, than a paper sconce[1] will keep out a bullet.

(iii) That which is but for a season cannot make one blessed; but all things under the sun are but 'for a season', therefore they cannot enrich with blessedness. Sublunary delights are like those meats which we say are a while in season, and then presently grow stale and are out of request. 'The world passeth away' (1 John 2:17). Worldly delights are winged. They may be compared to a flock of birds in the garden, that stay a little while, but when you come near to them they take their flight and are gone. So 'riches make themselves wings; they fly away as an eagle toward heaven' (Proverbs 23:5). They are like a meteor that blazes, but spends and annihilates.[2] They are like a castle made of snow, lying under the torrid beams of the sun. Augustine says of himself, that when any preferment smiled upon him, he was afraid to accept of it lest it should on a sudden give him the slip. Outward comforts are, as Plato says, like tennis balls which are bandied up and down from one to another. Had we the longest lease of worldly comforts, it would

[1] A protective screen or shelter.
[2] Fades out of existence.

soon be run out. Riches and honour are constantly in flight; they pass away like a swift stream, or like a ship that is going full sail. While they are with us they are going away from us. They are like a posy of flowers which withers while you are smelling it; like ice, which melts away while it is in your hand. The world, says Bernard,[1] cries out, 'I will leave you', and be gone. It takes its salute and farewell together.

(iv) Those things which do more vex than comfort cannot make a man blessed; but such are all things under the sun, therefore they cannot have blessedness affixed to them. As riches are compared to wind (Hosea 12:1) to show their vanity, so to thorns (Matthew 13:17) to show their vexation. Thorns are not more apt to tear our garments, than riches to tear our hearts. They are thorns in the gathering, they prick with care; and as they pierce the head with care of getting, so they wound the heart with fear of losing. God will have our sweetest wine run dregs, yea, and taste of a musty cask too, that we may not think this is the wine of paradise.

(v) Those things which (if we have nothing else) will make us cursed, cannot make us blessed; but the sole enjoyment of worldly things will make us cursed, therefore it is far from making us blessed. 'Riches are kept for the hurt of the owner' (Ecclesiastes 5:13). Riches to the wicked are fuel for pride: 'Thy heart is lifted up because of thy riches' (Ezekiel 28:5); and fuel for lust: 'when I had fed them to the full, they then committed adultery' (Jeremiah 5:7). Riches are a snare: 'But they that will be rich fall into temptation and a snare, and into many foolish and hurtful lusts which drown men in perdition' (1 Timothy 6:9). How many have pulled down their souls to build up an estate! A ship may be so laden with gold that it sinks; many a man's gold has sunk him to hell. The rich sinner seals up money in his bag, and God seals up a curse with it. 'Woe to him that ladeth himself with thick clay' (Habakkuk 2:6). Augustine says that Judas for money sold his salvation, and the Pharisees bought their damnation; so that happiness is not to be fetched out of the earth. They who go to the creature for blessedness go to the wrong box.

If blessedness does not consist in externals, then let us not place our blessedness here. This is to seek the living among the dead. As the angel told Mary concerning Christ, 'He is not here, he is risen' (Matthew 28:6), so I may say of blessedness, It is not here, it is risen; it is in a higher region. How do men thirst after the world, as if the pearl of

[1] Abbot of Clairvaux (France) in the 12th century.

[28]

blessedness hung upon an earthly crown! O, says one, if I had but such an estate, then I should be happy! Had I but such a comfort, then I should sit down satisfied! Well, God gives him that comfort and lets him suck out the very juice and spirits of it, but, alas, it falls short of his expectation. It cannot fill the hiatus and longing of his soul which still cries 'Give, give' (Proverbs 30:15); just like a sick man. If, says he, I had but such a meat, I could eat it; and when he has it, his stomach is bad, and he can hardly endure to taste it. God has put not only an emptiness, but bitterness into the creature, and it is good for us that there is no perfection here, that we may raise our thoughts higher to more noble and generous delights. Could we distil and draw out the quintessence of the creature, we should say as once the emperor Severus [1] said, who grew from a mean estate to be head of the greatest empire in the world: I have, says he, run through all conditions, yet could never find full contentment.

To such as are cut short in their allowance, whose cup does not overflow, but their tears – be not too much troubled; remember that these outward comforts cannot make you blessed. You might live rich and die cursed. You might treasure up an estate, and God might treasure up wrath. Be not perplexed about those things the lack of which cannot make you miserable, nor the enjoyment make you blessed.

Wherein blessedness consists

(2) Having shown wherein blessedness does not consist, I shall next show wherein it does consist. Blessedness stands in the fruition of the chief good.

(i)) It consists in fruition; there must not be only possession, but fruition. A man may possess an estate, yet not enjoy it. He may have the dominion of it, but not the comfort, as when he is in a lethargy or under the predominancy of melancholy. But in true blessedness there must be a sensible enjoyment of that which the soul possesses..
(ii) Blessedness lies in the fruition of the chief good. It is not every good that makes a man blessed, but it must be the supreme good, and that is God. 'Happy is that people whose God is the Lord' (Psalm 144:15). God is the soul's rest (Psalm 116:7). Now that only in which the soul acquiesces and rests can make it blessed. The globe or circle, as is observed in mathematics, is of all others the most perfect figure, because the last point of the figure ends in that first point where it began. So,

[1] Roman Emperor A.D. 193–211.

when the soul meets in God, whence it sprang as its first original, then it is completely blessed. That which makes a man blessed must have fixed qualifications or ingredients in it, and these are found nowhere but in God the chief good.

In true blessedness there must be *meliority*[1]; that which fills with blessedness must be such a good as is better than a man's self. If you would ennoble a piece of silver, it must be by putting something to it which is better than silver, as by putting gold or pearl to it. So that which ennobles the soul and enriches it with blessedness, must be by adding something to it which is more excellent than the soul, and that is God. The world is below the soul; it is but the soul's foot-stool; therefore it cannot crown it with happiness.

Another ingredient is *delectability*: that which brings blessedness must have a delicious taste in it, such as the soul is instantly ravished with. There must be in it spirits of delight and quintessence of joy, and where can the soul suck those pure comforts which amaze it with wonder and crown it with delight, but in God? 'In God', says Augustime, 'the soul is delighted with such sweetness as even transports it.' The love of God is a honeycomb which drops such infinite sweetness and satisfaction into the soul as is 'unspeakable and full of glory.' (1 Peter 1 : 8). A kiss from God's mouth puts the soul into a divine ecstasy, so that now it cries out, 'It is good to be here.'

The third ingredient in blessedness is *plenty*; that which makes a man blessed must not be too scanty. It is a full draught which quenches the soul's thirst; and where shall we find plenty but in Deity? 'Thou shalt make them drink of the river of thy pleasures' (Psalm 36 : 8); not drops but rivers! The soul bathes itself and is laid, as it were, a-steeping in the water of life. The river of paradise overflowed and empties its silver streams into the souls of the blessed.

In true blessedness there must be *variety*. Plenty without variety is apt to nauseate. In God there is 'all fulness'. (Colossians 1 : 19). What can the soul want, but it may be had in the chief good? God is 'the good in all good things'. He is a sun, a shield, a portion, a fountain, a rock of strength, an horn of salvation. In God there is a complication of all excellencies. There are every moment fresh beauties and delights springing from God.

To make up blessedness there must be *perfection*; the joy must be perfect, the glory perfect. 'Spirits of just men made perfect' (Hebrews 12 : 23). 'Blessedness must run through the whole.' If there be the least

---

[1] The quality of being better.

defect, it destroys the nature of blessedness, as the least symptom of a disease takes away the well-being and right temperature of the body.

True blessedness must have *eternity* stamped on it. Blessedness is a fixed thing; it admits of no change or alteration. God says of every child of his, 'I have blessed him and he shall be blessed.' As the sunshine of blessedness is 'without clouds', so it never sets. 'I give unto them eternal life' (John 10:28). 'And so shall we ever be with the Lord' (1 Thessalonians 4:17). Eternity is the highest link of blessedness. Thus we have seen that this diamond of blessedness is only to be found in the Rock of Ages. 'Blessed are the people whose God is the Lord.'

Blessedness in practice

If there is such a blessedness in reversion, be convinced of the truth of this; set it down as an article of your faith. We live in times wherein many are grown atheists. They have run through all opinions, and now of professors they are turned epicures; they have drunk in so much of the poison of error that they are quite intoxicated and fallen asleep, and begin to dream there is no such state of blessedness after this life; and this opinion is to them above the Bible. When men have the spiritual staggers, it sadly presages they will die. Oh, it is a dangerous thing to hesitate and waver about fundamentals; like Pythagoras, who doubted whether there was a God or no; so, whether there be a blessedness or no. Doubting of principles is the next way to the denying of principles. Let it be a maxim with every good Christian, there is a blessedness in reversion. 'There remains a rest for the people of God' (Hebrews 4:9).

Revolve this truth often in your mind. There are many truths swim in the brain, which do not sink into the heart, and those do us no good. Chew the cud. Let a Christian think seriously with himself, there is a blessedness feasible and I am capable of enjoying it, if I do not lay bars in the way and block up my own happiness. Though within I see nothing but guilt, and without nothing but curses, yet there is a blessedness to be had, and to be had for *me* too in the use of means.

The serious meditation of this will be a forcible argument to make the sinner break off his sins by repentance and sweat hard till he find the golden mine of blessedness. I say, it would be the break-neck of sin. How would a man offer violence to himself by mortification and to heaven by supplication, that at last he may arrive at a state of blessedness! What, is there a crown of blessedness to be set upon my head? A crown hung with the jewels of honour, delight, magnificence? a crown reached out by God himself? and shall I by sin hazard this? Can the pleasure of sin countervail the loss of blessedness? What more powerful motive to repentance than this? Sin will deceive me of the blessing! If a man knew certainly that a king would settle all his crown revenues on him after a term of years, would he offend that regal Majesty and cause him to reverse or alter his will? There is a blessedness promised to all that live godly. 'This is the promise he has promised us, even eternal life' (1 John 2 : 25). We are not excluded, but may come in for a child's part. Now shall we, by living in sin, provoke God and forfeit this blessedness? O what madness is this! Well may the apostle call them 'foolish and hurtful lusts' (1 Timothy 6 : 9), because every lust does what in it lies to cut off the entail of mercy and block up the way to happiness. Every sin may be compared to the 'flaming sword', which keeps the heavenly paradise that the sinner cannot enter.

Let us so deport ourselves, that we may express to others that we do believe a blessedness to come, and that is by seeking an interest in God. For the beams of blessedness shine only from his face. It is our union with God, the chief good, that makes us blessed. Oh, let us never rest till we can say, 'This God is our God for ever and ever' (Psalm 48 : 14). Most men think because God has blessed them with an estate, therefore they are blessed. Alas, God often gives these things in anger. 'God grants a thing when he is angry which he does not will to give when he is tranquil.' He loads his enemies with gold and silver; as Plutarch reports of Tarpeia, a vestal nun, who bargained with the enemy to betray the Capitol of Rome to them, if she might have the golden bracelets on their left hands, which they promised; and being entered into the Capitol, they threw not only their golden bracelets, but their bucklers too upon her, through the weight whereof she was pressed to death. God often lets men have the golden bracelets, the weight whereof sinks them into hell. Oh, let us pant after things heavenly, let us get our eyes fixed, and our hearts united to God, the supreme good. This is to pursue blessedness as in the chase.

Let us proclaim to the world that we do believe a blessedness to come by living blessed lives; walk as becomes the heirs of blessedness. A blessed crown and a cursed life will never agree. Many tell us they are bound for heaven, but they steer their course a quite contrary way. The Devil is their pilot, and they sail hell-ward, as if a man should say he were going a voyage to the east, but sails quite westward. The drunkard will tell you he hopes for blessedness, but he sails another way; you must go weeping to heaven, not reeling. The unclean person talks of blessedness, but he is fallen into that 'deep ditch' (Proverbs 23 : 27), where he is like sooner to find hell than heaven. A beast may as well be made an angel as an unclean person in his leprosy enter into the paradise of God. The covetous person (of whom it may be said, 'he is a worm and no man', for he is ever creeping in the earth) yet would lay a claim to blessedness; but can earth ascend? Shall a lump of clay be made a bright star in the firmament of glory? Be assured they shall never be blessed who bless themselves in their sins. If, says God, the sinner 'bless himself in his heart, saying, I shall have peace, though I walk in the imagination of my heart, to add drunkenness to thirst; the Lord will not spare him, but then the anger of the Lord and his jealousy shall smoke against that man, and the Lord shall blot out his name under heaven' (Deuteronomy 29:19). A man can no more extract blessedness out of sin than he can suck health out of poison. O let us lead blessed lives, and so 'declare plainly that we seek a country' (Hebrews 11:14).

To you that have any good hope through grace that you have a title to blessedness, let me say as the Levites did to the people, 'Stand up and bless the Lord your God for ever and ever' (Nehemiah 9:5). What infinite cause have you to be thankful that the lot of free grace is fallen upon you! Though you had forfeited all, yet God has provided a haven of happiness, and he is carrying you thither upon the sea of Christ's blood, the gale of his Spirit blowing your sails. You are in a better condition through Christ, than when you had the robes of innocency upon you. God has raised you a step higher by your fall. How many has God passed by and looked upon you! Millions there are who shall lie under the bitter vials of God's curses, whereas he will bring you into his banqueting-house and pour out the flagons of wine and feast you eternally with the delicacies of heaven. O adore free grace; triumph in this love of God. Spend and be spent for the Lord. Dedicate yourselves to him in a way of resignation, and lay out yourselves for him in a way of gratulation. Never think you can do enough for that God who will shortly set you ashore in the land of promise.

3 The godly are in some sense already blessed

I proceed now to the second aphorism or conclusion, that the godly are in some sense already blessed. The saints are blessed not only when they are apprehended by God, but while they are travellers to glory. They are blessed before they are crowned. This seems a paradox to flesh and blood. What, reproached and maligned, yet *blessed*! A man that looks upon the children of God with a carnal eye and sees how they are afflicted, and like the ship in the gospel which was 'covered with waves' (Matthew 8:24), would think they were far from blessedness. St Paul brings a catalogue of his sufferings: 'Thrice was I beaten with rods; once I was stoned, thrice I suffered shipwreck . . .' (2 Corinthians 11:24-26). And those Christians of the first magnitude, of whom the world was not worthy, 'had trial of cruel mockings and scourgings; they were sawn asunder; they were slain with the sword' (Hebrews 11:36, 37). What? and were all these during the time of their sufferings blessed? A carnal man would think, If this be to be blessed, God deliver him from it.

But, however sense and reason give their vote, our Saviour Christ pronounces the godly man blessed; though a mourner, though a martyr, yet blessed. Job on the dunghill was blessed Job. The saints are blessed when they are cursed. Shimei cursed David. 'He came forth and cursed him' (2 Samuel 16:5). Yet when he was cursed David, he was blessed David. The saints, though they are bruised, yet they are blessed. Not only shall they be blessed, they are so. 'Blessed are the undefiled' (Psalm 119:1). 'Thy blessing is upon thy people' (Psalm 3:8).

Evidences that the godly are already blessed

(1) How are the saints already blessed? In that they are enriched with heavenly blessings (Ephesians 1:3). They are 'partakers of the divine nature' (2 Peter 1:4), not by an incorporation into the divine essence,

[34]

but by transformation into the divine likeness. This is blessedness begun. As the new-born babe is said to have life in it as well as he who is fully grown, so the saints, who are partakers of the divine nature, have an inchoate blessedness, though they have not arrived yet at perfection. Believers have the seed of God abiding in them (1 John 3:9). And this is a seed of blessedness. The flower of glory grows out of the seed of grace. Grace and glory differ not in kind but degree. The one is the root, the other the fruit. Grace is glory in the dawning; glory is grace in the meridian. And in this sense that assertion of Augustine is true, 'Blessed are we in faith and in hope.' Grace is the first link in the chain of blessedness. Now he that has the first link of the chain in his hand, has the whole chain. The saints have the Spirit of God in them, 'The Holy Ghost which dwelleth in us' (2 Timothy 1:14). How can the blessed Spirit be in a man and he not blessed? A godly man's heart is a paradise, planted with the choicest fruit, and God himself walks in the midst of this paradise, and must the man not needs be blessed?

(2) The saints are already blessed because their sins are not imputed to them. 'Blessed is the man to whom the Lord imputeth not iniquity' (Psalm 32:2). God's not imputing iniquity, signifies God's making of sin not to be. It is as if the man had never sinned. The debt book is cancelled in Christ's blood, and if the debtor owe never so much, yet if the creditor cross the book, it is as if he had never owed anything. God's not imputing sin signifies that God will never call for the debt, or, if it should be called for, it shall be hid out of sight. 'In those days the iniquity of Israel shall be sought for, and there shall be none; and the sins of Judah, and they shall not be found' (Jeremiah 50:20). Now such a man who has not sin imputed to him, is blessed, and the reason is, because if sin be not imputed to a man, then the curse is taken away; and if the curse be taken away, then he must needs be blessed.

(3) The saints are already blessed because they are in covenant with God. This is clear by comparing two scriptures: 'I will be their God' (Jeremiah 31:33), and 'Happy is that people whose God is the Lord' (Psalm 144:15). This is the crowning blessing, to have the Lord for our God. Impossible it is to imagine that God should be our God, and we not be blessed.

This sweet word, 'I will be your God,' implies *propriety*, that all that is in God shall be ours. His love is ours, his Spirit ours, his mercy ours. It implies all *relations*: of a father, 'I will be a father unto you' (2 Corinthians 6:18). The sons of a prince are happy. How blessed are the saints who are of true blood royal? It implies the relation of an husband:

'Thy Maker is thy husband' (Isaiah 54 : 5). The spouse, being contracted to her husband, is happy by having an interest in all he has. The saints being contracted by faith are blessed, though the solemnity of the marriage be kept for heaven. It implies terms of *friendship*. They who are in covenant with God are favourites of heaven. 'Abraham my friend' (Isaiah 41 : 8). It is counted a subject's happiness to be in favour with his prince, though he may live a while from court. How happy must he needs be who is God's favourite!

(4) The saints are already blessed because they have a reversion of heaven, as, on the contrary, he who has hell in reversion is said to be already condemned. 'He that believeth not is condemned already' (John 3 : 18). He is as sure to be condemned, as if he were condemned already. So he who has heaven in reversion may be said to be already blessed. A man that has the reversion of an house, after a short lease is run out, he looks upon it as his already. This house, says he, is mine. So a believer has a reversion of heaven after the lease of life is run out, and he can say at present, Christ is mine and glory is mine. He has a title to heaven, and he is a blessed man who has a title to show; nay, faith turns the reversion into a possession.

(5) The saints are already blessed because they have the firstfruits of blessedness here. We read of the earnest of the Spirit, and the seal (2 Corinthians 1 : 22), and the firstfruits (Romans 8 : 23). Heaven is already begun in a believer. 'The kingdom of God is peace and joy in the Holy Ghost' (Romans 14 : 17). This kingdom is in a believer's heart (Luke 17 : 21). The people of God have a prelibation and taste of blessedness here. As Israel tasted a bunch of grapes before they were actually possessed of Canaan, so the children of God have those secret incomes of the Spirit, those smiles of Christ's face, those kisses of his lips, those love-tokens that are as bunches of grapes; and they think themselves sometimes in heaven. 'Paul was let down in a basket' (Acts 9 : 25). Oftentimes the Comforter is let down to the soul in an ordinance, and now the soul is in the suburbs of Jerusalem above. A Christian sees heaven by faith, and tastes it by joy; and what is this but blessedness?

(6) The saints may be said in this life to be blessed, because all things tend to make them blessed. 'All things work together for good to them that love God' (Romans 8 : 28). We say to him that has everything falling out for the best, You are a happy man. The saints are very happy, for all things have a tendency to their good. Prosperity does them good; adversity does them good. Nay, sin turns to their good. Every trip

makes them more watchful. Their maladies are their medicines. Are not they happy persons that have every wind blowing them to the right port?

(7) A saint may be said to be blessed, because part of him is already blessed. He is blessed in his head; Christ, his head, is in glory; Christ and believers make one body mystical; their head is gotten into heaven.

Practical issues

See the difference between a wicked man and a godly. Let a wicked man have never so many comforts, still he is cursed; let a godly man have never so many crosses, still he is blessed. Let a wicked man have the 'candle of God shining' on him (Job 29 : 3), let his way be so smooth that he meets with no rubs; let him have success; yet still there is a curse entailed upon him. You may read the sinner's inventory (Deuteronomy 28 : 16, 17, 18). He is not more full of sin than he is of a curse. Though perhaps he blesses himself in his wickedness, yet he is heir to God's curse. All the curses of the Bible are his portion, and at the day of death this portion is sure to be paid. But a godly man in the midst of all his miseries is blessed. He may be under the cross, but not under a curse.

It shows the privilege of a believer. He not only shall be blessed, but he is blessed. Blessedness is begun in him. 'You are blessed of the Lord' (Psalm 115 : 15). Let the condition of the righteous be never so sad, yet it is blessed; he is blessed in affliction. 'Blessed is he whom thou chastenest' (Psalm 94 : 12); blessed in poverty, 'poor in the world, rich in faith' (James 2 : 5); blessed in disgrace, 'The spirit of glory and of God resteth upon you' (1 Peter 4 : 14). This may be a cordial to the fainting Christian; he is blessed in life and death! Satan cannot supplant him of the blessing.

How may this take away murmuring and melancholy from a child of God? Will you repine and be sad when you are blessed? Esau wept because he wanted the blessing. 'Bless me, even me also, O my father, and Esau lifted up his voice and wept' (Genesis 27 : 38). But shall a child of God be immoderately cast down when he has the blessing? Adam sinned in the midst of paradise. How evil it is to be blessed, and yet murmur!

What an encouragement is this to godliness! We are all ambitious of a blessing, then let us espouse religion: 'Blessed is the man that feareth the Lord' (Psalm 112 : 1). But you will say, This way is every-where spoken against. It is no matter, seeing this is the way to get a blessing. Suppose a rich man should adopt another for his heir, and others should reproach him, he does not care as long as he is heir to the estate. So, what though others may reproach you for your religion, as long as it entails a blessing on you; the same day you become godly, you become blessed.

4. Blessed are the poor in spirit

Having spoken of the general notion of blessedness, I come next to consider the subjects of this blessedness, and these our Saviour has deciphered to be the poor in spirit, the mourners, etc. But before I touch upon these, I shall attempt a little preface or paraphrase upon this sermon of the beatitudes.

Various observations

1 Observe the divinity in this sermon, which goes beyond all philosophy. The philosophers use to say that one contrary expels another; but here one contrary begets another. Poverty is wont to expel riches, but here poverty begets riches, for how rich are they that have a kingdom! Mourning is wont to expel joy, but here mourning begets joy: 'they shall be comforted'. Water is wont to quench the flame but the water of tears kindles the flame of joy. Persecution is wont to expel happiness, but here it makes happy: 'Blessed are they that are persecuted.' These are the sacred paradoxes in our Saviour's sermon.

2 Observe how Christ's doctrine and the opinion of carnal men differ. They think, 'Blessed are the rich.' The world would count him blessed who could have Midas' wish, that all he touched might be turned into gold. But Christ says, 'Blessed are the poor in spirit.' The world thinks, Blessed are they on the pinnacle; but Christ pronounces them blessed who are in the valley. Christ's reckonings and the world's do not agree.

3 Observe the nature of true religion. Poverty leads the van, and persecution brings up the rear. Every true saint (says Luther) is heir to the cross! Some there are who would be thought religious, displaying Christ's colours by a glorious profession, but to be 'poor in spirit' and 'persecuted', they cannot take down this bitter pill. They would wear Christ's jewels, but waive his cross. These are strangers to religion.

4 Observe the certain connection between grace and its reward. They who are 'poor in spirit' shall have the 'kingdom of God'. They are as sure to go to heaven, as if they were in heaven already. Our Saviour would encourage men to religion by sweetening commands with promises. He ties duty and reward together. As in the body the veins carry the blood, and the arteries the spirits, so one part of these verses carries duty, and the other part carries reward. As that scholar of Apelles painted Helena richly drawn in costly and glorious apparel, hung all over with orient pearl, and precious stones; so our Lord Christ. having set down several qualifications of a Christian, 'poor in spirit'. 'pure in heart', etc., draws these heavenly virtues in their fair colours of blessedness, and sets the magnificent crown of reward upon them. that by this oriency,[1] he might the more set forth their unparalleled beauty, and entice holy love.

5 Observe hence the concatenation of the graces: poor in spirit, meek, merciful, etc. Where there is one grace there is all. As they say of the cardinal virtues that they are strung together, so we may say of the graces of the spirit, they are linked and chained together. He that has poverty of spirit is a mourner. He that is a mourner is meek. He that is meek is merciful, etc. The Spirit of God plants in the heart an habit of all the graces. The new creature has all the parts and lineaments, as in the body there is a composition of all the elements and a mixture of all the humours. The graces of the Spirit are like a row of pearls which hang together upon the string of religion and serve to adorn Christ's bride. This I note, to show you a difference between a hypocrite and a true child of God. The hypocrite flatters himself with a pretence of grace, but in the meantime he does not have an habit of all the graces. He does not have poverty of spirit, nor purity of heart, whereas a child of God has all the graces in his heart, at least radically, though not gradually. These things being premised, I come in particular to those heavenly dispositions of soul to which Christ has affixed blessedness. And the first is *Poverty of Spirit*: 'Blessed are the poor in spirit.'

The meaning of 'poor in spirit'

Chrysostom and Theophylact are of opinion that this was the first sermon that ever Christ made, therefore it may challenge our best attention. 'Blessed are the poor in spirit.' Our Lord Christ being to raise

[1] Brilliancy, lustre.

an high and stately fabric of blessedness, lays the foundation of it low, in poverty of spirit. But all poverty is not blessed. I shall use a fourfold distinction.

1 I distinguish between 'poor in estate', and 'poor in spirit'. There are the Devil's poor, poor and wicked, whose clothes are not more torn than their conscience. There are some whose poverty is their sin, who through improvidence or excess have brought themselves to want. These may be poor in estate but not poor in spirit.

2 I distinguish between 'spiritually poor' and 'poor in spirit'. He who is without grace is spiritually poor, but he is not poor in spirit; he does not know his own beggary. 'Thou knowest not that thou art poor' (Revelation 3 : 17). He is in the worst sense poor who has no sense of his poverty.

3 I distinguish between 'poor-spirited' and 'poor in spirit'. They are said to be poor-spirited who have mean, base spirits, who act below themselves. As they are *men*; such are those misers, who having great estates, yet can hardly afford themselves bread; who live sneakingly, and are ready to wish their own throats cut, because they are forced to spend something in satisfying nature's demands. This Solomon calls an evil under the sun. 'There is an evil which I have seen under the sun, a man to whom God has given riches, so that he wanteth nothing for his soul of all that he desireth, yet God giveth him not power to eat thereof' (Ecclesiastes 6 : 2). Religion makes no man a niggard. Though it teaches prudence, yet not sordidness.

Then there are those who act below themselves as they are *Christians*, while they sinfully comply and prostitute themselves to the humours of others; a base kind of metal that will take any stamp. They will for a piece of silver part with the jewel of a good conscience. They will be of the state religion. They will dance to the devil's pipe, if their superior commands them. These are poor-spirited but not poor in spirit.

4 I distinguish between poor in an evangelical sense and poor in a popish sense. The papists give a wrong gloss upon the text. By 'poor in spirit', they understand those who, renouncing their estates, vow a voluntary poverty, living retiredly in their monasteries. But Christ never meant these. He does not pronounce them blessed who make themselves poor, leaving their estates and callings, but such as are evangelically poor.

Well then, what are we to understand by 'poor in spirit'? The Greek word for 'poor' is not only taken in a strict sense for those who live upon alms, but in a more large sense, for those who are destitute as well of inward as outward comfort. 'Poor in spirit' then signifies those who are brought to the sense of their sins, and seeing no goodness in themselves, despair in themselves and sue wholly to the mercy of God in Christ. Poverty of spirit is a kind of self-annihilation. Such an expression I find in Calvin. The poor in spirit (says he) are they who see nothing in themselves, but fly to mercy for sanctuary. Such an one was the publican: 'God be merciful to me a sinner' (Luke 18:13). Of this temper was St Paul: 'That I may be found in Christ, not having mine own righteousness' (Philippians 3:9). These are the poor which are invited as guests to wisdom's banquet (Proverbs 7:3, 4).

Several questions propounded

Here several questions may be propounded.

(i) Why does Christ here begin with poverty of spirit? Why is this put in the forefront? I answer, Christ does it to show that poverty of spirit is the very basis and foundation of all the other graces that follow. You may as well expect fruit to grow without a root, as the other graces without this. Till a man be poor in spirit, he cannot mourn. Poverty of spirit is like the fire under the still, which makes the water drop from the eyes. When a man sees his own defects and deformities and looks upon himself as undone, then he mourns after Christ. 'The springs run in the valleys' (Psalm 104:10). When the heart becomes a valley and lies low by poverty of spirit, now the springs of holy mourning run there. Till a man be poor in spirit, he cannot 'hunger and thirst after righteousness'. He must first be sensible of want before he can hunger. Therefore Christ begins with poverty of spirit because this ushers in all the rest.

(ii) The second question is, what is the difference between poverty of spirit and humility? These are so alike that they have been taken one for the other. Chrysostom, by 'poverty of spirit', understands humility. Yet I think there is some difference. They differ as the cause and the effect. Tertullian says, none are poor in spirit but the humble. He seems to make humility the cause of poverty of spirit. I rather think poverty of spirit is the cause of humility, for when a man sees his want of Christ, and how he lives on the alms of free grace, this makes him humble. He that is sensible of his own vacuity and indigence, hangs his head in humility with the violet. Humility is the sweet spice that grows from poverty of spirit.

(iii) What is the difference between poverty of spirit and self-denial? I answer, in some things they agree, in some things they differ. In some things they agree; for the poor in spirit is an absolute self-denier. He renounces all opinion of himself. He acknowledges his dependence upon Christ and free grace. But in some things they differ. The self-denier parts with the world for Christ, the poor in spirit parts with himself for Christ, i.e. his own righteousness. The poor in spirit sees himself nothing without Christ; the self-denier will leave himself nothing for Christ. And thus I have shown what poverty of spirit is.

Why Christians must be 'poor in spirit'

The words thus opened present us with this truth: that Christians must be poor in spirit; or thus, poverty of spirit is the jewel which Christians must wear. As the best creature was made out of nothing, namely, light; so when a man sees himself nothing, out of this nothing God makes a most beautiful creature. It is God's usual method to make a man poor in spirit, and then fill him with the graces of the Spirit. As we deal with a watch, we take it first to pieces, and then set all the wheels and pins in order, so the Lord first takes a man all to pieces, shows him his undone condition, and then sets him in frame.

The reasons are:

1 Till we are poor in spirit we are not capable of receiving grace. He who is swollen with an opinion of self-excellency and self-sufficiency, is not fit for Christ. He is full already. If the hand be full of pebbles, it cannot receive gold. The glass is first emptied before you pour in wine. God first empties a man of himself, before he pours in the precious wine of his grace. None but the poor in spirit are within Christ's commission. 'The Spirit of the Lord God is upon me; he hath sent me to bind up the broken-hearted' (Isaiah 61:1), that is, such as are broken in the sense of their unworthiness.

2 Till we are poor in spirit, Christ is never precious. Before we see our own wants, we never see Christ's worth. Poverty of spirit is salt and seasoning, the sauce which makes Christ relish sweet to the soul. Mercy is most welcome to the poor in spirit. He who sees himself clad in filthy rags (Zechariah 3:4,5), what will he give for change of raiment, the righteousness of Christ! What will he give to have the fair mitre of salvation set upon his head! When a man sees himself almost wounded to death, how precious will the balm of Christ's blood be to him! When he sees himself deep in arrears with God, and is so far

from paying the debt that he cannot sum up the debt, how glad would he be of a surety! 'The pearl of price' is only precious to the poor in spirit. He that wants bread and is ready to starve, will have it whatever it cost. He will lay his garment to pledge; bread he must have or he is undone. So to him that is poor in spirit, that sees his want of Christ, how precious is a Saviour! Christ is Christ and grace is grace to him! He will do anything for the bread of life. Therefore will God have the soul thus qualified, to raise the price of his market, to enhance the value and estimate of the Lord Jesus.

3 Till we are poor in spirit we cannot go to heaven. 'Theirs is the kingdom of heaven.' This tunes and prepares us for heaven. By nature a man is big with self-confidence, and the gate of heaven is so strait that he cannot enter. Now poverty of spirit lessens the soul; it pares off its superfluity, and now he is fit to enter in at the 'strait gate'. The great cable cannot go through the eye of the needle, but let it be untwisted and made into small threads, and then it may. Poverty of spirit untwists the great cable. It makes a man little in his own eyes and now an entrance shall be made unto him, 'richly into the everlasting Kingdom' (2 Peter 1:11). Through this temple of poverty, we must go into the temple of glory.

Poverty of spirit is true riches

It shows wherein a Christian's riches consist, namely in poverty of spirit. Some think if they can fill their bags with gold, then they are rich. But they who are poor in spirit are the rich men. They are rich in poverty. This poverty entitles them to a kingdom. How poor are they that think themselves rich! How rich are they that see themselves poor! I call it the 'jewel of poverty'. There are some paradoxes in religion that the world cannot understand; for a man to become a fool that he may be wise (1 Corinthians 3:18); to save his life by losing it (Matthew 16:25); and by being poor to be rich. Reason laughs at it, but 'Blessed are the poor, for theirs is the kingdom'. Then this poverty is to be striven for more than all riches. Under these rags is hid cloth of gold. Out of this carcase comes honey.

If blessed are the poor in spirit, then by the rule of contraries, cursed are the proud in spirit (Proverbs 16:5). There is a generation of men who commit idolatry with themselves; no such idol as self! They admire their own parts, moralities, self-righteousness; and upon this stock graft the hope of their salvation. There are many too good to go to heaven. They have commodities enough of their own growth, and they scorn to live upon the borrow, or to be beholden to Christ. These bladders the Devil has blown up with pride, and they are swelled in their own conceit; but it is like the swelling of a dropsy man whose bigness is his disease. Thus it was with that proud justiciary: 'The Pharisee stood and prayed, God, I thank thee that I am not as other men are, extortioners, unjust, adulterers, or even as this publican; I fast twice in the week, I give tithes ...' (Luke 18:11). Here was a man setting up the top-sail of pride; but the publican, who was poor in spirit, stood afar off and would not lift up so much as his eyes unto heaven, but smote upon his breast saying, 'God be merciful to me a sinner.' This man carried away the garland. 'I tell you' (says Christ) 'this man went down to his house justified rather than the other.' St Paul, before his conversion, thought himself in a very good condition, 'touching the law, blameless' (Philippians 3:6). He thought to have built a tower of his own righteousness, the top whereof should have reached to heaven; but, at last, God showed him there was a crack in the foundation, and then he gets into the 'rock of ages'. 'That I may be found in him' (Philippians 3:9). There is not a more dangerous precipice than self-righteousness. This was Laodicea's temper: 'Because thou sayest I am rich and I have need of nothing ...' (Revelation 3:17). She thought she wanted nothing when indeed she had nothing. How many does this damn! We see some ships that have escaped the rocks, yet are cast away upon the sands; so some who have escaped the rocks of gross sins, yet are cast away upon the sands of self-righteousness; and how hard is it to convince such men of their danger! They will not believe but that they may be helped out of their dungeon with these rotten rags. They cannot be persuaded their case is so bad as others would make it. Christ tells them they are blind, but they are like Seneca's maid, who was born blind, but she would not believe it. The house, says she, is dark, but I am not blind. Christ tells them they are naked, and offers his white robe to cover them, but they are of a different persuasion; and because they are blind, they cannot see themselves naked. How many have perished by being their own saviours! O that this might drive the proud sinner out of himself! A man never comes to himself till he comes out of himself. And no man can come out, till first Christ comes in.

How we may know whether we are 'poor in spirit'

If poverty of spirit be so necessary, how shall I know that I am poor in spirit? By the blessed effects of this poverty, which are:

1 He that is poor in spirit is weaned from himself. 'My soul is even as a weaned child' (Psalm 131:2). It is hard for a man to be weaned from himself. The vine catches hold of everything that is near, to stay itself upon. There is some bough or other a man would be catching hold of to rest upon. How hard is it to be brought quite off himself! The poor in spirit are divorced from themselves; they see they must go to hell without Christ. 'My soul is even as a weaned child.'

2 He that is poor in spirit is a Christ-admirer. He has high thoughts of Christ. He sees himself naked and flies to Christ that in his garments he may obtain the blessing. He sees himself wounded, and as the wounded deer runs to the water, so he thirsts for Christ's blood, the water of life. Lord, says he, give me Christ or I die. Conscience is turned into a fiery serpent and has stung him; now all the world for a brazen serpent! He sees himself in a state of death; and how precious is one leaf of the tree of life, which is both for food and medicine! The poor in spirit sees all his riches lie in Christ, 'wisdom, righteousness, sanctification . . .' In every exigence he flies to this magazine and storehouse. He adores the all-fulness in Christ.

They say of the oil in Rheims, though they are continually almost spending it, yet it never wastes. And such is Christ's blood; it can never be emptied. He that is poor in spirit has recourse still to this fountain. He sets an high value and appreciation upon Christ. He hides himself in Christ's wounds. He bathes himself in his blood. He wraps himself in his robe. He sees a spiritual dearth and famine at home, but he makes out to Christ. 'Show me the Lord (says he) and it sufficeth.'

3 He that is poor in spirit is ever complaining of his spiritual estate. He is much like a poor man who is ever telling you of his wants; he has nothing to help himself with; he is ready to starve. So it is with him that is poor in spirit. He is ever complaining of his wants, saying, I want a broken heart, a thankful heart. He makes himself the most indigent creature. Though he dares not deny .the work of grace (which were a bearing false witness again the Spirit), yet he mourns he has no more grace. This is the difference between an hypocrite and a child of God. The hypocrite is ever telling what he has. A child of God complains of what he lacks. The one is glad he is so good, the other grieves he is so bad. The poor in spirit goes from ordinance to ordinance for a supply of his wants; he would fain have his stock increased. Try by this if you are poor in spirit. While others complain they want children, or they want estates, do you complain you want grace? This is a good sign.

'There is that maketh himself poor yet hath great riches' (Proverbs 13:7). Some beggars have died rich. The poor in spirit, who have lain all their lives at the gate of mercy and have lived upon the alms of free grace, have died rich in faith, heirs to a kingdom.

4 He that is poor in spirit is lowly in heart. Rich men are commonly proud and scornful, but the poor are submissive. The poor in spirit roll themselves in the dust in the sense of their unworthiness. 'I abhor myself in dust' (Job 42:6). He who is poor in spirit looks at another's excellencies and his own infirmities. He denies not only his sins but his duties. The more grace he has, the more humble he is, because he now sees himself a greater debtor to God. If he can do any duty, he acknowledges it is Christ's strength more than his own (Philippians 4:13). As the ship gets to the haven more by the benefit of the wind than the sail, so when a Christian makes any swift progress, it is more by the wind of God's Spirit than the sail of his own endeavour. The poor in spirit, when he acts most like a saint, confesses himself 'the chief of sinners'. He blushes more at the defect of his graces than others do at the excess of their sins. He dares not say he has prayed or wept. He lives, yet not he, but Christ lives in him (Galatians 2:20). He labours, yet not he, but the grace of God (1 Corinthians 15:10).

5 He who is poor in spirit is much in prayer. He sees how short he is of the standard of holiness, therefore begs for more grace; Lord, more faith, more conformity to Christ. A poor man is ever begging. You may know by this one that is poor in spirit. He is ever begging for a spiritual alms. He knocks at heaven-gate; he sends up sighs; he pours out tears; he will not away from the gate till he have his dole. God loves a modest boldness in prayer; such shall not be non-suited.

6 The poor in spirit is content to take Christ upon his own terms. The proud sinner will article and indent with Christ. He will have Christ and his pleasure, Christ and his covetousness. But he that is poor in spirit sees himself lost without Christ, and he is willing to have him upon his own terms, a Prince as well as a Saviour: 'Jesus my Lord' (Philippians 3:8). A castle that has long been besieged and is ready to be taken will deliver up on any terms to save their lives. He whose heart has been a garrison for the devil, and has held out long in opposition against Christ, when once God has brought him to poverty of spirit, and he sees himself damned without Christ, let God propound what articles he will, he will readily subscribe to them. 'Lord, what wilt thou have me to do' (Acts 9:6). He that is poor in spirit will do anything that he

may have Christ. He will behead his beloved sin. He will, with Peter, cast himself upon the water to come to Christ.

7 He that is poor in spirit is an exalter of free grace. None so magnify mercy as the poor in spirit. The poor are very thankful. When Paul had tasted mercy, how thankfully does he adore free grace! 'The grace of our Lord was exceeding abundant' (1 Timothy 1 : 14). It was super-exuberant. He sets the crown of his salvation upon the head of free grace. As a man that is condemned and has a pardon sent him, how greatly he proclaims the goodness and clemency of his prince! So St Paul displays free grace in its orient colours. He interlines all his epistles with free grace. As a vessel that has been perfumed makes the wine taste of it, so St Paul, who was a vessel perfumed with mercy, makes all his epistles to taste of this perfume of free grace. They who are poor in spirit, bless God for the least crumb that falls from the table of free grace. Labour for poverty of spirit. Christ begins with this, and we must begin here if ever we be saved. Poverty of spirit is the foundation stone on which God lays the superstructure of glory.

Four persuasions to be 'poor in spirit'

There are four things may persuade Christians to be poor in spirit.

1 This poverty is your riches. You may have the world's riches, and yet be poor. You cannot have this poverty without being made rich. Poverty of spirit entitles you to all Christ's riches.

2 This poverty is your nobility. God looks upon you as persons of honour. He that is vile in his own eyes is precious in God's eyes. The way to rise is to fall. God esteems the valley highest.

3 Poverty of spirit sweetly quiets the soul. When a man is brought off from himself to rest on Christ, what a blessed calm is in the heart! I am poor but 'my God shall supply all my need' (Philippians 4 : 19). I am un-worthy but Christ is worthy. I am indigent, Christ is infinite. 'Lead me to the rock that is higher than I' (Psalm 61 : 2). A man is safe upon a rock. When the soul goes out of itself and centres upon the rock, Christ, now it is firmly settled upon its basis. This is the way to comfort. You will be wounded in spirit till you come to be poor in spirit.

4 Poverty of spirit paves a causeway for blessedness. 'Blessed are the poor in spirit.' Are you poor in spirit? You are blessed persons. Happy for you that ever you were born! If you ask, Wherein does this blessed-ness appear?, read the next words, 'Theirs is the Kingdom of Heaven.'

5 The poor in spirit are enriched with a kingdom

Theirs is the kingdom of heaven.
MATTHEW 5 : 3

Here is high preferment for the saints. They shall be advanced to a kingdom. There are some who, aspiring after earthly greatness, talk of a temporal reign here, but then God's church on earth would not be militant but triumphant. But sure it is the saints shall reign in a glorious manner: 'Theirs is the Kingdom of Heaven.' A kingdom is held the acme and top of all worldly felicity, and 'this honour have all the saints'; so says our Saviour, 'Theirs is the kingdom of heaven.' All Christ's subjects are kings. By the kingdom of heaven is meant that state of glory which the saints shall enjoy when they shall reign with God and the angels for ever; sin, hell and death being fully subdued. For the illustration of this I shall show first wherein the saints in heaven are like kings.

Saints glorified may be compared to kings

Kings have their insignia or regalia, their ensigns of royalty and majesty.

1 Kings have their *crowns*. So the saints after death have their crown-royal. 'Be thou faithful unto death and I will give thee a crown of life' (Revelation 2:10). Believers are not only pardoned but crowned. The crown is an ensign of honour. A crown is not for every one. It will not fit every head. It is only for kings and persons of renown to wear (Psalm 21 : 3). The crown which the poor in spirit shall wear in heaven is an honourable crown. God himself installs them into their honour and sets the crown-royal upon their head. And this crown that the saints shall wear, which is divinely orient[1] and illustrious, exceeds all other.

(i) It is more pure. Other crowns, though they be made of pure gold, yet they are mixed metal; they have their troubles. A crown of gold cannot be made without thorns. It has so many vexations belonging to

[1] See p. 40 fn.

it, that it is apt to make the head ache. Which made Cyrus[1] say, did men but know what cares he sustained under the imperial crown, he thought they would not stoop to take it up. But the saints' crown is made without crosses. It is not mingled with care of keeping, or fear of losing. What Solomon speaks in another sense I may say of the crown of glory, 'It adds no sorrow with it' (Proverbs 10:22). This crown, like David's harp, drives away the evil spirit of sorrow and disquiet. There can be no grief in heaven any more than there can be joy in hell.

(ii) This crown of glory does not draw envy to it. David's own son envied him and sought to take his crown from his head. A princely crown is oftentimes the mark for envy and ambition to shoot at, but the crown the saints shall wear is free from envy. One saint shall not envy another, because all are crowned, and though one crown may be larger than another, yet everyone shall have as big a crown as he is able to carry.

(iii) This is a never-fading crown. Tertullian[2] says that this crown is not made out of either roses or gems. Other crowns quickly wear away and tumble into the dust: 'Doth the crown endure to all generations?' (Proverbs 27:24). Henry VI[3] was honoured with the crowns of two kingdoms, France and England. The first was lost through the faction of his nobles; the other was twice plucked from his head. The crown has many heirs and successors. The crown is a withering thing. Death is a worm that feeds in it; but the crown of glory is immarcescible'[4] 'it fadeth not away' (1 Peter 5:4). It is not like the rose that loses its gloss and vernancy. This crown cannot be made to wither, but like the flower we call Everlasting, it keeps always fresh and splendent. Eternity is a jewel of the saints' crown.

2 Kings have their *Robes*. The robe is a garment wherewith Kings are arrayed. 'The King of Israel and the King of Judah sat clothed in their robes' (2 Chronicles 18:9). The robe was of scarlet or velvet lined with ermine, sometimes of a purple colour, when it was called 'Purpura'; sometimes of an azure brightness. Thus the saints shall have their robes. 'I beheld a great multitude which no man could number of all nations and kindreds, clothed in white robes' (Revelation 7:9). The

---

[1] Cyrus the Great, founder of the Persian Empire (d. 529 B.C.).
[2] One of the 'fathers' of the church in the Province of Africa (d. 220).
[3] King of England, 1422–61.
[4] Unfading, imperishable.

saints' robes signify their glory and splendour; white robes denote their sanctity. They have no sin to taint or defile their robes. In these robes they shall shine as the angels.

3 Kings have their *Sceptres* in token of rule and greatness. King Ahasuerus held out to Esther the golden sceptre (Esther 5 : 2); and the saints in glory have their sceptre, and 'palms in their hands' (Revelation 7). It was a custom of great conquerors to have palm branches in their hand in token of victory. So the saints, those kings have 'palms', an emblem of victory and triumph. They are victors over sin and hell. 'They overcame by the blood of the Lamb' (Revelation 12 : 11).

4 Kings have their *Thrones*. When Caesar returned from conquering his enemies, there were granted to him four triumphs in token of honour, and there was set for him a chair of ivory in the senate and a throne in the theatre. Thus the saints in heaven returning from their victories over sin shall have a chair of state set them more rich than ivory or pearl, and a throne of glory (Revelation 3 : 21). (i) This shall be a high throne. It is seated above all the kings and princes of the earth. Nay, it is far above all heavens (Ephesians 4). There is the *airy* heaven, which is that space from the earth to the sphere of the moon; the *starry* heaven, the place where are the stars and those 'superior planets', as the philosophers call them, planets of higher elevation, as Saturn, Jupiter, Mars etc.; the *empyraean* heaven, which is called the 'third heaven' (2 Corinthians 12 : 2). In this glorious sublime place shall the throne of the saints be erected. (ii) It is a safe throne. Other thrones are unsafe; they stand tottering. 'Thou hast set them in slippery places' (Psalm 73 : 18); but the saints' throne is sure. 'He that overcomes shall sit with me upon my throne' (Revelation 3 : 21). The saints shall sit with Christ. He keeps them safe, that no hand of violence can pull them from their throne. O ye people of God, think of this; though now you may be called to the bar,[1] yet shortly you shall sit upon the throne.

The kingdom of heaven excels other kingdoms

Having shown wherein the saints in glory are like kings, let us see wherein the kingdom of heaven excels other kingdoms.

1 It excels in the *Founder and Maker*. Other kingdoms have men for their builders, but this kingdom has God for its builder (Hebrews 11 : 10). Heaven is said to be 'made without hands' (2 Corinthians 5 : 1),

---

[1] That is, to the bar of man's judgment.

to show the excellency of it. Neither man nor angel could ever lay stone in this building. God erects this kingdom. Its 'builder and maker is God'.

2 This kingdom excels in the *riches* of it. Gold does not so much surpass iron as this kingdom does all other riches. 'The gates are of pearl' (Revelation 21 : 21). 'And the foundations of the wall of it are garnished with all precious stones' (verse 19). It is enough for cabinets to have pearl; but were 'gates of pearl' ever heard of before? It is said that 'Kings shall throw down their crowns and sceptres before it (Revelation 4 : 10), as counting all their glory and riches but dust in comparison of it. This kingdom has deity itself to enrich it, and these riches are such as cannot be weighed in the balance; neither the heart of man can conceive, nor the tongue of angel express.

3 This kingdom excels in the *perfection* of it. Other kingdoms are defective. They have not all provisions within themselves, nor have they all commodities of their own growth, but are forced to traffic abroad to supply their wants at home. King Solomon sent for gold to Ophir (2 Chronicles 8 : 18), but there is no defect in the kingdom of heaven; here are all delights and rarities to be had. 'He that overcometh shall inherit all things' (Revelation 21 : 7). Here is beauty, wisdom, glory and magnificence. Here is the Tree of Life in the midst of this paradise. All things are to be found here but sin and sorrow, the absence whereof adds to the fulness of this kingdom.

4 It excels in *security*. Other kingdoms fear either foreign invasions or intestine divisions. Solomon's kingdom was peaceable awhile but at last he had an alarum given him by the enemy (1 Kings 11 : 11, 14). But the kingdom of heaven is so impregnable that it fears no hostile assaults or inroads. The devils are said to be locked up in chains (Jude 6). The saints in heaven shall no more need fear them than a man fears that thief's robbings who is hanged up in chains. The gates of this celestial kingdom 'are not shut at all by day' (Revelation 21 : 25). We shut the gates of the city in a time of danger, but the gates of that kingdom always stand open to show that there is no fear of the approach of an enemy. The kingdom has gates for the magnificence of it, but the gates are not shut because of the security of it.

5 This kingdom excels in its *stability*. Other kingdoms have vanity written upon them. They cease and are changed; though they may have a head of gold, yet feet of clay. 'I will cause the kingdom to cease' (Hosea

1 : 4). Kingdoms have their climacterical year. Where is the glory of Athens? the pomp of Troy? What is become of the Assyrian, Grecian, Persian monarchy? Those kingdoms are demolished and laid in the dust; but the kingdom of heaven has eternity written upon it. It is an 'everlasting kingdom' (2 Peter 1 : 11). Other kingdoms may be lasting but not everlasting. The apostle calls it 'a kingdom that cannot be shaken' (Hebrews 12 : 28). It is fastened upon a strong basis, the omnipotency of God. It runs parallel with eternity. 'They shall reign for ever and ever' (Revelation 22 : 5).

The kingdom of heaven is infallibly entailed upon the saints

I shall next clear the truth of this proposition that the saints shall be possessed of this kingdom.

1 In regard of God's free grace, 'It is your Father's good pleasure to give you the kingdom' (Luke 12 : 32). It is not any desert in us but free grace in God. The papists say we merit the kingdom, but we disclaim the title of merit. Heaven is a donative.

2 There is a price paid. Jesus Christ has shed his blood for it. All saints come to the kingdom through blood. Christ's hanging upon the cross was to bring us to the crown. As the kingdom of heaven is a gift in regard of the Father, so it is a purchase in regard of the Son.

Corollaries and inferences from the above

1 It shows us that religion is no unreasonable thing. God does not cut us out work and give no reward. Godliness enthrones us in a kingdom. When we hear of the doctrine of repentance, steeping our souls in brinish tears for sin; the doctrine of mortification, pulling out the right eye, beheading the king-sin; we are ready to think it is hard to take down this bitter pill, but here is that in the text may sweeten it. There is a kingdom behind, and that will make amends for all. This glorious recompense as far exceeds our thoughts as it surpasses our defects. No one can say without wrong to God that he is a hard master. God gives double pay. He bestows a kingdom upon those that fear him. Satan may disparage the ways of God, like those spies that raised an ill report of the good land (Numbers 13 : 32). But will Satan mend your wages if you serve him? He gives damnable pay; instead of a kingdom, 'chains of darkness' (Jude 6).

2 See here the mercy and bounty of God that has prepared a kingdom

for his people. It is a favour that we poor 'worms and no men' (Psalm 22:6) should be suffered to live. But that worms should be made kings, this is divine bounty. It is mercy to pardon us, but it is rich mercy to crown us. 'Behold, what manner of love' is this! Earthly princes may bestow great gifts and donatives on their subjects, but they keep the kingdom to themselves. Though Pharaoh advanced Joseph to honour and gave him a ring from his finger, yet he kept the kingdom to himself. 'Only in the throne will I be greater than thou' (Genesis 41:40); but God gives a kingdom to his people, he sets them upon the throne. How David admires the goodness of God in bestowing upon him a temporal kingdom! 'Then went king David in, and sat before the Lord and said, Who am I, O Lord God! and what is my house, that thou hast brought me hitherto?' (2 Samuel 7:18). He wondered that God should take him from the sheep-fold and set him on the throne! that God should turn his shepherd's staff into a sceptre! O then how may the saints admire the riches of grace, that God should give them a kingdom above all the princes of the earth, nay, far above all heavens! God thinks nothing too good for his children. We many times think much of a tear, a prayer, or to sacrifice a sin for him, but he does not think much to bestow a kingdom upon us. How will the saints read over the lectures of free grace in heaven and trumpet forth the praises of that God who has crowned them with lovingkindness!

3 It shows us that Christianity is no disgraceful thing. Wise men measure things by the end. What is the end of godliness? It brings a kingdom. A man's sin brings him to shame (Proverbs 13:5). What fruit had ye in those things whereof you are now ashamed? (Romans 6:21). But religion brings to honour (Proverbs 4:8). It brings a man to a throne, a crown, it ends in glory. It is the sinner's folly to reproach a saint. It is just as if Shimei had reproached David when he was going to be made king. It is a saint's wisdom to contemn a reproach. Say as David when he danced before the ark, 'I will yet be more vile' (2 Samuel 6:22). If to pray and hear and serve my God be to be vile, 'I will yet be more vile.' This is my excellency, my glory. I am doing now that which will bring me to a kingdom. O think it no disgrace to be a Christian! I speak it chiefly to you who are entering upon the ways of God. Perhaps you may meet with such as will reproach and censure you. Bind their reproaches as a crown about your head. Despise their censure as much as their praise. Remember there is a kingdom entailed upon godliness. Sin draws hell after it; grace draws a crown after it.

4 See here that which may make the people of God long for death.

Then they shall enter upon their kingdom. Indeed the wicked may fear death. It will not lead them to a kingdom but a prison. Hell is the gaol where they must lie rotting for ever with the devil and his angels. To every Christless person death is the king of terror; but the godly may long for death. It will raise them to a kingdom. When Scipio's father had told him of that glory the soul should be invested with in a state of immortality, why then, says Scipio, do I tarry thus long upon the earth? Why do I not hasten to die? Believers are not perfectly happy till death. When Croesus asked Solon whom he thought happy, he told him one Tellus, a man that was dead. A Christian at death shall be completely installed into his honour. The anointing oil shall be poured on him, and the crown-royal set upon his head. The Thracians, in their funerals, used music. The heathens (as Theocritus[1] observes) had their funeral banquet, because of that felicity which they supposed the parties deceased were entered into. The saints are now 'heirs of the kingdom' (James 2 : 5). Does not the heir desire to be crowned?

Truly there is enough to wean us and make us willing to be gone from hence. The saints 'eat ashes like bread'. They are here in a suffering condition. 'Our bones are scattered at the grave's mouth, as when one cutteth and cleaveth wood upon the earth' (Psalm 141 : 7). When a man hews and cuts a tree the chips fly up and down; here and there a chip. So here a saint wounded, there a saint massacred; our bones fly like chips up and down. 'For thy sake we are killed all the day long' (Romans 8 : 36). But there is a kingdom a-coming; when the body is buried the soul is crowned. Who would not be willing to sail in a storm if he were sure to be crowned as soon as he came at the shore? How is it that the godly look so ghastly at thoughts of death, as if they were rather going to their execution than their coronation? Though we should be willing to stay here awhile to do service, yet we should with St Paul, 'desire to be dissolved and be with Christ'. The day of a believer's dissolution is the day of his inauguration.

A scrutiny and trial whether we belong to the kingdom of heaven

But how shall we know that this glorious kingdom shall be settled upon us at death?

1. If God has set up his kingdom within us; 'The kingdom of God is within you' (Luke 17 : 21). By the kingdom of God there is meant the kingdom of grace in the heart. Grace may be compared to a kingdom. It

[1] Greek poet of the 3rd century B.C.

sways the sceptre; it gives out laws. There is the law of love. **Grace** beats down the devil's garrisons. It brings the heart into a sweet subjection to Christ. Now is this kingdom of grace set up in your heart? Do you rule over your sins? Can you bind those kings in chains? (Psalms 149:8). Are you a king over your pride, passion and unbelief? Is the kingdom of God within you? While others aspire after earthly greatness and labour for a kingdom *without* them, do you labour for a kingdom *within* you? Certainly if the kingdom of grace be in your heart, you shall have the kingdom of glory. If God's kingdom enter into you, you shall enter into his kingdom. But let not that man ever think to reign in glory, who lives a slave to his lusts.

2 If you are a believer, you will go to this blessed kingdom: 'Rich in faith, heirs of the kingdom' (James 2:5). Faith is an heroical act of the soul. It makes an holy adventure on God, by a promise. This is the crowning grace. Faith puts us into Christ, and our title to the crown comes in by Christ. By faith we are born of God, and so we become children of the blood-royal. By faith our hearts are purified (Acts 15:9, 10), and we are made fit for a kingdom; 'rich in faith, heirs of the kingdom'. Faith paves a causeway to heaven. Believers die heirs to the crown.

3 He that has a noble, kingly spirit shall go to the heavenly kingdom. 'Set your affection on things above' (Colossians 3:2). Do you live in the world, above the world? The eagle does not catch flies, she soars aloft in the air. Do you pant after glory and immortality? Do you have a brave majestic spirit, an heavenly ambition? Do you mind the favour of God, the peace of Sion, the salvation of your soul? Do you abhor that which is sordid and below you? Alexander [1] would not exercise at the Olympic games. Can you trample upon all sublunary things? Is heaven in your eye, and Christ in your heart and the world under your feet? He who has such a kingly spirit that looks no lower than a crown, 'he shall dwell on high', and have his throne mounted far above all heavens.

Serious exhortations to the wicked and to Christians

The exhortation has a double aspect.

1 It looks towards the wicked. It there a kingdom to be had, a kingdom so enamelled and bespangled with glory? Oh then, do not by your folly make yourselves incapable of this preferment. Do not for the satisfying of a base lust forfeit a kingdom. Do not drink away a kingdom. Do not

[1] Alexander the Great, King of Macedonia, 4th century B.C.

[56]

for the lap of pleasure lose the crown of life. If men, before they committed a sin, would but sit down and rationally consider whether the present gain and sweetness in sin would countervail the loss of a kingdom, I believe it would put them into a cold sweat, and give some check to their unbridled affections. Jacob took Esau by the heel. Look not upon the smiling face of sin, but 'take it by the heel'. Look at the end of it. It will deprive you of a kingdom, and can anything make amends for that loss? O, is it not madness, for the unfruitful works of darkness (Ephesians 5 : 11), to lose a kingdom? How will the devil at the last day reproach and laugh at men, that they should be so stupidly sottish as for a rattle to forgo a crown! Like those Indians who for pictures and glass beads will part with their gold. Surely it will much contribute to the vexation of the damned to think how foolishly they missed of a kingdom.

2 The exhortation looks toward the godly, and it exhorts to two things

(i) Is there a kingdom in reversion? Then let this be a motive to duty Do all the service you can for God while you live. 'Spend and be spent.' The reward is honourable. The thoughts of a kingdom should add wings to prayer, and fire to zeal. 'What honour and dignity has been done to Mordecai?' says King Ahasuerus (Esther 6 : 3). Inquire what has been done for God? What love have you shown to his name? What zeal for his glory? Where is the head of that Goliath lust you have slain for his sake? Methinks we should sometimes go aside into our closets and weep to consider how little work we have done for God. What a vast disproportion is there between our service and our reward! What is all our weeping and fasting compared to a kingdom! Oh improve all your interest for God. Make seasons of grace, opportunities for service.

And that you may act more vigorously for God, know and be assured. the more work you do, the more glory you shall have. Every saint shall have a kingdom, but the more service any man does for God, the greater will be his kingdom. There are degrees of glory which I will prove thus: First, because there are degrees of torment in hell. 'They shall receive greater damnation' (Luke 20 : 47). They who make religion a cloak for their sin, shall have an hotter place in hell. Now if there be degrees of torment in hell, then by the rule of contraries there are degrees of glory in the kingdom of heaven. Again, seeing God in his free grace rewards men according to their works, therefore, the more service they do the greater shall their reward be. 'Behold I come quickly and my reward is with me, to give every man according as his work shall be' (Revelation 22 : 12). He that has done more shall receive more

He whose pound gained ten, was made ruler over ten cities (Luke 19:16, 17). This may very much excite to eminency in religion. The more the lamp of your grace shines, the more you shall shine in the heavenly orb. Would you have your crown brighter, your kingdom larger, your palm-branches more flourishing? Be Christians of degrees. Do much work in a little time. While you are laying out, God is laying up. The more glory you bring to God, the more glory you shall have from God.

(ii) Walk worthy of this kingdom. 'That ye would walk worthy of God who hath called you to his kingdom' (1 Thessalonians 2:12). Live as kings. Let the majesty of holiness appear in your faces. Those who looked on Stephen, 'saw his face as it had been the face of an angel (Acts 6:15). A kind of angelical brightness was seen in his visage. When we shine in zeal, humility, gravity, this beautifies and honours us in the eyes of others, and makes us look as those who are heirs apparent to a crown.

Here is comfort to the people of God in case of poverty. God has provided them a kingdom: 'Theirs is the kingdom of heaven.' A child of God is often so low in the world that he has not a foot of land to in-herit. He is poor in purse as well as in spirit. But here is a fountain of consolation opened. The poorest saint who has lost all his golden fleece is heir to a kingdom, a kingdom which excels all the kingdoms and principalities of the world, more than pearl or diamond excels brass. It is peerless and endless. The hope of a kingdom, says Basil, should carry a Christian with courage and cheerfulness through all his afflictions. And it is a saying of Luther – 'The sea of God's mercy, overflowing in spiritual blessings, should drown all the sufferings of this life.' What though you go now in rags? You shall have your white robes. What though you are fed as Daniel with pulse and have coarser fare? You shall feast it when you come into the kingdom. Here you drink the water of tears, but shortly you shall drink the wine of paradise. Be comforted with the thoughts of a kingdom.

6 Blessed are they that mourn

Blessed are they that mourn.
MATTHEW 5:4

Here are eight steps leading to true blessedness. They may be compared to Jacob's Ladder, the top whereof reached to heaven. We have already gone over one step, and now let us proceed to the second: 'Blessed are they that mourn.' We must go through the valley of tears to paradise. Mourning were a sad and unpleasant subject to treat on, were it not that it has blessedness going before, and comfort coming after. Mourning is put here for repentance. It implies both sorrow, which is the cloud, and tears which are the rain distilling in this golden shower; God comes down to us.

The words fall into two parts, first, an *assertion* that mourners are blessed persons; second, a *reason*, because they shall be comforted.

1 I begin with the first, the assertion; mourners are blessed persons. 'Blessed are ye that weep now' (Luke 6:21). Though the saints' tears are bitter tears, yet they are blessed tears. But will all mourning entitle a man to blessedness? No, there is a two-fold mourning which is far from making one blessed. There is a carnal mourning. There is a diabolical mourning.

A two-fold mourning which does not make us blessed

There is a carnal mourning when we lament outward losses. 'In 'Rama there was a voice heard, lamentation and weeping, and great mourning; Rachel weeping for her children . . .' (Matthew 2:18). There are abundance of these tears shed. We have many can mourn over a dead child, that cannot mourn over a crucified Saviour. Worldly sorrow hastens our funerals. 'The sorrow of the world worketh death' (2 Corinthians 7:10).

2 There is a diabolical mourning and that is two-fold: When a man mourns that he cannot satisfy his impure lust, this is like the devil,

[59]

whose greatest torture is that he can be no more wicked. Thus Ammon mourned and was sick, till he defiled his sister Tamar (2 Samuel 13:2). Thus Ahab mourned for Naboth's vineyard: 'He laid him down upon his bed, and turned away his face, and would eat no bread' (1 Kings 21:4). This was a devilish mourning.

Again, when men are sorry for the good which they have done. Pharaoh grieved that 'he had let the children of Israel go' (Exodus 14:5). Many are so devilish that they are troubled they have prayed so much and have heard so many sermons. They repent of their repentance; but if we repent of the good which is past, God will not repent of the evil which is to come.

The object of holy mourning

To illustrate this point of holy mourning, I shall show you what is the adequate object of it. There are two objects of spiritual mourning, sin and misery. Sin, and that two-fold, our own sin; the sin of others.

Our own sin. Sin must have tears. While we carry the fire of sin about us, we must carry the water of tears to quench it (Ezekiel 7:16). They are not blessed (says Chrysostom) who mourn for the dead, but rather those who mourn for sin; and indeed it is with good reason we mourn for sin, if we consider the *guilt* of sin, which binds over to wrath. Will not a guilty person weep, who is to be bound over to the sessions? Every sinner is to be tried for his life and is sure to be cast [1] if mercy does not become an advocate for him.

The *pollution* of sin. Sin is a plague spot, and will you not labour to wash away this spot with your tears? Sin makes a man worse than a toad or serpent. The serpent has nothing but what God has put into it. Poison is medicinable [2]; but the sinner has that which the devil has put into him. 'Why hath Satan filled thine heart to lie to the Holy Ghost?' (Acts 5:3). What a strange metamorphosis has sin made! The soul, which was once of an azure brightness, sin has made of a sable colour. We have in our hearts the seed of the unpardonable sin. We have the seed of all those sins for which the damned are now tormented. And shall we not mourn? He that does not mourn has surely lost the use of his reason. But every mourning for sin is not sufficient to entitle a man to blessedness. I shall show what is not the right gospel-mourning for sin, and what is the right gospel-mourning for sin.

[1] Condemned.   [2] Capable of being used as a medicine.

A five-fold mourning which is spurious

What is not the right gospel-mourning for sin? There is a five-fold mourning which is false and spurious.

A *despairing* kind of mourning. Such was Judas' mourning. He saw his sin, he was sorry, he made confession, he justifies Christ, he makes restitution (Matthew 27). Judas, who is in hell, did more than many nowadays. He confessed his sin. He did not plead necessity or good intentions, but he makes an open acknowledgment of his sin. '*I* have sinned.' Judas made restitution. His conscience told him he came wickedly by the money. It was 'the price of blood', and he 'brought again the thirty pieces of silver to the chief priests' (Matthew 27:3). But how many are there who invade the rights and possessions of others, but not a word of restitution! Judas was more honest than they are. Well, wherein was Judas' sorrow blame-worthy? It was a mourning joined with despair. He thought his wound broader than the plaster. He drowned himself in tears. His was not repentance unto life (Acts 11:18), but rather unto death.

An *hypocritical mourning*. The heart is very deceitful. It can betray as well by a tear as by a kiss. Saul looks like a mourner, and as he was sometimes 'among the prophets' (1 Samuel 10:12) so he seemed to be among the penitents. 'And Saul said unto Samuel, I have sinned, for I have transgressed the commandment of the Lord' (1 Samuel 15:24). Saul played the hypocrite in his mourning, for he did not take shame to himself, but he did rather take honour to himself: 'honour me before the elders of my people' (verse 30). He pared and minced his sin that it might appear lesser, he laid his sin upon the people, 'because I feared the people' (verse 24). They would have me fly upon the spoil, and I dare do no other. A true mourner labours to draw out sin in its bloody colours, and accent it with all its killing aggravations, that he may be deeply humbled before the Lord. 'Our iniquities are increased over our head, and our trespass is grown up unto the heavens' (Ezra 9:6). The true penitent labours to make the worst of his sin. Saul labours to make the best of sin; like a patient that makes the best of his disease, lest the physician should prescribe him too sharp physic. How easy is it for a man to put a cheat upon his own soul, and by hypocrisy to sweep himself into hell!

A *forced* mourning. When tears are pumped out by God's judgements, these are like the tears of a man that has the stone, or that lies upon the rack. Such was Cain's mourning. 'My punishment is greater than I can bear' (Genesis 4:13). His punishment troubled him more than his sin; to mourn only for fear of hell is like a thief that weeps for the penalty rather than the offence. The tears of the wicked are forced by the fire of affliction.

An *extrinsic* mourning; when sorrow lies only on the outside. 'They disfigure their faces' (Matthew 6:16). The eye is tender, but the heart is hard. Such was Ahab's mourning. 'He rent his clothes and put sackcloth on his flesh, and went softly' (1 Kings 21:27). His clothes were rent, but his heart was not rent. He had sackcloth but no sorrow. He hung down his head like a bulrush, but his heart was like an adamant. There are many who may be compared to weeping marbles, they are both watery and flinty.

A *vain* fruitless mourning. Some will shed a few tears, but are as bad as ever. They will cozen¹ and be unclean. Such a kind of mourning there is in hell. The damned weep but they blaspheme.

The right gospel-mourning

What is the right gospel-mourning? That mourning which will entitle a man to blessedness has these qualifications:

It is *spontaneous* and free. It must come as water out of a spring, not as fire out of a flint. Tears for sin must be like the myrrh which drops from the tree freely without cutting or forcing. Mary Magdalene's repentance was voluntary. 'She stood weeping' (Luke 7). She came to Christ with ointment in her hand, with love in her heart, with tears in her eyes. God is for a free-will offering. He does not love to be put to distrain.²

Gospel-mourning is *spiritual*; that is, when we mourn for sin more than suffering. Pharaoh says, Take away the plague. He never thought of the plague of his heart. A sinner mourns because judgment follows at the heels of sin, but David cries out, 'My sin is ever before me' (Psalm 51:3). God had threatened that the sword should ride in circuit in his family, but David does not say, 'The sword is ever before me', but 'My sin is ever before me'. The offence against God troubled him. He grieved more for the treason than the bloody axe. Thus the penitent prodigal, 'I have sinned against heaven, and before thee' (Luke 15:18, 21). He does not say, 'I am almost starved among the husks', but 'I

¹ Cheat, defraud.
² That is, driven to the use of constraint or force to obtain what is due to him.

[62]

have offended my father'. In particular, our mourning for sin, if it be spiritual, must be under this three-fold notion:

1 We must mourn for sin as it is an act of hostility and enmity. Sin not only makes us unlike God, but contrary to God: 'They have walked contrary unto me' (Leviticus 26:40). Sin affronts and resists the Holy Ghost (Acts 7:51). Sin is contrary to God's nature; God is holy; sin is an impure thing. Sin is contrary to his will. If God be of one mind, sin is of another. Sin does all it can to spite God. The Hebrew word for 'sin' signifies 'rebellion'. A sinner fights against God (Acts 5:39). Now when we mourn for sin as it is a walking Antipodes [1] to heaven, this is a gospel-mourning. Nature will not bear contraries.

2 We must mourn for sin as it is a piece of the highest ingratitude. It is a kicking against the breasts of mercy. God sends his Son to redeem us, his Spirit to comfort us. We sin against the blood of Christ, the grace of the Spirit and shall we not mourn? We complain of the unkindness of others, and shall we not lay to heart our own unkindness against God? Caesar took it unkindly that his son, Brutus, should stab him – 'and thou, my son!' May not the Lord say to us, 'These wounds I have received in the house of my friend!' (Zechariah 13:6). Israel took their jewels and ear-rings and made a golden calf of them. The sinner takes the jewels of God's mercies and makes use of them to sin. Ingratitude dyes a sin in grain, [2] hence they are called 'crimson sins' (Isaiah 1:18). Sins against gospel-love are worse in some sense than the sins of the devils, for they never had an offer of grace tendered to them. 'The devil sinned though constituted in innocency, I indeed when restored. He continued in wickedness by reprobation of God, I indeed when recalled by God. He was hardened by punishment, I indeed by (divine) gentleness. And thus both of us went against God, the one by not seeking to know himself, I indeed against the one who died for me. Behold his (the devil's) dreadful likeness, but in many things I see myself even more dreadful' (Anselm [3]: Concerning the fall of the Devil.) Now when we mourn for sin as it has its accent of ingratitude upon it, this is an evangelical mourning.

3 We must mourn for sin as it is a privation; it keeps good things from us; it hinders our communion with God. Mary wept for Christ's absence. 'They have taken away my Lord' (John 20:13). So our sins

[1] That is, sin is in direct opposition to all that is of God. (Cf. Thomas Fuller's Holy and Profane State (1642): 'Christians were forced to be Antipodes to other men, so that when it was night with others, it was day with them.'
[2] Thoroughly, indelibly.   [3] Archbishop of Canterbury, 1093–1109.

have taken away our Lord. They have deprived us of his sweet presence. Will not he grieve who has lost a rich jewel? When we mourn for sin under this notion, as it makes the Sun of Righteousness withdraw from our horizon; when we mourn not so much that peace is gone, and trading is gone, but God is gone, 'My beloved had withdrawn himself' (Canticles 5 : 6); this is an holy mourning. The mourning for the loss of God's favour is the best way to regain his favour. If you have lost a friend, all your weeping will not fetch him again, but if you have lost God's presence, your mourning will bring your God again.

The accompaniments of gospel-mourning

Gospel-mourning sends the soul to God. When the prodigal son repented, he went to his father. 'I will arise and go to my father' (Luke 15 : 18). Jacob wept and prayed (Hosea 12 : 4). The people of Israel wept and offered sacrifice (Judges 2 : 4, 5). Gospel mourning puts a man upon duty. The reason is, that in true sorrow there is a mixture of hope, and hope puts the soul upon the use of means. That mourning which like the 'flaming sword' keeps the soul from approaching to God, and beats it off from duty, is a sinful mourning. It is a sorrow hatched in hell. Such was Saul's grief, which drove him to the witch of Endor (1 Samuel 28 : 7). Evangelical mourning is a spur to prayer. The child who weeps for offending his father goes to his presence and will not leave till his father be reconciled to him. Absalom could not be quiet 'till he had seen the king's face' (2 Samuel 14 : 32, 33).

Gospel mourning is for sin in particular. The deceitful man is occupied with generalities. It is with a true penitent as it is with a wounded man. He comes to the surgeon and shows him all his wounds. Here I was cut with the sword; here I was shot with a bullet. So a true penitent bewails all his particular sins. 'We have served Baalim' (Judges 10 : 10). They mourned for their idolatry. And David lays his fingers upon the sore and points to that very sin that troubled him (Psalm 51 : 4). I have done this evil. He means his blood-guiltiness. A wicked man will say he is a sinner, but a child of God says, I have done *this evil*. Peter wept for that particular sin of denying Christ. Clemens Alexandrinus [1] says, he never heard a cock crow, but he fell a-weeping. There must be a particular repentance before we have a general pardon.

Gospel tears must drop from the eye of faith. 'The father of the child cried out with tears, Lord, I believe' (Mark 9 : 24). Our disease must make us mourn, but when we look up to our Physician, who has

[1] Clement of Alexandria, theologian of the 2nd century A.D.

made a plaister of his own blood, we must not mourn without hope. Believing tears are precious. When the clouds of sorrow have over-cast the soul, some sunshine of faith must break forth. The soul will be swallowed up of sorrow, it will be drowned in tears, if faith be not the bladder to keep it up from sinking. Though our tears drop to the earth, our faith must reach heaven. After the greatest rain, faith must appear as the rainbow in the cloud. The tears of faith are bottled as precious wine (Psalm 56:8).

Gospel-mourning is joined with self-loathing. The sinner admires himself. The penitent loathes himself. 'Ye shall loath yourselves in your own sight for all your evils' (Ezekiel 20:43). A true penitent is troubled not only for the shameful consequence of sin, but for the loathsome nature of sin; not only the sting of sin but the deformed face. How did the leper loathe himself! (Leviticus 13:45). The Hebrew doctors say, the leper pronounced unclean was to put a covering on his upper lip, both as a mourner and in token of shame. The true mourner cries out, O these impure eyes! this heart which is a conclave of wickedness! He not only leaves sin but loathes sin. He that is fallen in the dirt loathes himself (Hosea 14:1).

Gospel-mourning must be purifying. Our tears must make us more holy. We must so weep for sin, as to weep out sin. Our tears must drown our sins. We must not only mourn but turn. 'Turn to me with weeping' (Joel 2:12). What is it to have a watery eye and a whorish heart? It is foolish to say it is day, when the air is full of darkness; so to say you repent, when you draw dark shadows in your life. It is an excellent saying of Augustine, 'He truly bewails the sins he has committed, who never commits the sins he has bewailed.' True mourning is like the 'water of jealousy' (Numbers 5:12–22). It makes the thigh of sin to rot. 'Thou breakest the heads of the dragons in the waters' (Psalm 74:14). The heads of our sins, these dragons, are broken in the waters of true repentance. True tears are cleansing. They are like a flood that carries away all the rubbish of our sins with it. The waters of holy mourning are like the river Jordan wherein Naaman washed and was cleansed of his leprosy. It is reported that there is a river in Sicily where, if the blackest sheep are bathed, they become white; so, though our sins be as scarlet, yet by washing in this river of repentance, they become white as snow. Naturalists say of the serpent, before it goes to drink it vomits out its poison. In this 'be wise as serpents'. Before you think to drink down the sweet cordials of the promises, cast up the poison that lies at your heart. Do not only mourn for sin, but break from sin.

Gospel mourning must be joined with hatred of sin. 'What indignation!' (2 Corinthians 7:11). We must not only abstain from sin, but abhor sin. The dove hates the least feather of the hawk. A true mourner hates the least motion to sin. A true mourner is a sin-hater. Amnon hated Tamar more than ever he loved her (2 Samuel 13:15). To be a sin-hater implies two things: first, to look upon sin as the most deadly evil, a complicated evil. It looks more ghastly than death or hell. Second, to be implacably incensed against it. A sin-hater will never admit of any terms of peace. The war between him and sin is like the war between Rehoboam and Jeroboam. 'There was war between Rehoboam and Jeroboam all their days' (1 Kings 14:30). Anger may be reconciled. Hatred cannot. True mourning begins in the love of God, and ends in the hatred of sin.

Gospel mourning in some cases is joined with restitution. It is as well a sin to violate the name as the chastity of another. If we have eclipsed the good name of others, we are bound to ask them for forgiveness. If we have wronged them in their estate by unjust, fraudulent dealing, we must make them some compensation. Thus Zacchaeus, 'If I have taken anything from any man by false accusation, I restore him four-fold' (Luke 19:8), according to the law of Exodus 22:1. St James bids us not only look to the heart but the hand: 'Cleanse your hands, ye sinners, and purify your hearts' (James 4:8). If you have wronged another, cleanse your hands by restitution. Be assured, without restitution, no remission.

Gospel mourning must be a speedy mourning. We must take heed of adjourning our repentance, and putting it off till death. As David said, 'I will pay my vows now' (Psalm 116:18), so should a Christian say, I will mourn for sin now. 'Blessed are ye that weep now' (Luke 6:21). As Popillius [1], the Roman Legate, when he was sent to Antiochus (Epiphanes) the king, made a circle round about the king and bade him make his answer before he went out of that circle, so God has encircled us in the compass of a little time, and charges us immediately to bewail our sins. 'Now God calleth all men everywhere to repent' (Acts 17:30). We know not whether we may have another day granted us. Oh let us not put off our mourning for sin till the making of our will. Do not think holy mourning is only a death-bed duty. You may seek the blessing with tears, as Esau,[2] when it is too late. 'During tomorrow?' says Augustine. How long shall I say that I will repent tomorrow? Why not at this instant? 'Delay brings danger.' Caesar's deferring to read his

---

[1] As Roman ambassador he acted thus towards the King of Syria, to intimidate him into compliance with Rome's demands (168 B.C.).
[2] 'Isaac' appears in the text of 1671.

letter before he went to the Senate-house, cost him his life. The true mourner makes haste to meet an angry God, as Jacob did his brother; and the present he sends before is the sacrifice of tears.

Gospel mourning for sin is constant. There are some who at a sermon will shed a few tears, but this land-flood is soon dried up. The hypocrite's sorrow is like a vein opened and presently stopped. The Hebrew word for 'eye' signifies also 'a fountain', to show that the eye must run like a fountain for sin and not cease; but it must not be like the Libyan fountain of the sun which the ancients speak of; in the morning the water is hot, at mid-day cold. The waters of repentance must not overflow with more heat in the morning, at the first hearing of the gospel, and at mid-day, in the midst of health and prosperity, grow cold and be ready to freeze. No, it must be a daily weeping. As Paul said, 'I die daily' (1 Corinthians 15:31), so a Christian should say, 'I mourn daily.' Therefore keep open an issue of godly sorrow, and be sure it be not stopped till death. 'Let not the apple of thine eye cease' (Lamentations 2:18). It is reported of holy John Bradford[1] that scarce a day passed him wherein he did not shed some tears for sin. Daily mourning is a good antidote against backsliding. I have read of one that had an epilepsy, or falling sickness, and being dipped in sea-water, was cured. The washing of our souls daily in the brinish waters of repentance is the best way both to prevent and cure the falling into relapses.

Even God's own children must mourn after pardon; for God, in pardoning, does not pardon at one instant sins past and future; but as repentance is renewed, so pardon is renewed. Should God by one act pardon sins future as well as past, this would make void part of Christ's office. What need were there of his intercession, if sin should be pardoned before it be committed? There are sins in the godly of daily incursion, which must be mourned for. Though sin be pardoned still it rebels; though it be covered, it is not cured (Romans 7:23). There is that in the best Christian which is contrary to God. There is that in him which deserves hell, and shall he not mourn? A ship that is always leaking must have the water continually pumped out. While the soul leaks by sin, we must be still pumping at the leak by repentance. Think not, O Christian, that your sins are washed away only by Christ's blood, but by water and blood. The brazen laver (Exodus 30:18) that the people of Israel were to wash in might be a fit emblem of this spiritual laver, tears and blood; and when holy mourning is thus qualified, this is that 'sorrowing after a godly sort' (2 Corinthians 7:11), which makes a Christian eternally blessed.

[1] Burned at Smithfield, London (1555), during the Marian Persecution.

We must mourn for the sins of others

As we must mourn for our own sins, so we must lay to heart the sins of others. The poets feign that Biblis[1] was turned into a fountain. Thus we should wish with Jeremiah, that our eyes were a fountain of tears, that we might weep day and night for the iniquity of the times. Our blessed Saviour mourned for the sins of the Jews: 'Being grieved for the hardness' (or brawniness) 'of their hearts' (Mark 3:5). And holy David, looking upon the sins of the wicked, his heart was turned into a spring, and his eyes into rivers. 'Rivers of tears run down mine eyes, because they keep not thy law' (Psalm 119:136). Lot's righteous soul 'was vexed with the unclean conversation of the wicked' (2 Peter 2:7). Lot took the sins of Sodom and made spears of them to pierce his own soul. Cyprian[2] says that in the primitive times, when a virgin who vowed herself to religion had defiled her chastity, shame and grief filled the whole face of the congregation.

Have not we cause to mourn for the sins of others? The whole axle-tree of the nation is ready to break under the weight of sin. What an inundation of wickedness is there amongst us? Mourn for the hypocrisy of the times. Jehu says 'Come see my zeal for the Lord', but it was zeal for the throne (2 Kings 10:16). This is the hypocrisy of some. They entitle God to whatever they do. They make bold with God to use his name to their wickedness; as if a thief should pretend the king's warrant for his robbery. 'They build up Sion with blood; the heads thereof judge for reward; yet will they lean upon the Lord and say, Is not the Lord among us?' (Micah 3:10, 11). Many with a religious kiss smite the gospel under the fifth rib. Could not Ahab be content to kill and take possession, but must he usher it in with religion, and make fasting a preface to his murder? (1 Kings 21:12). The white devil is worst. A burning torch in the hand of a ghost is most affrighting. To hear the name of God in the mouths of scandalous hypocrites is enough to affright others from the profession of religion.

Mourn for the errors and blasphemies of the nation. There is now a free trade of error. Toleration gives men a patent to sin. What cursed opinion that has been long ago buried in the church, but is now digged out of the grave, and by some worshipped! England is grown as wanton in her religion, as she is antic[3] in her fashions. The Jesuits' Exchange is open, and every one almost is for an opinion of the newest cut. Did men's faces alter as fast as their judgments, we should not know them.

[1] The Roman poet Ovid tells how Biblis, becoming enamoured of her brother, was changed into a fountain near Miletus. [2] Bishop of Carthage in the 3rd century.
[3] Grotesque, bizarre.

Mourn for covenant violation. This sin is a flying roll against England. Breach of covenant is spiritual harlotry, and for this God may name us 'Lo-ammi', and give us a bill of divorce (Hosea 1 : 9).

Mourn for the pride of the nation. Our condition is low, but our hearts are high. Mourn for the profaneness of the land. England is like that man in the gospel who had 'a spirit of an unclean devil' (Luke 4 : 33). Mourn for the removing of landmarks (Deuteronomy 27 : 17). Mourn for the contempt offered to magistracy, the spitting in the face of authority. Mourn that there are so few mourners. Surely if we mourn not for the sins of others, it is to be feared that we are not sensible of our own sins. God looks upon us as guilty of those sins in others which we do not lament. Our tears may help to quench God's wrath.

We must mourn for the miseries of the church

The saints are members of the body mystical as well as political, therefore they must be sensible of the injuries of God's church. 'We wept when we remembered Sion' (Psalm 137 : 1). The people of Israel, being debarred from the place of public worship, sat by the rivers weeping. They laid aside all their musical instruments. 'We hanged our harps upon the willows' (verse 2). We were as far from joy as those willows were from fruit. 'How shall we sing the Lord's song in a strange land?' (verse 4). We were fitter to weep than to sing. The sound of song is not agreeable to mourning.

When we consider the miseries of many Christians in Germany,[1] the Dukedom of Savoy,[2] and other foreign parts, who have been driven from their habitations because they would not desert the Protestant and espouse the Popish religion; when instead of a Bible, a crucifix; instead of prayers, mass; instead of going to church, they should go on pilgrimage to some saint or relic. When we consider these things, our eyes should run down. Mourn to see God's church a bleeding vine. Mourn to see Christ's spouse with 'garments rolled in blood'.

Methinks I hear England's passing bell go. Let us shed some tears over dying England. Let us bewail our intestine divisions. England's divisions have been fatal. They brought in the Saxons, Danes, Normans. If 'a kingdom divided cannot stand', how do we stand but by a miracle of free grace? Truth is fallen and peace is fled. England's fine coat of peace is torn and, like Joseph's coat, dipped in blood. Peace is the

[1] Miseries occasioned by the Thirty Years' War (1618–48).
[2] Miseries suffered by the Waldenses (cf. Milton's sonnet: 'Avenge, O Lord, thy slaughtered saints whose bones lie scattered on the Alpine mountains cold . . .').

glory of a nation. Some observe, if the top of the beech tree be taken off, the whole tree withers. Peace is the apex and top of all earthly blessings. This top being cut off, we may truly say the body of the whole nation begins to wither apace.

Mourn for the oppressions of England. The people of this land have laid out their money only to buy mourning.

The seasons of holy mourning

Though we must always keep open the issue of godly sorrow, yet there are some seasons wherein our tears should overflow, as the water sometimes rises higher. There are three special seasons of extraordinary mourning, when it should be as it were high-water in the soul:

1 When there are tokens of God's wrath breaking forth in the nation. England has been under God's black rod these many years. The Lord has drawn his sword and it is not yet put up. O that our tears may blunt the edge of this sword! When it is a time of treading down, now is a time of breaking up the fallow ground of our hearts. 'Therefore said I, look away from me, I will weep bitterly for it is a time of treading down' (Isaiah 22:4, 5). 'A day of darkness and of gloominess, a day of clouds . . . therefore turn ye even to me with weeping and with mourning' (Joel 2: 2, 12). Rain follows thunder. When God thunders in a nation by his judgments, now the showers of tears must distil. When God smites upon our back, we must 'smite upon our thigh' (Jeremiah 31:19). When God seems to stand upon the 'threshold of the temple' (Ezekiel 10:4), as if he were ready to take his wings and fly, then is it a time to lie weeping between 'the porch and the altar'. If the Lord seems to be packing up and carrying away his gospel, it is now high time to mourn, that by our tears possibly his 'repentings may be kindled' (Hosea 11:8).

2 Before the performing solemn duties of God's worship, as fasting or receiving the Lord's Supper. Christian, are you about to seek God in an extraordinary manner? 'Seek him sorrowing' (Luke 2:48). Would you have the smiles of God's face, the kisses of his lips? Set open all the springs of mourning, and then God will draw nigh to you in an ordinance and say, 'Here I am' (Isaiah 58:9). When Jacob wept, then he 'found God in Bethel' (Hosea 12:4). 'He called the name of the place Peniel, for (says he) I have seen God face to face' (Genesis 32:30). Give Christ the wine of your tears to drink, and in the sacrament he will give you the wine of his blood to drink.

3 After scandalous relapses. Though I will not say with Novatus that there is no mercy for sins of recidivation or relapse, yet I say there is no mercy without bitter mourning. Scandalous sins reflect dishonour upon religion (2 Samuel 12:14). Therefore now our cheeks should be covered with blushing, and our eyes bedewed with tears. Peter, after his denying Christ, wept bitterly. Christian, has God given you over to any enormous sin as a just reward of your pride and security? Go into the 'weeping bath'. Sins of infirmity injure the soul, but scandalous sins wound the gospel. Lesser sins grieve the Spirit, but greater sins vex the Spirit (Isaiah 63:10). And if that blessed Dove weeps, shall not we weep? When the air is dark then the dew falls. When we have by scandalous sin darkened the lustre of the gospel, now is the time for the dew of holy tears to fall from our eyes.

The degrees of mourning

Next to the seasons of mourning, let us consider the degree of it. The mourning for sin must be a very great mourning. The Greek word imports a great sorrow, such as is seen at the funeral of a dear friend. 'They shall look on me whom they have pierced, and they shall mourn for him, as one that mourneth for his only son' (Zechariah 12:10). The sorrow for an only child is very great. Such must be the sorrow for sin. 'In that day there shall be great mourning, as the mourning of Hadad-rimmon in the valley of Megiddon (verse 11). In that valley Josiah, that famous and pious prince, was cut off by an untimely death, at whose funeral there was bitter lamentation. Thus bitterly must we bewail, not the death, but the life of our sins. Now then, to set forth the graduation of sorrow.

Our mourning for sin must be so great as to exceed all other grief. Eli's mourning for the ark was such that it swallowed up the loss of his two children. Spiritual grief must preponderate over all other. We should mourn more for sin than for the loss of friends or estate.

We should endeavour to have our sorrow rise up to the same height and proportion as our sin does. Manasseh was a great sinner and a great mourner. 'He humbled himself greatly' (2 Chronicles 33:12). Manasseh made the streets run with blood and he made the prison in Babylon run with tears. Peter wept bitterly. A true mourner labours that his repentance may be as eminent as his sin is transcendent.

The opposite to holy mourning

Having shown the nature of mourning, I shall next show what is the
opposite to holy mourning. The opposite to mourning is 'hardness of
heart', which in Scripture is called 'an heart of stone' (Ezekiel 36:26).
An heart of stone is far from mourning and relenting. This heart of
stone is known by two symptoms:

One symptom is *insensibility*. A stone is not sensible of anything.
Lay weight upon it; grind it to powder; it does not feel. So it is with
an hard heart. It is insensible of sin or wrath. The stone in the kidneys
is felt but not the stone in the heart. 'Who being past feeling . . .' (Ephesians 4:19).

An heart of stone is known by its *inflexibility*. A stone will not bend.
That is hard which does not yield to the touch. So it is with an hard
heart. It will not comply with God's command. It will not stoop to
Christ's sceptre. An heart of stone will sooner break than bend by repentance. It is so far yielding to God that like the anvil it beats back
the hammer. It 'resists the Holy Ghost' (Acts 7:51).

Oh Christians, if you would be spiritual mourners, take heed of this
stone of the heart. 'Harden not your hearts' (Hebrews 3:7, 8). A stony
heart is the worst heart. If it were brazen, it might be melted in the furnace of iron; it might be bowed with the hammer. But a stony heart is
such that only the arm of God can break it and the blood of God soften
it. Oh the misery of an hard heart! An hard heart is void of all grace.
While the wax is hard, it will not take the impression of the seal. The
heart, while it is hard, will not take the stamp of grace. It must first be
made tender and melting. The plough of the Word will not go upon
an hard heart. An hard heart is good for nothing but to make fuel for
hell-fire. 'After thy hardness of heart thou treasurest up wrath' (Romans
2:5). Hell is full of hard hearts, there is not one soft heart there. There
is weeping there but no softness. We read of 'vessels fitted to destruction' (Romans 9:22). Impenitency fits these vessels for hell, and makes
them like sere wood which is fit to burn. Hardness of heart makes a
man's condition worse than all his other sins besides. If one be guilty
of great sins, yet if he can mourn, there is hope. Repentance unravels
sin, and makes sin not to be. But hardness of heart binds guilt fast upon
the soul. It seals a man under wrath. It is not heinousness of sin, but
hardness of heart that damns. This makes the sin against the Holy
Ghost incapable of mercy, because the sinner that has committed it is
incapable of repentance.

7 Sundry sharp reproofs

This doctrine draws up a charge against several sorts:

1 Those that think themselves good Christians, yet have not learned this art of holy mourning. Luther calls mourning 'a rare herb'. Men have tears to shed for other things, but have none to spare for their sins. There are many murmurers, but few mourners. Most are like the stony ground which 'lacked moisture' (Luke 8:6).

We have many cry out of hard times, but they are not sensible of hard hearts. Hot and dry is the worst temper of the body. Sure I am that to be hot in sin, and to be so dry as to have no tears, is the worst temper of the soul. How many are like Gideon's dry fleece, and like the mountains of Gilboa! There is no dew upon them. Did Christ bleed for sin, and can you not weep? If God's bottle be not filled with tears, his vial will be filled with wrath. We have many sinners in Sion, but few mourners in Sion. It is with most people as with a man on the top of a mast; the winds blow and the waves beat, and the ship is in danger of shipwreck, and he is fast asleep. So when the waves of sin have even covered men and the stormy wind of God's wrath blows, and is ready to blow them into hell, yet they are asleep in security.

2 This doctrine reproves them who instead of weeping for sin, spend their days in mirth and jollity. Instead of mourners we have ranters. 'They take the timbrel and harp, they spend their days in wealth' (Job 21:12, 13). 'They pursue the Sybarite[1] life,' says Luther. 'They do not give themselves to mourning, but follow after their enjoyments.' They live epicures and die atheists. St James bids us 'turn our laughter to mourning' (James 4:9). But they turn their mourning to laughter. Samson was brought forth to make the Philistines sport (Judges 16:25). The jovial sinner makes the devil sport. It is a saying of Theophylact,

[1] Sybaris, in ancient Italy, had the reputation of a pleasure-loving city, given over to luxury and effeminacy.

'It is one of the worst sights to see a sinner go laughing to hell.' How unseasonable is it to take the harp and viol when God is taking the sword! 'A sword, a sword is sharpened and also furbished; should we then make mirth?' (Ezekiel 21 : 9, 10). This is a sin that enrages God. 'In that day did the Lord of hosts call to weeping and to mourning, and behold joy and gladness, slaying oxen and killing sheep, eating flesh and drinking wine; and it was revealed in mine ears by the Lord of hosts. Surely this iniquity shall not be purged from you till ye die, saith the Lord God of hosts' (Isaiah 22: 12–14). That is, this your sin shall not be done away by any expiatory sacrifice, but vengeance shall pursue you for ever.

3 This doctrine reproves those who, instead of mourning for sin, rejoice in sin (Proverbs 2 : 14); 'Who take pleasure in iniquity' (2 Thessalonians 2 : 12). Wicked men in this sense are worse than the damned in hell, for I dare say *they* take little pleasure in their sins. There are some so impudently profane, that they will make themselves and others merry with their sins. Sin is a soul sickness (Luke 5 : 31). Will a man make merry with his disease? Ah wretch, did Christ bleed for sin, and do you laugh at sin? Is that your mirth which grieves the Spirit? Is it a time for a man to break jests when he is upon the scaffold, and his head is to be stricken off? You who laugh at sin now, the time is coming when God will 'laugh at your calamity' (Proverbs 1 : 26).

4 This doctrine reproves those that cry down mourning for sin. They are like the Philistines who stopped the wells (Genesis 26 : 15). These would stop the wells of godly sorrow. Antinomians say this is a legal doctrine, but Christ here preaches it: 'Blessed are they that mourn.' And the apostles preached it, 'And they went out and preached that men should repent' (Mark 6 : 12). Holy ingenuity will put us upon mourning for sin. He that has the heart of a child cannot but weep for his unkindness against God. Mourning for sin is the very fruit and product of the Spirit of grace (Zechariah 12 : 10). Such as cry down repentance, cry down the Spirit of grace. Mourning for sin is the only way to keep off wrath from us. Such as with Samson would break this pillar, go about to pull down the vengeance of God upon the land. To all such I say, as Peter to Simon Magus, 'Repent therefore of this thy wickedness and pray God if perhaps the thought of thine heart may be forgiven thee', O sinner (Acts 8 : 22). Repent that you have cried down repentance.

8 Motives to holy mourning

Let me exhort Christians to holy mourning. I now persuade to such a mourning as will prepare the soul for blessedness. Oh that our hearts were spiritual limbecs,[1] distilling the water of holy tears! Christ's doves weep. 'They that escape shall be like doves of the valleys, all of them mourning, every one for his iniquity' (Ezekiel 7: 16).

Eleven divine motives to holy mourning

There are several divine motives to holy mourning:

1 Tears cannot be put to a better use. If you weep for outward losses, you lose your tears. It is like a shower upon a rock, which does no good; but tears for sin are blessed tears. 'Blessed are they that mourn.' These poison our corruptions; salt-water kills the worms. The brinish water of repenting tears will help to kill that worm of sin which should gnaw the conscience.

2 Gospel-mourning is an evidence of grace. 'I will pour upon the house of David and the inhabitants of Jerusalem, the Spirit of grace, and they shall mourn . . .' (Zechariah 12: 10). The Holy Ghost descended on Christ like a dove (Luke 3: 22). The dove is a weeping creature. Where there is a dove-like weeping, it is a good sign the Spirit of God has descended there. Weeping for sin is a sign of the new birth. As soon as the child is born, it weeps: 'And behold the babe wept' (Exodus 2: 6). To weep kindly for sin is a good sign we are born of God. Mourning shows a 'heart of flesh' (Ezekiel 36: 26). A stone will not melt. When the heart is in a melting frame, it is a sign the heart of stone is taken away.

3 The preciousness of tears. Tears dropping from a mournful, penitent eye, are like water dropping from the roses, very sweet and precious to

[1] Apparatus formerly used in distillation (now spelt, 'alembic').

God. A fountain in the garden makes it pleasant. That heart is most delightful to God which has a fountain of sorrow running in it. 'Mary stood at Christ's feet weeping' (Luke 7:38). Her tears were more fragrant and odoriferous than her ointment. The incense, when it is broken, smells sweetest. When the heart is broken for sin, then our services give forth their sweetest perfume. 'There is joy in heaven over one sinner that repenteth' (Luke 15:7). Whereupon St Bernard calls tears 'the wine of angels'. And sure, God delights much in tears, else he would not keep a bottle for them (Psalm 56:8). One calls tears 'a fat sacrifice', which under the law was most acceptable (Leviticus 3:3). St Jerome calls mourning a plank after shipwreck. Chrysostom calls tears a spunge to wipe off sin. Tears are powerful orators for mercy. Eusebius [1] says there was an altar at Athens, on which they poured no other sacrifice but tears, as if the heathens thought there was no better way to pacify their angry gods, than by weeping. Jacob wept and 'had power over the angel' (Hosea 12:4). Tears melt the heart of God. When a malefactor comes weeping to the bar, this melts the judge's heart towards him. When a man comes weeping in prayer and smites on his breast, saying, 'God be merciful to me a sinner' (Luke 18:13), this melts God's heart towards him. Prayer (says Jerome) inclines God to shew mercy; tears compel him. God seals his pardons upon melting hearts. Tears, though they are silent, yet have a voice (Psalm 6:8). Tears wash away sin. Rain melts and washes away a ball of snow. Repenting tears wash away sin. That sin, says Ambrose,[2] which cannot be defended by argument, may be washed away by tears.

4 The sweetness of tears. Mourning is the way to solid joy. 'The sweetest wine is that which comes out of the wine-press of the eyes', says Chrysostom. The soul is never more enlarged than when it can weep. Closet tears are better than court music. When the heart is sad, weeping eases it by giving vent. The soul of a Christian is most eased when it can vent itself by holy mourning. Chrysostom observes that David who was the great mourner in Israel was the sweet singer in Israel. 'My tears were my meat' (Psalm 42:3). On which place Ambrose gives this gloss: 'No meat so sweet as tears.' 'The tears of the penitent,' says Bernard, 'are sweeter than all worldly joy.' A Christian thinks himself sometimes in the suburbs of heaven when he can weep. When Hannah had wept, she went away and was no more sad. Sugar

---

[1] The 'Father of Church History'. He was the Bishop of Caesarea from about 315 to 340.
[2] Bishop of Milan in the 4th century.

when it melts is sweetest. When a Christian melts in tears, now he has the sweetest joy. When the daughter of Pharaoh descended into the river, she found a babe there among the flags; so when we descend into the river of repenting tears, we find the babe Jesus there who shall wipe away all tears from our eyes. Well therefore might Chrysostom solemnly bless God for giving us this laver of tears to wash in.

5 A mourner for sin not only does good to himself but to others. He helps to keep off wrath from a land. As when Abraham was going to strike the blow, the angel stayed his hand (Genesis 22 : 12), so when God is going to destroy a nation, the mourner stays his hand. Tears in the child's eye sometimes move the angry father to spare the child. Penitential tears melt God's heart and bind his hand. Jeremiah, who was a weeping prophet, was a great intercessor. God says to him, 'Pray not for this people' (Jeremiah 7 : 16), as if the Lord had said, Jeremiah, so powerful are your prayers and tears, that if you pray I cannot deny you. 'This kind of labour bears sway,' as he said in Plautus.[1] Tears have a mighty influence upon God. Surely God has some mourners in the land, or he had destroyed us before now.

6 Holy mourning is preventing physic. Our mourning for sin here will prevent mourning in hell. Hell is a place of weeping (Matthew 8 : 12). The damned mingle their drink with weeping. God is said to hold his bottle for our tears (Psalm 56 : 8). They who will not shed a bottle-full of tears shall hereafter shed rivers of tears. 'Woe to you that laugh now, for ye shall mourn and weep' (Luke 6 : 25). You have sometimes seen sugar lying in a damp place dissolve to water. All the sugared joys of the wicked dissolve at last to the water of tears. Now tears will do us good. Now it is seasonable weeping. It is like a shower in the spring. If we do not weep now it will be too late. Could we hear the language of the damned, they are now cursing themselves that they did not weep soon enough. Oh is it not better to have our hell here, than hereafter? Is it not better to shed repenting tears than despairing tears? He that weeps here is a blessed mourner. He that weeps in hell is a cursed mourner. The physician by bleeding the patient prevents death. By the opening a vein of godly sorrow, we prevent the death of our souls.

7 There is no other way the Gospel prescribes to blessedness but this: 'Blessed are they that mourn.' This is the road that leads to the new Jerusalem. There may be several ways leading to a city; some go one way, some another; but there is but one way to heaven, and that is by

[1] Latin dramatist of the 2nd century B.C.

the house of weeping (Acts 26:20). Perhaps a man may think thus, If I cannot mourn for sin, I will get to heaven some other way. I will go to church; I will give alms; I will lead a civil life. Nay, but I tell you there is but one way to blessedness, and that is, through the valley of tears. If you do not go this way, you will miss of Paradise. 'I tell you, except ye repent, ye shall all likewise perish' (Luke 13:3). There are many lines leading to the centre, but the heavenly centre has but one line leading to it, and that is a tear dropping from the eye of faith. A man may have a disease in his body that twenty medicines will heal. Sin is a disease of the soul which makes it sick unto death. Now there is but one medicine will heal, and that is the medicine of repentance.

8 Consider what need every Christian has to be conversant in holy mourning. A man may take physic when he has no need of it. Many go to the Bath [1] when they have no need. It is rather out of curiosity than necessity. But O what need is there for everyone to go into the weeping bath! Think what a sinner you have been. You have filled God's book with your debts, and what need you have to fill his bottle with your tears! You have lived in secret sin. God enjoins you this penance, 'Mourn for sin.' But perhaps some may say, I have no need of mourning, for I have lived a very civil life. Go home and mourn because you are but civil. Many a man's civility, being rested upon, has damned him. It is sad for men to be without repentance, but it is worse to need no repentance (Luke 15:7).

9 Tears are but finite. It is but a while that we shall weep. After a few showers that fall from our eyes, we shall have a perpetual sunshine. In heaven the bottle of tears is stopped. 'God shall wipe away all tears . . .' (Revelation 7:17). When sin shall cease, tears shall cease. 'Weeping may endure for a night, but joy cometh in the morning' (Psalm 30:5). In the morning of the ascension, then shall all tears be wiped away.

10 The benefit of holy mourning. The best of our commodities come by water. Mourning makes the soul fruitful in grace. When a shower falls, the herbs and plants grow. 'I will water thee with my tears, O Heshbon!' (Isaiah 16:9). I may allude to it; tears water our graces and make them flourish. 'He sends his springs into the valleys' (Psalm 104:10). That is the reason the valleys flourish with corn, because the springs run there. Where the springs of sorrow run, there the heart bears a fruitful crop. Leah was tender-eyed; she had a watery eye and was fruitful. The

[1] The city of Bath. It was customary in the late 17th century to speak of going to 'the Bath'.

tender-eyed Christian usually brings forth more of the fruits of the Spirit. A weeping eye is the water-pot to water our graces.

Again, mourning fences us against the devil's temptations. Temptations are called 'fiery darts' (Ephesians 6 : 16), because indeed they set the soul on fire. Temptations enrage anger, inflame lust. Now the waters of holy mourning quench these fiery darts. Wet powder will not soon take the fire. When the heart is wetted and moistened with sorrow, it will not so easily take the fire of temptation. Tears are the best engines and water-works to quench the devil's fire; and if there be so much profit and benefit in gospel-sorrow, then let every Christian wash his face every morning in the laver of tears.

11 And lastly, to have a melting frame of spirit is a great sign of God's presence with us in an ordinance. It is a sign that the Sun of Righteousness has risen upon us, when our frozen hearts thaw and melt for sin. It is a saying of Bernard, 'By this you may know whether you have met with God in a duty, when you find yourselves in a melting and mourning frame'. We are apt to measure all by comfort. We think we never have God's presence in an ordinance, unless we have joy. Herein we are like Thomas. 'Unless (says he) I shall see in his hands the print of the nails, I will not believe' (John 20 : 25). So are we apt to say that, unless we have incomes of comfort, we will not believe that we have found God in a duty; but if our hearts can melt kindly in tears of love, this is a real sign that God has been with us. As Jacob said, 'Surely the Lord is in this place, and I knew it not' (Genesis 28 : 16). So, Christian, when your heart breaks for sin and dissolves into holy tears, God is in this duty, though you do not know it.

Methinks all that has been said should make us spiritual mourners. Perhaps we have tried to mourn and cannot. But as a man that has digged so many fathoms deep for water and can find none, at last digs till he finds a spring; so though we have been digging for the water of tears and can find none, yet let us weigh all that has been said and set our hearts again to work, and perhaps at last we may say, as Isaac's servants said, 'We have found water' (Genesis 26 : 32). When the herbs are pressed, the watery juice comes out. These eleven serious motives may press out tears from the eye.

An objection answered

But some may say, My constitution is such that I cannot weep. I may as well go to squeeze a rock as think to get a tear.

I answer, but if you cannot weep for sin, can you not grieve? Intellectual mourning is best. There may be sorrow where there are no tears. The vessel may be full though it wants vent. It is not so much the weeping eye God respects, as the broken heart. Yet I would be loath to stop their tears who can weep. God stood looking on Hezekiah's tears: 'I have seen thy tears' (Isaiah 38:5). David's tears made music in God's ears. 'The Lord hath heard the voice of my weeping' (Psalm 6:8). It is a sight fit for angels to behold, tears as pearls dropping from a penitent eye.

9 The hindrances to mourning

What shall we do to get our heart into this mourning frame? Do two things. Take heed of those things which will stop these channels of mourning; put yourselves upon the use of all means that will help forward holy mourning. Take heed of those things which will stop the current of tears.

Nine hindrances considered

There are nine hindrances of mourning.

1 *The love of sin.* The love of sin is like a stone in the pipe which hinders the current of water. The love of sin makes sin taste sweet and this sweetness in sin bewitches the heart. Jerome says it is worse to love sin than to commit it. A man may be overtaken with sin (Galatians 6:1). He that has stumbled upon sin unawares will weep, but the love of sin hardens the heart and keeps the devil in possession. In true mourning there must be a grieving for sin. But how can a man grieve for that sin which his heart is in love with? Oh, take heed of this sweet poison. The love of sin freezes the soul in impenitency.

2 *Despair.* Despair affronts God, undervalues Christ's blood and damns the soul. 'They said there is no hope, but we will walk after our own devices, and we will every one do the imagination of his evil heart' (Jeremiah 18:12). This is the language of despair. I had as good follow my sins still and be damned for something. Despair presents God to the soul as a judge clad in the garments of vengeance (Isaiah 59:17). The despair of Judas was in some sense worse than his treason. Despair destroys repentance, for the proper ground of repentance is mercy. 'The goodness of God leadeth thee to repentance' (Romans 2:4), but despair hides mercy out of sight as the cloud covered the Ark. Oh, take heed of this. Despair is an irrational sin; there is no ground for it. The Lord

shews mercy to thousands. Why may you not be one of a thousand? The wings of God's mercy, like the wings of the Cherubim, are stretched out to every humble penitent. Though you have been a great sinner, yet if you are a weeping sinner, there is a golden sceptre of mercy held forth (Psalm 103 : 11). Despair locks up the soul in impenitency.

3 *A conceit that this mourning will make us melancholy:* we shall drown all our joy in our tears. But this is a mistake. Lose our joy? Tell me, What joy can there be in a natural condition? What joy does sin afford? Is not sin compared to a wound and bruise? (Isaiah 1 : 6). David had his broken bones (Psalm 51 : 8). Is there any comfort in having the bones out of joint? Does not sin breed a palpitation and trembling of heart? (Deuteronomy 28 : 65, 66). Is it any joy for a man to be a 'magor-missabib' (Jeremiah 20 : 4), a terror to himself? Surely of the sinner's laughter it may be said, 'It is mad' (Ecclesiastes 2 : 2), whereas holy mourning is the breeder of joy. It does not eclipse but refines our joy and makes it better. The prodigal dated his joy from the time of his repentance. 'Then they began to be merry' (Luke 15 : 24).

4 *Checking the motions of the Spirit.* The Spirit sets us a-mourning. It causes all our spring-tides. 'All my springs are in thee' (Psalm 87 : 7). Oft we meet with gracious motions to prayer and repentance. Now when we stifle these motions, which is called a quenching the Spirit (I Thessalonians 5 : 19), then we do, as it were, hinder the tide from coming in. When the dew falls, then the ground is wet. When the Spirit of God falls as dew in its influences upon the soul, then it is moistened with sorrow. But if the Spirit withdraw, the soul is like Gideon's dry fleece. A ship can as well sail without the wind, a bird can as well fly without wings, as we can mourn without the Spirit. Take heed of grieving the Spirit. Do not drive away this sweet Dove from the ark of your soul. The Spirit is 'gentle and tender'. If he be grieved, he may say, 'I will come no more', and if he once withdraw we cannot mourn.

5 *Presumption of mercy.* Who will take pains with his heart or mourn for sin that thinks he may be saved at a cheaper rate? How many, spider-like, suck damnation out of the sweet flower of God's mercy? Jesus Christ, who came into the world to save sinners, is the occasion of many a man's perishing. Oh, says one, Christ died for me. He has done all. What need I pray or mourn? Many a bold sinner plucks death from the tree of life, and through presumption, goes to hell by that ladder of Christ's blood, by which others go to heaven. It is sad when

the goodness of God, which should 'lead to repentance' (Romans 2:4), leads to presumption. O sinner, do not hope thyself into hell. Take heed of being damned upon a mistake. You say God is merciful, and therefore you go on securely in sin. But whom is mercy for? The presuming sinner or the mourning sinner? 'Let the wicked forsake his way, and return to the Lord, and he will have mercy upon him' (Isaiah 55:7). No mercy without forsaking sin, and no forsaking sin without mourning! If a king should say to a company of rebels, 'Whosoever comes in and submits shall have mercy', such as stood out in rebellion could not claim the benefit of the pardon. God makes a proclamation of mercy to the mourner, but such as are not mourners have nothing to do with mercy. The mercy of God is like the ark, which none but the priests were to meddle with. None may touch this golden ark of mercy but such as are 'priests unto God' (Revelation 1:6), and have offered up the sacrifice of tears.

6 *A conceit of the smallness of sin*. 'Is it not a little one?' (Genesis 19:20). The devil holds the small end of the perspective-glass to sinners. To fancy sin less than it is, is very dangerous. An opinion of the littleness of sin keeps us from the use of means. Who will be earnest for a physician that thinks it is but a trivial disease? And who will seek to God with a penitent heart for mercy that thinks sin is but a slight thing? But to take off this wrong conceit about sin, and that we may look upon it with watery eyes, consider that sin cannot be little because it is against the Majesty of heaven. There is no treason small, it being against the king's person. Every sin is sinful, therefore damnable. A penknife or stiletto makes but a little wound, but either of them may kill as well as a greater weapon. There is death and hell in every sin (Romans 6:23). What was it for Adam to pluck an apple? But that lost him his crown. It is not with sin as it is with diseases. Some are mortal, some not mortal. The least sin without repentance will be a lock and bolt to shut men out of heaven.

View sin in the red glass of Christ's sufferings. The least sin cost 'the price of blood'. Would you take a true prospect of sin? Go to Golgotha. Jesus Christ was fain to vail his glory and lose his joy, and pour out his soul an offering for the least sin. Read the greatness of your sin in the deepness of Christ's wounds. Let not Satan cast such a mist before your eyes that you cannot see sin in its right colours. Remember, not only do great rivers fall into the sea, but little brooks. Not only do great sins carry men to hell, but lesser.

7 *Procrastination*; or an opinion that it is too soon as yet to tune the

penitential string. When the lamp is almost out, the strength exhausted, and old age comes on, then mourning for sin will be in season, but it is too soon yet. That I may show how pernicious this opinion is, and that I may roll away this stone from the mouth of the well, that so the waters of repentance may be drawn forth, let me propose these four serious and weighty considerations:

First, do you know what it is to be in the state of nature? and will you say it is too soon to get out of it? You are under 'the wrath of God' (John 3:36), and is it too soon to get from under the dropping of this vial? You are under 'the power of Satan' (Acts 26:18), and is it too soon to get out of the enemy's quarters?

Second, men do not argue thus in other cases. They do not say, Is it too soon to be rich? They will not put off getting the world till old age. No, here they take the first opportunity. It is not too soon to be rich, and is it too soon to be good? Is not repentance a matter of the greatest consequence? Is it not more needful for men to lament their sin, than augment their estate?

Third, God's call to mourning looks for present entertainment. 'To-day, if you will hear his voice, harden not your hearts' (Hebrews 3:7, 8). A general besieging a garrison summons it to surrender upon such a day or he will storm it. Such are God's summons to repentance. 'To-day if ye will hear his voice.' Sinners, when Satan has tempted you to any wickedness, you have not said, 'It is too soon, Satan', but have immediately embraced his temptation. You have not put the devil off, and will you put God off?

Fourth, it is a foolish thing to adjourn and put off mourning for sin, for the longer you put off holy mourning, the harder you will find the work when you come to it. A bone that is out of joint is easier to set at first than if you let it go longer. A disease taken in time is sooner cured than if it be let alone till it comes to a paroxysm. You may easily wade over the waters when they are low; if you stay till they are risen, then they will be beyond your depth. O sinner, the more treasons you commit, the more do you incense heaven against you, and the harder it will be to get your pardon. The longer you spin out the time of your sinning, the more work you make for repentance.

To adjourn, and put off mourning for sin is folly in respect of the uncertainty of life. How does the procrastinating sinner know that he shall live to be old? 'What is your life? it is but a vapour' (James 4:14). How soon may sickness arrest you, and death strike off your head? May not your sun set at noon? Oh then what impudence is it to put off mourning for sin, and to make a long work, when death is about to

[84]

make a short work? Caesar, deferring to read the letter sent him, was stabbed in the senate house.

It is folly to put off all till the last in respect of the improbability of finding mercy. Though God has given you space to repent, he may deny you grace to repent. When God calls for mourning and you are deaf, when you call for mercy God may be dumb (Proverbs 1 : 24, 28). Think of it seriously. God may take the latter time to judge you in, because you did not take the former time to repent in.

To put off our solemn turning to God till old age, or sickness, is high imprudence, because these late acts of devotion are for the most part dissembled and spurious. Though true mourning for sin be never too late, yet late mourning is seldom true. That repentance is seldom true-hearted which is gray-headed. It is disputable whether these autumn-tears are not shed more out of fear of hell than love to God. The mariner in a storm throws his goods overboard, not but that he loves them, but he is afraid they will sink the ship. When men fall to weeping-work late and would cast their sins overboard, it is for the most part only for fear lest they should sink the ship and drown in hell. It is a great question whether the sick-bed penitent does not mourn because he can keep his sins no longer. All which considered may make men take heed of running their souls upon such a desperate hazard as to put all their work for heaven upon the last hour.

8 *Delay in the execution of justice.* 'Because sentence against an evil work is not executed speedily, therefore the heart of the sons of men is fully set in them to do evil' (Ecclesiastes 8 : 11). God forbears punishing, therefore men forbear repenting. He does not smite upon their back by correction, therefore they do not smite upon their thigh by humiliation (Jeremiah 31 : 19). The sinner thinks thus: God has spared me all this while; he has eked out patience into longsuffering; surely he will not punish. 'He hath said in his heart, God hath forgotten' (Psalm 10 : 11). In infinite patience God sometimes adjourns his judgments and puts off the sessions a while longer. He is not willing to punish (2 Peter 3 : 9). The bee, naturally gives honey, but stings only when it is angered. The Lord would have men make their peace with him (Isaiah 27 : 5). God is not like an hasty creditor that requires the debt, and will give no time for the payment. He is not only gracious, but 'waits to be gracious' (Isaiah 30 : 18), but God by his patience would bribe sinners to repentance. But, alas, how is this patience abused! God's longsuffering hardens. Because God stops the vial of his wrath, sinners stop the con-

duit of tears. That the patience of God may not (through our corruption) obstruct holy mourning, let sinners remember:

First, God's patience has bounds set to it (Genesis 6:3). Though men will not set bounds to their sin, yet God sets bounds to his patience. There is a time when the sun of God's patience will set, and, being once set, it never returns any degrees backwards. The lease of patience will soon be run out. There is a time when God says, 'My Spirit shall no longer strive.' The angel cried, 'The hour of judgment is come' (Revelation 14:7). Perhaps at the next sin you commit God may say, 'Your hour is now come.'

Second, to be hardened under patience makes our condition far worse. Incensed justice will revenge abused patience. God was patient towards Sodom, but when they did not repent he made the fire and brimstone flame about their ears. Sodom, that was once the wonder of God's patience, is now a standing monument of God's severity. All the plants and fruits were destroyed, and, as Tertullian says, that place still smells of fire and brimstone. Long forbearance is no forgiveness. God may keep off the stroke awhile, but justice is not dead, but sleeps. God has leaden feet but iron hands. The longer God is taking his blow, the sorer it will be when it comes. The longer a stone is falling, the heavier it will be at last. The longer God is whetting his sword, the sharper it cuts. Sins against patience are of a deeper dye; they are worse than the sins of the devils. The lapsed angels never sinned against God's patience. How dreadful will their condition be, who sin because God is patient. For every crumb of patience, God puts a drop of wrath into his vial. The longer God forbears a sinner, the more interest he is sure to pay in hell.

9 *Mirth and music.* 'That chant to the sound of the viol, and drink wine in bowls' (Amos 6:5, 6). Instead of the dirge, the anthem. Many sing away sorrow and drown their tears in wine. The sweet waters of pleasure destroy the bitter waters of mourning. How many go dancing to hell, like those fish which swim down pleasantly into the Dead Sea! Let us take heed of all these hindrances to holy tears. 'Let our harp be turned into mourning and our organ into the voice of them that weep,' (Job 30:31).

10 *Some helps to mourning*

Having removed the obstructions, let me in the last place propound some helps to holy mourning.

1 *Set David's prospect continually before you.* 'My sin is ever before me' (Psalm 51 : 3). David, that he might be a mourner, kept his eye full upon sin. See what sin is, and then tell me if there be not enough in it to draw forth tears. I know not what name to give it bad enough. One calls it the devil's excrement. Sin is a complication of all evils. It is the spirits of mischief distilled. Sin dishonours God, it denies God's omniscience, it derides his patience, it distrusts his faithfulness. Sin tramples upon God's law, slights his love, grieves his Spirit. Sin wrongs us; sin shames us. 'Sin is a reproach to any people' (Proverbs 14 : 34). Sin has made us naked. It has plucked off our robe and taken our crown from us. It has spoiled us of our glory. Nay, it has not only made us naked, but impure. 'I saw thee polluted in thy blood' (Ezekiel 16:6). Sin has not only taken off our cloth of gold, but it has put upon us 'filthy garments' (Zechariah 3:3). God made us 'after his likeness' (Genesis 1:26), but sin has made us 'like the beasts that perish' (Psalm 49:20). We are all become brutish in our affections. Nor has sin made us only like the beasts, but like the devil (John 8:44). Sin has drawn the devil's picture upon man's heart. Sin stabs us. The sinner, like the gaoler, draws a sword to kill himself (Acts 16:27). He is bereaved of his judgment and, like the man in the gospel, possessed with the devils, 'he cuts himself with stones' (Mark 5:5), though he has such a stone in his heart that he does not feel it. Every sin is a stroke at the soul. So many sins, so many wounds! Every blow given to the tree helps forward the felling of the tree. Every sin is an hewing and chopping down the soul for hell-fire. If then there be all this evil in sin, if this forbidden fruit has such a bitter core, it may make us mourn. Our hearts should be the spring, and our eyes the rivers.

[87]

2 *If we would be mourners, let us be orators.* Beg a spirit of contrition. Pray to God that he will put us in mourning, that he will give us a melting frame of heart. Let us beg Achsah's blessing, even 'springs of water' (Joshua 15:19). Let us pray that our hearts may be spiritual limbecs,[1] dropping tears into God's bottle. Let us pray that we who have the poison of the serpent may have the tears of the dove. The Spirit of God is a spirit of mourning. Let us pray that God would pour out that Spirit of grace on us, whereby we may 'look on him whom we have pierced and mourn for him' (Zechariah 12:10). God must breathe in his Spirit before we can breathe out our sorrows. The Spirit of God is like the fire in a still, that sends up the dews of grace in the heart and causes them to drop from the eyes. It is this blessed Spirit whose gentle breath causes our spices to smell and our waters to flow; and if the spring of mourning be once set open in the heart, there can want no joy. As tears flow out, comfort flows in; which leads to the second part of the text, 'They shall be comforted.'

[1] See footnote, page 75.

11 The comforts belonging to mourners

Having already presented to your view the dark side of the text, I shall now show you the light side, 'They shall be comforted.'

The relationship of comfort to mourning

Where observe:

1 *Mourning goes before comfort* as the lancing of a wound precedes the cure. The Antinomian talks of comfort, but cries down mourning for sin. He is like a foolish patient who, having a pill prescribed him, licks the sugar but throws away the pill. The libertine is all for joy and comfort. He licks the sugar but throws away the bitter pill of repentance. If ever we have true comfort we must have it in God's way and method. Sorrow for sin ushers in joy: 'I will restore comforts to him, and to his mourners' (Isaiah 57:18). That is the true sunshine of joy which comes after a shower of tears. We may as well expect a crop without seed, as comfort without gospel-mourning.

2 Observe that *God keeps his best wine till last*. First he prescribes mourning for sin and then sets abroach the wine of consolation. The devil does quite contrary. He shows the best first and keeps the worst till last. First, he shows the wine sparkling in the glass, then comes the 'biting of the serpent' (Proverbs 23:32). Satan sets his dainty dishes before men. He presents sin to them coloured with beauty, sweetened with pleasure, silvered with profit, and then afterwards the sad reckoning is brought in. He showed Judas first the silver bait, and then struck him with the hook. This is the reason why sin has so many followers, because it shows the best first. First, the golden crowns, then comes the lions' teeth (Revelation 9:7, 8).

But God shows the worst first. First he prescribes a bitter portion, and then brings a cordial, 'They shall be comforted.'

3 Observe, *gospel tears are not lost; they are seeds of comfort*. While the penitent pours out tears, God pours in joy. If you would be cheerful (says Chrysostom), be sad. 'They that sow in tears shall reap in joy' (Psalm 126:5). It was the end of Christ's anointing and coming into the world, that he might comfort them that mourn (Isaiah 61:3). Christ had the oil of gladness poured on him (as Chrysostom says) that he might pour it upon the mourner. Well then may the apostle call it 'a repentance not to be repented of' (2 Corinthians 7:10). A man's drunkenness is to be repented of; his uncleanness is to be repented of; but his repentance is never to be repented of, because it is the inlet to joy. 'Blessed are they that mourn, for they shall be comforted.' Here is sweet fruit from a bitter stock. Christ caused the earthen vessels to be filled with water, and then turned the water into wine (John 2:9). So when the eye, that earthen vessel, has been filled with water brim-full, then Christ will turn the water of tears into the wine of joy. Holy mourning, says Basil, is the seed out of which the flower of eternal joy grows.

The reason why the mourner shall be comforted is:

(i) Because mourning is made on purpose for this end. Mourning is not prescribed for itself but that it may lead on to something else, that it may lay a train for comfort. Therefore we sow in tears that we may reap in joy. Holy mourning is a spiritual medicine. Now a medicine is not prescribed for itself, but for the sake of health. So gospel-mourning is appointed for this very end, to bring forth joy.

(ii) The spiritual mourner is the fittest person for comfort. When the heart is broken for sin, now it is fittest for joy. God pours the golden oil of comfort into broken vessels. The mourner's heart is emptied of pride and God fills the empty with his blessing. The mourner's tears have helped to purge out corruption, and after purging physic God gives a julep. The mourner is ready to faint away under the burden of sin, and then the bottle of strong water comes seasonably. The Lord would have the incestuous person (upon his deep humiliation) to be comforted, lest 'he should be swallowed up with overmuch sorrow' (2 Corinthians 2:7).

This is the mourner's privilege: 'He shall be comforted.' The valley of tears brings the soul into a paradise of joy. A sinner's joy brings forth sorrow. The mourner's sorrow brings forth joy. 'Your sorrow shall be turned into joy' (John 16:20). The saints have a wet seed-time but a joyful harvest. 'They shall be comforted.'

[90]

Now to illustrate this, I shall show you what the comforts are the mourners shall have. These comforts are of a divine infusion, and they are two-fold, either here or hereafter.

The nature of the comforts during the earthly life

They are called 'the consolations of God' (Job 15:11); that is, 'great comforts', such as none but God can give. They exceed all other comforts as far as heaven exceeds earth. The root on which these comforts grow is the blessed Spirit. He is called 'the Comforter' (John 14:26), and comfort is said to be a 'fruit of the Spirit' (Galatians 5:22). Christ purchased peace, and the Spirit speaks peace.

How does the Spirit comfort? Either mediately or immediately.

(i) Mediately, by helping us to apply the promises to ourselves and draw water out of those 'wells of salvation'. We lie as dead children at the breast, till the Spirit helps us to suck the breast of a promise; and when the Spirit has taught faith this art, now comfort flows in. O how sweet is the breast-milk of a promise!

(ii) The Spirit comforts immediately. The Spirit by a more direct act presents God to the soul as reconciled. It 'sheds his love abroad in the heart', from whence flows infinite joy (Romans 5:5). The Spirit secretly whispers pardon for sin, and the sight of a pardon dilates the heart with joy. 'Be of good cheer, thy sins are forgiven thee' (Matthew 9:2).

That I may speak more fully to this point, I shall show you the qualifications and excellencies of these comforts which God gives his mourners. These comforts are *real comforts*. The Spirit of God cannot witness to that which is untrue. There are many in this age who pretend to comfort, but their comforts are mere impostures. The body may as well swell with wind as with flesh. A man may as well be swelled with false as true comforts. The comforts of the saints are certain. They have the seal of the Spirit set to them (2 Corinthians 1:22; Ephesians 1:13). A seal is for confirmation. When a deed is sealed, it is firm and unquestionable. When a Christian has the seal of the Spirit stamped upon his heart, now he is confirmed in the love of God.

Ten differences between true and false comfort

Wherein do these comforts of the Spirit which are unquestionably sure, differ from those which are false and pretended? Three ways:

First, the comforts of God's Spirit are laid in deep conviction: 'And when he (that is, the Comforter) is come, he shall reprove (or, as the Greek word is, he shall convince) the world of sin' (John 16:7, 8).

Why does conviction go before consolation? Conviction fits for comfort. By conviction the Spirit sweetly disposes the heart to seek after Christ and then to receive Christ. Once the soul is convinced of sin and of the hell that follows it, a Saviour is precious. When the Spirit has shot in the arrow of conviction, now, says a poor soul, where may I meet with Christ? In what ordinance may I come to enjoy Christ? 'Saw ye him whom my soul loves?' All the world for one glimpse of my Saviour!

Again, the Spirit by conviction makes the heart willing to receive Christ upon his own terms. Man, by nature, would article and indent[1] with Christ. He would take half Christ. He would take him for a Saviour, not a prince. He would accept of Christ as he has 'an head of gold' (Canticles 5:11), but not as he has 'the government upon his shoulder' (Isaiah 9:6). But when God lets loose the spirit of bondage and convinces a sinner of his lost, undone condition, now he is content to have Christ upon any terms. When Paul was struck down to the ground by a spirit of conviction, he cries out, 'Lord, what wilt thou have me to do?' (Acts 9:6). Let God propound what articles he will, the soul will subscribe to them. Now when a man is brought to Christ's terms, to believe and obey, then he is fit for mercy. When the Spirit of God has been a spirit of conviction, then He becomes a spirit of consolation. When the plough of the law has gone upon the heart and broken up the fallow ground, now God sows the seed of comfort. Those who brag of comfort, but were never yet convinced, nor broken, for sin, have cause to suspect their comfort to be a delusion of Satan. It is like a madman's joy, who fancies himself to be king, but it may be said of 'his laughter, it is mad' (Ecclesiastes 2:2). The seed which wanted 'depth of earth' withered (Matthew 13:5). That comfort which wants 'depth of earth', deep humiliation and conviction, will soon wither and come to nothing.

The Spirit of God is a sanctifying, before a comforting Spirit. As God's Spirit is called the 'Comforter', so he is called 'a Spirit of grace' (Zechariah 12:10). Grace is the work of the Spirit. Comfort is the seal of the Spirit. The work of the Spirit goes before the seal. The graces of the Spirit are compared to water (Isaiah 44:3) and to oil (Isaiah 61:3). First, God pours in the water of the Spirit and then comes the oil of gladness. The oil (in this sense) runs above the water. Hereby we

[1] That is, the natural man wishes to fix his own terms for receiving Christ.

shall know whether our comforts are true and genuine. Some talk of the comforting Spirit, who never had the sanctifying Spirit. They boast of assurance but never had grace. These are spurious joys. These comforts will leave men at death. They will end in horror and despair. God's Spirit will never set seal to a blank. First, the heart must be an epistle written with the finger of the Holy Ghost, and then it is 'sealed with the Spirit of promise'.

The comforts of the Spirit are humbling. Lord, says the soul, what am I that I should have a smile from heaven, and that thou shouldest give me a privy seal of thy love? The more water is poured into a bucket, the lower it descends. The fuller the ship is laden with sweet spices, the lower it sails. The more a Christian is filled with the sweet comforts of the Spirit, the lower he sails in humility. The fuller a tree is of fruit, the lower the bough hangs. The more full we are of 'the fruit of the Spirit, joy and peace' (Galatians 5:22), the more we bend in humility. St. Paul, a 'chosen vessel' (Acts 9:15), filled with the wine of the Spirit (2 Corinthians 1:5), did not more abound in joy, than in lowliness of mind. 'Unto me who am less than the least of all saints, is this grace given . . .'' (Ephesians 3:8). He who was the chief of the apostles calls himself the least of the saints.

Those who say they have comfort, but are proud; who have learned to despise others and are climbed above ordinances; their comforts are delusions. The devil is able, not only to 'transform himself into an angel of light' (2 Corinthians 11:14), but he can transform himself into the comforter. It is easy to counterfeit money, to silver over brass and put the king's image upon it. The devil can silver over false comforts and make them look as if they had the stamp of the King of heaven upon them. The comforts of God are humbling. Though they lift the heart up in thankfulness, yet they do not puff it up in pride.

Second, the comforts God gives his mourners are unmixed. They are not tempered with any bitter ingredients. Worldly comforts are like wine that runs dregs. 'In the midst of laughter the heart is sad' (Proverbs 14:13). Queen Mary Tudor once said, if she were opened, they would find Calais graven on her heart. And if the breast of a sinner were anatomized and opened, you would find a worm gnawing at his heart. Guilt is a wolf which feeds in the breast of his comfort. A sinner may have a smiling countenance, but a chiding conscience. His mirth is like the mirth of a man in debt, who is every hour in fear of arrest. The comforts of wicked men are spiced with bitterness. They are worm-wood wine.

'These are the men who tremble, and grow pale at every lightning flash, and when it thunders are half-dead with terror at the very first rumbling of the heavens.'[1]

But spiritual comforts are pure. They are not muddied with guilt, nor mixed with fear. They are the pure wine of the Spirit. What the mourner feels is joy, and nothing but joy.

Third, the comforts God gives his mourners are sweet. 'Truly the light is sweet' (Ecclesiastes 11:7); so is the light of God's countenance. How sweet are those comforts which bring the Comforter along with them! (John 14:16). Therefore the love of God shed into the heart is said to be 'better than wine' (Canticles 1:2). Wine pleases the palate, but the love of God cheers the conscience. The 'lips' of Christ 'drop sweet-smelling myrrh' (Canticles 5:13). The comforts God gives are a Christian's music. They are the golden pot of manna, the nectar and ambrosia of a Christian. They are the saints' festival, their banqueting stuff. So sweet are these divine comforts, that the church had her 'fainting fits' for want of them. 'Stay me with flagons' (Canticles 2:5). In metonymy the name of an accompanying thing is substituted for the thing meant. The 'flagons' are put for the wine. By these flagons are meant the comforts of the Spirit. The Hebrew word signifies 'all variety of delights' to show the abundance of delectability and sweetness in these comforts of the Spirit. 'Comfort me with apples.' Apples are sweet in taste, fragrant in smell; so sweet and delicious are those apples which grow upon the tree in paradise. These comforts from above are so sweet that they make all other comforts sweet; health, estate, relations. They are like sauce which makes all our earthly possessions and enjoyments come off with a bitter relish. So sweet are these comforts of the Spirit that they do much abate and moderate our joy in worldly things. He who has been drinking spirits of wine, will not much thirst after water; and that man who has once 'tasted how sweet the Lord is' (Psalm 34:8), and has drunk the cordials of the Spirit, will not thirst immoderately after secular delights. Those who play with dogs and birds, it is a sign they have no children; such as are inordinate in their desire and love of the creature, declare plainly that they never had better comforts.

Fourth, these comforts which God gives his mourners are holy comforts. They are called 'the comfort of the Holy Ghost' (Acts 9:31). Everything propagates in its own kind. The Holy Ghost can no more produce impure joys in the soul than the sun can produce darkness. He

[1] Juvenal, Satires, V, 13, lines 223–4.

[94]

who has the comforts of the Spirit looks upon himself as a person engaged to do God more service. Has the Lord looked upon me with a
smiling face? I can never pray enough. I can never love God enough.
The comforts of the Spirit raise in the heart an holy antipathy against
sin. The dove hates every feather that has grown upon the hawk. So
there is an hatred of every motion and temptation to evil. He who has a
principle of life in him opposes everything that would destroy life. He
hates poison. So he that has the comforts of the Spirit living in him, sets
himself against those sins which would murder his comforts. Divine
comforts give the soul more acquaintance with God. 'Our fellowship
is with the Father and with his Son, Jesus.' (1 John 1 : 3).

Fifth, the comforts reserved for the mourners are 'filling comforts':
'The God of hope fill you with all joy . . .' (Romans 15 : 13). 'Ask . . .
that your joy may be full' (John 16 : 24). When God pours in the joys
of heaven, they fill the heart and make it run over. 'I am exceeding
joyful . . .' (2 Corinthians 7 : 4); the Greek word is 'I overflow with
joy', as a cup that is filled with wine till it runs over. Outward comforts can no more fill the heart than a triangle can fill a circle. Spiritual
joys are satisfying. 'My soul shall be satisfied as with marrow, and I
will praise thee with joyful lips' (Psalm 63 : 5). David's heart was full,
and the joy broke out at his lips. 'Thou hast put gladness in my heart'
(Psalm 4 : 7). Worldly joys put gladness into the face: 'They rejoice
in the face' (2 Corinthians 5 : 12), but the Spirit of God puts gladness
into the heart. Divine joys are heart joys (Zechariah 10 : 7). "Your heart
shall rejoice' (John 16 : 22). A believer rejoices in God: 'My Spirit re-
joiceth in God . . .' (Luke 1 : 47). And to show how filling these comforts are which are of an heavenly extraction, the Psalmist says they
create greater joy than when 'wine and oil increase' (Psalm 4 : 7). Wine
and oil may delight but not satisfy; they have their vacuity and
indigence. We may say as Zechariah 10 : 2, 'They comfort in vain.'
Outward comforts sooner cloy than cheer, and sooner weary than fill.
Xerxes[1] offered great rewards to him that could find out a new pleasure, but the comforts of the Spirit are satisfactory. They recruit the
heart. 'Thy comforts delight my soul' (Psalm 94 : 19). There is as much
difference between heavenly comforts and earthly, as between a banquet that is eaten and one that is painted on the wall.

Sixth, the comforts God gives his mourners in this life are 'glorious
comforts': 'Joy full of glory' (1 Peter 1 : 8). They are glorious because
they are a prelibation and foretaste of that joy which we shall have in

[1] King of Persia, 6th century **B.C.**

a glorified estate. These comforts are an handsel[1] and earnest of glory. They put us in heaven before our time. 'Ye were sealed with that Holy Spirit, which is the earnest of the inheritance' (Ephesians 1 : 13, 14). The earnest is part of the sum behind. So the comforts of the Spirit are the earnest, the 'cluster of grapes' at Eshcol (Numbers 13 : 23), the first-fruits of the heavenly Canaan. The joys of the Spirit are glorious, in opposition to other joys, which compared with these, are inglorious and vile. A carnal man's joy, as it is airy and flashy, so it is sordid. He sucks nothing but dregs. 'Ye rejoice in a thing of nought' (Amos 6 : 13). A carnal spirit rejoices because he can say this house is his, this estate is his. But a gracious spirit rejoices because he can say this God is his : 'For this God is our God for ever and ever' (Psalm 48 : 14). The ground of a Christian's joy is glorious. He rejoices in that he is an heir of the promise. The joy of a godly man is made up of that which is the angels' joy. He triumphs in the light of God's countenance. His joy is that which is Christ's own joy. He rejoices in the mystical union which is begun here and consummated in heaven. Thus the joy of the saints is a joy 'full of glory'.

Seventh, the comforts which God gives his mourners are infinitely transporting and ravishing. So delightful are they and amazing, that they cause a jubilation which, as some of the learned say, is so great that it cannot be expressed. Of all things joy is the most hard to be deciphered. It is called 'joy unspeakable' (1 Peter 1 : 8). You may sooner taste honey than tell how sweet it is. The most pathetic words can no more set forth the comforts of the Spirit than the most curious pencil can draw the life and breath of a man. The angels cannot express the joys they feel. Some men have been so overwhelmed with the sweet raptures of joy that they have not been able to contain, but as Moses, have died with a kiss from God's mouth. Thus have we seen the glass oft breaking with the strength of the liquor put into it.

Eighth, these comforts of the Spirit are powerful. They are strong cordials, strong consolation, as the apostle phrases it (Hebrews 6 : 18). Divine comfort strengthens for duty. 'The joy of the Lord is your strength' (Nehemiah 8 : 10). Joy whets and sharpens industry. A man that is steeled and animated with the comfort of God's Spirit, goes with vigour and alacrity through the exercises of religion. He believes firmly, he loves fervently, he is carried full sail in duty. 'The joy of the Lord is his strength.' Divine comfort supports under affliction : 'Having received the Word in much affliction, with joy' (1 Thessalonians 1 : 6).

[1] Earnest-money; a gift at the beginning of a New Year, or at the start of a new era in life.

The wine of the Spirit can sweeten 'the waters of Marah'. They who are possessed of these heavenly comforts can 'gather grapes of thorns', and fetch honey out of the 'lion's carcase'. They are 'strong consolations' indeed, that can stand it out against the 'fiery trial', and turn the flame into a bed of roses. How powerful is that comfort which can make a Christian glory in tribulations (Romans 5:3)! A believer is never so sad but he can rejoice. The bird of paradise can sing in the winter. 'As sorrowing, yet alway rejoicing' (2 Corinthians 6:10). Let sickness come, the sense of pardon takes away the sense of pain. 'The inhabitant shall not say, I am sick' (Isaiah 33:24). Let death come, the Christian is above it. 'O death, where is thy sting?' (1 Corinthians 15:55). At the end of the rod a Christian tastes honey. These are 'strong consolations'.

Ninth, the comforts God's mourners have are heart-quieting comforts. They cause a sweet acquiescence and rest in the soul. The heart of a Christian is in a kind of ataxy [1] and discomposure, like the needle in the compass; it shakes and trembles till the Comforter comes. Some creatures cannot live but in the sun. A Christian is even dead in the nest, unless he may have the sunlight of God's countenance. 'Hide not thy face from me, lest I be like them that go down into the pit' (Psalm 143:7). Nothing but the breast will quiet the child. It is only the breast of consolation quiets the believer.

Tenth, the comforts of the Spirit are abiding comforts. As they abound in us so they abide with us. 'He shall give you another Comforter that he may abide with you for ever' (John 14:16). Worldly comforts are always upon the wing, ready to fly. They are like a land-flood, or a flash of lightning. 'They will oft-times pass away and glide from thy closest embrace.' [2] All things here are transient, but the comforts with which God feeds his mourners are immortal: 'Who hath loved us and given us everlasting consolation' (2 Thessalonians 2:16). Though a Christian does not always have a full beam of comfort, yet he has a dawning of it in his soul. He always has a ground of hope and a root of joy. There is that within him which bears up his heart, and which he would not on any terms part with.

Behold, then, the mourner's privilege, 'He shall be comforted'. David who was the great mourner of Israel, was the 'sweet singer of Israel'. The weeping dove shall be covered with the golden feathers of comfort. O how rare and superlative are these comforts!

---

[1] State of unsteadiness.   [2] Martial, *Epigrams*, I, 16.

Five reasons why mourners may lack comfort

But the question may be asked, May not God's mourners lack these comforts? Spiritual mourners have a title to these comforts, yet they may sometimes lack them. God is a free agent. He will have the timing of our comforts. He has a self-freedom to do what he will. The Holy One of Israel will not be limited. He reserves his prerogative to give or suspend comfort as he will; and if we are awhile without comfort, we must not quarrel with his dispensations, for as the mariner is not to wrangle with providence because the wind blows out of the east when he desires it to blow out of the west; nor is the husbandman to murmur when God stops the bottles of heaven in time of drought; so neither is any man to dispute or quarrel with God, when he stops the sweet influence of comfort, but he ought rather to acquiesce in his sacred will

But though the Lord might by virtue of his sovereignty withhold comfort from the mourner, yet there may be many pregnant causes assigned why mourners lack comfort in regard of God and also in regard of themselves.

1 *In regard of God*: He sees it fit to withhold comfort that he may raise the value of grace. We are apt to esteem comfort above grace, therefore God locks up our comforts for a time, that he may enhance the price of grace. When farthings go better than gold the king will call in farthings, that the price of gold may be the more raised. God would have his people serve him for himself and not for comfort only. It is an harlot love to love the husband's money and tokens[1] more than his person. Such as serve God only for comfort, do not so much serve God, as serve themselves of him.

2 That God's mourners lack comfort, it is most frequently *in regard of themselves*.

(i) Through mistake, which is two-fold. They do not go to the right spring for comfort. They go to their tears, when they should go to Christ's blood. It is a kind of idolatry to make our tears the ground of our comfort. Mourning is not meritorious. It is the way to joy, not the cause. Jacob got the blessing in the garments of his elder brother. True comfort flows out of Christ's sides. Our tears are stained, till they are washed in the blood of Christ. 'In me peace' (John 16:33). The second mistake is that mourners are privileged persons, and may take more

[1]Coins.

liberty. They may slacken the strings of duty, and let loose the reins to sin. Christ has indeed purchased a liberty for his people, but an holy liberty, not a liberty for sin, but from sin. 'Ye are a royal priesthood, a peculiar people' (1 Peter 2:9). You are not in a state of slavery, but royalty. What follows? Do not make Christian liberty a cloak for sin. 'As free, and not using your liberty for a cloak of maliciousness' (*v* 16). If we quench the sanctifying Spirit, God will quench the comforting Spirit. Sin is compared to a 'cloud' (Isaiah 44:22). This cloud intercepts the light of God's countenance.

(ii) God's mourners sometimes lack comfort through discontent and peevishness. David makes his disquiet the cause of his sadness. 'Why art thou cast down, O my soul? Why art thou disquieted within me?' (Psalm 43:5). A disquieted heart, like a rough sea, is not easily calmed. It is hard to make a troubled spirit receive comfort. This disquiet arises from various causes: sometimes from outward sorrow and melancholy, sometimes from a kind of envy. God's people are troubled to see others have comfort, and they lack it; and now in a pet they refuse comfort, and like a forward child, put away the breast. 'My soul refused to be comforted' (Psalm 77:2). Indeed a disquieted spirit is no more fit for comfort, than a distracted man is fit for counsel. And whence is the mourner's discontent, but pride? As if God had not dealt well with him in stopping the influences of comfort. O Christian, your spirit must be more humbled and broken, before God empty out his golden oil of joy.

(iii) The mourner is without comfort for want of applying the promises. He looks at sin which may humble him, but not at that Word which may comfort him. The mourner's eyes are so full of tears that he cannot see the promise. The virtue and comfort of a medicine is in the applying. When the promises are applied by faith, they bring comfort (Hosea 2:19; Isaiah 49:15, 16). Faith milks the breast of a promise. That Satan may hinder us of comfort, it is his policy either to keep the promise from us that we may not know it, or to keep us from the promise that we may not apply it. Never a promise in the Bible but belongs to the mourner, had he but the skill and dexterity of faith to lay hold on it.

(iv) The mourner may lack comfort through too much earthly-mindedness; by feeding immoderately on earthly comforts we miss of heavenly comforts. 'For the iniquity of his covetousness was I wroth, and I hid me' (Isaiah 57:17). The earth puts out the fire. Earthliness extinguishes the flame of divine joy in the soul. An eclipse occurs when the moon, which is a dense body, comes between the sun and the earth. The moon is an emblem of the world (Revelation 12:1). When this comes between, then there is an eclipse in the light of God's face. Such as dig in mines say there is such a damp comes from the earth as puts out the light of a candle. Earthly comforts send forth such a damp as puts out the light of spiritual joy.

(v) Perhaps the mourner has had comfort and lost it. Adam's rib was taken from him when he was asleep (Genesis 2:21). Our comforts are taken away when we fall asleep in security. The spouse lost her beloved when she lay upon the bed of sloth (Canticles 5:2, 6).

For these reasons God's mourners may lack comfort, but that the spiritual mourner may not be too much dejected, I shall reach forth 'the cup of consolation' (Jeremiah 16:7), and speak a few words that may comfort the mourner in the want of comfort. Jesus Christ was without comfort, therefore no wonder if we are. Our comforts are not better than his. He who was the Son of God's love was without the sense of God's love. The mourner has a seed of comfort: 'Light is sown for the righteous' (Psalm 97:11). Light is a metaphor put for comfort, and it is sown. Though a child of God does not have comfort always in the flower, yet he has it in the seed. Though he does not feel comfort from God yet he takes comfort in God. A Christian may be high in grace and low in comfort. The high mountains are without flowers. The mines of gold have little or no corn growing on them. A Christian's heart may be a rich mine of grace, though it be barren of comfort. The mourner is heir to comfort, and though for a small moment God may forsake his people (Isaiah 54:7), yet there is a time shortly coming when the mourner shall have all tears wiped away, and shall be brim full of comfort. This joy is reserved for heaven, and this brings me to the second particular.

The nature of the comforts in the world to come

'They shall be comforted'. Though in this life some interviews and love-tokens pass between God and the mourner, yet the great comforts are kept in reversion. 'In God's presence is fulness of joy' (Psalm 16:11). There is a time coming (the day-star is ready to appear) when the saints shall bathe themselves in the river of life, when they shall never see a wrinkle on God's brow more, but his face shall shine, his lips drop honey, his arms sweetly embrace them. The saints shall have a spring-tide of joy, and it shall never be low water. The saints shall at that day put off their mourning and exchange their sables for white robes. Then shall the winter be past, the rain of tears be over and gone (Canticles 2:11, 12). The flowers of joy shall appear, and after the weeping of the dove 'the time of the singing of birds shall come'. This is the 'great consolation', the Jubilee of the blessed which shall never expire. In this life the people of God taste of joy, but in heaven the full vessels shall be broached. There is a river in the midst of the heavenly paradise which has a fountain to feed it (Psalm 36:8, 9).

The times we are cast into, being for the present sad and cloudy, it will not be amiss for the reviving the hearts of God's people, to speak a little of these comforts which God reserves in heaven for his mourners. 'They shall be comforted.'

The greatness of these celestial comforts is most fitly in Scripture expressed by the joy of a feast. Mourning shall be turned into feasting, and it shall be a marriage-feast, which is usually kept with the greatest solemnity. 'Blessed are they which are called unto the marriage-supper of the Lamb' (Revelation 19:9). Bullinger[1] and Gregory the Great[2] understand this supper of the Lamb to be meant of the saints, supping with Christ in heaven. Men after hard labour go to supper. So when the saints shall 'rest from their labours' (Revelation 14:13), they shall sup with Christ in glory. Now to speak something of the last great supper.

(i) It will be a great supper in regard of the *Founder* of this feast, *God*. It is the supper of a king, therefore sumptuous and magnificent. 'The Lord is a great God, and a great King above all gods' (Psalm 95:3). Where should there be state and magnificence but in a king's court?

(ii) It will be a great supper in regard of the *cheer* and *provision*. This exceeds all hyperboles. What blessed fruit does the tree of life in paradise yield! (Revelation 2:7). Christ will lead his spouse into the 'banqueting house' and feast her with those rare viands, and cause her to drink that spiced wine, that heavenly nectar and ambrosia[3] wherewith the angelical powers are infinitely refreshed.

First, every dish served in at this heavenly supper shall be sweet to our palate. There is no dish here we do not love. Christ will make such 'savoury meat' as he is sure his spouse loves.

Second, there shall be no want here. There is no want at a feast. The various fulness in Christ will prevent a scarcity, and it will be a fulness without surfeit, because a fresh course will continually be served in.

[1] Swiss theologian of the Reformation Period (d. 1575).
[2] Bishop of Rome (d. 604).
[3] The food of the immortals.

Third, they who eat of this supper shall 'never hunger more'. Hunger is a sharp sauce. The 'Lamb's supper' shall not only satisfy hunger, but prevent it. 'They shall hunger no more!' (Revelation 7:16).

(iii) It will be a great supper in regard of the *company invited*. Company adds to a feast, and is of itself sauce to sharpen and provoke the appetite. Saints, angels, archangels will be at this supper. Nay, Christ himself will be both Founder and Guest. The Scripture calls it 'an innumerable company . . .' (Hebrews 12:22); and that which makes the society sweeter is that there shall be perfect love at this feast. The motto shall be 'one heart and one way'. All the guests shall be linked together with the golden chain of charity.

(iv) It will be a great supper in regard of the *holy mirth*. 'A feast is made for mirth' (Ecclesiastes 10:19). At this supper there shall be joy, and nothing but joy (Psalm 16:11). There is no weeping at a feast. O what triumph and acclamations will there be! There are two things at this 'supper of the Lamb' which will create joy and mirth. First, when the saints shall think with themselves that they are kept from a worse supper. The devils have a supper (such an one as it is), a black banquet. There are two dishes served in, weeping and gnashing of teeth. Every bit they eat makes their hearts ache. Who would envy them their dinner here, who must have such a supper? Second, it will be a matter of joy at the 'supper of the Lamb', that the Master of the feast bids all his guests welcome. The saints shall have the smiles of God's face, the kisses of his lips. He will lead them into the wine cellar, and display the banner of love over them. The saints shall be as full of solace as sanctity. What is a feast without mirth? Worldly mirth is flashy and empty. This will be infinitely delightful and ravishing.

(v) It will be a great supper for the *music*. This will be a marriage supper, and what better music than the Bridegroom's voice, saying, 'My spouse, my undefiled, take thy fill of love.' There will be the angels' anthems, the saints' triumphs. The angels, those trumpeters of heaven, shall sound forth the excellencies of Jehovah, and the saints, those noble choristers, shall take 'down their harps from the willows', and join in consort with the angels, praising and blessing God. 'I saw them that had gotten the victory over the beast, having the harps of God, and they sing the song of Moses and the song of the Lamb, saying, Great and marvellous are thy works, Lord God Almighty, just and true are thy ways thou king of saints . . .' (Revelation 15:2, 3). O the sweet harmony at this feast! it shall be music without discord.

(vi) This supper is great in regard of the *place* where it shall be celebrated, in the 'paradise of God' (Revelation 2:7). It is a stately palace.
Stately: for its *situation*. It is of a very great height (Revelation 21:10):
for its *prospect*. All sparkling beauties are there concentred, and the delight of the prospect is propriety.[1] That is the best prospect, where a
man can see furthest on his own ground: for its *amplitude*. This royal
feast shall be kept in a most spacious room, a room infinitely greater
than the whole firmament, one star whereof (if we may believe astro-
nomers) is bigger than the whole earth. Though there be such a multitude as no man can number, 'of all nations, kindreds, people and
tongues' (Revelation 7:9), yet the table is long enough and the room
spacious enough for all the guests. Aulus Gellius[2] in his thirteenth
book, makes this to be one of those four things which are requisite to a
feast—'a fit place'. The empyrean heaven bespangled with light, arrayed
with rich hangings, embroidered with glory, seated above all the visible
orbs, is the place of the marriage-supper. This infinitely transcends the
most profound search. I am no more able to express it, than I can span
the firmament, or weigh the earth in a pair of balances.

(vii) It will be a great supper in regard of its *continuance*. It has no end.
Epicures have a short feast, and a long reckoning, but those who shall
sit down at the heavenly banquet, shall not rise from the table. The
cloth shall never be taken away, but they shall always be feeding upon
those sweet junkets and delicacies which are set before them. We read
that King Ahasuerus made a feast for his princes that lasted 'an hundred and fourscore days' (Esther 1:4). But this blessed feast reserved for
the saints, is 'for ever'. 'At thy right hand there are pleasures for evermore' (Psalm 16:11).

An exhortation to comfort

For your consolation, consider how this may be as Bezar stone[3] to keep
the hearts of God's people from fainting! 'They shall be comforted.'
They shall sit with Christ 'upon the throne' (Revelation 3:21), and sit
down with him 'at the table'. Who would not mourn for sin that are

[1] Used here with the meaning of 'ownership'.

[2] A Roman writer of the 1st century. His work, entitled *Noctes Atticae* (in twenty
books), was praised by Augustine.

[3] A counter-poison or antidote. It consists of a 'stone' found in the stomach or
intestines of certain animals and is formed of concentric layers of animal matter
deposited round some foreign substance which serves as a nucleus. The modern
spelling is *Bezoar*.

sure to meet with such rewards! 'They shall be comforted.' The marriage-supper will make amends for 'the valley of tears'. O saint of God, you who are now watering your plants and weeping bitterly for sin, at this last and great feast your 'water shall be turned into wine'. You who now mortify your corruptions, and 'beat down your body' by prayer and fasting, shall shortly sup with Christ and angels. You who refused to touch the forbidden tree shall feed upon 'the tree of life in the paradise of God'. You impoverished saint, who have scarce a bit of bread to eat, remember for your comfort, 'in thy father's house there is bread enough', and he is making ready a feast for you, where all the dainties of heaven are served in. O feed with delight upon the thoughts of this marriage supper! After your funeral begins your festival. Long for supper-time. 'The delay is long which separates us from our honeysweet joys.' Christ has paid for this supper upon the cross, and there is no fear of a 'reckoning' to be brought in. 'Wherefore comfort one another with these words.'

12 Christian meekness

Blessed are the meek, for they shall inherit the earth
                                                    MATTHEW 5:5

We are now got to the third step leading in the way to blessedness, *Christian meekness*. 'Blessed are the meek.' See how the Spirit of God adorns 'the hidden man of the heart' with multiplicity of graces! The workmanship of the Holy Ghost is not only curious, but various. It makes the heart meek, pure, peaceable etc. The graces therefore are compared to needlework, which is different and various in its flowers and colours (Psalm 45:14). In the words there is a duty, and that duty like the dove brings an olive leaf in the mouth of it, 'they shall inherit the earth'.

The proposition I shall insist on is that *meek persons are blessed persons*. For the right understanding of this, we must know there is a two-fold meekness. Meekness towards God, meekness towards man.

Meekness towards God and towards man

1 *Meekness towards God*, which implies two things: submission to his will; flexibleness to his Word.

(i) Submission to God's will: when we carry ourselves calmly, without swelling or murmuring, under the dispensations of providence. 'It is the Lord, let him do what seemeth him good' (1 Samuel 3:18). The meek-spirited Christian saith thus: Let God do what he will with me, let him carve out what condition he please, I will submit. God sees what is best for me, whether a fertile soil or a barren. Let him chequer his work as he please, it suffices that God has done it. It was an unmeek spirit in the prophet to struggle with God: 'I do well to be angry to the death' (Jonah 4:9).

(ii) Flexibleness to God's Word: when we are willing to let the Word bear sway in our souls and become pliable to all its laws and maxims. He is spiritually meek who conforms himself to the mind of God, and does not quarrel with the instructions of the Word, but with the corruptions of his heart. Cornelius' speech to Peter savoured of a meek spirit: 'Now therefore we are all here present before God, to hear all things that are commanded thee of God' (Acts 10:33). How happy is it when the Word which comes with majesty is received with meekness! (James 1:21).

2 *Meekness towards man.* Basil the Great calls this the indelible character of a gracious soul. 'Blessed are the meek.' To illustrate this, I shall show what this meekness is. Meekness is a grace whereby we are enabled by the Spirit of God to moderate our passion. It is a grace. The philosopher calls it a virtue, but the apostle calls it a grace, and therefore reckons it among the 'fruits of the Spirit' (Galatians 5:23). It is of a divine extract and original. By it we are enabled to moderate our passion. By nature the heart is like a troubled sea, casting forth the foam of anger and wrath. Now meekness calms the passions. It sits as moderator in the soul, quieting and giving check to its distempered motions. As the moon serves to temper and allay the heat of the sun, so Christian meekness allays the heat of passion. Meekness of spirit not only fits us for communion with God, but for civil converse with men; and thus among all the graces it holds first place. Meekness has a divine beauty and sweetness in it. It brings credit to religion; it wins upon all. This meekness consists in three things: the bearing of injuries, the forgiving of injuries, the recompensing good for evil.

Meekness in the bearing of injuries

First, meekness consists in the *bearing of injuries*. I may say of this grace, 'it is not easily provoked'. A meek spirit, like wet tinder, will not easily take fire. 'They that seek my hurt spake mischievous things, but I, as a deaf man, heard not' (Psalm 38:12, 13). Meekness is 'the bridle of anger'. The passions are fiery and headstrong; meekness gives check to them. Meekness 'bridles the mouth', it ties the tongue to its good behaviour. Meekness observes that motto, Bear and forbear. There are four things opposite to meekness.

(i) Meekness is opposed to *hastiness of spirit*. 'Be not hasty in thy spirit to be angry, for anger rests in the bosom of fools' (Ecclesiastes 7:9). When the heart boils in passion, and anger (as Seneca says) sparkles forth in the eye, this is far from meekness. 'Anger rests in the bosom of fools.' Anger may be in a wise man, but it rests in a fool. The angry man is like flax or gunpowder. No sooner do you touch him but he is all on fire. Saint Basil calls anger drunkenness, and Jerome says there are more drunken with passion than with wine. Seneca calls anger 'a short fit of madness'. Sometimes it suspends the use of reason. In the best things we are cool enough. In religion we are all ice, in contention all fire. How unbeseeming is rash anger! How it disguises and disfigures! Homer says of Agamemnon[1] that when he moderated his passion, he resembled the gods. He was like Jupiter in feature, like Pallas in wisdom, but when he was in his fury, he was a very tiger. Nothing of Jupiter appeared in him. As Plato[2] counselled the great revellers and drinkers of his time, that they should view themselves in a glass when they were in their drunken humour, and they would appear loathsome to themselves, so let a man disguised with passion view himself in the glass, and sure he would ever after be out of love with himself. 'The face swells with anger, the veins become black with blood.' 'Let not the sun go down upon your wrath, neither give place to the devil' (Ephesians 4 : 26, 27). Oh, says one, he has wronged me and I will never give place to him; but better give place to him than to the devil. An hasty spirit is not a meek spirit. Not but that we may in some cases be angry. There is an holy anger. That anger is without sin which is against sin. Meekness and zeal may stand together. In matters of religion, a Christian must be clothed with the spirit of Elias, and be 'full of the fury of the Lord' (Jeremiah 6 : 11). Christ was meek (Matt. 11 : 29), yet zealous (John 2 : 14, 15). The zeal of God's house ate him up.

(ii) Meekness is opposed to *malice*. Malice is the devil's picture (John 8 : 44). Malice is mental murder (1 John 3 : 15). It unfits for duty. How can such a man pray? I have read of two men that lived in malice, who being asked how they could say the Lord's prayer, one answered, he thanked God there were many good prayers besides. The other answered, when he said the Lord's prayer he left out those words, 'as we forgive them that trespass against us'. But Augustine brings in God replying, 'Because thou dost not say my prayer, I will not hear thine.' Were it not a sad judgment if all that a man ate should turn to poison! To a malicious man all the holy ordinances of God turn to poison. 'The table of the Lord' is a snare; 'he eats and drinks his own damnation'. A malicious spirit is not a meek spirit.

(iii) Meekness is opposed to *revenge*. Malice is the scum of anger, and revenge is malice boiling over. Malice is a vermin which lives on blood.

[1] Leader of the ancient Greek expedition against Troy, described by Homer in *The Iliad*.
[2] Greek philosopher, the pupil of Socrates and tutor of Aristotle (4th century B.C.).

Revenge is Satan's nectar and ambrosia. This is the savoury meat which the malicious man dresses for the devil. The Scripture forbids revenge: 'Dearly beloved, avenge not yourselves' (Romans 12:19). This is to take God's office out of his hand, who is called 'the God of recompences' (Jeremiah 51:56) and the 'God of vengeance' (Psalm 94:1). This I urge against those who challenge one another to duels. Indeed, spiritual duels are lawful. It is good to fight with the devil. 'Resist the devil' (James 4:7). It is good to duel with a man's self, the regenerate part against the carnal. Blessed is he that seeks a revenge upon his lusts. 'Yea, what revenge!' (2 Corinthians 7:11). But other duels are unlawful. 'Avenge not yourselves.' The Turks, though a barbarous people, in ancient times burnt such as went to duel, applying hot coals of fire to their sides. They who were in heat of revenge were punished suitably with fire.

Some may object. But if I am thus meek and tame in bearing of injuries and incivilities, I shall lose my credit. It will be a strain to my reputation. I answer: To pass by an injury without revenge is no eclipse to a man's credit. Solomon tells us it is the glory of a man to 'pass over a transgression' (Proverbs 19:11). It is more honour to bury an injury than revenge it; and to slight it than to write it down. The weakest creatures soonest turn head, and sting upon every touch. The lion, a more majestic creature, is not easily provoked. The bramble tears. The oak and cedar are more peaceable. Passion imports weakness. A noble spirit overlooks an injury.

Again, suppose a man's credit should suffer an impair[1] with those whose censure is not to be valued. Yet think which is worse, shame or sin? Will you sin against God to save your credit? Surely it is little wisdom for a man to venture his blood that he may fetch back his reputation, and to run into hell to be counted valorous.

Not but that a man may stand up in defence of himself when his life is endangered. Some of the Anabaptists hold it unlawful to take up the sword upon any occasion (though when they get the power, I would be loath to trust them, their river water often turning to blood), but questionless a man may take up the sword for self-preservation, else he comes under the breach of the sixth commandment. He is guilty of self-murder. In taking up the sword he does not so much seek another's death, as the safeguard of his own life. His intention is not to do hurt, but to prevent it. Self-defence is consistent with Christian meekness. The law of nature and religion justify it. That God who bids us 'put up our sword' (Matthew 26:52) yet will allow us a 'buckler' in our own

[1] Damage.

defence, and he that will have us 'innocent as doves' not to offend others,
will have us 'wise as serpents' in preserving ourselves.

Though revenge may be contrary to meekness, yet not but that a
magistrate may revenge the quarrels of others. Indeed, it is not revenge
in him, but doing justice. The magistrate is God's lieutenant on earth.
God has put the sword in his hand, and he is not 'to bear the sword in
vain'. He must be 'for the punishment of evil-doers' (1 Peter 2:14).
Though a private person must not render to any man 'evil for evil'
(Romans 12:17), yet a magistrate may; the evil of punishment for the
evil of offence. This rendering of evil is good. Private men must 'put
their sword into the sheath', but the magistrate sins if he does not draw
it out. As his sword must not surfeit through cruelty, so neither must
it rust through partiality. Too much lenity in a magistrate is not meekness, but injustice. For him to indulge offences, and say with a gentle
reproof as Eli, 'Why do you such things? Nay, my sons, for it is no
good report that I hear' (1 Samuel 2:23, 24), this is but to shave the
head that deserves to be cut off. Such a magistrate makes himself guilty.

(iv) Meekness is *opposed to evil-speaking*. 'Let all evil-speaking be put
away' (Ephesians 4:31). Our words should be mild, like the waters of
Shiloah which run softly. It is too usual for passionate spirits to break
out into opprobrious language. The tongues of many are fired, and it is
the devil lights the match. Therefore they are said in Scripture to be
'set on fire of hell' (James 3:6). Men have learned of the 'old serpent' to
spit their venom one at another in disgraceful revilings. 'Whosoever
shall say, Thou fool, shall be in danger of hell-fire' (Matthew 5:22).
Under that word 'fool', all vilifying terms are by our Saviour forbidden. Let us take heed of this. It is hateful to God. God is not in this fire,
but in the 'still small voice' (1 Kings 19:12).

Some may say, But did not the apostle Paul call the Galatians fools?
(Galatians 3:1). I answer, Paul had an infallible spirit, which we do not
have. Besides, when Paul uttered those words, it was not by way of reproach, but reproof. It was not to defame the Galatians but to reclaim
them; not to vilify them but to humble them. Paul was grieved to see
them so soon fall into a relapse. Well might he say 'foolish Galatians' in
an holy zeal, because they had suffered so much in the cause of religion,
and now made a defection and fell off. 'Have ye suffered so many things
in vain?' (verse 4). But though Paul, guided by the Spirit of God, did
give this epithet to the Galatians, it is no warrant for us when any have
wronged us to use disgraceful terms. Meekness does not vent itself in
scurrility. It does not retaliate by railing. 'Yet Michael the archangel,

when contending with the devil he disputed about the body of Moses, durst not bring against him a railing accusation, but said, The Lord rebuke thee' (Jude 9). Some understand by Michael, Christ, but more truly it is meant of one of the chief of the angels. The contest or dispute between the archangel and the devil was about the body of Moses. Some divines say that when God disposed of Moses' body, he employed the archangel to inter him so secretly that his burying place might not be known. It is likely if his dead body had been found, the Israelites might have been ready in a preposterous zeal to have adored it. The devil opposes the archangel and contends about the dead body, but the archangel 'durst not', or, as some read it, he could not endure to 'bring a railing accusation'. It seems the devil provoked him with evil language, and would fain have extorted passion from him, but the archangel was mild, and said only, 'The Lord rebuke thee.' The angel would not so much as rail against the devil. We may learn meekness of the archangel : 'Not rendering railing for railing' (1 Peter 3 : 9).

Not but that a Christian ought prudentially to clear himself from slanders. When the apostle Paul was charged to be mad he vindicated himself. 'I am not mad, most noble Festus' (Acts 26 : 25). Though a Christian's retorts must not be vulnerating,[1] they may be vindicating. Though he may not scandalize another, yet he may apologize[2] for himself. There must be Christian prudence, as well as Christian meekness. It is not mildness but weakness to part with our integrity (Job 27 : 6). To be silent when we are slanderously traduced, is to make ourselves appear guilty. We must so affect meekness as not to lose the honour of innocence. It is lawful to be our own compugnators.[3] The fault lies only in this, when we retort injuries with reproachful terms, which is to pay a man back in the devil's coin.

Meekness in the forgiving of injuries

The second branch of meekness is in *forgiving of injuries*. 'And when ye stand praying, forgive' (Mark 11 : 25); as if Christ had said, It is to little purpose to pray, unless you forgive. A meek spirit is a forgiving spirit. This is an Herculean work. Nothing more crosses the stream of corrupt nature. Men forget kindnesses, but remember injuries. I once heard of a woman that lived in malice, and being requested by some of her neighbours when she lay on her death-bed, to forgive, she answered,

---

[1] Wounding, injurious.   [2] Used here in the former sense of 'defend'.
[3] Those who fight (in self-defence). The word is so rare that it does not appear in the large (12-vol.) Oxford Dictionary.

'I cannot forgive though I go to hell.' This is cutting against the grain. Some can rather sacrifice their lives than their lusts, but forgive we must, and forgive as God forgives. Forgiveness must be:

(i) *Really*. God does not make a show of forgiveness and keep our sins by him. He 'blots out' our debts (Isaiah 43:25). God passes an act of oblivion (Jeremiah 31:34). He forgives and forgets. So the meek spirit not only makes a show of forgiving his neighbour, but he does it from the heart (Matthew 18:27).

(ii) *Fully*. God forgives all our sins. He does not for 'fourscore write down fifty', but he gives a general release. 'Who forgiveth all thy iniquities' (Psalm 103:3). Thus a meek-spirited Christian forgives all injuries. False hearts pass by some offences, but retain others. This is but half forgiving. Is this meekness? Would you have God deal so with you? Would you have him forgive your trespasses, as you forgive others?

(iii) God forgives *often*. We are often peccant.[1] We run every day afresh upon the score, but God often forgives. Therefore he is said to 'multiply pardon' (Isaiah 55:7). So a meek spirit reiterates and sends one pardon after another. Peter asks the question, 'Lord, how oft shall my brother sin against me, and I forgive him? till seven times?' (Matthew 18:21) Christ answers him, 'I say not unto thee, Until seven times, but until seventy times seven' (verse 22).

Some may object that such an affront has been offered that flesh and blood cannot put up? I answer: 'Flesh and blood cannot inherit the Kingdom of God' (1 Corinthians 15:50). Christians must walk antipodes[2] to themselves, and with the sword of the Spirit fight against the lusts of the flesh (Galatians 5:24).

Again, you may say: But if I forgive one injury I shall invite more. I answer: It argues a devilish nature to be the worse for kindness; but suppose we should meet with such monsters, yet it is our duty to be ready to forgive (Colossians 3:13). Shall we cease from doing good because others will not cease from being evil? If the more you forgive injuries, the more injuries you meet with, this will make your grace shine the more. Another's vice will be a greater demonstration of your virtue. Often forgiving will add the more to the weight of his sin, and the weight of your glory. If any shall say to me, I strive to excel in

[1] Sinning.   [2] See p. 63 fn. 1.

other graces, but as for this grace of meekness, the bearing and for-giving of injuries, I cannot arrive at it; I desire in this to be excused. What do you talk of other graces? Where there is one grace, there is all. If meekness be wanting, it is but a counterfeit chain of grace. Your faith is a fable: your repentance is a lie; your humility is hypocrisy.

And whereas you say you cannot forgive, think of your sin. Your neighbour is not so bad in offending you as you are in not forgiving him. Your neighbour, in offending you, but trespasses against a man, but you, refusing to forgive him, trespass against God. Think also of your danger. You who are implacable, and though you may smother the fire of your rage, yet will not extinguish it, know that if you die this night, you die in an unpardoned condition. If you will not believe me, believe Christ. 'If you do not forgive, neither will your Father which is in heaven forgive your trespasses' (Mark 11:26). He who lives without meekness, dies without mercy.

Meekness in recompensing good for evil

The third branch of meekness is in *recompensing good for evil*. This is an higher degree than the other. 'Love your enemies, do good to them that hate you, pray for them which despitefully use you' (Matthew 5:44). 'If thine enemy hunger, feed him' (Romans 12:20). 'Not render-ing evil for evil, but contrariwise blessing' (1 Peter 3:9). This three-fold cord of Scripture should not easily be broken. To render evil for evil is brutish: to render evil for good is devilish; to render good for evil is Christian. The heathens thought it lawful to wrong none unless first provoked with an injury, but the sunlight of Scripture shines brighter than the lamp of reason. 'Love your enemies.' When grace comes into the heart, it works a strange alteration. When a scion is ingrafted into the stock, it partakes of the nature and sap of the tree and brings forth the same fruit. Take a crab, ingraft it into a pippin, it brings forth the same fruit as the pippin. So he who was once of a sour crabby disposi-tion, given to revenge, when he once partakes of the sap of the heavenly olive, he bears generous fruits. He is full of love to his enemies. Grace allays the passion and melts the heart into compassion. As the sun draws up many thick noxious vapours from the earth and sea, and returns them in sweet showers, so a gracious heart returns all the unkindness and discourtesies of his enemies with the sweet influences and distilla-tions of love. Thus David, 'They rewarded me evil for good; but as for me, when they were sick, my clothing was sack-cloth, I humbled my soul with fasting . . .' (Psalm 35:12, 13). Some would have rejoiced;

he wept. Some would have put on scarlet; David put on sack-cloth. This is the rarity or rather miracle of meekness. It retorts good for evil. Thus we have seen the nature of meekness.

Meekness shows the character of a true saint

Meekness shows us the badge of a true saint. He is of a meek, candid spirit. 'He is not easily provoked.' He takes everything in the best sense and conquers malice with mildness. I would to God all who profess themselves saints were bespangled with this grace. We are known to belong to Christ when we wear his livery. He is a saint whose spirit is made so meek that he can smother prejudices and bury unkindnesses. A passion of tears better becomes a Christian than a passion of anger. Every saint is Christ's spouse (Canticles 4:8). It becomes Christ's spouse to be meek. If any injury be offered to the spouse, she leaves it to her husband to revenge. It is unseemly for Christ's spouse to strike.

Ten reasons why Christians should be meek

Let me beseech all Christians to labour to be eminent in this superlative grace of meekness. 'Seek meekness' (Zephaniah 2:3). Seeking implies we have lost it. Therefore, we must make an hue and cry after it to find it. 'Put on therefore as the elect of God, meekness' (Colossians 3:12). Put it on as a garment, never to be left off. Meekness is a necessary ingredient in everything. It is necessary in *instruction*: 'In meekness instructing . . .' (2 Timothy 2:25). Meekness conquers the opposers of truth. Meekness melts the heart. 'Soft words' are softening. Meekness is necessary in hearing the Word. 'Receive with meekness the ingrafted Word' (James 1:21). He who come to the Word with either passion or prejudice gets no good, but hurt. He turns wine into poison, and stabs himself with the sword of the Spirit. Meekness is needful in reproof. 'If a man be overtaken with a fault, restore such an one with the spirit of meekness' (Galatians 6:1). The Greek word is 'put him in joint again'. If a bone be out of joint, the surgeon must not use a rough hand that may chance break another bone. But he must come gently to work, and afterwards bind it up softly. So if a brother be through inadvertency overtaken, we must not come to him in a fury of passion, but with a spirit of meekness labour to restore him. I shall lay down several motives or arguments to meeken the spirits of men.

1 *Let me propound examples of meekness*

(i) The example of Jesus Christ. 'Thy king cometh unto thee meek' (Matthew 21:5). Christ was the samplar and pattern of meekness. 'When he was reviled, he reviled not again' (1 Peter 2:23). His enemies' words were more bitter than the gall they gave him, but Christ's words were smoother than oil. He prayed and wept for his enemies. He calls us to learn of him: 'Learn of me, for I am meek' (Matthew 11:29). Christ does not bid us (says Augustine) learn of him to work miracles, to open the eyes of the blind, to raise the dead, but he would have us learn of him to be meek. If we do not imitate his life, we cannot be saved by his death.

(ii) Let us set before our eyes the examples of some of the saints who have shined in this grace. Moses was a man of unparalleled meekness. 'Now the man Moses was very meek, above all the men which were upon the face of the earth' (Numbers 12:3). How many injuries did he put up? When the people of Israel murmured against him, instead of falling into a rage, he falls to prayer for them (Exodus 15:24, 25). The text says, they murmured at the waters of Marah. Sure the waters were not so bitter as the spirits of the people, but they could not provoke him to passion, but to petition. Another time when they wanted water, they fell a chiding with Moses. 'Wherefore is this that thou hast brought us up out of Egypt, to kill us and our children with thirst?' (Exodus 17:3). As if they had said, If we die we will lay our death to your charge. Would not this exasperate? Surely it would have required the meekness of an angel to bear this; but behold Moses' meekness. He did not give them an unbecoming word! Though they were in a storm, he was in a calm. They chide, but he prays. Oh that as the spirit of Elijah rested upon Elisha, so may some of the spirit of Moses, this meek man (or rather earthly angel), rest upon us! Another eminent pattern of meekness was David. When Shimei cursed David, and Abishai, one of David's life-guard, would have beheaded Shimei; No, says king David, 'Let him alone, and let him curse' (2 Samuel 16:11). And when Saul had wronged and abused David and it was in David's power to have taken Saul napping, and have killed him (1 Samuel 26:7, 12), yet he would not touch Saul, but called God to be umpire (verse 23). Here was a mirror of meekness.

(iii) The examples of heathens. Though their meekness could not properly be called grace, because it did not grow upon the right stock of faith, yet it was very beautiful in its kind. When one reviled Pericles [1]

[1] Athenian statesman of 5th century B.C.

and followed him home to his gate at night, railing upon him, he answered not a word, but commanded one of his servants to light a torch, and bring the railer home to his own house. Frederick, Duke of Saxony,[1] when he was angry, would shut himself up in his closet and let none come near him, till he had mastered his passion. Plutarch[2] reports of the Pythagoreans,[3] if they chanced to fall out in the day, they would embrace and be friends ere sun-set. Cicero,[4] in one of his Orations, reports of Pompey[5] the Great that he was a man of a meek disposition. He admitted all to come to him so freely, and heard the complaints of them that were wronged so mildly, that he excelled all the princes before him. He was of that sweet temper that it was hard to say whether his enemies more feared his valour, or his subjects loved his meekness. Julius Caesar not only forgave Brutus and Cassius, his enemies, but advanced them. He thought himself most honoured by acts of clemency and meekness. Did the spring-head of nature rise so high, and shall not grace rise higher? Shall we debase faith below reason? Let us write according to these fair copies.

2 *Meekness is a great ornament to a Christian.* 'The ornament of a meek spirit' (1 Peter 3:4). How amiable is a saint in God's eye when adorned with this jewel! What the psalmist says of praise (Psalm 33:1), the same may I say of meekness. It is 'comely for the righteous'. No garment is more becoming to a Christian than meekness. Therefore we are bid to put on this garment. 'Put on therefore as the elect of God, meekness' (Colossians 3:12) A meek spirit brings credit to religion and silences malice. It is the varnish that puts lustre upon holiness, and sets off the gospel with a better gloss.

3 *This is the way to be like God.* God is meek towards them that provoke him. How many black mouths are opened daily against the Majesty of heaven? How do men tear his Name! vex his Spirit! crucify his Son afresh! They walk up and down the earth as so many devils covered with flesh, yet the Lord is meek, 'not willing that any should perish' (2 Peter 3:9). How easily could God crush sinners, and kick them into hell! But he moderates his anger. Though he be full of majesty, yet full of meekness. In him is mixed princely greatness and

---

[1] Known as 'the Wise': he was a supporter of the Lutheran Reformation.
[2] Greek historian of the 1st century A.D.
[3] Disciples of Pythagoras, philosopher and mathematician of the 6th century B.C.
[4] Roman orator, philosopher, statesman of the 1st century B.C.
[5] Roman general, a contemporary of Julius Caesar (1st century B.C.).

fatherly mildness. As he has his sceptre of royalty, so his throne of grace. Oh how should this make us fall in love with meekness! Hereby we bear a kind of likeness to God. It is not profession makes us like God, but imitation. Where meekness is wanting, we are not like men. Where it is present, we are like God.

4 *Meekness argues a noble and excellent spirit.* A meek man is a valorous man. He gets a victory over himself. Passion arises from imbecility and weakness. Therefore we may observe old men and children are more choleric than others. Strength of passion argues weakness of judgment, but the meek man who is able to conquer his fury, is the most puissant[1] and victorious. 'He that is slow to anger is better than the mighty; and he that ruleth his spirit than he that taketh a city' (Proverbs 16:32). To yield to one's passion is easy. It is swimming along with the tide of corrupt nature, but to turn against nature, to resist passion, to 'overcome evil with good', this is like a Christian. This is that spiritual chivalry and fortitude of mind that deserves the trophies of victory and the garland of praise.

5 *Meekness is the best way to conquer and melt the heart of an enemy.* When Saul lay at David's mercy and David only cut off the skirt of his robe, how was Saul's heart affected with David's meekness? 'Is this thy voice, my son David? And Saul lift up his voice and wept, and he said to David, Thou art more righteous than I, for thou hast rewarded me good, whereas I have rewarded thee evil; forasmuch as when the Lord had delivered me into thine hand, thou killedst me not; wherefore the Lord reward thee good . . .' (1 Samuel 24:16, 17). This 'heaping of coals' melts and thaws the heart of others. It is the greatest victory to overcome an enemy without striking a blow. The fire will go where the wedge cannot. Mildness prevails more than fierceness. Passion makes an enemy of a friend. Meekness makes a friend of an enemy. The meek Christian shall have letters testimonial even from his adversary. It is reported of Philip,[2] king of Macedon, that when it was told him Nicanor openly railed against his Majesty, the king instead of putting him to death (as his council advised), sent Nicanor a rich present, which so overcame the man's heart, that he went up and down to recant what he had said against the king, and highly extolled the king's clemency. Roughness hardens men's hearts; meekness causes them to relent (2 Kings 6:22). When the king of Israel feasted the captives he had taken in war, they were more conquered by his meekness than by his sword.

[1] Powerful.

[2] Father of Alexander the Great (4th century B.C.)

'The bands of Syria came no more into the land of Israel' (2 Kings 6:23).

6 *Consider the great promise in the text.* 'The meek shall inherit the earth'. This argument perhaps will prevail with those who desire to have earthly possessions. Some may object, If I forbear and forgive, I shall lose my right at last and be turned out of all? No! God has here entered into bond, 'The meek shall inherit the earth.' The unmeek man is in a sad condition. There is no place remains for him but hell, for he has no promise made to him either of earth or heaven. It is the 'meek shall inherit the earth'.

How do the meek inherit the earth when they are strangers in the earth? (Hebrews 11:37).

The meek are said to inherit the earth, not that the earth is their chief inheritance, or that they have always the greatest share there, but:

(i) They are the inheritors of the earth because, though they have not always the greatest part of the earth, yet they have the best right to it. The word 'inherit', says Ambrose, denotes the saints' 'title to the earth'. The saints' title is best, being 'members of Christ', who is Lord of all. Adam not only lost his title to heaven when he fell, but to the earth too; and till we are incorporated into Christ, we do not fully recover our title. I do not deny that the wicked have a civil right to the earth which the laws of the land give them, but not a sacred right. Only the meek Christian has a Scripture-title to his land. We count that the best title which is held in capite. The saints hold their right to the earth *in capite*, in their head, Christ, who is 'the prince of the kings of the earth (Revelation 1:5). In this sense, he who has but a foot of land inherits more than he who has a thousand acres, because he has a better and more juridical right to it.

(ii) The meek Christian is said to inherit the earth, because he inherits the blessing of the earth. The wicked man has the earth, but not as a fruit of God's favour. He has it as a dog has poisoned bread. It does him more hurt than good. A wicked man lives in the earth as one that lives in an infectious air. He is infected by his mercies. The fat of the earth will but make him fry and blaze the more in hell. So that a wicked man may be said not to have what he has, because he has not the blessing; but the meek saint enjoys the earth as a pledge of God's love. The curse and poison is taken out of the earth: 'The meek shall inherit the earth and shall delight themselves in the abundance of peace' (Psalm 37:11), on which words Augustine gives this gloss: Wicked men (says he) may

[117]

delight themselves in the abundance of cattle and riches, but the meek man delights himself in the abundance of peace. What he has he possesses with inward serenity and quietness.

When it is said the meek shall inherit the earth, it does not intimate that they shall not inherit more than the earth. They shall inherit heaven too. If they should only inherit the earth, then (says Chrysostom) how could it be said, 'Blessed are the meek?' The meek have the earth only for their sojourning-house: they have heaven for their mansion-house. 'He will beautify the meek with salvation' (Psalm 149:4). The meek beautify religion, and God will beautify them with salvation. Salvation is the port we all desire to sail to. It is the harvest and vintage of souls. The meek are they which shall reap this harvest. The meek shall wear the embroidered robe of salvation. The meek are lords of the earth and 'heirs of salvation' (Hebrews 1:14).

7 *Consider the mischief of an unmeek spirit.* There is nothing makes such room for the devil to come into the heart and take possession, as wrath and anger. 'Let not the sun go down upon your wrath, neither give place to the devil' (Ephesians 4:26, 27). When men let forth passion, they let in Satan. The wrathful man has the devil for his bedfellow. Passion hinders peace. The meek Christian has sweet quiet and harmony in his soul, but passion puts the soul into a disorder. It not only clouds reason, but disturbs conscience. He does not possess himself whom passion possesses. It is no wonder if they have no peace of conscience who make so little conscience of peace. Wrathfulness grieves the Spirit of God (Ephesians 4:30, 31), and if the Spirit be grieved, he will be gone. We do not care to stay in smoky houses. The Spirit of God does not love to be in that heart which is so full of the vapours and fumes of distempered passion.

8 *Another argument to cool the intemperate heat of our cursed hearts,* is to consider that all the injuries and unkind usages we meet with from the world, do not fall out by chance, but are disposed of by the all-wise God for our good. Many are like the foolish cur that snarls at the stone, never looking to the hand that threw it; or like the horse, who being spurred by the rider, bites the snaffle. If we looked higher than instruments our hearts would grow meek and calm. David looked beyond Shimei's rage: 'Let him curse, for the Lord hath bidden him' (2 Samuel 16:11). What wisdom were it for Christians to see the hand of God in all the barbarisms and incivilities of men! Job eyed God in his affliction, and that meekened his spirit. 'The Lord hath taken away, blessed be the name of the Lord' (Job 1:21). He does not say, The Chaldeans have

taken away, but 'The Lord hath taken away'. What made Christ so meek in his sufferings? He did not look at Judas or Pilate, but at his Father. 'The cup which my Father hath given me' (John 18:11). When wicked men revile and injure us, they are but God's executioners. Who is angry with the executioner?

And as God has an hand in all the affronts and discourtesies we receive from men (for they but hand them over to us), so God will do us good by all if we belong to him. 'It may be' (says David) 'that the Lord will look upon mine affliction, and requite me good for his cursing' (2 Samuel 16:12). Usually, when the Lord intends us some signal mercy, he fits us for it by some eminent trial. As Moses' hand was first leprous before it wrought salvation (Exodus 4:6), so God may let his people be belepered with the cursings and revilings of men before he shower down some blessings upon them. 'It may be the Lord will requite me good for his cursing this day.'

9 *Want of meekness evidences want of grace.* True grace inflames love and moderates anger. Grace is like the file which smoothes the rough iron. It files off the ruggedness of a man's spirit. Grace says to the heart as Christ did to the angry sea, 'Peace, be still' (Mark 4:39). So where there is grace in the heart, it stills the raging of passion and makes a calm. He who is in a perpetual frenzy, letting loose the reins to wrath and malice, never yet felt the sweet efficacy of grace. It is one of the sins of the heathen to be 'implacable' (Romans 1:31). A revengeful cankered heart is not only heathenish, but devilish. 'If ye have bitter envying and strife in your hearts, this wisdom descendeth not from above, but is devilish' (James 3:14, 15). The old serpent spits forth the poison of malice and revenge.

10 If all that has been said will not serve to master this bedlam-humour of wrath and anger, let me tell you, you are the *persons whom God speaks of, who hate to be reformed.* You are rebels against the Word. Read and tremble: 'Now go, write it before them in a table, and note it in a book, that it may be for the time to come for ever and ever; that this is a rebellious people, children that will not hear the law of the Lord' (Isaiah 30:8, 9). If nothing yet said will charm down the wrathful devil, let me tell you, God hath charged every man not to meddle or have any league of friendship with you. 'Make no friendship with an angry man, and with a furious man thou shalt not go' (Proverbs 22:24). What a monster is he among men, that every one is warned to beware of, and not to come near, as one who is unfit for humane society! Make no league, says God, with THAT MAN. If you take him into your

society, you take a snake into your bosom. 'With a furious man thou shalt not go.' Will you walk with the devil? The furious man is possessed with a wrathful devil.

Oh that all this might help to meeken and sweeten Christians' spirits!

But some will say, It is my nature to be passionate! I answer:

(i) This is sinful arguing. It is secretly to lay our sin upon God. We learned this from Adam. 'The woman whom thou gavest to be with me, she gave me of the tree, and I did eat' (Genesis 3:12); rather than Adam would confess his sin, he would father it upon God. 'The woman thou gavest me.' As if he had said, If you had not given this woman to me, I had not eaten. So, says one, It is my nature; this is the froward, peevish nature God has given me. Oh no! you charge God falsely. God did not give you such a nature. 'He made man upright' (Ecclesiastes 7:29). God made you straight; you made yourself crooked. All your affections at first, your joy, love, anger were set in order as the stars in their right orb, but you misplaced them and made them move eccentric. At first the affections like several musical instruments well tuned, made a sweet consort, but sin was the jarring string that brought all out of tune. Vain man, do not plead that it is your nature to be angry; thank yourself for it. Nature's spring was pure till sin poisoned the spring.

(ii) Is it your nature to be fierce and angry? This is so far from being an excuse, that it makes it so much the worse. It is the nature of a toad to poison that makes it the more hateful. If a man were indicted for stealing, and he should say to the judge, 'Spare me; it is my nature to steal', were this any excuse? The judge would say, 'You deserve the rather to die.' Sinner, get a new nature. 'Flesh and blood cannot enter into the kingdom of God.'

How to attain the grace of meekness

What shall I do to be possessed of this excellent grace of meekness?

1 Often look upon the meekness of Christ. The scholar that would write well has his eye often upon the copy.

2 Pray earnestly that God will meeken your spirit. God is called 'the God of all grace' (1 Peter 5:10). He has all the graces in his gift. Sue to him for this grace of meekness. If one were patron of all the livings in the land, men would sue to him for a living. God is patron of all the graces. Let us sue to him. Mercy comes in at the door of prayer. 'I will yet for this be enquired of by the house of Israel to do it for them'

(Ezekiel 36:26, 37). Meekness is the commodity we want. Let us send prayer as our factor [1] over to heaven to procure it for us; and pray in faith. When faith sets prayer on work, prayer sets God on work. All divine blessings come streaming to us through this golden channel of prayer.

[1] Merchant-agent.

13 The nature of spiritual hunger

Blessed are they which do hunger and thirst after righteousness

We are now come to the fourth step of blessedness: 'Blessed are they that hunger.' The words fall into two parts: a duty implied; a promise annexed.

A duty implied: 'Blessed are they that hunger.' Spiritual hunger is a blessed hunger.

What is meant by hunger? Hunger is put for desire (Isaiah 26:9). Spiritual hunger is the rational appetite whereby the soul pants after that which it apprehends most suitable and proportionable to itself.

Whence is this hunger? Hunger is from the sense of want. He who spiritually hungers, has a real sense of his own indigence. He wants righteousness.

Hungering after righteousness

What is meant by righteousness? There is a two-fold righteousness: of imputation; of implantation.

A righteousness of *Imputation*, namely, Christ's righteousness. 'He shall be called the Lord our righteousness' (Jeremiah 23:6). This is as truly ours to justify, as it is Christ's to bestow. By virtue of this righteousness God looks upon us as if we had never sinned (Numbers 23:21). This is a perfect righteousness. 'Ye are complete in him' (Colossians 2:10). This does not only cover but adorn. He who has this righteousness is equal to the most illustrious saints. The weakest believer is justified as much as the strongest. This is a Christian's triumph. When he is defiled in himself, he is undefiled in his Head. In this blessed righteousness we shine brighter than the angels. This righteousness is worth hungering after.

A righteousness of *Implantation*: that is, inherent righteousness, namely, the graces of the Spirit, holiness of heart and life, which Cajetan [1] calls 'universal righteousness'. This a pious soul hungers after.

This is a blessed hunger. Bodily hunger cannot make a man so miserable as spiritual hunger makes him blessed. This evidences life. A dead man cannot hunger. Hunger proceeds from life. The first thing the child does when it is born, is to hunger after the breast. Spiritual hunger follows upon the new birth (1 Peter 2:2). Saint Bernard in one of his Soliloquies comforts himself with this, that sure he had the truth of grace in him, because he had in his heart a strong desire after God. It is happy when, though we have not what we should, we desire what we have not. The appetite is as well from God as the food.

The inferences drawn from the proposition

1 See here at what a low price God sets heavenly things. It is but hungering and thirsting. 'Ho, every one that thirsteth, come ye to the waters, buy without money' (Isaiah 55:1). We are not bid to bring any merits as the Papists would do, nor to bring a sum of money to purchase righteousness. Rich men would be loath to do that. All that is required is to bring an appetite. Christ 'hath fulfilled all righteousness'. We are only to 'hunger and thirst after righteousness'. This is equal and reasonable. God does not require rivers of oil, but sighs and tears. The invitation of the gospel is free. If a friend invites guests to his table, he does not expect they should bring money to pay for their dinner, only come with an appetite. So, says God, It is not penance, pilgrimage, self-righteousness I require. Only bring a stomach: 'hunger and thirst after righteousness'. God might have set Christ and salvation at an higher price, but he has much beaten down the price. Now as this shows the sweetness of God's nature – he is not a hard master – so it shows us the inexcusableness of those who perish under the gospel. What apology can any man make at the day of judgment, when God shall ask that question, Friend, why did you not embrace Christ? I set Christ and grace at a low rate. If you had but hungered after righteousness, you might have had it, but you slighted Christ. You had such low thoughts of righteousness that you would not hunger after it. How do you think to escape who have neglected 'so great salvation'? The easier the terms of the gospel are, the sorer punishment shall they be thought worthy of who unworthily refuse such an offer.

2 It shows us a true character of a godly man. He hungers and thirsts after spiritual things (Isaiah 26:9; Psalm 73:25). A true saint is carried

[1] A Roman Catholic bishop opposed to Luther (he takes his name from Gaeta in Italy).

upon the wing of desire. It is the very temper and constitution of a gracious soul to thirst after God (Psalm 42:2). *In the word preached*, how he is big with desire! These are some of the pantings of his soul: Lord, thou hast led me into thy courts. O that I may have thy sweet presence, that thy glory may fill the temple! This is thy limning house; wilt thou draw some sacred lineaments of grace upon my soul that I may be more assimilated and changed into the likeness of my dear Saviour. *In prayer*, how is the soul filled with passionate longings after Christ! Prayer is expressed by 'groans unutterable' (Romans 8:26). The heart sends up whole volleys of sighs to heaven; Lord, one beam of thy love! one drop of thy blood!

A reproof for such as do not hunger after righteousness

It reproves such as have none of this spiritual hunger. They have no winged desires. The edge of their affections is blunted. Honey is not sweet to them that are sick of a fever and have their tongues embittered with choler.[1] So those who are soul-sick and 'in the gall of bitterness', find no sweetness in God or religion. Sin tastes sweeter to them; they have no spiritual hunger. That men do not have this 'hunger after righteousness' appears by these seven demonstrations:

1 They never felt any emptiness. They are full of their own righteousness (Romans 10:3). Now 'the full stomach loathes the honey-comb'. This was Laodicea's disease. She was full and had no stomach either to Christ's gold or eye-salve (Revelation 3:17). When men are filled with pride, this flatulent distemper hinders holy longings. As when the stomach is full of wind it spoils the appetite. None so empty of grace as he that thinks he is full. He has most need of righteousness that least wants it.

2 That men do not hunger after righteousness appears because they can make a shift well enough to be without it. If they have oil in the cruse, the world coming in, they are well content. Grace is a commodity that is least missed. You shall hear men complain they lack health, they lack trading, but never complain they lack righteousness. If men lose a meal or two they think themselves half undone, but they can stay away from ordinances which are the conduits of grace. Do they hunger after righteousness who are satisfied without it? nay, who desire to be

[1] Bile.

excused from feeding upon the gospel banquet (Luke 14:18). Sure he has no appetite, who entreats to be excused from eating.

3. It is a sign they have none of this spiritual hunger, who desire rather sleep than food. They are more drowsy than hungry. Some there are who come to the Word that they may get a nap, to whom I may say as Christ did to Peter, 'Couldest thou not watch one hour?' (Mark 14: 37). It is strange to see a man asleep at his meat. Others there are who have a 'deep sleep' fallen upon them. They are asleep in security and they hate a soul-awakening ministry. While they sleep, 'their damnation slumbereth not' (2 Peter 2: 3).

4 It appears that men have no spiritual hunger because they refuse their food. Christ and grace are offered, nay, pressed upon them, but they put away salvation from them as the froward child puts away the breast (Psalm 81: 11; Acts 13: 46). Such are your fanatics and enthusiasts who put away the blessed ordinances and pretend to revelations. That is a strange revelation that tells a man he may live without food. These prefer husks before manna. They live upon airy notions, being fed by the 'prince of the air'.

5. It is a sign they have none of this spiritual hunger who delight more in the garnishing of the dish than in food. These are they who look more after elegancy and notion in preaching than solid matter. It argues either a wanton palate or a surfeited stomach to feed on sallets[1] and kickshaws,[2] neglecting wholesome food. 'If any man consent not to wholesome words, he is proud, knowing nothing . . .' (1 Timothy 6: 3, 4). The plainest truth has its beauty. They have no spiritual hunger that desire only to feast their fancy. Of such the prophet speaks: 'Thou art to them as a very lovely song of one that hath a pleasant voice, and can play well on an instrument' (Ezekiel 33: 32). If a man were invited to a feast, and there being music at the feast, he should so listen to the music that he did not mind his meat, you would say, Sure he is not hungry. So when men are for jingling words and like rather gallantry of speech than spirituality of matter, it is a sign they have surfeited stomachs and 'itching ears'.

6 They evidence little hunger after righteousness that prefer other things before it, namely, their profits and recreations. If a boy when he should be at dinner is playing in the street, it is a sign that he has no appetite to his meat. Were he hungry he would not prefer his play before his food.

[1] Salads.
[2] Fancy dishes (word is derived from the French 'quelque chose').

So when men prefer 'vain things which cannot profit' before the blood of Christ and the grace of the Spirit, it is a sign they have no palate or stomach to heavenly things.

7 It is a sign men have no spiritual hunger when they are more for disputes in religion than practice. Robert of Gaul thought he saw in his dream a great feast, and some were biting on hard stones. When men feed only on hard questions and controversies (1 Timothy 6:3, 4) (like some of the schoolmen's 'utrums'[1] and distinctions), as whether one may partake with him that does not have the work of grace in his heart, whether one ought not to separate from a church in case of maladministration, what is to be thought of paedobaptism, etc. When these niceties and criticisms in religion take men's heads, neglecting faith and holiness, these pick bones and do not feed on the meat. Sceptics in religion have hot brains but cold hearts. Did men hunger and thirst after righteousness they would propound to themselves such questions as these, How shall we do to be saved? How shall we make our calling and election sure? How shall we mortify our corruptions? But such as ravel out their time in frothy and litigious disputes, I call heaven to witness, they are strangers to this text. They do not 'hunger and thirst after righteousness'.

A reproof for such as hunger but not after righteousness

The Word reproves them who, instead of hungering and thirsting after righteousness, thirst after riches. This is the thirst of covetous men. They desire mammon not manna. 'They pant after the dust of the earth' (Amos 2:7). This is the disease most are afflicted with, an immoderate appetite after the world, but these things will no more satiate than drink will quench the thirst of a man with the dropsy. Covetousness is idolatry (Colossians 3:5). Too many Protestants set up the idol of gold in the temple of their hearts. This sin of covetousness is the most hard to root out. Commonly, when other sins leave men, this sin abides. Wantonness is the sin of youth; worldliness the sin of old age.

The Word reproves them who hunger and thirst after unrighteousness. Here I shall indict three sorts of persons:

1 It reproves such as thirst after other men's lands and possessions. This the Scripture calls a 'mighty sin' (Amos 5:12). Thus Ahab thirsted after Naboth's vineyard. This is an hungry age wherein we live. We have a great deal of this hungering and thirsting, which has made so

[1] The introduction of alternative questions – this or that?

many State-thieves. Men have fleeced others to feather themselves. What a brave challenge did Samuel make; 'Behold, here I am, witness against me before the Lord, and before his anointed: Whose ox have I taken? or whose ass have I taken? or whom have I defrauded? Of whose hand have I received any bribe? ...' (1 Samuel 12:3). Few that have been in power that can say thus, Whose ox have we taken? whose house have we plundered? whose estate have we sequestered? Nay, whose ox have they not taken? 'Goods unjustly gotten seldom go to the third heir.'¹ Read the plunderer's curse: 'Woe to thee that spoilest, and thou wast not spoiled; when thou shalt cease to spoil, thou shalt be spoiled' (Isaiah 33:1). Ahab paid dear for the vineyard when the devil carried away his soul and the 'dogs licked his blood' (1 Kings 21:19). He that lives on rapine dies a fool. 'He that getteth riches, and not by right, at his end shall be a fool' (Jeremiah 17:11).

2 It reproves such as hunger and thirst after revenge. This is a devilish thirst. Though it were more Christian and safe to smother an injury, yet our nature is prone to this disease of revenge. We have the sting of the bee, not the honey. Malice having broken the bars of reason grows savage and carries its remedy in the scabbard. Heathens who have stopped the vein of revengeful passion when it has begun to vent, will rise up against Christians. I have read of Phocion² who, being wrongfully condemned to die, desired that his son might not remember the injuries which the Athenians had done to him, nor revenge his blood.

3 It reproves such as hunger and thirst to satisfy their impure lusts. Sinners are said to sin 'with greediness' (Ephesians 4:19). So Amnon was sick till he had defiled Tamar's chastity (2 Samuel 13). Never does an hungry man come with more eagerness to his food than a wicked man does to his sin. And when Satan sees men have such an appetite, commonly he will provide a dish they love. He will set the 'forbidden tree' before them. They that thirst to commit sin shall thirst as Dives did in hell and not have a drop of water to cool their tongue.

Five signs of spiritual hunger

Let us put ourselves upon a trial whether we hunger and thirst after righteousness. I shall give you five signs by which you may judge of this hunger.

¹A mediaeval epigram.
²An Athenian statesman of the 4th century B.C.

1 Hunger is a painful thing. Esau, when he was returning from hunting, was almost dead with hunger (Genesis 25 : 32). 'Hungry and thirsty, their soul fainted in them' (Psalm 107:5). So a man that hungers after righteousness is in anguish of soul and ready to faint away for it. He finds a want of Christ and grace. He is distressed and in pain till he has his spiritual hunger stilled and allayed.

2 Hunger is satisfied with nothing but food. Bring an hungry man flowers, music; tell him pleasant stories; nothing will content him but food. 'Shall I die for thirst?' says Samson (Judges 15:18). So a man that hungers and thirsts after righteousness says, Give me Christ or I die. Lord, what wilt thou give me seeing I go Christless? What though I have parts, wealth, honour and esteem in the world? All is nothing without Christ. Shew me the Lord and it will suffice me. Let me have Christ to clothe me, Christ to feed me, Christ to intercede for me. While the soul is Christless, it is restless. Nothing but the water-springs of Christ's blood can quench its thirst.

3 Hunger wrestles with difficulties and makes an adventure for food. We say hunger breaks through stone walls (cf. Genesis 42:1, 2). The soul that spiritually hungers is resolved; Christ it must have; grace it must have. And to use Basil's expression, the hungry soul is almost distracted till it enjoys the thing it hungers after.

4 An hungry man falls to his meat with an appetite. You need not make an oration to an hungry man and persuade him to eat. So he who hungers after righteousness feeds eagerly on an ordinance. 'Thy words were found, and I did eat them' (Jeremiah 15:16). In the sacrament he feeds with appetite upon the body and blood of the Lord. God loves to see us feed hungrily on the bread of life.

5 An hungry man tastes sweetness in his meat. So he that hungers after righteousness relishes a sweetness in heavenly things. Christ is to him all marrow, yea the quintessence of delights. 'If so be ye have tasted that the Lord is gracious' (1 Peter 2:3). He that spiritually hungers tastes the promises sweet, nay tastes a reproof sweet. 'To the hungry soul every bitter thing is sweet' (Proverbs 27:7). A bitter reproof is sweet. He can feed upon the myrrh of the gospel as well as the honey. By these notes of trial we may judge of ourselves whether we hunger and thirst after righteousness.

Comforts for such as know spiritual hunger

The words may serve to comfort the hearts of those who hunger and thirst after righteousness; I doubt not but it is the grief of many a good heart that he cannot be more holy, that he cannot serve God better. 'Blessed are they that hunger.' Though you do not have so much righteousness as you would, yet you are blessed because you hunger after it. Desire is the best discovery [1] of a Christian. Actions may be counterfeit. A man may do a good action for a bad end. So did Jehu. Actions may be compulsory. A man may be forced to do that which is good, but not to will that which is good. Therefore we are to cherish good desires and to bless God for them. Oftentimes a child of God has nothing to show for himself but desires. 'Thy servants, who desire to fear thy name' (Nehemiah 1:11). These hungerings after righteousness proceed from love. A man does not desire that which he does not love. If you did not love Christ, you could not hunger after him.

Six differences between spiritual and carnal hunger

But some may say, If my hunger were right then I could take comfort in it, but I fear it is counterfeit. Hypocrites have their desires.

In reply, that I may the better settle a doubting Christian I shall show the difference between true and false desires, spiritual hunger and carnal.

1 The hypocrite does not desire grace for itself. He desires grace only as a bridge to lead him over to heaven. He does not so much search after grace as glory. He does not so much desire the way of righteousness as the crown of righteousness. His desire is not to be made like Christ, but to reign with Christ. This was Balaam's desire. 'Let me die the death of the righteous' (Numbers 23:10). Such desires as these are found among the damned. This is the hypocrite's hunger. But a child of God desires grace for itself and Christ for himself. To a believer not only is heaven precious but Christ is precious (1 Peter 2:7).

2 The hypocrite's desire is conditional. He would have heaven and his sins too, heaven and his pride, heaven and his covetousness. The young man in the gospel would have had heaven, provided he might keep his

---

[1] That is, evidence that a person is a true Christian.

earthly possessions. Many a man would have Christ, but there is some sin he must not be uncivil to, but gratify. This is the hypocrites' hunger; but true desire is absolute. Give me, says the soul, Christ on any terms. Let God propound what articles he will, I will subscribe to them. Would he have me deny myself? Would he have me mortify sin? I am content to do anything so I may have Christ. Hypocrites would have Christ, but they are loath to part with a lust for him. They are like a man that would have a lease, but is loath to pay down the fine.[1]

3 Hypocrites' desires are but desires. They are lazy and sluggish. When one excited Lipsius[2] to the study of virtue, says he, 'My mind is to it.' 'The desire of the slothful killeth him, for his hands refuse to labour' (Proverbs 21:25). Many stand as the waggoner in the fable crying, 'Help, Hercules', when his wain stuck in the mud, when he should rather have put his shoulder to the wheel.[3] Men would be saved but they will take no pains. Does he desire water that will not let down the bucket into the well? But true desire is quickened into endeavour. 'With my soul have I desired thee in the night; yea, with my spirit within me will I seek thee early' (Isaiah 26:9). The 'violent' take heaven by force (Matthew 11:12). The love-sick spouse, though she was wounded, and her vail taken away, yet she follows after Christ (Canticles 5:7). Desire is the weight of the soul which sets it a going; as the eagle which desires her prey makes haste to it. 'Where the slain are, there is she' (Job 39:30). The eagle has sharpness of sight to discover her prey, and swiftness of wing to fly to it. So the soul that hungers after righteousness is carried swiftly to it in the use of all holy ordinances.

4 The hypocrite's desires are cheap. He would have spiritual things, but will be at no charges for them. He cares not how much money he parts with for his lusts; he has money to spend upon a drunken companion; but he has no money to part with for the maintaining of God's ordinances. Hypocrites cry up religion, but cry down maintenance of ministers. But true desires are costly. David would not offer burnt-offerings without cost (1 Chronicles 21:24). An hungry man will give anything for food; as it fell out in the siege of Samaria (2 Kings 6:25). That man never hungered after Christ who thinks much of parting with a little silver for 'the Pearl of price'.

[1] A payment made by an incoming tenant in consideration of a small rent.
[2] A Flemish classical scholar of the 16th century.
[3] Aesop's Fables, No. 78.

5 Hypocrites' desires are flashy and transient. They are quickly gone, like the wind that does not stay long in one corner. Or like an hot fit which is soon over. While the hypocrite is under legal terror, or in affliction, he has some good desires, but the hot fit is soon over. His goodness, like a fiery comet, soon spends and evaporates; but true desire is constant. It is observable that the Greek word in the text is in the participle: 'Blessed are they that are hungering.' Though they have righteousness, yet they are still hungering after more. Hypocrites desire it like the motion of a watch which is quickly down. The desire of a godly man is like the beating of the pulse which lasts as long as life. 'My soul breaketh for the longing that it hath to thy judgments' (Psalm 119:20). And that we might not think this pang of desire would soon be over he adds, 'at all times'. David's desire after God was not an high colour in a fit, but the constant complexion of his soul. In the temple the fire was not to go out by night. 'The fire shall ever be burning upon the altar' (Leviticus 6:13). There was, says Cyril, a mystery in it, to show that we must be ever burning in holy affections and desires.

6 Hypocrites' desires are unseasonable. They are not well-timed. They put off their hungering after righteousness till it be too late. They are like the foolish virgins that came knocking when the door was shut (Matthew 25:11). In time of health and prosperity the stream of the affections ran another way. It was sin the hypocrite desired, not righteousness. When he is to die and can keep his sins no longer, now he would have grace as a passport to carry him to heaven (Luke 13:25). This is the hypocrite's fault. His faith is too early and his desires are too late. His faith began to bud in the morning of his infancy; he believed ever since he could remember, but his desires after Christ begin not to put forth till the evening of old age. He sends forth his desires when his last breath is going forth; as if a man should desire a pardon after the sentence is passed. These bed-rid desires are suspicious; but true desires are timely and seasonable. A gracious heart 'seeks first the Kingdom of God' (Matthew 6:33). David's thirst after God was early (Psalm 63:1). The wise virgins got their oil betimes before the bridegroom came. Thus we see the difference between a true and false hunger. They who can find this true hunger are blessed and may take comfort in it.

Believers' objections answered

But some may object: My hunger after righteousness is so weak, that I fear it is not true.

I answer: Though the pulse beats but weak it shows there is life. And that weak desires should not be discouraged, there is a promise made to them. 'A bruised reed he will not break' (Matthew 12:20). A reed is a weak thing, but especially when it is bruised, yet this 'bruised reed' shall not be broken, but like Aaron's dry rod, 'bud and blossom'. In case of weakness look to Christ your High Priest. He is merciful, therefore will bear with your infirmities; he is mighty, therefore will help them.

Further, if your desires after righteousness seem to be weak and languid, yet a Christian may sometimes take a measure of his spiritual estate as well by the judgment as by the affections. What is that you esteem most in your judgment? Is it Christ and grace? This is good evidence for heaven. It was a sign that Paul bore entire love to Christ because he esteemed this Pearl above all. He counted other things 'but dung, that he might win Christ' (Philippians 3:8).

But, says a child of God, that which much eclipses my comfort is, I have not that hunger which I once had. Time was when I did hunger after a Sabbath because then the manna fell. 'I called the Sabbath a delight.' I remember the time when I hungered after the body and blood of the Lord. I came to a sacrament as an hungry man to a feast, but now it is otherwise with me. I do not have those hungerings as formerly.

I answer: It is indeed an ill sign for a man to lose his stomach, but, though it be a sign of the decay of grace to lose the spiritual appetite, yet it is a sign of the truth of grace to bewail the loss. It is sad to lose our first love, but it is happy when we mourn for the loss of our first love.

If you do not have that appetite after heavenly things as formerly, yet do not be discouraged, for in the use of means you may recover your appetite. The ordinances are for the recovering of the appetite when it is lost. In other cases feeding takes away the stomach, but here, feeding on an ordinance begets a stomach.

A persuasion to spiritual hunger

The text exhorts us all to labour after this spiritual hunger. Novarinus [1] says, 'It is too small a thing merely to wish for righteousness; but we

[1] This seems to refer to Novatian, a Roman presbyter of the 3rd century, whose name appears in a variety of forms.

must hunger for it on account of a vast longing making itself felt.'
Hunger less after the world and more after righteousness. Say concerning spiritual things, 'Lord, evermore give us this bread. Feed me with
this angels' food.' That manna is most to be hungered after which will
not only preserve life but prevent death (John 6:50). That is most desirable which is most durable. Riches are not for ever (Proverbs 27:24)
but righteousness is for ever (Proverbs 8:18). 'The beauty of holiness'
never fades (Psalm 110:3). 'The robe of righteousness' (Isaiah 61:10)
never waxes old! Oh hunger after that righteousness which 'delivereth
from death' (Proverbs 10:12). This is the righteousness which God himself is in love with. 'He loveth him that followeth after righteousness'
(Proverbs 15:9). All men are ambitious of the king's favour. Alas,
what is a prince's smile but a transient beatitude? This sunshine of his
royal countenance soon masks itself with a cloud of displeasure, but
those who are endued with righteousness are God's favourites, and
how sweet is his smile! 'Thy lovingkindness is better than life' (Psalm
63:3).

To persuade men to hunger after this righteousness, consider two
things.

1 Unless we hunger after righteousness we cannot obtain it. God will
never throw away his blessings upon them that do not desire them. A
king may say to a rebel, Do but desire a pardon and you shall have it;
but if through pride and stubbornness he disdains to sue out his pardon,
he deserves justly to die. God has set spiritual blessings at a low rate.
Do but hunger and you shall have righteousness; but if we refuse to
come up to these terms there is no righteousness to be had for us. God
will stop the current of his mercy and set open the sluice of his indignation.

2 If we do not thirst here we shall thirst when it is too late. If we do
not thirst as David did – 'My soul thirsteth for God' (Psalm 42:2) – we
shall thirst as Dives did for a drop of water (Luke 16:24). They who do
not thirst for righteousness shall be in perpetual hunger and thirst. They
shall thirst for mercy, but no mercy to be had. Heat increases thirst.
When men shall burn in hell and be scorched with the flames of God's
wrath, this heat will increase their thirst for mercy but there will be
nothing to allay their thirst. O is it not better to thirst for righteousness
while it is to be had, than to thirst for mercy when there is none to
be had? Sinners, the time is shortly coming when the drawbridge of
mercy will be quite pulled up.

Helps to spiritual hunger

I shall next briefly describe some helps to spiritual hunger.

1 Avoid those things which will hinder your appetite: As *'windy things'*. When the stomach is full of wind a man has little appetite to his food. So when one is filled with a windy opinion of his own righteousness, he will not hunger after Christ's righteousness. He who, being puffed up with pride, thinks he has grace enough already will not hunger after more. These windy vapours spoil the stomach. *'Sweet things'* destroy the appetite. So by feeding immoderately upon the sweet luscious delights of the world, we lose our appetite to Christ and grace. You never knew a man surfeit himself upon the world, and at the same time be 'sick of love' to Christ. While Israel fed with delight upon garlic and onions, they never hungered after manna. The soul cannot be carried to two extremes at once. As the eye cannot look intent on heaven and earth at once, so a man cannot at the same instant hunger excessively after the world, and after righteousness! The earth puts out the fire. The love of earthly things will quench the desire of spiritual. 'Love not the world' (1 John 2:15). The sin is not in the having, but in the loving.

2 Do all that may provoke spiritual appetite. There are two things that provoke appetite. *Exercise*: a man by walking and stirring gets a stomach to his meat. So by the exercise of holy duties the spiritual appetite is increased. 'Exercise thyself unto godliness' (1 Timothy 4:7). Many have left off closet prayer. They hear the Word but seldom, and for want of exercise they have lost their stomach to religion. *Sauce*: sauce whets and sharpens the appetite. There is a two-fold sauce provokes holy appetite: first, the *'bitter herbs'* of repentance. He that tastes gall and vinegar in sin hungers after the body and blood of the Lord. Second, *affliction*. God often gives us this sauce to sharpen our hunger after grace. 'Reuben found mandrakes in the field' (Genesis 30:14). The mandrakes are an herb of a very strong savour, and among other virtues they have, they are chiefly medicinal for those who have weak and bad stomachs. Afflictions may be compared to these mandrakes, which sharpen men's desires after that spiritual food which in time of prosperity they began to loathe and nauseate. Penury is the sauce which cures the surfeit of plenty. In sickness people hunger more after righteousness than in health. 'The full soul loathes the honey-comb' (Proverbs 27:7). Christians, when full fed, despise the rich cordials of

the gospel. I wish we did not slight those truths now which would taste sweet in a prison. How precarious was a leaf of the Bible in Queen Mary's days! the wise God sees it good sometimes to give us the sharp sauce of affliction, to make us feed more hungrily upon the bread of life. And so much for the first part of the text, 'Blessed are they that hunger.'

14 Spiritual hunger shall be satisfied

They shall be filled.

MATTHEW 5:6

I proceed now to the second part of the text. *A promise annexed*. 'They shall be filled.' A Christian fighting with sin is not like one that 'beats the air' (1 Corinthians 9:26), and his hungering after righteousness is not like one that sucks in only air, 'Blessed are they that hunger, for they shall be filled.'

Those that hunger after righteousness shall be filled. God never bids us seek him 'in vain' (Isaiah 45:19). Here is an honey-comb dropping into the mouths of the hungry, 'they shall be filled'. 'He hath filled the hungry with good things' (Luke 1:53). 'He satisfieth the longing soul' (Psalm 107:9). God will not let us lose our longing. Here is the excellency of righteousness above all things. A man may hunger after the world and not be filled. The world is fading, not filling. Cast three worlds into the heart, yet the heart is not full. But righteousness is a filling thing; nay, it so fills that it satisfies. A man may be filled and not satisfied. A sinner may take his fill of sin, but that is a sad filling. It is far from satisfaction. 'The backslider in heart shall be filled with his own ways' (Proverbs 14:14). He shall have his belly full of sin; he shall have enough of it, but this is not a filling to satisfaction. This is such a filling that the damned in hell have. They shall be full of the fury of the Lord. But he that hungers after righteousness shall be satisfyingly filled. 'My people shall be satisfied with my goodness' (Jeremiah 31:14). 'My soul shall be satisfied as with marrow' (Psalm 63:5). Joseph first opened the mouth of the sacks, and then filled them with corn and put money in them (Genesis 42:25). So God first opens the mouth of the soul with desire and then fills it with good things (Psalm 81:10). For the illustration of this, consider these three things: that God can fill the hungry soul; why he fills the hungry soul; how he fills the hungry soul.

God can fill the hungry soul: why and how he does so

1 That God can fill the hungry soul. He is called a fountain. 'With thee is the fountain of life' (Psalm 36:9). The cistern may be empty and cannot fill us. Creatures are often 'broken cisterns' (Jeremiah 2:13). But the fountain is filling. God is a fountain. If we bring the vessels of our desires to this fountain, he is able to fill them. The fulness in God is an infinite fulness. Though he fill us and the angels which have larger capacities to receive, yet he has never the less himself. As the sun, though it shines, has never the less light. 'I perceive that virtue is gone out of me' (Luke 8:46). Though God lets virtue go out of him, yet he has never the less. The fulness of the creature is limited. It arises just to such a degree and proportion; but God's fulness is infinite; as it has its resplendency, so its redundancy.[1] It knows neither bounds nor bottom.

It is a constant fulness. The fulness of the creature is a mutable fulness; it ebbs and changes. I could, says one, have helped you, but now my estate is low. The blossoms of the fig-tree are soon blown off. Creatures cannot do that for us which once they could. But God is a constant fulness. 'Thou art the same' (Psalm 102:27). God can never be exhausted. His fulness is overflowing and ever-flowing. Then surely 'it is good to draw nigh to God' (Psalm 73:28). It is good bringing our vessels to this spring-head. It is a never-failing goodness.

2 Why God fills the hungry soul. The reasons are:

(i) God will fill the hungry soul out of his tender compassion. He knows that else 'the spirit would fail before him and the soul which he has made' (Isaiah 57:16). If the hungry man be not satisfied with food he dies. God has more bowels than to suffer an hungry soul to be famished. When the multitude had nothing to eat, Christ was moved with compassion and he wrought a miracle for their supply (Matthew 15:32). Much more will he compassionate such as hunger and thirst after righteousness. When a poor sinner sees himself almost starved in his sins (as the prodigal among his husks) and begins to hunger after Christ, saying, 'there is bread enough and to spare in my Father's house', God will then out of his infinite compassions bring forth the fatted calf and refresh his soul with the delicacies and provisions of the gospel. Oh the melting of God's bowels to an hungry sinner! 'Mine heart is turned within me, my repentings are kindled' (Hosea 11:8). We cannot see a poor creature at the door ready to perish with hunger,

[1] Copiousness.

but our bowels begin to relent and we afford him some relief. And will the Father of mercies let a poor soul that hungers after the blessings of the gospel go away without an alms of free grace? No, he will not; he cannot. Let the hungry sinner think thus, Though I am full of wants, yet my God is full of bowels.

(ii) God will fill the hungry that he may fulfil his Word. 'Blessed are ye that hunger now: for ye shall be filled' (Psalm 107:9; Jeremiah 31:14; Luke 6:21). 'I will pour water upon him that is thirsty, I will pour my Spirit upon thy seed ...' (Isaiah 44:3). Has the Lord spoken and shall it not come to pass? Promises are obligatory. If God has passed a promise, he cannot go back. You who hunger after righteousness have God engaged for you. He has (to speak with reverence) pawned his truth for you. As 'his compassions fail not' (Lamentations 3:22), so 'he will not suffer his faithfulness to fail' (Psalm 89:33). If the hungry soul should not be filled, the promise would not be fulfilled.

(iii) God will fill the hungry soul because he himself has excited and stirred up this hunger. He plants holy desires in us, and will not he satisfy those desires which he himself has wrought in us? As in the case of prayer, when God prepares the heart to pray, he prepares his ear to hear (Psalm 10:17); so in the case of spiritual hunger, when God prepares the heart to hunger, he will prepare his hand to fill. It is not rational to imagine that God should deny to satisfy that hunger which he himself has caused. Nature does nothing in vain. Should the Lord inflame the desire after righteousness and not fill it, he might seem to do something in vain.

(iv) God will fill the hungry because of those sweet relations he stands unto them; they are his children. We cannot deny our children when they are hungry. We will rather spare it from our own selves (Luke 11:13). When he that is born of God shall come and say, Father, I hunger, give me Christ; Father, I thirst, refresh me with the living streams of thy Spirit, can God deny? Does God hear the raven when it cries, and will he not hear the righteous when they cry? When the earth opens its mouth and thirsts God satisfies it (Psalm 65:9, 10). Does the Lord satisfy the thirsty earth with showers and will he not satisfy the thirsty soul with grace?

(v) God will satisfy the hungry because the hungry soul is most thankful for mercy. When the restless desire has been drawn out after God, and God fills it, how thankful is a Christian! The Lord loves to bestow his mercy where he may have most praise. We delight to give to them that are thankful. Musicians love to play where there is the best sound. God loves to bestow his mercies where he may hear of them again. The hungry soul sets the crown of praise upon the head of free grace. 'Whoso offereth praise glorifies me' (Psalm 50:23).

3 How God fills the hungry soul. There is a three-fold filling: with grace; with peace; with bliss.

(i) God fills the hungry soul with grace. Grace is filling because suitable to the soul. Stephen was 'full of the Holy Ghost' (Acts 7:55). This fulness of grace is in respect of parts, not of degrees. There is something of every grace, though not perfection in any grace.

(ii) God fills the hungry soul with peace. 'The God of hope fill you with all joy and peace' (Romans 15:13). This flows from Christ. Israel had honey out of the rock. This honey of peace comes out of the rock, Christ. 'That in me ye might have peace' (John 16:33). So filling is this peace that it sets the soul a-longing after heaven. This cluster of grapes quickens the appetite and pursuit after the full crop.

(iii) God fills the hungry soul with bliss. Glory is a filling thing. 'When I awake I shall be satisfied with thy image' (Psalm 17:15). When a Christian awakes out of the sleep of death then he shall be satisfied, having the glorious beams of God's image shining upon him. Then shall the soul be filled brimfull. The glory of heaven is so sweet that the soul shall still thirst, yet so infinite that it shall be filled. 'They who drink of thee, O Christ, being refreshed with sweet torrents, shall not continue to thirst – yet they shall thirst.'

What an encouragement is this to hunger after righteousness! Such shall be filled. God charges us to fill the hungry (Isaiah 58:10). He blames those who do not fill the hungry (Isaiah 32:6). And do we think he will be slack in that which he blames us for not doing? Oh come with hungerings after Christ and be assured of satisfaction. God keeps open house for hungry sinners. He invites his guests and bids them come without money (Isaiah 55:1, 2). God's nature inclines him and his promise obliges him to fill the hungry. Consider, why did Christ receive 'the Spirit without measure'? (John 3:34). It was not for himself. He was infinitely full before. But he was filled with the holy unction for this end, that he might distil his grace upon the hungry soul. Are you ignorant? Christ was filled with wisdom that he might teach you. Are you polluted? Christ was filled with grace that he might cleanse you. Shall not the soul then come to Christ who was filled on purpose to fill the hungry? We love to knock at a rich man's door. In our Father's house there is bread enough. Come with desire and you shall go away with comfort. You shall have the virtues of Christ's blood, the influences of his Spirit, the communications of his love.

The objections of carnal and godly men considered

There are two objections made against this.

The carnal man's objection. I have (says he) hungered after righteousness, yet am not filled.

You say you hunger and are not satisfied? Perhaps God is not satisfied with your hunger. You have 'opened your mouth wide' (Psalm 81 : 10), but have not 'opened your ear' (Psalm 49 : 4). When God has called you to family prayer and mortification of sin, you have, like the 'deaf adder', stopped your ear against God (Zechariah 7 : 11). No wonder then that you have not that comfortable filling as you desire. Though you have opened your mouth you have stopped your ear. The child that will not hear his parent, is made to do penance by fasting.

Perhaps you thirst as much after a temptation as after righteousness. At a sacrament you seem to be inflamed with desire after Christ, but the next temptation that comes either to drunkenness or lasciviousness, you fall in and close with the temptation. Satan but beckons to you and you come. You open faster to the tempter than to Christ; and do you wonder you are not filled with the fat things of God's house?

Perhaps you hunger more after the world than after righteousness. The young man in the gospel would have Christ, but the world lay nearer his heart than Christ. Hypocrites pant more after the dust of the earth (Amos 2 : 7) than the 'water of life'. Israel had no manna while their dough lasted. Such as feed immoderately upon the dough of earthly things, must not think to be filled with manna from heaven. If your money be your God, never look to receive another God in the sacrament.

The godly man's objection. I have had unfeigned desires after God, but am not filled.

You may have a filling of grace, though not of comfort. If God does not fill you with gladness, yet with goodness (Psalm 107 : 9). Look into your heart and see the distillations of the Spirit. The dew may fall though the honey-comb does not drop.

Wait a while and you shall be filled. The gospel is a spiritual banquet. It feasts the soul with grace and comfort. None eat of this banquet but such as wait at the table. 'In this mountain shall the Lord of hosts make unto all people a feast of fat things, a feast of wines on the lees well refined. And it shall be said in that day, Lo, this is our God, we have waited for him; we will be glad and rejoice in his salvation' (Isaiah 25 : 6,9). Spiritual mercies are not only worth desiring, but worth waiting for.

If God should not fill his people to satisfaction here, yet they shall be filled in heaven. The vessels of their desires shall be filled as those water pots (John 2 : 7) 'up to the brim'.

15 A discourse of mercifulness

Blessed are the merciful, for they shall obtain mercy.

MATTHEW 5:7

These verses, like the stairs of Solomon's temple, cause our ascent to the holy of holies. We are now mounting up a step higher. 'Blessed are the merciful . . .' There was never more need to preach of mercifulness than in these unmerciful times wherein we live. It is reported in the life of Chrysostom that he preached much on this subject of mercifulness, and for his much pressing Christians to mercy, he was called of many, 'the alms-preacher' or 'the preacher for mercy'. Our times need many Chrysostoms.

'Blessed are the merciful.' Mercy stands both in the van and rear of the text. In the beginning of the text it stands as a duty. In the end of the text it stands as a reward. The Hebrew word for 'godly' signifies 'merciful': the more godly, the more merciful. The doctrine I shall gather out of the words, which will comprehend and bring in the whole, is this:

That the merciful man is a blessed man; as there is a curse hangs over the head of the unmerciful man. 'Let Satan stand at his right hand; when he shall be judged let him be condemned, and let his prayer become sin; let his children be fatherless and his wife a widow; let his children be continually vagabonds and beg; let the extortioner catch all that he hath, and let strangers spoil his labour; let there be none to extend mercy to him. Let his posterity be cut off, and in the generation following let their name be blotted out. Let the iniquity of his fathers be remembered with the Lord, and let not the sin of his mother be blotted out' (Psalm 109:6–9). Why, what is this crime? 'Because he remembered not to show mercy' (verse 16). See what a long vial full of the plagues of God is poured out upon the unmerciful man! So by the rule of contraries, the blessings of the Almighty crown and encompass the merciful man. 'The merciful man is a blessed man' (2 Samuel 22:26; Psalm 37:26; Psalm 41:1). For the illustrating this I shall show, first, what is meant by mercifulness; second, the several kinds of mercy.

The nature and source of mercifulness

1 What is meant by mercifulness? I answer, it is a melting disposition whereby we lay to heart the miseries of others and are ready on all occasions to be instrumental for their good.

How do mercy and love differ?

In some things they agree, in some things they differ, like waters that may have two different spring-heads, but meet in the stream. Love and mercy differ thus: love is more extensive. The diocese that love walks and visits in is larger. Mercy properly respects them that are miserable. Love is of a larger consideration. Love is like a friend that visits them that are well. Mercy is like a physician that visits only them that are sick. Again, love acts more out of affection. Mercy acts out of a principle of conscience. Mercy lends its help to another. Love gives its heart to another. Thus they differ, but love and mercy agree in this, they are both ready to do good offices. Both of them have soundings of bowels, and healing under their wings.

Whence does mercy spring?

Its spring-head rises higher than nature. Mercy taken in its full latitude proceeds from a work of grace in the heart. Naturally we are far enough from mercy. The sinner is a bramble, not a fig tree yielding sweet fruit. It is the character and sign of a natural man to be 'unmerciful' (Romans 1 : 31). A wicked man, like Jehoram, has 'his bowels fallen out' (2 Chronicles 21 : 19). Therefore he is compared to an adamant (Zechariah 7 : 12) because his heart does not melt in mercy. Before conversion the sinner is compared to a wolf for his savageness, to a lion for his fierceness (Isaiah 11 : 6), to a bee for his sting (Psalm 118 : 12), to an adder for his poison (Psalm 140 : 3). By nature we do not send forth oil, but poison; not the oil of mercifulness, but the poison of maliciousness.

Besides that inbred unmercifulness which is in us, there is something infused too by Satan. 'The prince of the air works in men' (Ephesians 2 : 2). He is a fierce spirit, therefore called 'the Red Dragon' (Revelation 12 : 3). And if he possesses men no wonder if they are implacable and without mercy. What mercy can be expected from hell? So that, if the heart be tuned into mercifulness, it is from the change that grace has made (Colossians 3 : 12). When the sun shines the ice melts. When the Sun of righteousness once shines with beams of grace upon the soul, then it melts in mercy and tenderness. You must first be a new man before a merciful man. You cannot help a member of Christ till you yourself are a member.

2 The several kinds of mercy, or how many ways a man may be said to be merciful. Mercy is a fountain that runs in five streams. We must be merciful to the souls, names, estates, offences, wants of others.

Mercy is to be extended to the souls of others

We must be merciful to the souls of others. This is a spiritual alms. Indeed soul-mercy is the chief of mercies. The soul is the most precious thing; it is a vessel of honour; it is a bud of eternity; it is a sparkle lighted by the breath of God; it is a rich diamond set in a ring of clay. The soul has the blood of God to redeem it, the image of God to beautify it. It being therefore of so high a descent, sprung from the Ancient of days, that mercy which is shown to the soul must needs be the greatest. This soul-mercy to others stands in four things.

1 In pitying them. If I weep, says Augustine, for that body from which the soul is departed, how should I weep for that soul from which God is departed? Had we seen that man in the gospel cutting himself with stones and fetching blood of himself it would have moved our pity (Mark 5:5). To see a sinner stabbing himself and having his hands imbrued in his own blood should cause relenting in our bowels. Our eye should affect our heart. God was angry with Edom because he 'cast off all pity' (Amos 1:11).

2 Soul-mercy is in advising and exhorting sinners. Tell them in what a sad condition they are, even 'in the gall of bitterness'. Show them their danger. They tread upon the banks of the bottomless pit. If death gives them a jog they tumble in. And we must dip our words in honey; use all the mildness we can: 'In meekness instructing those ...' (2 Timothy 2:25). Fire melts; ointment mollifies. Words of love may melt hard hearts into repentance. This is soul-mercy. God made a law that whosoever saw 'his enemy's ass lying under a burden, he should help him' (Exodus 23:5). On which words, says Chrysostom, we will help a beast that is fallen under a burden; and shall we not extend relief to those who are fallen under a worse burden of sin?

3 Soul-mercy is in reproving refractory sinners. There is a cruel mercy when we see men go on in sin and we let them alone, and there is a merciful cruelty when we are sharp against men's sins and will not let

them go to hell quietly. 'Thou shalt not hate thy brother in thine heart; thou shalt in any wise rebuke thy neighbour and not suffer sin upon him' (Leviticus 19:17). Fond pity is no better than cruelty. 'Rebuke them sharply', cuttingly (Titus 1:13). The surgeon cuts and lances the flesh, but it is in order to a cure. They are healing wounds. So by cutting reproof when we lance men's consciences and let out the blood of sin, we exercise spiritual surgery. This is showing mercy. 'Others save with fear, pulling them out of the fire' (Jude 23). If a man were in the fire, though you did hurt him a little in pulling him out, he would be thankful and take it as a kindness. Some men, when we tell them of sin say, 'O this is bitterness.' No, it is showing mercy. If a man's house were on fire, and another should see it and not tell him of it for fear of waking him, were not this cruelty? When we see others 'sleeping the sleep of death' and the fire of God's wrath ready to burn about their ears, and we are silent, is not this to be accessory to their death?

4 Soul-mercy is in praying for others. This is like physic used in a desperate case and often it recovers the sick patient. 'The effectual fervent prayer of a righteous man avails much' (James 5:16). As it cures the sick body, so also the sin-sick soul. There is a story of one who gave his soul to the devil, who was saved through the prayers of Luther. When 'Eutychus fell down from an high loft and was taken up dead, Paul fell on him', that is, he effectually prayed over him and he prayed him alive (Acts 20:9–12). By sin the soul is fallen from an high loft, namely, a state of innocency. Now fervent prayer oft-times fetcheth life in such a dead soul.

See what a blessed work the work of the ministry is! The preaching of the Word is nothing but showing mercy to souls. This is a mighty and glorious engine in the hand of the Lord of hosts for the beating down of the devil's strongholds. The ministry of the Word not only brings light with it, but eye-salve, anointing the eyes to see that light. It is a sin-killing and soul-quickening ordinance. It is the 'power of God to salvation'. What enemies are they to their own souls that oppugn the ministry! They say, the people that live 'under the line',[1] curse the sun and are glad when the sun sets because of its burning heat. Foolish sinners curse the sun-rising of the ministry and are offended at the light of it because it comes near their sins and scorches their consciences, though in the end it saves their souls.

[1] In the tropics, the 'line' being the equator.

Reproofs for such as have no mercy to souls

It reproves them that have no mercy to souls: evil magistrates; evil ministers.

Evil magistrates who either 'take away the key of knowledge' (Luke 11:52), or give a toleration to wickedness, suffering men to sin by a licence. The meaning of toleration is this, that if men will themselves to hell none shall stop them. Is not nature enough poisoned? Do not men sin fast enough, but must have such political engines as serve them up higher in wickedness? Must they have such favourable gales from the breath of great ones as serve to carry them full sail to the devil? This is far from soul-mercy. What an heavy reckoning will these 'statists' [1] have in the day of the Lord!

Evil ministers are such as have no bowels to the souls of their people. They do not pity them or pray for them. They seek not them but theirs. They preach not for love but lucre. Their care is more for tithes than souls. How can they be called spiritual fathers, who are without bowels? These are mercenaries, not ministers.

Such men feed not the souls of their people with solid truths. When Christ sent out his apostles, he gave them their text, and told them what they must preach, 'Preach, saying the kingdom of heaven is at hand' (Matthew 10:7). Upon which place, says Luther, the ministers of Christ must preach 'things that pertain to the kingdom of God' – pardon of sin, sanctification, living by faith – not otherwise, at the bidding of the church. They are unmerciful to souls who, instead of breaking the bread of life, fill their people's heads with airy speculations and notions; who rather tickle the fancy than touch the conscience and give precious souls rather music than food.

Some there are who darken knowledge with words, and preach as if they were speaking in 'an unknown tongue'. Some ministers love to soar aloft like the eagle and fly above their people's capacities, endeavouring rather to be admired than understood. They are like some crabbed authors which cannot be read without a comment. Indeed God calls his ministers 'ambassadors' (2 Corinthians 5:20), but they must not be like those outlandish ambassadors that cannot be understood without an interpreter. It is unmercifulness to souls to preach so as not to be understood. Ministers should be stars to give light, not clouds

[1] One skilled in state affairs, a politician, a statesman.

to obscure the truth. Saint Paul was learned, yet plain. Clearness and perspicuity is the grace of speech. It is cruelty to souls when we go about to make easy things hard. This many are guilty of in our age, who go into the pulpit only to tie knots, and think it their glory to amuse the people. This savours more of pride than mercifulness.

Such there are, too, as see others going on in sin but do not tell them of it. When men declare their sin as Sodom, it is the minister's duty to 'lift up his voice like a trumpet and show the house of Jacob their sin' (Isaiah 58:1). Zeal in the ministry is as proper as fire on the altar. He who lets another sin and holds his peace is a manslayer. That sentinel deserves death who sees the enemy approaching, and gives not warning (Ezekiel 3:20).

Some ministers poison souls with error. How dangerous is the leprosy of the head! A frenzy is worse than a fever. What shall we say to such ministers as give poison to their people in a golden cup? Are not these unmerciful? Others there are (unworthy the name of ministers), itineraries, the devil's journey-men, who ride up and down, and with Satan compass the earth to devour souls. It would pity one's heart to see poor unstable creatures misled by rude and illiterate men, who diet the people with blasphemy and nonsense, and make them fitter for bedlam than the New Jerusalem. All these are unmerciful to souls.

Let me beseech all that fear God to show soul-mercy. Strengthen the weak; reduce the wandering; raise up them that are fallen. 'He which converteth the sinner from the error of his way shall save a soul from death' (James 5:20).

Christians must be tender of one another's names

We must be merciful to the names of others. A good name is one of the greatest blessings upon earth. No chain of pearl so adorns as this. It being so, we ought to be very tender of names. They are to be accounted in an high degree unmerciful, who make no conscience of taking away the good names of their brethren. Their throats are open sepulchres to bury the fame and renown of men (Romans 3:13). It is a great cruelty to murder a man in his name. 'The keepers of the walls took away my vail from me' (Canticles 5:7). Some expositors interpret it of her honour and fame which covered her as a beautiful vail. The ground of this unmercifulness to names is

1 *Pride*. Pride is such a thing as cannot endure to be outshined. It loves not to see itself exceeded in parts and eminency; therefore it will behead another in his good name that he may appear something lower. The

proud man will be pulling down of others in their reputation, and so by their eclipse he thinks he shall shine the brighter. The breath of a proud man causes a blast or mildew upon fame.

2 *Envy* (1 Peter 2:1). An envious man maligns the dignity of another, therefore seeks to mischief him in his name. Religion teaches us to rejoice in the esteem and fame of others. 'I thank my God for you all, that your faith is spoken of throughout the whole world'; it is 'divulged with fame' (Romans 1 : 8). A good report is a credit to religion (Hebrews 11 : 2). If persons professing godliness do not have a good name, religion will not have a very good name, but envy consulting with the devil lays a train and fetches fire from hell to blow up the good name of another.

In how many ways may we be unmerciful to the names of others?

Divers ways: First, by mis-reporting them, a sin forbidden. 'Thou shalt not raise a false report' (Exodus 23:1). Eminency is commonly blasted by slander. 'Their tongues are as arrows shot out' (Psalm 64 : 3). The tongue of a slanderer shoots out words to wound the fame of another and make it bleed to death. The saints of God in all ages have met with unmerciful men who have fathered things upon them that they have not been guilty of. Surius, the Jesuit, reported of Luther that he learned his divinity of the Devil and that he died drunk; but Melanchthon,[1] who wrote his life, affirms that he died in a most pious holy manner and made a most excellent prayer before his death. It was David's complaint, 'They laid to my charge things which I knew not' (Psalm 35:11). The Greek word for 'devil' signifies slanderer (1 Timothy 3:11). 'Not slanderers' – in the Greek it is 'not devils'. Some think that it is no great matter to defame and traduce another, but know, this is to act the part of a devil. O how many unmerciful men are there, who indeed pass for Christians, but play the devil in venting their lies and calumnies! Wicked men in Scripture are called 'dogs' (Psalm 22:16). Slanderers are not like those dogs which licked Lazarus' sores to heal them, but like the dogs which ate Jezebel. They rend and tear the precious names of men. Valentinian the Emperor[2] decreed that he who was openly convicted of this crime of slander should die for it. And Pope Gregory decreed that such a person should be excommunicate, and not have the communion given him. I think it was a just decree.

Second, we are unmerciful to the names of others when we receive

---

[1] Professor of Greek at Wittenberg and a friend and colleague of Luther.
[2] Roman emperor of the 4th century A.D.

a slander, and then report what we hear. 'Thou shalt not go up and down as a tale-bearer among thy people' (Leviticus 19 : 16). A good man is one that 'doeth not evil to his neighbour, nor taketh up a reproach against his neighbour' (Psalm 15 : 3). We must not only not raise a false report, but not take it up. To divulge a report before we speak with the party and know the truth of it is unmercifulness and cannot acquit itself of sin. The same word in the Hebrew, 'to raise a slander', signifies to receive it (Exodus 23 : 1). The receiver is even as bad as the thief. It is well if none of us have (in this sense) received stolen goods. When others have stolen away the good names of their brethren, have not we received these stolen goods? There would not be so many to broach false rumours, but that they see this liquor pleases other men's taste.

Third, we deal unmercifully with the names of others when we diminish from their just worth and dignity; when we make more of their infirmities and less of their virtues. 'Speak not evil one of another' (James 4 : 11). I have read a story of one, Idor, an abbot, that he was never heard to speak evil of any man. Augustine could not endure that any should eclipse and lessen the fame of others, therefore he wrote those two verses upon his table:

> *Whoever loves another's name to blast,*
> *This table's not for him; so let him fast.*

Wicked men are still paring off the credit of their neighbours, and they make thick parings. They pare off all that is good. Nothing is left but the core, something that may tend to their disparagement. Unmerciful men know how to boil a quart to a pint. They have a devilish art so to extenuate and lessen the merit of others, that it is even boiled away to nothing. Some, though they have not the power of creation, yet they have the power of annihilation. They can sooner annihilate the good which is in others than imitate it.

Fourth, we are unmerciful to the names of others when we know them to be calumniated yet do not vindicate them. A man may sometimes as well wrong another by silence as slander. He who is merciful to his brother is an advocate to plead in his behalf when he is injuriously traduced. When the apostles, who were filled with the wine of the Spirit, were charged with drunkenness, Peter vindicated them openly (Acts 2 : 15). A merciful man will take the dead fly out of the box of ointment.

Fifth, they are in an high degree unmerciful to the names of others who 'bear false witness against' them (Psalm 27 : 12). 'Put not thy hand with the wicked to be a false witness' (Exodus 23 : 1). 'Putting the hand'

[149]

is taking an oath falsely, as when a man puts his hand upon the book and swears to a lie. So Tostatus expounds it. This 'false-witness' is a two-edged sword. The party forsworn wounds another's name and his own soul. A false witness is compared to a maul or hammer (Proverbs 25:18). It is true in this sense, because he is hardened in impudency – he blushes at nothing – and in unmercifulness. There is no softness in a maul or hammer, nor is there any relenting or bowels to be found in a false witness. In all these ways men are unmerciful to the names of others.

Let me persuade all Christians, as they make conscience of religion, so to show mercy to the names of others. Be very chary and tender of men's good name.

Consider what a sin it is to defame any man. 'Laying aside all envies and evil speakings' (Titus 3:2; 1 Peter 2:1). Envy and evil speaking are put together: 'laying aside', 'putting away', as a man would put away a thing from him with indignation; as Paul shook off the viper (Acts 28:5).

Consider also the injuriousness of it. You, who take away the good name of another, wound him in that which is most dear to him. Better take away a man's life than his name. By eclipsing his name you bury him alive. It is an irreparable injury; something will remain. A wound in the name is like a flaw in a diamond or a stain in azure, which will never die out. No physician can heal the wounds of the tongue.

God will require it at men's hands. If idle words must be accountable for, shall not reproachful slanders? God will make inquisition one day as well for names as for blood. Let all this persuade to caution and circumspection. You would be loath to steal the goods of others. A man's name is of more worth, and he that takes away the good name of another sins more than if he had taken the corn out of his field or the wares out of his shop.

Especially take heed of wounding the names of the godly. God has set a crown of honour on their head, and will you take it off? 'Wherefore then were ye not afraid to speak against my servant Moses?' (Numbers 12:8). To defame the saints is no less than the defaming God himself, they having his picture drawn upon them and being members of Christ. Oh think how ill Christ will take this at your hand another day! It was under the old law a sin to defame a virgin, and what is it to calumniate Christ's spouse? Are the names of the saints written in heaven, and will you blot them out upon earth? Be merciful to the names of others.

Mercy is to be extended to the estates, offences and wants of others

Be merciful to the estates of others. If a man be your debtor and providence has frowned upon him that he has not wherewithal to pay, do not crush him when he is sinking, but remit something of the rigour of the law. 'Blessed are the merciful.' The wicked are compared to beasts of prey that live upon rapine and spoil. They do not care what mischief they do. 'He lieth in wait secretly as a lion in his den; he doth catch the poor when he draweth him into his net' (Psalm 10 : 9). Chrysostom says the drawing into the net is when the rich draw the poor into bonds, and in case of non-payment at the day, the bond being forfeited, seize upon all they have. It is not justice but cruelty, when others lie at our mercy, to be like that hard-hearted creditor in the gospel who took his debtor by the throat saying, 'Pay me what thou owest' (Matthew 18 : 28). God made a law, 'No man shall take the nether or the upper millstone to pledge, for he taketh a man's life to pledge' (Deuteronomy 24 : 6). If a man had lent another money, he must not take both his millstones for a pawn. He must show mercy and leave the man something to get a livelihood with. We should in this imitate God who in the midst of anger remembers mercy. God does not take the extremity of the law upon us, but when we have not to pay, if we confess the debt, he freely forgives (Proverbs 28 : 13; Matthew 18 : 27).

Not but that we may justly seek what is our own, but if others be brought low and submit, we ought in conscience to remit something of the debt. 'Blessed are the merciful.'

We must be merciful to the offences of others. Be ready to show mercy to them which have injured you. Thus Stephen the proto-martyr, 'He kneeled down and cried with a loud voice, Lord, lay not this sin to their charge' (Acts 7 : 60). When he prayed for himself he stood, but when he came to pray for his enemies, he kneeled down, to show, says Bernard, his earnestness in prayer and how greatly he desired that God would forgive them. This is a rare kind of mercy. 'It is a man's glory to pass over a trangression' (Proverbs 19 : 11). Mercy in forgiving injuries, as it is the touchstone, so the crown of Christianity. Bishop Cranmer [1] was of a merciful disposition. If any who had wronged him came to desire a courtesy from him, he would do all that lay in his power for him, insomuch that it grew to a proverb : Do Cranmer an injury and he will be your friend as long as he lives. To 'overcome evil with good', and answer malice with mercy is truly heroical and renders religion glorious in the eyes of all. But I leave this and proceed.

[1] Archbishop of Canterbury, 1533–55.

We must be merciful to the wants of others. This the text chiefly intends. A good man does not, like the snake, twist within himself. His motion is direct, not circular. He is ever merciful and lendeth (Psalm 37:26). This merciful charity to the wants of others stands in three things.

1 A judicious consideration. 'Blessed is he that considereth the poor' (Psalm 41:1); and you must consider four things.

(i) It might have been your own case. You yourselves might have stood in need of another's charity and then how welcome and refreshing would those streams have been to you!

(ii) Consider how sad a condition poverty is. Though Chrysostom calls poverty the highway to heaven, yet he that keeps this road will go weeping thither. Consider the poor; behold their tears, their sighs, their dying groans. Look upon the deep furrows made in their faces, and consider if there be not reason why you should scatter your seed of mercy in these furrows. 'For a cloak he has a tattered vesture, for a couch a stone.' The poor man feeds upon sorrow; he drinks tears, (Psalm 80:5). Like Jacob, in a windy night he has the clouds for his canopy and a stone for his pillow.

Nay further, consider that oftentimes poverty becomes not only a cross but a snare. It exposes to much evil, which made Agur pray, 'Give me not poverty' (Proverbs 30:8). Want puts men upon indirect courses. The poor will venture their souls for money, which is like throwing diamonds at pear-trees. If the rich would wisely consider this, their alms might prevent much sin.

Consider why the wise God has suffered an inequality in the world. It is for this very reason, because he would have mercy exercised. If all were rich, there were no need of alms, nor could the merciful man have been so well known. If he that travelled to Jericho had not been wounded and left half dead, the good Samaritan who poured oil and wine into his wounds had not been known.

> *'Had Ilium stood, who'd known of Hector's name'?* [1]

Consider how quickly the balance of providence may turn. We ourselves may be brought to poverty and then it will be no small comfort to us that we relieved others while we were in a capacity to do it. 'Give a portion to seven and also to eight, for thou knowest not what evil shall be upon the earth' (Ecclesiastes 11:2). We cannot promise ourselves always halcyon days. God knows how soon many of us may

[1] Ovid: Tristia, iv. iii. 75 (Ilium is Troy; Hector was the chief Trojan warrior).

change our pasture. The cup which now runs over with wine may be filled with the waters of Marah. 'I went out full and the Lord hath brought me home again empty' (Ruth 1:21). How many have we seen like Bajazet[1] and Belisarius[2] invested with great lordships and possessions who have on a sudden brought their manor[3] to a morsel?

'Suddenly he becomes Irus, he who was formerly a Croesus for wealth.'[4]

So that it is wisdom (in this sense) to consider the wants of others. Remember how soon the scene may alter. We may be put in the poor's dress and, if adversity come, it will be no trouble of mind to us to think that while we had an estate we laid it out upon Christ's indigent members. This is the first thing in mercifulness, a judicious consideration

2 A tender commiseration. 'If thou draw out thy soul to the hungry' (Isaiah 58:10). Bounty begins in pity. The Hebrew word for 'mercy' signifies 'bowels'. Christ first 'had compassion on the multitude'. Then he wrought a miracle to feed them (Matthew 15:32). Charity which lacks compassion is brutish. The brute creatures can relieve us in many ways, but cannot pity us. It is a kind of cruelty (says Quintilian[5]) to feed one in want and not to sympathize with him. True religion begets tenderness. As it melts the heart in tears of contrition towards God, so in bowels of compassion towards others. 'My bowels shall sound as an harp' (Isaiah 16:11). Likewise, when our bowels of pity sound, then our alms make sweet music in the ears of God.

3 Mercifulness consists in a liberal contribution. 'If there be a poor man within thy gates, thou shalt open thy hand wide unto him' (Deuteronomy 15:7, 8). The Hebrew word to 'disperse' (Psalm 112:9) signifies 'a largeness of bounty'. It must be like water that overflows the banks. 'Not a meagre dispersing of a mere trifle.' If God has enriched men with estates and made 'his candle (as Job says) to shine upon their tabernacle', they must not encircle and engross all to themselves but be

[1] A 14th-century Turkish Sultan (surnamed 'Ilderim' – 'lightning' – on account of his rapid movements and conquests). Marlowe, the Elizabethan dramatist, speaks of him (though without historical warrant) as imprisoned by his Tartar conqueror, Tamerlane, in an iron cage, and fed with broken scraps like a dog.
[2] The greatest general of the Byzantine Empire (6th century). There is no historical basis for the tradition that in old age he was obliged to beg his bread from door to door.
[3] Used here with the meaning of 'estate'.
[4] Ovid, Tristia, iii. vii. 42. Irus was a beggar in the house of Ulysses at Ithaca. Croesus was a king of Lydia, celebrated for his riches.
[5] Roman writer of 1st century A.D., famous for a treatise on Oratory.

as the moon which, having received its light from the sun, lets it shine to the world. The ancients, as Basil and Lorinus observe, made oil to be the emblem of charity. The golden oil of mercy must, like Aaron's oil, run down upon the poor which are the lower skirts of the garment. This liberal disbursement to the wants and necessities of others God commands and grace compels.

God Commands. There is an express statute law, 'If thy brother be waxen poor and fallen in decay with thee, then thou shalt relieve him' (Leviticus 25:35). The Hebrew word is 'Thou shalt strengthen him'; put under him a silver crutch when he is falling. It is worth our observation what great care God took of the poor, besides what was given them privately. God made many laws for the public and visible relief of the poor. 'The seventh year thou shalt let the land rest and lie still, that the poor of the people may eat' (Exodus 23:11). God's intention in his law was that the poor should be liberally provided for. They might freely eat of any thing which grew of itself this seventh year, whether of herbs, vines or olive trees. If it be asked how the poor could live only on these fruits, there being (as it is probable) no corn growing then, for answer Cajetan is of opinion that they lived by selling these fruits and, so converting them into money, lived upon the price of the fruits.

There is another law made: 'And when ye reap the harvest of your land, thou shalt not wholly reap the corners of thy field, neither shalt thou gather the gleanings of thy harvest' (Leviticus 19:9). See how God indulged the poor. Some corners of the field were for the poor's sake to be left uncut, and when the owners reaped they must not go too near the earth with their sickle. The Vulgate Latin reads it, 'Thou shalt not shear to the very ground.' Something like an aftercrop must be left. The shorter ears of corn and such as lay bending to the ground, were to be reserved for the poor, says Tostatus.

And God made another law in favour of the poor. 'At the end of three years thou shalt bring forth the tithe of thy increase the same year, and thou shalt lay it up in thy gates: and the Levite and the fatherless and the widow which are within thy gates shall come and shall eat and be satisfied' (Deuteronomy 14:28, 29). The Hebrews write that every third year, besides the first tithe given to Levi which was called the perpetual tithe (Numbers 18:21), the Jews set apart another tithe of their increase for the use of the widows and orphans, and that was called 'the tithe of the poor'. Besides, at the Jews' solemn festivals, the poor were to have a share (Deuteronomy 16:11).

And as relieving the necessitous was commanded under the law, so it stands in force under the gospel. 'Charge them that are rich in this world that they do good, that they be rich in good works ...' (1 Timothy 6 : 17, 18). It is not only a counsel but a charge, and non-attendance to it runs men into a gospel-praemunire.[1] Thus we have seen the mind of God in this particular of charity. Let all good Christians comment upon it in their practice. What benefit is there of gold while it is embowelled and locked up in the mine? and what is it the better to have a great estate if it be so hoarded and cloistered up as never to see the light?

As God commands, so *grace compels* to works of mercy and beneficence. 'The love of Christ constraineth' (2 Corinthians 5 : 14). Grace comes with majesty upon the heart. Grace does not lie as a sleepy habit in the soul but will put forth itself in vigorous and glorious actings. Grace can no more be concealed than fire. Like new wine it will have vent. Grace does not lie in the heart as a stone in the earth, but as seed in the earth. It will spring up into good works.

A vindication of the Church of England and its doctrine of good works

This doctrine may serve to justify the Church of England against the calumny of malevolent men. Julian [2] upbraided the Christians that they were Solifidians,[3] and the Church of Rome lays upon us this aspersion, that we are against good works. Indeed we plead not for the *merit* of them but we are for the *use* of them. 'Let ours also learn to maintain good works for necessary uses' (Titus 3 : 14). We preach that they are needful both as they are enforced by the precept and as they are needful for the general good of men. We read that the angels had wings, and hands under their wings (Ezekiel 1 : 8). It may be emblematical of this truth. Christians must not only have the wings of faith to fly, but hands under their wings to work the works of mercy. 'This is a faithful saying, and these things I will that thou affirm constantly, that they which have believed in God might be careful to maintain good works' (Titus 3:8). The lamp of faith must be filled with the oil of charity. Faith alone justifies but justifying faith is not alone. You may as well separate weight from lead or heat from fire as works from faith. Good works, though they are not the causes of salvation, yet they are evidences. Though they are not the foundation yet they are the superstructure. Faith must not be built upon works, but works must be built upon

[1] Gospel-warning.
[2] Julian the Apostate, Roman Emperor (d. 363); upon his accession he turned from Christianity to paganism.
[3] Those who hold that faith alone, without works, suffices.

faith. 'Ye are married to another that we should bring forth fruit unto God' (Romans 7:4). Faith is the grace which marries Christ and good works are the children which faith bears. For the vindication of the doctrine of our Church, and in honour of good works, I shall lay down four aphorisms.

1 Works are distinct from faith. It is vain to imagine that works are included in faith as the diamond is enclosed in the ring. No, they are distinct, as the sap in the vine is different from the clusters that grow upon it.

2 Works are the touchstone of faith. 'Show me thy faith by thy works' (James 2:18). Works are faith's letters of credence to show. If, says Saint Bernard, you see a man full of good works, then by the rule of charity you are not to doubt of his faith. We judge the health of the body by the pulse where the blood stirs and operates. O Christian, judge of the health of your faith by the pulse of mercy and charitableness. It is with faith as with a deed in law. To make a deed valid, there are three things requisite – the writing, the seal, the witnesses. So for the trial and confirmation of faith there must be these three things – the writing, the Word of God; the seal, the Spirit of God; the witnesses, good works. Bring your faith to this Scripture touchstone. Faith justifies works; works testify faith.

3 Works honour faith. These fruits adorn the 'trees of righteousness'. Let the liberality of your hand (says Clemens Alexandrinus) be the ornament of your faith, and wear it as an holy bracelet about your wrists. 'I was eyes to the blind and feet was I to the lame. I put on righteousness and it clothed me. My judgment was as a robe and a diadem' (Job 29:14-15). While Job was the poor's benefactor and advocate, this was the ensign of his honour; it clothed him as a robe and crowned him as a diadem. This is that which takes off the odium and obloquy and makes others speak well of religion when they see good works as handmaids waiting upon this queen.

4 Good works are in some sense more excellent than faith; in two respects:
Because they are of a more noble diffusive nature. Though faith be more needful for ourselves, yet good works are more beneficial to others. Faith is a receptive grace. It is all for self-interest. It moves within its own sphere. Works are for the good of others, and it is a more blessed thing to give, than to receive.

Good works are more visible and conspicuous than faith. Faith is a more occult grace. It may lie hidden in the heart and not be seen, but when works are joined with it, now it shines forth in its native beauty. Though a garden be never so decked with flowers, yet they are not seen till the light comes. So the heart of a Christian may be enriched with faith, but it is like a flower in the night. It is not seen till works come. When this light shines before men, then faith appears in its orient[1] colours.

A check to the unmerciful

If this be the effigy[2] of a good man, that he is of a merciful disposition, then it sharply reproves those that are far from this temper. Their hearts are like the scales of the Leviathan, 'shut up together as with a close seal' (Job 41:15). They move only within their own circle, but do not indulge the necessities of others. They have a flourishing estate, but like the man in the gospel, they have a withered hand and cannot stretch it out to good uses. They have all as for themselves, not for Christ. These are akin to the churl Nabal. 'Shall I take my bread and my water and give it unto men, whom I know not whence they be?' (1 Samuel 25:11). It was said of the emperor Pertinax,[3] that he had a large empire but a narrow scanty heart.

There was a temple at Athens which was called the Temple of Mercy. It was dedicated to charitable uses; and it was the greatest reproach to upbraid one with this, that he had never been in the Temple of Mercy. It is the greatest disgrace to a Christian to be unmerciful. Covetous men, while they enrich themselves, debase themselves, setting up a monopoly and committing idolatry with Mammon, thus making themselves lower than *their* angels, as God made them lower than *his* angels. In the time of pestilence, it is sad to have your houses shut up, but it is worse to have your hearts shut up. How miserable is it to have a sea of sin and not a drop of mercy! Covetous hearts, like the Leviathan, are 'firm as a stone' (Job 41:24). One may as well extract oil out of a flint, as the golden oil of charity out of their flinty hearts. The philosopher says that the coldness of the heart is a presage of death. When men's affections to works of mercy are frozen, this coldness of heart is ominous and sadly portends that they are dead in sin. We read in the law that the shell-fish was accounted unclean. This might probably be one reason, because the meat of it was enclosed in the shell and it was hard to come by. They are to be reckoned among the unclean who enclose all their

[1] See p. 40 fn.   [2] Image.
[3] Roman Emperor in 193 A.D. He reigned for less than a year.

estate within the shell of their own cabinet and will not let others be the better for it. How many have lost their souls by being so saving!

There are some who perhaps will give the poor good words and that is all. 'If a brother or sister be naked and destitute of food and one of you say to them, Depart in peace, be ye warmed and filled; notwithstanding ye give them not those things which are needful to the body, what doth it profit?' (James 2:15). Good words are but a cold kind of charity. The poor cannot live as the chameleon upon this air.[1] Let your words be as smooth as oil, they will not heal the wounded. Let them drop as the honey-comb, they will not feed the hungry. 'Though I speak with the tongues of angels and have not charity, I am but as a tinkling cymbal' (1 Corinthians 13:1). It is better to be charitable as a saint than eloquent as an angel. Such as are cruel to the poor, let me tell you, you unchristian yourselves. Unmercifulness is the sin of the heathen (Romans 1:31). While you put off the bowels of mercy you put off the badge of Christianity. Saint Ambrose says that when we do not relieve one whom we see ready to perish with hunger, we are guilty of his death. If this rule hold true there are more guilty of the breach of the sixth commandment than we are aware of. St James speaks a sad word: 'For he shall have judgment without mercy that hath showed no mercy' (James 2:13). How do they think to find mercy *from* Christ, who never showed mercy *to* Christ in his members? Dives denied Lazarus a crumb of bread and Dives was denied a drop of water. At the last day behold the sinner's indictment, 'I was an hungred and ye gave me no meat; I was thirsty and ye gave me no drink' (Matthew 25:42). Christ does not say, 'Ye took away my meat', but 'Ye gave me none; ye did not feed my members'. Then follows the sentence, 'Depart from me, ye cursed.' When Christ's poor come to your doors and you bid them depart from you, the time may come when you shall knock at heaven's gate, and Christ will say, Go from my door, 'Depart from me, ye cursed'.

In short, covetousness is a foolish sin. God gave the rich man in the gospel that appellation, 'Thou fool' (Luke 12:20). The covetous man does not enjoy what he possesses. He embitters his own life. He discruciates[2] himself with care either how to get or how to increase or how to secure an estate. And what is the issue and result? Often as a just reward of sordid penuriousness,[3] God blasts and withers him in his

---

[1] In the 17th century it was widely, though erroneously believed, that the chameleon could live on air alone.

[2] Tortures.   [3] Stinginess.

outward estate. That saying of Gregory Nazianzen [1] is to be seriously weighed: God many times lets the thief take away and the moth consume that which is injuriously and unmercifully withheld from the poor.

Before I leave this matter, I am sorry that any who pass for honest men should be brought into the indictment. I mean, sorry that any who profess Christianity should be impeached as guilty of this sin of covetousness and unmercifulness. Sure I am that God's elect put on 'bowels of mercies' (Colossians 3:12); but I tell you that devout misers are the reproach of Christianity. They are wens and spots in the face of religion. I remember Aelian [2] in his History reports that in India there is a griffin having four feet and wings, his bill like the eagle's. It is hard whether to rank him among the beasts or the fowl. So I may say of penurious votaries,[3] they have the wings of profession by which they seem to fly to heaven, but the feet of beasts, walking on earth and even licking the dust. It is hard where to rank these, whether among the godly or the wicked. Oh take heed that, seeing your religion will not destroy your covetousness, at last your covetousness does not destroy your religion. The fabulist tells a story of the hedge-hog that came to the coney-burrows in stormy weather and desired harbour, promising that he would be a quiet guest, but when once he had gotten entertainment, he set up his prickles and never left till he had thrust the poor conies out of their burrows. So covetousness, though it has many fair pleas to insinuate and wind itself into the heart, yet as soon as you have let it in, this thorn will never leave pricking till it has choked all good beginnings and thrust all religion out of your hearts.

Persuasions to mercifulness

I proceed next to the exhortation to beseech all Christians to put on 'bowels of mercies'. Be ready to indulge the miseries and necessities of others. Saint Ambrose calls charity the sum of Christianity, and the apostle makes it the very definition of religion. 'Pure religion and undefiled before God and the Father is this, to visit the fatherless and the widows in their affliction' (James 1:27). The Hebrew word for 'poor' signifies 'one that is empty' or 'drawn dry'. So the poor are exhausted of their strength, beauty, substance; like ponds they are dried up. Therefore let them be filled again with the silver streams of charity. The poor are as it were in the grave. The comfort of their life is buried. Oh

---

[1] One of the 'fathers' of Cappadocia (4th century A.D.).
[2] A Roman writer on Natural History (largely anecdotal) of the 2nd century.
[3] Persons vowed to the service of God, but miserly.

Christians, help with your merciful hands to raise them out of the sepulchre. God 'sendeth his springs into the valleys' (Psalm 104:10). Let the springs of your liberality run among the valleys of poverty. Your sweetest and most benign influence should fall upon the lower grounds. What is all your seeming devotion without bounty and mercifulness? I have known many, says Basil, pray and fast, but relieve not such as are in distress. They are for a zeal that will put them to no charges. What are they the better (says he) for all their seeming virtue? We read that the incense was to be laid upon the fire (Levicticus 16:13). The flame of devotion must be perfumed with the incense of charity. Aaron was to have a bell and a pomegranate. The pomegranate, as some of the learned observe, was a symbol of good works. They lack the pomegranate (says Gregory Nazianzen) who have no good works. The wise men not only bowed the knee to Christ, but presented him with gold, myrrh and frankincense (Matthew 2:11). Pretences of zeal are insufficient. We must not only worship Christ but bestow something upon his members. This is to present Christ with gold and frankincense. Isaac would not bless Jacob by the voice, but he feels and handles him, and supposing them to be Esau's hands, he blessed him. God will not bless men by their voice, their loud prayers, their devout discourses, but if he feel Esau's hands, if their hands have wrought good works, then he blesses them.

Let me exhort you therefore to deeds of mercy. Let your fingers drop with the myrrh of liberality. Sow your golden seed. In this sense it is lawful to put out your money to use [1] when you lay it out for good uses. Remember that excellent saying of Augustine, Give those things to the poor which you cannot keep that you may receive those things which you cannot lose. There are many occasions of exercising your mercifulness. 'The poor goes to the wall.' [2] Hear the orphans' cry; pity the widows' tears. Some there are who want employment. It would do well to set their wheel a-going. Others who are past employment: be as eyes to the blind and feet to the lame. In some cases whole families are sinking if some merciful hand does not help to shore them up. Before I press arguments to liberality and munificence, there are three objections lie in the way which I shall endeavour to remove:

1 We may give and so in time come ourselves to want.

Let Basil answer this. Wells (says he), which have their water drawn, spring ever more freely. 'The liberal soul shall be made fat '(Proverbs 11:25). Luther speaks of a monastery in Austria which was very rich

[1] That is, to 'interest'.   [2] Quoted from Ovid's Fasti, Book I, 218.

while it gave annually to the poor, but when it left off giving the monastery began to decay. There is nothing lost by doing our duty. An estate may be imparted, yet not impaired. The flowers yield honey to the bee yet do not hurt their own fruit. When the candle of prosperity shines upon us we may light our neighbour that is in the dark and have never the less light ourselves. Whatever is disbursed to pious uses, God brings it in some other way. As the loaves in breaking multiplied or as the widow's oil increased by pouring out (1 Kings 17 : 16).

2 I cannot do so much as others – erect churches, build hospitals, augment libraries, maintain scholars at the university.

If you cannot do so much, yet do something. Let there be much good-will though there be not much wealth to go with it. The widow's two mites cast into the treasury were accepted (Luke 21 : 1–4). God (as Chrysostom observes) looked not at the smallest of her gift, but at the largeness of her heart. In the law, he that could not bring a lamb for an offering, if he brought but two turtle-doves, it sufficed. We read that the people brought 'gold and silver, and goats' hair' to the building of the tabernacle' (Exodus 35 : 22–24); on which place (says Origen [1]), 'I desire, Lord, to bring something to the building of thy temple, if not gold to make the mercy-seat on, if not silk to make the curtains on, yet a little goats' hair, that I may not be found in the number of those that have brought nothing to thy temple.'

3 But I do not have anything to bestow upon the necessities of others.

Have you anything to bestow upon your lusts? Have you money to feed your pride, your Epicurism [2]? And can you find nothing to relieve the poor members of Christ?

Admit this excuse to be real, that you do not have such an estate; yet you may do something wherein you may express your mercy to the poor. You may sympathize with them, pray for them, speak a word of comfort to them. 'Speak ye comfortably to Jerusalem' (Isaiah 40:2). If you can give them no gold, you may speak a word in season which may be as 'apples of gold in pictures of silver'. Nay more, you may be helpful to the poor in stirring up others who have estates to relieve them. As it is with the wind, if a man be hungry the wind will not fill him, but it can blow the sails of the mill and make it grind corn for the use of man. So though you do not have an estate yourself to help him who is in want, yet you may stir up others to help him. You may blow the sails of their

[1] Christian theologian of Alexandria (3rd century).
[2] Devotion to the pleasures of eating and drinking.

affections, causing them to show mercy, and so you may help your brother by a proxy.

Nine persuasions to works of mercy

Having answered these objections let me now pursue the exhortation to mercifulness. I shall lay down several arguments which I desire may be weighed in the balance of reason and conscience.

1 To be diffusively good is the great end of our creation. 'Created in Christ Jesus unto good works' (Ephesians 2:10). Every creature answers the end of its creation. The star shines, the bird sings, the plant bears; the end of life is service. He that does not answer his end in respect of usefulness, cannot enjoy his end in respect of happiness. Many, says Seneca, have been long in the world, but have not lived. They have done no good: 'a useless weight of earth'. A useless person serves for nothing but to 'cumber the ground'. And because he is barren in figs he shall be fruitful in curses (Hebrews 6:8).

2 By mercifulness we resemble God who is a God of mercy. He is said to 'delight in mercy' (Micah 7:18). 'His tender mercies are over all his works') (Psalm 145:9). He requires good for evil, like the clouds which receive ill vapours from us but return them to us again in sweet showers. There is not a creature lives but tastes of the mercies of God. Every bird, says Ambrose, in its kind sings hymns of praise to God for his bounty, but men and angels in a more particular manner taste the cream and quintessence of God's mercies.

What temporal mercies have you received! Every time you draw your breath you suck in mercy. Every bit of bread you eat, the hand of mercy carves it to you. You never drink but in a golden cup of mercy.

What spiritual mercies has God enriched some of you with! Pardoning, adopting, saving mercy! The picture of God's mercy can never be drawn to the full. You cannot take the breadth of his mercy, for it is infinite, nor the height of it, for it 'reacheth above the clouds', nor the length of it, for it is 'from everlasting to everlasting' (Psalm 103:17). The works of mercy are the glory of the Godhead. Moses prays, 'Lord, show me thy glory' (Exodus 33:18). Says God, 'I will make all my goodness to pass before thee' (verse 19). God accounts himself most glorious in the shining robes of his mercy. Now by works of mercy we resemble the God of mercy. We are bid to draw our lines according to this copy. 'Be ye merciful, as your Father also is merciful' (Luke 6:36).

3 Alms are a sacrifice. 'To do good and to communicate, forget not, for

with such sacrifices God is well pleased' (Hebrew 13:16). When you are distributing to the poor, it is as if you were praying, as if you were worshipping God. There are two sorts of sacrifices; expiatory – the sacrifice of Christ's blood; and gratulatory – the sacrifice of alms. This (says holy Greenham [1]) is more acceptable to God than any other sacrifice. The angel said to Cornelius, 'Thy alms are come up for a memorial before God' (Acts 10:4). The backs of the poor are the altar on which this sacrifice is to be offered.

4 We ourselves live upon alms. Other creatures liberally contribute to our necessities. The sun does not have its light for itself but for us; it enriches us with its golden beams. The earth brings us a fruitful crop, and to show how joyful a mother she is in bringing forth, the psalmist says 'The valleys are covered over with corn, they shout for joy, they also sing' (Psalm 65:13). One creature gives us wool, another oil, another silk. We are fain to go a-begging to the creation. Shall every creature be for the good of man and man only be for himself? How absurd and irrational is this!

5 We are to extend our liberality by virtue of a membership: 'That thou hide not thyself from thine own flesh' (Isaiah 58:7). The poor are 'of the same clay'. The members by a law of equity and sympathy contribute one to another. The eye conveys light to the body, the heart blood, the head spirits. That is a dead member in the body which does not communicate to the rest. Thus it is in the body politic. Let no man think it is too far below him to mind the wants and necessities of others. It is pity but that hand should be cut off which disdains to pluck a thorn out of the foot. It is spoken in the honour of that renowned princess, the Empress of Theodosius the Great,[2] that she herself visited the sick and prepared relief for them with her own imperial hands.

6 We are not lords of an estate, but stewards, and how soon may we hear the word, 'Give an account of thy stewardship, for thou mayest be no longer steward!' (Luke 16:2). An estate is a talent to trade with. It is as dangerous to hide our talent as to spend it (Matthew 25:25, 30). If the covetous man keeps his gold too long, it will begin to rust, and the rust of it will witness against him (James 5:3).

7 The examples of others who have been renowned for acts of mercy and munificence.

[1] Richard Greenham (1531–91) of Drayton (near Cambridge) and London. His collected works were published in one volume in 1601.
[2] Roman Emperor in 4th century A.D.

Our Lord Christ is a great example of charity, he was not more full of merit than bounty. Trajan the Emperor[1] rent off a piece of his own robe to wrap his soldiers' wounds. Christ did more. He rent his flesh; He made a medicine of his body and blood to heal us. 'By his stripes we are healed' (Isaiah 53:5). Here was a pattern of charity without a parallel.

The Jews are noted in this kind. It is a rabbinical observation that those who live devoutly among the Jews distribute a tenth part of their estate among the poor, and they give so freely (says Philo[2] the Jew) as if by giving they hope to receive some great gratuity. Now if the Jews are so devoted to works of mercy, who live without priest, without temple, without Messiah, shall not we much more profess our faith in the blessed Messiah!

Let me tell you of heathens. I have read of Titus Vespasian,[3] he was so inured to works of mercy that remembering he had given nothing that day, cried out, 'I have lost a day.' It is reported of some of the Turks that they have servants whom they employ on purpose to enquire what poor they have and they send relief to them. And the Turks have a saying in their Alcoran, that if men knew what a blessed thing it were to distribute alms, rather than spare, they would give some of their own flesh to relieve the poor. And shall not a Christian's creed be better than a Turk's Alcoran[4]?

Let all this persuade to works of mercy. 'Believe me, it is a royal deed to succour the fallen.'[5]

When poor indigent creatures like Moses are laid in the ark of bulrushes weeping and ready to sink in the waters of affliction, be as temporal saviours to them and draw them out of the waters with a golden cord. Let the breasts of your mercy nurse the poor. Be like the trees of the sanctuary both for food and medicine (Ezekiel 47:12). When distressed and even starved souls are fainting, let your costly ingredients revive and fetch spirits in them. Let others see the coats and garments which you have made for the poor (Acts 9:39).

8 The sin of unmercifulness. The unmerciful man is an unthankful man, and what can be said worse? You to whom the Lord has given an estate, your cup runs over, but you have a miserly heart and will not part

[1] Roman Emperor (d. A.D. 117).
[2] A learned Jew of Alexandria (1st century A.D.), famed for his allegorical interpretation of the Old Testament.
[3] The son of the Emperor Vespasian; it was he who captured Jerusalem in A.D. 70.
[4] Commonly called the Koran.
[5] Quoted from Ovid's Epistolae ex Ponto, Lib. II, Epis. ix, 11.

with anything for good uses; it is death to you to relieve them that are dying. Know that you are in the highest degree ungrateful; you are not fit for human society. The Scripture has put these two together – 'unthankful, without natural affection' (2 Timothy 3:2, 3). God may repent that ever he gave such men estates, and may say as Hosea 2:9: 'Therefore will I return and take away my corn and my wine in the season thereof and will recover my wool and my flax.'

The unmerciful man lacks love to Christ. All men would be thought to love Christ and would be very angry with them that should question their love; but do they love Christ who let the members of Christ starve? No, these love their money more than Christ, and come under that fearful 'Anathema' (1 Corinthians 16:22).

9 Lastly, I shall use but one argument more to persuade to works of mercy, and that is the reward which follows alms-deeds. Giving of alms is a glorious work, and let me assure you it is not unfruitful work. Whatsoever is disbursed to the poor is given to Christ. 'Inasmuch as you have done it to one of the least of these my brethren, ye have done it unto me' (Matthew 25:40). The poor man's hand is Christ's treasury, and there is nothing lost that is put there. 'Whatsoever you give by stretching forth your hand on earth is as it were given in heaven.' The text says, 'the merciful shall obtain mercy'. In the Greek it is, 'they shall be be-mercied'. What is it we need most? Is it not mercy? Pardoning and saving mercy? What is it we desire on our death-bed? Is it not mercy? You that show mercy shall find mercy. You that pour in the oil of compassion to others, God will pour in the golden oil of salvation unto you (Matthew 7:2). The Shunammite woman showed mercy to the prophet and she received kindness from him another way (2 Kings 4:8–37). She welcomed him to her house, and he restored her dead child to life. They that sow mercy shall reap in kind; 'they shall obtain mercy'. Such is the sweetness and mercifulness of God's nature, that he will not suffer any man to be a loser. No kindness shown to him shall be unregarded or unrewarded. God will be in no man's debt. For a cup of cold water he shall have a draught of Christ's warm blood to refresh his soul. 'For God is not unrighteous to forget your work and labour of love, which you have shown toward his name, in that ye have ministered to the saints . . .' (Hebrews 6:10). God's mercy is a tender mercy, a pure mercy, a rich mercy. Mercy shall follow and overtake the merciful man. He shall be rewarded in this life and in the life to come.

Rewards for the merciful man in this life

The merciful man shall be rewarded in this life. He shall be blessed –

In his *person*: 'Blessed is he that considers the poor' (Psalm 41:1). Let him go whither he will, a blessing goes along with him. He is in favour with God. God casts a smiling aspect upon him.

Blessed in his *name*: 'He shall be had in everlasting remembrance' (Psalm 112:6). When the niggard's name shall rot, the name of a merciful man shall be embalmed with honour, and give forth its scent as the wine of Lebanon.

Blessed in his *estate*: 'He shall abound in all things.' 'The liberal soul shall be made fat' (Proverbs 11:25). He shall have the fat of the earth and the dew of heaven. He shall not only have the venison, but the blessing.

Blessed in his *posterity*: 'He is ever merciful and lendeth; and his seed is blessed' (Psalm 37:26). He shall not only leave an estate behind, but a blessing behind to his children, and God will see that the entail of that blessing shall not be cut off.

Blessed in his *negotiations*[1]: 'For this thing the Lord thy God shall bless thee in all thy works, and in all that thou puttest thine hand unto' (Deuteronomy 15:10). The merciful man shall be blessed in his building, planting, journeying. Whatever he is about, a blessing shall empty itself upon him. 'Wherever he treads there shall be a rose.' He shall be a prosperous man. The honeycomb of a blessing shall be still dropping upon him.

Blessed with *long life*: 'The Lord will preserve him and keep him alive' (Psalm 41:2). He has helped to keep others alive, and God will keep him alive. Is there anything then lost by mercifulness? It spins out the silver thread of life. Many are taken away the sooner for their unmercifulness. Because their hearts are straitened, their lives are shortened.

Again, the merciful man shall be rewarded in the life to come. Aristotle joins these two together, liberality and utility. God will reward the merciful man hereafter, though not for his works, yet according to his works. 'I saw the dead, small and great, stand before God, and the books were opened, and the dead were judged out of those things which were written in the books, according to their works' (Revelation 20:12). As God has a bottle to put our tears in, so he has a book to write our alms in. As God will put a veil over his people's sins, so he will in

[1] Trading, traffic.

free grace set a crown upon their works. The way to lay up is to lay out. Other parts of our estate are left behind (Ecclesiastes 2:18), but that which is given to Christ's poor is hoarded up in heaven. That is a blessed kind of giving which though it makes the purse lighter, it makes the crown heavier.

You that are mercifully inclined, remember whatever alms you distribute:

You shall have good security. 'He that gives to the poor lends to the Lord; and that which he hath given will he pay him again' (Ecclesiastes 11:1; Luke 6:38; Proverbs 19:17). There is God's counter-band to save you harmless, which is better security than any public faith. Yet here is our unbelief and atheism; we will not take God's bond. We commonly put our deeds of mercy among our desperate debts.

You shall be paid with over-plus. For a wedge of gold which you have parted with you shall have a weight of glory. For a cup of cold water you shall have rivers of pleasure, which run at God's right hand for evermore. The interest comes to infinitely more than the principal. Pliny [1] writes of a country in Africa where the people for every bushel of seed they sow receive an hundred and fifty-fold increase. For every penny you drop into Christ's treasury, you shall receive above a thousandfold increase. Your after-crop of glory will be so great that, though you are still reaping, you will never be able to inn [2] the whole harvest. Let all this persuade rich men to honour the Lord with their substance.

Six rules concerning works of mercy

Before I conclude this subject, let me lay down some rules briefly concerning works of mercy.

1 Charity must be free. 'Thou shalt give, and thy heart must not be grieved ...' (Deuteronomy 15:10). That is, you must not be troubled at parting with your money. He that gives grievingly, gives grudgingly. It is not a gift, but a tax. Charity must flow like spring-water. The heart must be the spring, the hand the pipe, the poor the cistern. God loves a cheerful giver. Do not be like the crab [3] which has all the verjuice squeezed and pressed out. You must not give to the poor as if you were delivering your purse on the highway. Charity without alacrity is

---

[1] Latin author, famous for his Natural History. He died in the eruption of Vesuvius in A.D. 79.
[2] To lodge, to house.
[3] Apple.

rather a fine than an offering. It is rather doing of penance than giving of alms. Charity must be like the myrrh which drops from the tree without cutting or forcing.

2 We must give that which is our own (Isaiah 58:7). To deal bread to the hungry, it must be 'thy bread'. The word for 'alms' in the Syriac signifies 'justice', to show that alms must be of that which is justly gotten. The Scripture puts them together, 'To do justice, to love mercy.' (Micah 6:8). We must not make 'a sacrifice out of robbery', a sacrifice of sacrilege. 'For I the Lord love judgment, I hate robbery for burnt offering' (Isaiah 61:8). He that shall build an alms-house or hospital with goods ill-gotten displays the ensign of his pride and sets up the monument of his shame.

3 Do all *in* Christ and *for* Christ.

Do all *in* Christ. Labour that your persons may be in Christ. We are 'accepted in him' (Ephesians 1:6). Origen, Chrysostom, and Peter Martyr [1] affirm that the best works not springing from faith are lost. The Pelagians thought to have posed Augustine with that question, Whether it was sin in the heathen to clothe the naked? Augustine answered rightly: 'The doing of good is not in itself simply evil, but proceeding from infidelity it becomes evil.' 'To them that are unbelieving is nothing pure' (Titus 1:15). That fruit is most sweet and genuine which is brought forth in the vine (John 15:4). Out of Christ all our alms-deeds are but the fruit of the wild olive. They are not good works but dead works.

Do all for Christ, namely, for his sake, that you may testify your love to him. Love mellows and ripens our alms-deeds. It makes them a precious perfume to God. As Mary did out of love bring her ointments and sweet spices to anoint Christ's dead body, so out of love to Christ bring your ointments and anoint his living body, viz, saints and members.

4 Works of mercy are to be done in humility. Away with ostentation! The worm breeds in the fairest fruit, the moth in the finest cloth. Pride will be creeping into our best things. Beware of this dead fly in the box of ointment. When Moses' face shone, he put a veil over it. So while your light shines before men and they see your good works, cover yourselves with the veil of humility. As the silk-worm, while she weaves her curious works, hides herself within the silk and is not seen, so we should hide ourselves from pride and vain-glory.

It was the sin of the Pharisees while they were distributing alms that

[1] Italian Protestant Reformer, resident in England 1547–54.

they blew the trumpet (Matthew 6:2). They did not give their alms, but sold them for applause. A proud man 'casts his bread upon the waters', as a fisherman casts his angle upon the waters. He angles for vain-glory. I have read of one Cosmus Medices,[1] a rich citizen of Florence, that he confessed to a near friend of his, he built so many magnificent structures, and spent so much on scholars and libraries, not for any love to learning but to raise up to himself trophies of fame and renown. An humble soul denies himself, yes, even annihilates himself. He thinks how little it is he can do for God, and if he could do more, it were but a due debt. Therefore he looks upon all his works as if he had done nothing. The saints are brought in at the last day as disowning their works of charity. 'Lord, when saw we thee an hungred and fed thee . . .?' (Matthew 25:37). A good Christian not only empties his hand of alms, but empties his heart of pride. While he raises the poor out of the dust, he lays himself in the dust. Works of mercy must be like the cassia which is a sweet spice, but grows low.

5 Dispose your alms prudentially. It is said of the merciful man, 'He orders his affairs with discretion' (Psalm 112:5). There is a great deal of wisdom in distinguishing between those that have sinned themselves into poverty, and those who by the hand of God are brought into poverty. Discretion in the distribution of alms consists of two things: in finding out a fit object; in taking a fit season.

The finding out a fit object comes under a double notion. Give to those who are in most need. Raise the hedge where it is lowest. Feed the lamp which is going out. Give to those who may probably be more serviceable. Though we bestow cost and dressing upon a weak plant, yet not upon a dead plant. Breed up such as may help to build the house of Israel (Ruth 4:11), that may be pillars in church and state, not caterpillars making your charity to blush.

Discretion in giving alms is in taking the fit season. Give to charitable uses in time of health and prosperity. Distribute your silver and gold to the poor before 'the silver cord be loosed or the golden bowl be broken' (Ecclesiastes 12:6). 'He who gives quickly gives double.' Make your hands your executors; not as some who reserve all they give till the term of life is ready to expire, and truly what is then bestowed is not given away, but taken away by death. It is not charity, but necessity. Oh do not so marry yourselves to money that you are resolved nothing

[1] Cosmo de Medici, of the Renaissance period. His palace became the place of refuge of Greek scholars exiled from Constantinople after its capture by the Turks in 1453.

shall part you but death. Be not like the medlar[1] which is never good till it be rotten. A covetous man may be compared to a Christmas-box. He receives money, but parts with none till death breaks this box in pieces. Then the silver and the gold come tumbling out. Give in time of health. These are the alms which God takes notice of, and (as Calvin says) puts in his book of accounts.

6 Give thankfully. They should be more thankful that give an alms than they that receive it. We should (says Nazianzen)[2] give a thank-offering to God that we are in the number of givers and not receivers. Bless God for a willing mind. To have not only an estate, but an heart, is matter of gratulation.

[1] A tree bearing a fruit like a small brown apple, but not eaten until decayed.
[2] See p. 159, fn 1.

16 A description of heart-purity

Blessed are the pure in heart, for they shall see God.

MATTHEW 5:8

The holy God, who is 'of purer eyes than to behold iniquity' calls here for heart-purity, and to such as are adorned with this jewel, he promises a glorious and beatifical vision of himself: 'they shall see God'. Two things are to be explained – the nature of purity; the subject of purity.

The nature of heart-purity

1 The nature of purity. Purity is a sacred refined thing. It stands diametrically opposed to whatsoever defiles. We must distinguish the various kinds of purity. First, there is a primitive purity which is in God originally and essentially as light is in the sun. Holiness is the glory of the Godhead: 'Glorious in holiness' (Exodus 15:11). God is the pattern and prototype of all holiness. Second, there is a created purity. Thus holiness is in the angels and was once in Adam. Adam's heart did not have the least spot or tincture of impurity. We call that wine pure which has no sophistication[1]; and that gold pure which has no dross mingled with it. Such was Adam's holiness. It was like the wine which comes from the grape, having no mixture. But this is not to be found on earth. We must go to heaven for it.

Third, there is an evangelical purity; whence grace is mingled with some sin, like gold in the ore, like air in the twilight, like wine that has a dash in it, like fine cloth with a coarse list,[2] like Nebuchadnezzar's image, part of silver, and part of clay (Daniel 2:35). This mixture God calls purity in a gospel-sense; as a face may be said to be fair which has some freckles in it. Where there is a study of purity and a loathing ourselves for our impurity, this is to be 'pure in heart'.

Some by pure in heart, understand chastity, others sincerity (Psalm 32:2). But I suppose purity here is to be taken in a larger sense for the several kinds and degrees of holiness. They are said to be pure who are

[1] Adulteration. [2] Selvage.

consecrated persons, having the oil of graces poured upon them. This purity is much mistaken.

Civility is not purity. A man may be clothed with moral virtues – justice, prudence, temperance – yet go to hell.

Profession is not purity. A man may have a name to live and yet be dead (Revelation 3:1). He may be swept by civility and garnished by profession, yet the devil may dwell in the house. The blazing comet is no star. The hypocrite's tongue may be silver, yet his heart stone. Purity consists in two things; rectitude of mind, a prizing holiness in the judgment (Psalm 119:30); conformity of will, an embracing of holiness in the affections (Psalm 119:97). A pure soul is cast into the mould of holiness. Holiness is a blood that runs in his veins.

2 The subject of purity: the heart: 'pure in heart'. Purity of heart does not exclude purity of life, no more than the pureness of the fountain excludes the pureness of the stream. But it is called purity of heart, because this is the main thing in religion, and there can be no purity of life without it. A Christian's great care should be to keep the heart pure, as one would especially preserve the spring from being poisoned. In a duel, a man will chiefly guard and fence his heart, so a wise Christian should above all things keep his heart pure. Take heed that the love of sin does not get in there, lest it prove mortal.

Christians should above all things breathe after heart purity: 'Holding the mystery of the faith in a pure conscience' (1 Timothy 3:9). Justification causes our happiness, sanctification evidences it.

Reasons for purity of heart

1 The reasons for purity are: (i) Purity is a thing called for in Scripture: 'Be ye holy for I am holy' (1 Peter 1:16). It is not only the minister bids you be holy, but God himself calls for it. What should the Holy God do with unholy servants?

(ii) Because of that filthy and cursed condition we are in before purity be wrought in us. We are a lump of clay and sin mingled together. Sin not only blinds us, but defiles us. It is called filthiness (James 1:21). And to show how befilthying a thing it is, it is compared to a plague-sore (1 Kings 8:38), to spots (Deuteronomy 32:5), to a vomit (2 Peter 2:22), to the infants 'tumbling in blood' (Ezekiel 16:6), and to a 'menstruous cloth' (Isaiah 30:22), which (as Jerome says) was the most defiling thing under the law. All the legal warnings which God appointed were but to put men in mind of their loathsomeness before they were washed in the blood of Christ. If all the evils in the world were put together and their quintessence strained out, they could not make a thing so black and polluted as sin does. A sinner is a devil in man's shape. When Moses' rod was turned into a serpent, he fled from it. Would God open men's eyes and show them their deformities and damnable spots, they would be afraid and fly from themselves as serpents! This shows what need we have of purity. When grace comes it washes off this hellish filth. Of Ethiopians it makes us Israelites. It turns ravens into swans. It makes them who are as black as hell to become white as snow.

(iii) Because none but the pure in heart are interested in the covenant of grace. Covenanted persons have 'the sprinkling with clean water' (Ezekiel 36:25). Now, till we are thus sprinkled, we have nothing to do with the new covenant and by consequence with the new Jerusalem. If a will be made only to such persons as are so qualified, none can come in for a part, but such as have those qualifications. So, God has made a will and covenant that he will be our God, and will settle heaven upon us by entail, but with this clause or proviso in the will, that we be purified persons, having the 'clean water sprinkled' upon us. Now till then, we have nothing to do with God or mercy.

(iv) Purity is the end of our election. 'He has chosen us that we should be holy' (Ephesians 1:4). Not *for* holiness, but *to* holiness. 'Whom he did foreknow, he also did predestinate to be conformed to the image of his Son' (Romans 8:29). God predestinates us to Christ's image, which image consists 'in righteousness and true holiness' (Ephesians 4:24). So that till you are holy, you cannot show any sign of election upon you, but rather the devil's brand-mark.

(v) Purity is the end of our redemption. If we could have gone to heaven in our sins, Christ needed not have died. Why did he shed his blood but to redeem us from 'a vain conversation'? (I Peter:18, 19); and, 'who gave himself for us that he might redeem us from all iniquity, and purify unto himself a peculiar people' (Titus 2:14). Christ shed his blood to wash off our filth. The cross was both an altar and a laver. Jesus died not only to save us from wrath (1 Thessalonians 1:10), but to save us from sin (Matthew 1:21). Out of his side came water which signifies our cleansing, as well as blood which signifies our justifying (1 John 5:6). The truth is, it were to make the body of Christ monstrous, if the head should be pure and not the members.

2 Why purity must be chiefly in the heart.

(i) Because if the heart be not pure, we differ nothing from a Pharisaical purity. The Pharisees' holiness consisted chiefly in externals. Theirs was an outside purity. They never minded the inside of the heart. 'Woe unto you, scribes and Pharisees, hypocrites! for ye make clean the outside of the cup and of the platter, but within they are full of extortion', and 'Ye are like unto whited sepulchres, which indeed appear beautiful outward, but are within full of dead men's bones' (Matthew 23:25, 27). The Pharisees were good only on the surface. They were whited over, not white. They were like a rotten post laid in vermilion colour, like a fair chimney-piece gilded without, but within nothing but soot. Of such hypocrites Salvian [1] complains, who had Christ in their mouths but to no purpose. We must go further. Be 'pure in heart', like the king's daughter 'all glorious within' (Psalm 45:13); else ours is but a Pharisaical purity; and Christ says, 'Except your righteousness shall exceed the righteousness of the scribes and Pharisees, ye shall in no case enter into the kingdom of heaven' (Matthew 5:20).

(ii) The heart must especially be kept pure, because the heart is the chief seat or place of God's residence. God dwells in the heart. He takes up the heart for his own lodging (Isaiah 57:15; Ephesians 3:17), therefore it must be pure and holy. A king's palace must be kept from defilement, especially his presence-chamber. How holy ought that to be! If the body be the temple of the Holy Ghost (1 Corinthians 6:19), the heart is the holy of holies. Oh take heed of defiling the room where God is to come. Let that room be washed with holy tears.

(iii) The heart must especially be pure, because it is the heart that sanctifies all we do. If the heart be holy, all is holy – our affections holy, our duties holy. 'The altar sanctifieth the gift' (Matthew 23:19). The heart is the altar that sanctifies the offering. The Romans kept their springs from being poisoned. The heart is the spring of all our actions; let us keep this spring from poison. Be 'pure in heart'.

Showing the true purity of the soul

See here what is the beauty that sets off a soul in God's eye, namely, purity of heart. You who are never so beautiful are but a spiritual leper till you are pure in heart. God is in love with the pure heart for he sees his own picture drawn there. Holiness is a beam of God; it is the angels' glory. They are pure virgin-spirits. Take away purity from an angel and

[1] A Christian writer of the 5th century who spent most of his life at Marseilles.

he is no more an angel but a devil. You who are pure in heart have the angels' glory shining in you. You have the embroidery and workmanship of the Holy Ghost upon you. The pure heart is God's paradise where he delights to walk. It is his lesser heaven. The dove delights in the purest air. The Holy Ghost who descended in the likeness of a dove delights in the purest soul. God says of the pure in heart as of Zion, 'This is my rest for ever, here will I dwell' (Psalm 132:14). God loves the fairest complexion. The pure in heart is Christ's bride, decked and bespangled with the jewels of holiness. 'Thou hast ravished my heart with one of thine eyes' (Canticles 4:9). Thine eyes, that is, thy graces; these as a chain of pearl have drawn mine heart to thee. Of all hearts God loves the pure heart best. You who dress yourself by the glass of the Word and adorn 'the hidden man of thy heart' (1 Peter 3:4), are most precious in God's eyes, though you may be blear-eyed as Leah, lame as Barzillai,[1] yet being 'pure in heart' you are the mirror of beauty and may say 'Yet shall I be glorious in the eyes of the Lord' (Isaiah 49:5). How may this raise the esteem of purity! This is a beauty that never fades and which makes God himself fall in love with us.

Christians must not rest in outside purity

If we must be pure in heart then we must not rest in outward purity. Civility is not sufficient. A swine may be washed, yet a swine still. Civility does but wash a man, grace changes him. Civility, like a star may shine in the eyes of the world, but it differs as much from purity as the crystal from the diamond. Civility is but strewing flowers on a dead corpse. A man may be wonderfully moralized, yet but a tame devil. How many have made civility their saviour! Morality may damn as well as vice. A vessel may be sunk with gold, as well as with dung.

Observe two things:

1 The civil person, though he will not commit gross sins, yet he is not sensible of heart sins. He does not discern the 'law in his members' (Romans 7:23). He is not troubled for unbelief, hardness of heart, vanity of thoughts. He abhors gaol-sins, not gospel-sins.

2 The civil person has an aching tooth at religion. His heart rises against holiness. The snake is of a fine colour, but has a deadly sting. The civil man is fair to look to, but has a secret antipathy against the ways of God. He hates grace as much as vice. Zeal is as odious to him as uncleanness. So that civility is not to be rested in. The heart must be

[1] This seems to be in mistake for Mephibosheth.

pure. God would have Aaron wash the inwards of the sacrifice (Leviticus 9:14). Civility does but wash the outside; the inwards must be washed. 'Blessed are the pure in heart.'

Signs of an impure heart

Let us put ourselves on trial whether we are pure-hearted or no. Here I shall do two things to show the signs, first, of an impure heart; second, of a pure heart.

1 An ignorant heart is an impure heart. To be ignorant of sin or Christ argues impurity of heart. Nahash the Ammonite would enter into covenant with the men of Jabesh-Gilead so he might thrust out their right eyes (1 Samuel 11:2). Satan leaves men their left eye. In worldly knowledge they are quick-sighted enough but the right eye of spiritual knowledge is quite put out (2 Corinthians 4:4). Ignorance is Satan's stronghold (Acts 26:18). The devils are bound in chains of darkness (Jude 6). So are all ignorant persons. Impossible it is that an ignorant heart should be good. It is knowledge makes the heart good. 'That the soul be without knowledge is not good' (Proverbs 19:2). For any to say that, though their mind be ignorant yet their heart is good, they may as well say that, though they are blind yet their eyes are good. In the law, when the plague of leprosy was in a man's head the priest was to pronounce him unclean. This is the case of an ignorant man. The leprosy is in his head, 'he is unclean'. That heart cannot be very pure which is a dungeon. Grace cannot reign where ignorance reigns. An ignorant man can have no love to God. 'He cannot love that which he does not know.' [1] He can have no faith. Knowledge must usher in faith (Psalm 9:10). He cannot worship God aright (John 4:22). Though he may worship the true God, yet in a wrong manner. Ignorance is the root of sin. Blindness leads to lasciviousness (Ephesians 4:18, 19; Proverbs 7:23). Ignorance is the mother of pride (Revelation 3:17). It is the cause of error (2 Timothy 3:7), and, which is worse, an affected ignorance. 'It is one thing to be ignorant; it is another thing to be unwilling to know'.[1] Many are in love with ignorance. They hug their disease (Job 21:14; 2 Peter 3:5). Ignorant minds are impure. There is no going to heaven in the dark.

2 That heart is impure which sees no need of purity. 'I am rich and have need of nothing' (Revelation 3:17). Not to be sensible of a disease is worse than the disease. You shall hear a sick man say, 'I am well, I

[1] Quoted from Ovid: Artis Amatoriae III, 397.

ail nothing.' There are some who 'need no repentance' (Luke 15:7). Some sinners are too well to be cured. Heart purity is as great a wonder to the natural man as the new birth was to Nicodemus (John 3:4). It is sad to think how many go on confidently and are ready to bless themselves, never suspecting their condition till it be too late.

3 He has an impure heart who regards iniquity in his heart. 'If I regard iniquity in my heart, the Lord will not hear me' (Psalm 66:18). In the original it is 'If I look upon sin', that is, with a lustful look. Sin-regarding is inconsistent with heart-purity.

What is it to 'regard iniquity'?

(i) When we indulge in sin. When sin not only lives in us, but when we live in sin. Some will leave all their sins but one. Jacob would let all his sons go but Benjamin. Satan can hold a man by one sin. The fowler holds the bird fast enough by a wing or a claw. Others hide their sins like one that shuts up his shop-windows but follows his trade within doors. Many deal with their sins as Moses' mother dealt with her son. She hid him in the ark of bulrushes, as if she had left him quite, but her eye was still upon him and in conclusion she became his nurse (Exodus 2:9). So, many seem to leave their sins, but they only hide them from the eye of others. Their heart still goes after them and at last they nurse and give breast to their sins.

(ii) To regard iniquity is to delight in iniquity. A child of God, though he sins, yet he does not take a complacency in sin. 'What I hate, that do I' (Romans 7:15). But impure souls make a recreation of sin. 'They had pleasure in unrighteousness' (2 Thessalonians 2:12). Never did one feed with more delight on a dish he loves than a wicked man does upon the forbidden fruit. This delight shows that the will is in the sin. And 'the will is the rule and measure of the deed'.

(iii) To regard iniquity is to lay in provision for sin. 'Make not provision for the flesh' (Romans 13:14). Sinners are caterers for their lusts. It is a metaphor taken from such as make provision for a family, or victual a garrison. The Greek word here signifies a projecting and forecasting in the mind how to bring a thing about. This is to make provision for the flesh when one studies to satisfy the flesh and lay in fuel for lust. Thus Amnon made provision for the flesh (2 Samuel 13:5). He fains himself sick, and his sister, Tamar, must be his nurse. She must cook and dress his meat for him. By which means he defiled the breasts of her virginity. It is sad when men's care is not to discharge conscience, but to satisfy lust.

[177]

(iv) To regard iniquity is to give it respect and entertainment, as Lot showed respect to the angels. 'He bowed himself with his face toward the ground and said, Behold now, my lords, turn in I pray you . . .' (Genesis 19:2). When the Spirit of God comes He is repulsed and grieved, but when temptation comes, the sinner bows to it, sets open the gates, and says 'Turn in, my lord.' This is to regard iniquity.

(v) He is said to regard sin that does not regard the threatenings of God against sin. We read of 'seven thunders uttering their voices' (Revelation 10:3). How many thunders in Scripture utter their voice against sin! 'God shall wound the hairy scalp of such an one as goeth on still in his trespasses' (Psalm 68:21). Here is a thundering scripture, but sinners fear not this thunder. Let a minister come as a Boanerges, clothed with the spirit of Elijah, and denounce all the curses of God against men's sins, they regard it not. They can laugh at the shaking of a spear (Job 41:29). This is to regard iniquity, and argues an impure heart.

4 An unbelieving heart is an impure heart. The Scripture calls it expressly 'an evil heart of unbelief' (Hebrews 3:12). An unbelieving heart is evil in the highest degree. It is full of the poison of hell. Unbelief is the foul medley of all sins, the root and receptacle of sin.

(i) Unbelief is a God-affronting sin. It puts the lie upon God. It calls in question his power (Psalm 78:19), mercy and truth. 'He that believeth not hath made God a liar' (1 John 5:10). And can a greater affront be cast upon the God of glory? It makes us trust to second causes, which is setting the creature in the room of God. 'Asa in his disease sought not to the Lord, but to the physicians' (2 Chronicles 16:12). He relied more on the physician than upon God. Saul seeks to the witch of Endor. O high affront, to lean upon the reed and neglect the Rock of Ages!

(ii) Unbelief hardens the heart. These two sins are linked together. 'He upbraided them with their unbelief and hardness of heart' (Mark 16:14). Unbelief breeds the stone of the heart. He that believes not God's threatenings will never fear him. He that believes not God's promises will never love him. What is said of the Leviathan is true of the unbeliever. 'His heart is as firm as a stone' (Job 41:24). Unbelief first pollutes the heart and then hardens it.

(iii) Unbelief breeds hypocrisy. Atheists do not believe that God is a jealous God and will call them to account. Therefore it is they put on a mask of religion and are saints in jest, that they may play the devil in earnest (2 Timothy 3:4, 5). They pretend God, but Self is the idol they worship. Like barge-men they look one way and row another. The unbeliever is the greatest hypocrite.

(iv) Unbelief causes the fear of men. 'Fear is proof of a base-born soul.'[1] Fear is a debasing thing. It unmans a man. It makes him afraid to be good. The fearful man studies rather compliance than conscience. 'The fear of man bringeth a snare' (Proverbs 29:25). What made Abraham equivocate, David feign himself mad, Peter deny Christ? Was it not their fear? And whence does fear spring, but from unbelief? Therefore the Scripture joins them together. 'The fearful and unbelieving' (Revelation 21:8).

(v) Unbelief is the root of apostasy: 'an evil heart of unbelief in departing from the living God' (Hebrews 3:12). What is the reason those who seemed once zealous now despise prophesying and leave off prayer in their families? is it not their unbelief? They believed not that God is, and that he is a rewarder of them that diligently seek him (Hebrews 11:6). Infidelity is the cause of apostasy. In the Greek, 'apistia' (unbelief) leads to 'apostasia' (apostasy). And if infidelity be the breeder and fomenter of so much sin, then the unbelieving heart must needs be an impure heart.

5 A covetous heart is an impure heart. The earth is the most impure element. The purity of the heart lies in the spirituality of it, and what more opposite to spiritualness than earthiness? Covetousness is 'the root of all evil' (1 Timothy 6:10). 'To what dost thou not drive mortal hearts, thou accursed lust for gold?'[2]

(i) Covetousness is the root of discontent. Why do any repine at their condition, but because they think they do not have enough? The Greek word for covetousness signifies an immoderate desire of getting. Covetousness is a dry dropsy, and because the thirst is not satisfied, therefore the heart frets through discontent and impatiency.

(ii) Covetousness is the root of theft. Achan's covetous humour made him steal that wedge of gold which served to cleave asunder his soul from God (Joshua 7:21).

(iii) Covetousness is the root of treason. It made Judas betray Christ. 'What will ye give me and I will deliver him unto you?' (Matthew 26:15). Absalom's covetousness made him attempt to pluck the crown

[1] Quoted from Virgil, most famous of Roman poets (1st century B.C.).
[2] Virgil: Aeneid III, 56 (Watson erroneously refers the Latin original to the poet Horace).

from his father's head. He that is a Demas will soon prove a Judas. 'Men shall be covetous' (2 Timothy 3:2), and it follows in the next verse, 'traitors'. Where covetousness is in the premises, treason will be in the conclusion.

(iv) Covetousness is the root of murder. Why did Ahab stone Naboth to death but to possess his vineyard? (1 Kings 21:13). Covetousness has made many swim to the crown in blood. And can the heart be pure, when the 'hands are full of blood'? (Isaiah 1:15).

(v) Covetousness is the root of perjury. 'Men shall be covetous' and it follows, 'truce-breakers' (2 Timothy 3:2, 3). For love of money will take a false oath and break a just oath. He that lives a Midas, will die a perjurer.

(vi) Covetousness is the root of necromancy. Why do persons indent with the devil, but for money? They study the black art for yellow gold. Alexander the Sixth[1] pawned his soul to the devil for a popedom.

(vii) It is the root of fraud and cozenage in dealings. Such as would be over-rich, will over-reach. It is the covetous hand that holds false weights (Amos 8:5).

(viii) Covetousness is the root of bribery and injustice. It makes the courts of judicature, 'great places of robbery', as Augustine speaks. At Athens causes were bought and sold for money.

(ix) It is the cause of uncleanness. The Scripture mentions 'the hire of a whore' (Deuteronomy 23:18). For money both conscience and chastity are set to sale.

(x) Covetousness is the root of idolatry: 'Covetousness which is idolatry' (Colossians 3:5). The covetous person bows down to the image of gold. His money is his god, for he puts his trust in it. Money is his creator. When he has abundance of wealth, then he thinks he is made. It is his redeemer. If he be in any strait or trouble, he flies to his money and that must redeem him. It is his comforter. When he is sad he counts over his money and with this golden harp he drives away the evil spirit. When you see a covetous man, you may say, There goes an idolater.

(xi) Covetousness is the cause of unprofitableness under the means. In the parable the thorns choked the seed (Matthew 13:7). This is the reason the Word preached does no more good. The seed often falls among thorns. Thousands of sermons lie buried in earthly hearts.

[1] Pope, 1493–1503: the most famous member of the infamous Borgia family

[180]

(xii) Covetousness is the root of penuriousness and baseness. It hinders hospitality. A covetous man has a withered hand. He cannot reach it out to clothe or feed such as are in want. The covetous person is so sordid that if his estate may flourish he is content to let his name lie dead and buried. What a cursed sin is avarice! And can he be pure in heart that has such a 'root of bitterness' growing in him? We may as well say the wine is pure which runs dregs or the body is pure which is full of plague-spots.

6 Those hearts are impure which are 'haters of purity' (Micah 3:2), which 'hate knowledge' (Proverbs 1:29). Some things in nature have an antipathy; the serpent will not come near the boughs of the wild ash. There is an antipathy in a carnal heart against holiness; and when hatred is boiled up to malice, it is dangerous. Thus Julian [1] maliciously opposed holiness. Making war against the Persians, and receiving a mortal wound through his armour, he threw up an handful of his blood into the air in indignation saying, 'Thou Galilean, hast thou overcome me?'

7 He that decries purity has an impure heart. 'There shall come in the last days scoffers' (Luke 16:14; 2 Peter 3:3). There are some that make a jeer of religion. These are (say they) 'your holy brethren'! It is a sign of an Ishmael spirit to scoff at holiness. Are we not commanded to be perfect as God is? (Matthew 5:48). One would wonder that those who dare open their mouths in derision against holiness, the earth does not open her mouth to swallow them up as it did Korah and Dathan. These are devils covered over with flesh. They have damnation written on their foreheads. Lucian who in the time of the Emperor Trajan had professed religion, afterwards became so profane as to make a mock at the Christians and by his jeers and taunts went about to rend religion. At last he himself was rent asunder and devoured by dogs. When the scab of the leper appeared, he was to be shut out of the camp (Leviticus 13:8, 46). Those who flout at religion, if God give them not repentance, are sure to be shut out of the camp of heaven.

Seven signs of a pure heart

I shall next show you the signs of a pure heart.

1 A sincere heart is a pure heart: 'In whose spirit there is no guile' (Psalm 32:2). There are four characters of a sincere-hearted Christian.

[1] Julian the Apostate (see p. 155, fn 2).

(i) A sincere heart serves God with the whole heart.

First, he serves God with the heart. The hypocrite does but make a show of obedience. 'Thou art near in their mouth and far from their reins' (Jeremiah 12:2). There may be a fair complexion when the lungs and vitals are rotten. The hypocrite is fair to look on. He has a devout eye but a hollow heart. But he who is sincere, his inside is his best side. In the law God would have 'the inwards' offered up (Leviticus 4:11). A good Christian gives God 'the inwards'. When he prays his heart prays. 'Hannah prayed in her heart' (1 Samuel 1:13). In his thanksgiving the heart is the chief instrument of praise (Psalm 111:1). Then is the sweetest music when we 'make melody in our hearts to the Lord' (Ephesians 5:19).

Secondly, the sincere Christian serves God with the 'whole heart' (Psalm 119:2). Hypocrites have a double heart (Psalm 12:2). An heart for God and an heart for sin. 'Their heart is divided' (Hosea 10:2). God loves a broken heart, but not a divided heart. An upright heart is a whole heart. The full stream and torrent of the affections runs out after God. A sincere heart 'follows God fully' (Numbers 14:24).

(ii) A sincere heart is willing to come under a trial. 'Search me, O God, and try me' (Psalm 139:23). That metal is to be suspected which men are afraid to bring to the touch-stone. A sound heart likes the touch-stone of the Word. It is for a searching ministry. Hypocrites fly from the light of truth; they fly from that light which would discover sin. They hate that physic of the Word which, meeting with their ill humours, begins to make them sick and trouble their conscience. A gracious soul loves that preaching best which makes an heart-anatomy.

Thirdly, a man of sincere heart dares not act in the least against his conscience. He is the most magnanimous, yet the most pusillanimous. He is bold in suffering (Proverbs 28:1) but fearful of sin (Genesis 39:9). He dares not get an estate by sinful shifts, or rise upon the ruins of another. Jacob got his father's blessing by fraud, but that is not the way to get God's blessing.

Fourthly, a sincere heart is a suspicious heart. The hypocrite suspects others and has charitable thoughts of himself. The sincere Christian has charitable thoughts of others and suspects himself. He calls himself often to account: O my soul, have you any evidences for heaven? Are they not to seek when they should be to show? Is there no flaw in your evidences? You may mistake common for saving grace. Weeds in the corn-fields look like flowers. The foolish virgins' lamps looked as if they had oil in them. O my soul, is it not so with you? The man of sin-

cere soul, being ever jealous, plays the critic upon himself and so tra-
verses things in the court of conscience as if he were presently [1] to be
cited to God's bar. This is to be pure in heart.

2 A pure heart breathes after purity. If God should stretch out the
golden sceptre and say to him, 'Ask, and it shall be given thee, to half
the kingdom', he would say, 'Lord, a pure heart!' Let my heart have
this inscription, 'Holiness to the Lord.' Let my heart be thy temple and
do thou dwell in it. Lord, what should I do in heaven with this unholy heart? What converse could I have with God or angels? A
gracious soul is so in love with purity that he prizes a pure heart above
all blessings.

(i) Above riches; he knows he may be clothed in purple and fine linen,
and yet go to hell. He is content to be poor, so long as he may be pure.
He knows heart-purity is a special certificate of God's love. 'The pure
in heart' shall see God.

(ii) Above gifts: gifts do not at all set us off in God's eye. A pure
heart is the jewel. 'O woman, great is thy faith!' (Matthew 15:28). It
was not her rhetorical language Christ was taken with, but her faith.
Hypocrites have had rare gifts. Saul had the spirit of prophecy. Judas
no doubt could make an elegant oration. Hypocrites have come into
God's church loaded with the Egyptian gold of human learning. There
may be illumination without sanctification. A small diamond is better
than a great deal of brass. A little grace excels the most flourishing
parts. Now if the out-goings of your soul are after holiness, you desire
rather a pure heart than an eloquent tongue. You have the oil of the
Spirit poured on you and you shall be crowned with a sight of God.

3 A pure heart abhors all sin. A man may forbear and forsake sin, yet
not have a pure heart.

(i) He may forbear sin as one may hold his breath while he dives under
water, and then take breath again. And a man may forbear sin for want
of occasion. The gun-powder makes no noise till the fire be put to it.
The clock stands still till the weights are put on. Let a temptation come,
which is like the hanging on of the weights, and the heart goes as fast in
sin as ever.

(ii) He may forbear sin for fear of the penalty. A man forbears a dish
he loves for fear it should bring his disease upon him of the stone or
gout. There is conflict in a sinner between the passions of desire and fear.

[1] Immediately.

Desire spurs him on to sin, but fear as a curb and bit checks him. Nor is it the crookedness of the serpent he fears, but the sting of the serpent.

(iii) He may forbear sin out of a design. He has a plot in hand and his sin might spoil his plot. Some rich heir would fly out in excess, but he carries it fair to prevent a cutting off the entail. How good was Joash while Jehoiada the priest lived! Prudence as well as conscience may restrain from sin.

Again, a man may forsake sin yet not have a pure heart. It is a great matter, I confess, to forsake sin. So dear is sin to men that they will part with the fruit of their body for the sin of their souls. Sin is the Delilah that bewitches, and it is much to see men divorced from it. This is some fruit of the ministry to civilize, but there may be a forsaking of sin, yet no heart purity. Sin may be forsaken upon wrong principles.

From *morality*: moral arguments may suppress sin. I have read of a debauched heathen who, hearing Socrates [1] read an ethical lecture of virtue and vice (though he came with a purpose to deride Socrates, yet) he went away changed and no more followed his former exorbitancies. Cato,[2] Seneca, Aristides,[3] seeing beauty in virtue, led unblameable lives.

From *policy*: a man may forsake sin, not out of respect to God's glory, but his own credit. Vice will waste his estate, eclipse the honour of his family, therefore out of policy he will divorce his sin.

From *necessity*. Perhaps he can now follow the trade of sin no longer. The adulterer is grown old, the drunkard poor. His heart is toward sin, but either his purse fails him or his strength; as a man that loves hunting, but his prison-fetters will not suffer him to follow the sport. This man, who is necessitated to put a stop to sin, does not so much forsake sin as sin forsakes him.

But he is pure in God's eye who abhors sin. 'I hate every false way' (Psalm 119:104). This is excellent indeed, because now the love of sin is crucified. A hypocrite may leave sin, yet love it; as the serpent casts her coat, yet keeps her sting. But when a man can say he abhors sin, now is sin killed in the root. A pure heart abstains from sin, as a man does from a dish that he has an antipathy against. This is a sign of a new nature, when a man hates what he once loved; and because he hates sin therefore he fights against it with the 'sword of the Spirit', as a man that hates a serpent seeks the destruction of it.

[1] Athenian philosopher, 5th century B.C.
[2] Roman statesman and soldier, surnamed 'The Censor' (d. 149 B.C.).
[3] Athenian statesman and soldier, surnamed 'The Just' (5th century B.C.).

4 A pure heart avoids the appearance of evil. 'Abstain from all show of evil' (1 Thessalonians 5:22). A pure heart avoids that which may be interpreted as evil. He that is loyal to his prince not only forbears to have his hand in treason, but he takes heed of that which has a show of treason. A gracious heart is shy of that which looks like sin. When Joseph's mistress took hold of him and said, 'Lie with me', he left his garment in her hand and fled from her (Genesis 39:12). He avoided the appearance of evil. He would not be seen in her company. Thus a pure heart avoids whatever may have the suspicion of sin:

(i) In regard of himself, and that two ways. First, because the appearance of evil is oftentimes an occasion of evil. Effeminate dalliance is an appearance of evil, and many times occasions evil. Had Joseph been familiar with his mistress in a wanton sporting manner, he might in time have been drawn to commit folly with her. Some out of novelty and curiosity have gone to hear mass, and afterwards have lent the idol not only their ear but their knee. In our times are there not many who have gone with itching ears into sectarian company and have come home with the plague in their head? When Dinah would be gadding, she lost her chastity (Genesis 34:2). A pure heart foreseeing the danger avoids the appearance of evil. It is dangerous to go near a hornets' nest. The men who went near the furnace were burned (Daniel 3:22). Second, because the appearance of evil may eclipse his good name. A good name is a precious ointment. It is better than 'fine gold' (Proverbs 22:1). It commends us to God and angels, which riches cannot do. Now a godly man avoids the appearance of evil, lest he wound his good name. What comfort can there be of life, when the name lies buried?

(ii) A pure heart avoids the suspicion of sin out of reverence and respect to the holiness of God. God hates the very appearance of evil. God abhors hypocrites because they have no more than the appearance of good, and he is angry with his children if they have so much as the appearance of evil. A gracious heart knows God is a jealous God and cannot endure that his people should border upon sin. Therefore he keeps aloof off and will not come near the smell of infection.

(iii) A pure heart avoids the show of sin in regard of the godly. The appearance of evil may scandalize a weak brother. A gracious heart is not only fearful lest he should defile his own conscience, but lest he should offend his brother's conscience. Were it only a thing indifferent, yet if it be an appearance of evil and may grieve another, we are to forbear (1 Corinthians 10:25-28). For 'when we sin against the brethren and wound their weak conscience, we sin against Christ' (1 Corinthians

8:12). The weak Christian is a member of Christ. Therefore the sinning against a member is a sinning against Christ.

(iv) A pure heart avoids the very appearance of evil in regard of the wicked. The apostle would have us walk wisely 'towards them that are without' (1 Thessalonians 4:12). The wicked watch for our halting. How glad would they be of anything to reproach religion? Professors are placed as stars in the highest orb of the church, and if there be but the appearance of any eccentric, or irregular motion, the wicked would presently open their mouths with a fresh cry against religion. Now to a godly heart the fame and honour of the gospel is so dear that he had rather die than impeach or eclipse it. By this then let us try ourselves whether we are pure in heart. Do we avoid the least apparition[1] of sin? Alas, how many run themselves into the occasions of sin! They tempt the devil to tempt them. Some go to masques and comedies, the very fuel and temptation to lust. Others frequent erroneous meetings, and truly God often in just judgment leaves them to the acts of sin, that do not avoid the appearance of sin. 'They were mingled among the heathen and learned their works' (Psalm 106:35). Pure hearts fly the occasion. John would not endure the company of Cerinthus[2] in the bath, as Nicephorus notes. Polycarp[3] would have no conference with Marcion the heretic, but called him 'the devil's firstborn'. Basil says that the Christians in his time avoided the meetings of sectaries as the 'very schools of error'. Oh, avoid the appearance of evil. The apostle bids us to follow those things which are 'of good report' (Philippians 4:8).

5 A pure heart performs holy duties in an holy manner. This holy manner, or due order, consists in three things:

(i) Preparing the heart before a duty. An unholy heart does not care how it rushes upon an ordinance. It comes without preparation and goes away without profit. The pure heart is a prepared heart. It dresses itself, before it comes to a duty, by examination and ejaculation. When the earth is prepared, then it is fit to receive the seed. When the instrument is prepared and tuned it is fit for music.

(ii) Watching the heart in a duty. An holy heart labours to be affected and wrought upon. His heart burns within him. There was no sacrifice

[1] Appearance.

[2] A Gnostic heretic: the apostle John is said to have hurried out of the bath-house of Ephesus, fearing that it would fall on the enemy of the truth. The story is to be found in the *History of the Church* by Eusebius, III. 28, 6 (4th century). Nicephorus is a much later writer (9th century).

[3] The martyred Bishop of Smyrna in the 2nd century.

without fire. A pure saint labours to have his heart broken in a duty (Psalm 51:17). The incense, when it was broken, cast the sweetest savour. Impure souls care not in what a dead or perfunctory manner they serve God (Ezekiel 33:31). They pray more out of fashion than out of faith. They are no more affected with an ordinance than the tombs of the church. God complains of offering up the blind (Malachi 1:8). And is it not as bad to offer up the dead? O Christian, say to yourself, How can this deadness of heart stand with pureness of heart? Do not dead things putrify?

(iii) Outward reverence. Purity of heart will express itself by the reverend gesture of the body, the lifting up of the eye and hand, the uncovering the head, the bending the knee. Constantine the Emperor[1] bore great reverence to the Word. When God gave the law, 'the mount was on fire and trembled' (Exodus 19:18). The reason was that the people might prostrate themselves more reverently before the Lord. The ark wherein the law was put was carried upon bars that the Levites might not touch it (Exodus 25:11, 14). To show what reverence God would have about holy things: sitting in prayer (unless in case of weakness) and having the hat half on in prayer, is a very indecent, irreverent practice. Let such as are guilty reform it. We must not only offer up our souls, but our bodies (Romans 12:1). The Lord takes notice what posture and gesture we use in his worship. If a man were to deliver a petition to the king, would he deliver it with his hat half on? The careless irreverence of some would make us think they did not much regard whether God heard them or no. We are run from one extreme to another, from superstition to unmannerliness. Let Christians think of the dreadful majesty of God who is present. 'How dreadful is this place! This is none other but the house of God and this is the gate of heaven' (Genesis 28:17). The blessed angels 'cover their faces crying, Holy, holy holy' (Isaiah 6:3). An holy heart will have an holy gesture.

6 A pure heart will have a pure life. 'Let us cleanse ourselves from all filthiness of the flesh and spirit, perfecting holiness in the fear of God.' (2 Corinthians 7:1). Where there is a good conscience there will be a good conversation. Some bless God they have good hearts, but their lives are evil. 'There is a generation that are pure in their own eyes and yet is not washed from their filthiness' (Proverbs 30:12). If the stream be corrupt we may suspect the spring-head to be impure. Aaron was called the saint of the Lord (Psalm 106:16). He had not only an holy

---

[1] Roman Emperor (surnamed the Great) d. A.D. 337. He gave Christianity state recognition.

heart, but there was a golden plate on his forehead on which was written 'Holiness to the Lord'. Purity must not only be woven into the heart but engraven upon the life. Grace is most beautiful when it shines abroad with its golden beams. The clock has not only its motion within, but the finger moves without upon the dial. Pureness of heart shows itself upon the dial of the conversation.

(i) A pure soul talks of God (Psalm 37:30). His heart is seen in his tongue. The Latins call the roof of the mouth Caelum (heaven). He that is pure in heart, his mouth is full of heaven.

(ii) He walks with God (Genesis 6:9). He is still doing angel's work, praising God, serving God. He lives as Christ did upon earth. Holy duties are the Jacob's ladder by which he is still ascending to heaven. Purity of heart and life are in Scripture made twins. 'I will put my Spirit within you' (Ezekiel 36:27); there is purity of heart. 'And cause you to walk in my statutes'; there is purity of life. Shall we account them pure whose conversation is not in heaven (Philippians 3:20), but rather in hell? 'Shall I count them pure with the wicked balances and with the bag of deceitful weights? (Micah 6:11). How justly may others reproach religion when they see it kicked down with our unholy feet! A pure heart has a golden frontispiece. Grace like new wine will have vent; it can be no more concealed than lost. The saints are called 'jewels' (Malachi 3:17), because of that shining lustre they cast in the eyes of others.

7 A pure heart is so in love with purity that nothing can draw him off from it.

(i) Let others reproach purity, he loves it. As David, when he danced before the ark, and Michal scoffed, if (says he) this be to be vile, 'I will yet be more vile' (2 Samuel 6:22). So says a pure heart: If to follow after holiness be to be vile, I will yet be more vile. Let water be sprinkled upon the fire, it burns the more. The more others deride holiness, the more a gracious soul burns in love and zeal to it. If a man had an inheritance befallen him, would he be laughed out of it? What is a Christian the worse for another's reproach? A blind man's disparaging a diamond does not make it sparkle the less.

(ii) Let others persecute holiness, a pure heart will pursue it. Holiness is the queen every gracious soul is espoused to and he will rather die than be divorced. Paul would be holy, 'though bonds and persecutions did abide him' (Acts 20:23). The way of religion is often thorny and bloody, but a gracious heart prefers inward purity before outward peace.

I have heard of one who, having a jewel he much prized, the king sent for his jewel. Tell the king (says he) I honour his Majesty, but I will rather lose my life than part with my jewel. He who is enriched with the jewel of holiness will rather die than part with this jewel. When his honour and riches will do him no good, his holiness will stand him instead. 'Ye have your fruit unto holiness, and the end everlasting life.'

Nine exhortations to heart-purity

Let me persuade Christians to heart purity. The harlot 'wipes her mouth' (Proverbs 30:20). But that is not enough. 'Wash thine heart, O Jerusalem' (Jeremiah 4:14). And here I shall lay down some arguments or motives to persuade to heart purity.

1 The necessity of heart-purity. It is necessary:

(i) In respect of ourselves. Till the heart be pure, all our holy things are polluted. They are 'splendid sins'. To the unclean all things are unclean (Titus 1:15). Their offering is unclean. Under the law, if a man who was unclean by a dead body, carried a piece of holy flesh in his skirt, the holy flesh could not cleanse him, but he polluted that. (Haggai 2:12, 13). He who had the leprosy, whatever he touched was unclean. If he had touched the altar or sacrifice, the altar had not cleansed him, but he had defiled the altar. A foul hand defiles the purest water. An impure heart defiles prayers, sacraments. He drops poison upon all. A pure stream running through muddy ground is polluted. The holiest ordinances are stained, running through an impure heart. A sinner's works are called 'dead works' (Hebrews 6:1). And those works which are dead cannot please God. A dead wife cannot please her husband.

(ii) Heart purity is necessary in respect of God. God is holy. Purity is the chief robe wherewith God himself is clothed. 'Thou art of purer eyes than to behold evil' (Habakkuk 1:13). And will this holy God endure to have an impure heart come near him? Will a man lay a viper in his bosom? The holy God and the sinner cannot dwell together. None can dwell together but friends, but there is no friendship between God and the sinner, both of them being of a contrary judgment and disposition. An impure heart is more odious to God than a serpent. God gave the serpent its venom, but Satan fills the heart with sin. 'Why hath Satan filled thine heart?' (Acts 5:3). The Lord abhors a sinner. He will not come near him, having his plague-sores running. 'My soul loathed them' (Zechariah 11:8).

(iii) Heart purity is necessary in regard of angels. They are pure creatures. The Cherubims, which typified the angels, were made of fine gold to denote the purity of their essence. No unholy thought enters into the angels, therefore there must be purity of heart that there may be some resemblance between us and them. What should unholy hearts do among those pure angelical spirits?

(iv) In regard of the saints glorified. They are pure, being refined from all lees and dregs of sin. Their title is 'spirits of just men made perfect' (Hebrews 12:23). Now what should profane spirits do among 'spirits made perfect'? I tell you, if you who wallow in your sins could come near God and angels and spirits of men made perfect, and have a sight of their lustre, you would soon wish yourselves out of their company. As a man that is dirty and in his rags, if he should stand before the king and his nobles and see them glistering in their cloth of gold and sparkling with their jewels, he would be ashamed of himself, and wish himself out of their presence.

(v) There must be heart purity in regard of heaven. Heaven is a pure place. It is an 'inheritance undefiled' (1 Peter 1:4). No unclean beasts come into the heavenly ark. There shall not enter into it 'anything that defileth' (Revelation 21:27). The Lord will not put the new wine of glory into a musty impure heart, all which considered shows the necessity of heart purity.

2 It is the will of God that we should be pure in heart. 'This is the will of God, your sanctification' (1 Thessalonians 4:3). Are you low in the world? Perhaps it is not the will of God that you should be rich, but it is the will of God that you should be holy. 'This is the will of God, your sanctification' (1 Thessalonians 4:3). Let God have his will by being holy, and you shall have your will by being happy. God's will must either be fulfilled by us or upon us.

3 Purity of heart is the characteristic note of God's people. 'God is good to Israel, even to such as are of a clean heart' (Psalm 73:1). Heart-purity denominates us the 'Israel of God'. It is not profession which makes us the Israel of God. It makes us of Israel indeed, but 'all are not Israel, which are of Israel' (Romans 9:6). Purity of heart is the jewel which is hung only upon the elect. As chastity distinguishes a virtuous woman from an harlot, so the true saint is distinguished from the hypocrite by his heart-purity. This is like the nobleman's star or garter, which is a peculiar ensign of honour, differing him from the

vulgar. When the bright star of purity shines in a Christian's heart, it distinguishes him from a formal professor.

4 Purity of heart makes us like God. It was Adam's unhappiness once, that he aspired to be like God in omnisciency; but we must endeavour to be like God in sanctity. God's image consists in holiness. To those who do not have this image and superscription upon them, he will say 'I know you not'. God delights in no heart but where he may see his own face and likeness. You cannot see your face in a glass when it is dusty. God's face cannot be seen in a dusty impure soul. A pure heart (like a clean glass) gives forth some idea and representation of God. There is little comfort in being like God in other things besides purity. Are we like God in that we have a being? So have stones. Are we like him in that we have motion? So have stars. Are we like him in that we have life? So have trees and birds. Are we like him in that we have knowledge? So have devils. There is no likeness to God will prove comfortable and blissful, but our being like him in purity. God loves the pure in heart. Love is founded upon likeness.

5 The excellency of the heart lies in the purity of it. Purity was the glory of the soul in innocency. The purer a thing is, the better. The purer the air is, and the more free from noxious vapours, the better it is. The spirits of water distilled are most precious. The purer the gold is, the more valuable. The purer the wine is when it is taken off from the lees and dregs, the more excellent it is. The more the soul is clarified by grace and taken off from the lees and dregs of sin, the more precious account God makes of it. The purer the heart is, the more spiritual it is, and the more spiritual the more fit to entertain him who is a Spirit.

6 God is good to the pure in heart. 'God is good to Israel, even to such as are of a clean heart' (Psalm 73:1). We all desire that God should be good to us. It is the sick man's prayer, 'The Lord be good to me.' God is good to such as are of a clean heart.

But how is God good to them? Two ways –

(i) To them that are pure, all things are sanctified. 'To the pure all things are pure' (Titus 1:15). Estate is sanctified, relations are sanctified, as the temple sanctified the gold and the altar sanctified the offering. To the unclean nothing is clean. Their table is a snare; their temple-devotion is sin. There is a curse entailed upon a wicked man (Deuteronomy 28:15–20), but holiness removes the curse and cuts off the entail. 'To the pure all things are pure.'

(ii) The pure-hearted have all things work for their good (Romans 8:28). Mercies and afflictions shall turn to their good. The most poisonful drug shall be medicinable. The most cross providence shall carry on the design of their salvation. Who then would not be pure in heart? 'God is good to such as are of a clean heart.'

7 Heart purity makes way for heaven. The pure in heart 'shall see God'. Happiness is nothing but the quintessence of holiness. Purity of heart is heaven begun in a man. Holiness is called in Scripture 'the anointing of God' (1 John 2:27). Solomon was first anointed with the holy oil, and then he was made king (1 Kings 1:39). The people of God are first anointed with the oil of the Spirit and made pure in heart, and then the crown of glory is set upon their head. And is not purity to be highly valued? It lays a train for glory. 'Purity of heart' and 'seeing of God' are linked together.

8 Note the examples of those who have been eminent for heart-purity. The Lord Jesus was a pattern of purity. 'Which of you convinceth me of sin?' (John 8:46). In this we are to imitate Christ. We are not to imitate him in raising the dead or in working miracles, but in being holy (1 Peter 1:16). Besides this golden pattern of Christ, we are to write after the fair copy of those saints who have been of a dove-like purity. David was so pure in heart, that he was a man 'after God's heart'. Abraham was so purified by faith that he was one of God's cabinet-counsel (Genesis 18:17). Moses was so holy that God spake with him face to face. What were the rest of the patriarchs but so many plants of renown flourishing in holiness? The fathers in the primitive church were exemplary for purity. Gregory Nazianzen, Basil, Augustine, they were so inlaid and adorned with purity that envy itself could not tax them. Therefore, as Caesar wished he had such soldiers as were in the time of Alexander the Great, so we may wish we had such saints as were in the primitive times, so just were they in their dealings, so decent in their attire, so true in their promises, so devout in their religion, so unblameable in their lives that they were living sermons, walking Bibles, real pictures of Christ, and helped to keep up the credit of godliness in the world.

9 Heart-purity is the only jewel you can carry out of the world. Have you a child you delight in, or an estate? You can 'carry nothing out of the world' (1 Timothy 6:7). Purity of heart is the only commodity that can be with comfort transported. This is that will stay longest with you. Usually we love those things which last longest. We prize a dia-

mond or piece of gold above the most beautiful flower, because fading. Heart-purity has perpetuity. It will go with us beyond the grave.

Eight means to be used to obtain heart-purity

But how shall we attain to heart-purity?

1 Often look into the Word of God. 'Now ye are clean through the word' (John 15:3). 'Thy word is very pure' (Psalm 119:140). God's Word is pure, not only for the matter of it, but the effect, because it makes us pure. 'Sanctify them through thy truth; thy word is truth' (John 17:17). By looking into this pure crystal we are changed into the image of it. The Word is both a glass to show us the spots of our souls and a laver to wash them away. The Word breathes nothing but purity; it irradiates the mind; it consecrates the heart.

2 Go to the bath. There are two baths Christians should wash in.

(i) The bath of tears. Go into this bath. Peter had sullied and defiled himself with sin and he washed himself with penitential tears. Mary Magdalene, who was an impure sinner, 'stood at Jesus' feet weeping' (Luke 7:38). Mary's tears washed her heart as well as Christ's feet. Oh sinners, let your eyes be a fountain of tears! Weep for those sins which are so many as have passed all arithmetic. This water of contrition is healing and purifying.

(ii) The bath of Christ's blood. This is that 'fountain opened for sin and uncleanness' (Zechariah 13:1). A soul steeped in the brinish tears of repentance and bathed in the blood of Christ is made pure. This is that 'spiritual washing'. All the legal washings and purifications were but types and emblems representing Christ's blood. This blood lays the soul a-whitening.

3 Get faith. It is a soul-cleansing grace. 'Having purified their hearts by faith' (Acts 15:9). The woman in the gospel that but touched the hem of Christ's garment was healed. A touch of faith heals. If I believe Christ and all his merits are mine, how can I sin against him? We do not willingly injure those friends who, we believe, love us. Nothing can have a greater force and efficacy upon the heart to make it pure than faith. Faith will remove mountains, the mountains of pride, lust, envy. Faith and the love of sin are inconsistent.

4 Breathe after the Spirit. He is called the Holy Spirit (Ephesians 1:13).

It purgeth the heart as lightning purgeth the air. That we may see what a purifying virtue the Spirit has, it is compared:

(i) To fire (Acts 2:3). Fire is of a purifying nature. It refines and cleans metals. It separates the dross from the gold. The Spirit of God in the heart refines and sanctifies it. It burns up the dross of sin.

(ii) The Spirit is compared to wind. 'There came a sound from heaven as of a mighty rushing wind, and they were all filled with the Holy Ghost' (Acts 2:2-4). The wind purifies the air. When the air by reason of foggy vapours is unwholesome, the wind is a fan to winnow and purify it. Thus when the vapours of sin arise in the heart, vapours of pride and covetousness, earthly vapours, the Spirit of God arises and blows upon the soul and so purges away these impure vapours. The spouse in the Canticles prays for a gale of the Spirit, that she might be made pure (4:16).

(iii) The Spirit is compared to water. 'He that believeth on me, out of his belly shall flow rivers of living water; but this spake he of the Spirit' (John 7:38, 39). The Spirit is like water, not only to make the soul fruitful, for it causes the desert to blossom as the rose (Isaiah 32:15; 35:1), but the Spirit is like water to purify. Whereas, before, the heart of a sinner was unclean and whatever he touched had a tincture of impurity (Numbers 19:22), when once the Spirit comes into the heart, it does with its continual showers wash off the filthiness of it, making it pure and fit for the God of spirits to dwell in.

5 Take heed of familiar converse and intercourse with the wicked. One vain mind makes another. One hard heart makes another. The stone in the body is not infectious, but the stone in the heart is. One profane spirit poisons another. Beware of the society of the wicked.

Some may object: But what hurt is in this? Did not Jesus converse with sinners? (Luke 5:29).

(i) There was a necessity for that. If Jesus had not come among sinners, how could any have been saved? He went among sinners, not to join with them in their sins. He was not a companion of sinners but a physician of sinners.

(ii) Though Christ did converse with sinners, he could not be polluted with their sin. His divine nature was a sufficient antidote to preserve him from infection. Christ could be no more defiled with their sin than the sun is defiled by shining on a dunghill. Sin could no more stick on Christ than a burr on a glass of crystal. The soil of his heart was so pure that no viper of sin could breed there. But the case is altered with us. We have a stock of corruption within and the least thing will increase this stock. Therefore it is dangerous mingling ourselves among the wicked. If we would be pure in heart let us shun their society. He that would preserve his garment clean avoids the dirt. The wicked are as the mire (Isaiah 57:20). The fresh waters running among the salt taste brackish.

6 If you would be pure, walk with them that are pure. As the communion of the saints is in our Creed, so it should be in our company. 'He that walketh with the wise shall be wise' (Proverbs 13:20), and he that walketh with the pure shall be pure. The saints are like a bed of spices. By inter-mixing ourselves with them we shall partake of their savouriness. Association begets assimilation. Sometimes God blesses good society to the conversion of others.

7 Wait at the posts of wisdom's doors. Reverence the word preached. The Word of God sucked in by faith (Hebrews 4:2) transforms the heart into the likeness of it (Romans 6:17). The word is an holy seed (James 1:18), which being cast into the heart makes it partake of the divine nature (2 Peter 1:4).

8 Pray for heart purity. Job propounds the question, 'Who can bring a clean thing out of an unclean?' (Job 14:4; 15:14). God can do it. Out of an impure heart he can produce grace. Pray that prayer of David, 'Create in me a clean heart, O God' (Psalm 51:10). Most men pray more for full purses than pure hearts. We should pray for heart-purity fervently. It is a matter we are most nearly concerned in. 'Without holiness no man shall see the Lord' (Hebrews 12:14). Our prayer must be with sighs and groans (Romans 8:23–26). There must not only be elocution but affection. Jacob wrestled in prayer (Genesis 32:24). Hannah poured out her soul (1 Samuel 1:15). We often pray so coldly (our petitions even freezing between our lips), as if we would teach God to deny. We pray as if we cared not whether God heard us or no. Oh Christian, be earnest with God for a pure heart. Lay your heart before the Lord and say, Lord, Thou who hast given me a heart, give me a pure heart. My heart is good for nothing as it is. It defiles everything it touches. Lord, I am not fit to live with this heart, for I cannot honour thee; nor to die with it, for I cannot see thee. Oh purge me with hyssop. Let Christ's blood be sprinkled upon me. Let the Holy Ghost descend upon me. 'Create in me a clean heart, O God.' Thou who biddest me give thee my heart, Lord, make my heart pure and thou shalt have it.

17 The blessed privilege of seeing God explained

They shall see God.
MATTHEW 5:8

The sight of God in this life and in the life to come

These words are linked to the former and they are a great incentive to heart-purity. The pure heart shall see the pure God. There is a double sight which the saints have of God.

1 In this life; that is, spiritually by the eye of faith. Faith sees God's glorious attributes in the glass of his Word. Faith beholds him showing forth himself through the lattice of his ordinances. Thus Moses saw him who was invisible (Hebrews 11:27). Believers see God's glory as it were veiled over. They behold his 'back parts' (Exodus 33:23).

2 In the life to come; and this glorious sight is meant in the text, 'They shall see God.' A pleasant prospect! This divines call 'the beatifical vision'. At that day the veil will be pulled off, and God will show himself in all his glory to the soul, as a king on a day of coronation shows himself in all his royalty and magnificence. This sight of God will be the heaven of heaven. We shall indeed have a sight of angels and that will be sweet, but the quintessence of happiness and the diamond in the ring will be this, 'We shall see God.' If the sun be absent it is night for all the stars. The angels are called 'stars' (Job 38:7). But it would be night in heaven if the Sun of Righteousness did not shine there. It is the king's presence makes the court. Absalom counted himself half-alive unless he might see the king's face (2 Samuel 14:32). 'Blessed are the pure in heart for they shall see God.' This sight of God in glory is, first, partly mental and intellectual. We shall see him with the eyes of our mind. If there be not an intellectual sight of God, how do the 'spirits of just men made perfect' see him? But second, it is partly corporeal; not that we can with bodily eyes behold the bright essence of God. Indeed the Anthromorphites[1] and Vorstians[2] erroneously held

---

[1] A name applied to all who attribute human characteristics to God.

[2] Followers of Konrad von Vorstius (1569–1622), who succeeded Arminius as professor of theology at Leyden. The Synod of Dort condemned his teachings as heretical.

that God had a visible shape and figure. As man was made in God's image so they thought that God was made in man's image; but God is a Spirit (John 4:24), and being a Spirit is invisible (1 Timothy 1:17). He cannot be beheld by bodily eyes. 'Whom no man hath seen nor can see' (1 Timothy 6:16). A sight of his glory would overwhelm us. This wine is too strong for our weak heads.

But when I say our seeing of God in heaven is corporeal, my meaning is that we shall with bodily eyes behold Jesus Christ, through whom the glory of God, his wisdom, holiness, and mercy, shall shine forth to the soul. Put a back of steel to the glass and you may see a face in it. So the human nature of Christ is as it were a back of steel through which we may see the glory of God (2 Corinthians 4:6). In this sense that scripture is to be understood, 'With these eyes shall I see God' (Job 19:26, 27).

Nine excellencies of the beatific vision

Now concerning this blessed sight of God, it is so sublime and sweet that I can but draw a dark shadow of it. We shall better understand it when we come to heaven. Only at present I shall lay down these nine aphorisms or maxims.

1 Our sight of God in heaven shall be a transparent sight. Here we see him 'through a glass darkly' (1 Corinthians 13:12). But through Christ we shall behold God in a very illustrious manner. God will unveil himself and show forth his glory so far as the soul is capable to receive. If Adam had not sinned yet it is probable he should never have had such a clear sight of God as the saints in glory shall have. 'We shall see him as he is' (1 John 3:2). Now we see him as he is not. He is not mutable, not mortal. There we shall see him 'as he is' in a very transparent manner. 'Then shall I know even as also I am known' (1 Corinthians 13:12), that is, 'clearly'. Does not God know us clearly and fully? Then shall the saints know him (according to their capacity) as they are known. As their love to God, so their sight of God shall be perfect.

2 This sight of God will be a transcendent sight. It will surpass in glory. Such glittering beams shall sparkle forth from the Lord Jesus as shall infinitely amaze and delight the eyes of the beholders. Imagine what a blessed sight it will be to see Christ wearing the robe of our human nature and to see that nature sitting in glory above the angels. If God be so beautiful here in his ordinances, Word, prayer, sacraments; if there be such excellency in him when we see him by the eye of faith through the prospective glass of a promise, O what will it be when we shall see

him 'face to face'! When Christ was transfigured on the mount he was full of glory (Matthew 17:2). If his transfiguration were so glorious, what will his inauguration be? What a glorious time will it be when (as it was said of Mordecai) we shall see him in the presence of his Father, 'arrayed in royal apparel, and with a great crown of gold upon his head' (Esther 8:15). There will be glory beyond hyperbole. If the sun were ten thousand times brighter than it is, it could not so much as shadow out this glory. In the heavenly horizon we behold beauty in its first magnitude and highest elevation. There we shall 'see the king in his glory' (Isaiah 33:17). All lights are but eclipses compared with that glorious vision. Apelles'[1] pencil would blot, angels' tongues would but disparage it.

3 This sight of God will be a transforming sight. 'We shall be like him' (1 John 3:2). The saints shall be changed into glory. As when the light springs into a dark room, the room may be said to be changed from what it was; the saints shall so see God as to be changed into his image (Psalm 17:15). Here God's people are blackened and sullied with infirmities, but in heaven they shall be as the dove covered with silver wings. They shall have some rays and beams of God's glory shining in them. As a man that rolls himself in the snow is of a snow-like whiteness; as the crystal, by having the sun shine on it, sparkles and looks like the sun; so the saints by beholding the brightness of God's glory shall have a tincture of that glory upon them. Not that they shall partake of God's very essence, for as the iron in the fire becomes fire, yet remains iron still, so the saints by beholding the lustre of God's majesty shall be glorious creatures but yet creatures still.

4 This sight of God will be a joyful sight: 'Thou shalt make me glad with the light of thy countenance' (Acts 2:28). After a sharp winter, how pleasant will it be to see the Sun of Righteousness displaying himself in all his glory! Does faith breed joy? 'In whom, though now ye see him not, yet believing, ye rejoice with joy unspeakable' (1 Peter 1:8). If the joy of faith be such, what will the joy of vision be? The sight of Christ will amaze the eye with wonder and ravish the heart with joy. If the face of a friend whom we entirely love so affects us and drives away sorrow, O how cheering will the sight of God be to the saints in heaven! Then indeed it may be said, 'Your heart shall rejoice' (John 16:22). And there are two things which will make the saints' vision of God in heaven joyful.

[1] The most famous of ancient Greek painters; he lived at the time of Alexander the Great (4th century B.C.).

(i) Through Jesus Christ the dread and terror of the divine essence shall be taken away. Majesty shall appear in God to preserve reverence, but withal majesty clothed with beauty and tempered with sweetness to excite joy in the saints. We shall see God as a friend, not as guilty Adam did, who was afraid, and hid himself (Genesis 3:10), but as Queen Esther looked upon King Ahasuerus holding forth the golden sceptre (Esther 5:2). Surely this sight of God will not be formidable but comfortable!

(ii) The saints shall not only have vision but fruition. They shall so see God as to enjoy him. Aquinas[1] and Scotus[2] dispute the case whether the 'formalis ratio', the very formality and essence of blessedness, be an act of the understanding or the will. Aquinas says that happiness consists in the intellectual part, 'the bare seeing of God'. Scotus says that happiness is an act of the will, the enjoying of God. But certainly true blessedness comprehends both. It lies partly in the understanding, by seeing the glory of God richly displayed, and partly in the will, by a sweet delicious taste of it and acquiescence of the soul in it. We shall so see God as to love him, and so love him as to be filled with him. The seeing of God implies fruition. 'Enter thou into the joy of thy Lord' (Matthew 25:21) – not only behold it but enter into it. 'In thy light we shall see light' (Psalm 36:9); there is vision. 'At thy right hand there are pleasures for evermore' (Psalm 16:11); there is fruition. So great is the joy which flows from the sight of God as will make the saints break forth into triumphant praises and hallelujahs.

5 This sight of God will be a satisfying sight. Cast three worlds into the heart and they will not fill it, but the sight of God satisfies. 'I shall be satisfied when I awake with thy likeness' (Psalm 17:15). Solomon says 'The eye is not satisfied with seeing' (Ecclesiastes 1:8). But there the eye will be satisfied with seeing. God and nothing but God can satisfy. The saints shall have their heads so full of knowledge and their hearts so full of joy that they shall find no want.

6 It will be an unweariable sight. Let a man see the rarest sight that is, he will soon be cloyed. When he comes into a garden and sees delicious walks, fair arbours, pleasant flowers, within a little while he grows weary; but it is not so in heaven. There is no surfeit. We shall never be weary of seeing God, for the divine essence being infinite, there shall be

[1] Thomas Aquinas, an Italian, the great Roman Catholic theologian of the 13th century, known as 'Doctor Angelicus'.
[2] Duns Scotus, a Scotsman and a theologian contemporary with Aquinas, and known as 'Doctor Subtilis'.

every moment new and fresh delights springing forth from God into the glorified soul. The soul shall not so desire God but it shall still be full. Nor shall it be so full but it shall still desire. So sweet will God be that the more the saints behold God the more they will be ravished with desire and delight.

7 It will be a beneficial sight. It will tend to the bettering and advantaging of the soul. Some colours, while they delight the eyes, hurt them. But this intuition and vision of God shall better the soul and tend to its infinite happiness. Eve's looking upon the tree of knowledge prejudiced her sight. She afterwards grew blind upon it, but the saints can receive no detriment from the inspection of glory. This sight will be beneficial. The soul will never be in its perfection till it comes to see God. This will be the crowning blessing.

8 This sight of God shall be perpetuated. Here we see objects awhile, and then our eyes grow dim and we need spectacles, but the saints shall always behold God. As there shall be no cloud upon God's face, so the saints shall have no mote in their eye. Their sight shall never grow dim, but they shall be to all eternity looking on God, that beautiful and beatifical object. O what a soul-ravishing sight will this be! God must make us able to bear it. We can no more endure a sight of glory than a sight of wrath. But the saints after this life shall have their capacities enlarged, and they shall be qualified and made fit to receive the penetrating beams of glory.

9 It will be a speedy sight. There are some who deny that the soul is immediately after death admitted to the sight of God, but I shall make good this assertion that the saints shall have an immediate transition and passage from death to glory. As soon as death has closed their eyes they shall see God. If the soul be not presently[1] after death translated to the beatifical vision, then what becomes of the soul in that juncture of time till the resurrection?

Does the soul go into torment? That cannot be, for the soul of a believer is a member of Christ's body mystical, and if this soul should go to hell a member of Christ might be for a time damned. But that is impossible.

Does the soul sleep in the body as some drowsily imagine? How then shall we make good sense of that scripture – 'We are willing rather to be absent from the body and to be present with the Lord (2 Corinthians

[1] Immediately.

5:8)? If the soul at death be absent from the body then it cannot sleep in the body.

Does the soul die? So the Lucianists [1] held that the soul was mortal and died with the body, but as Scaliger [2] observes, it is impossible that the soul being of a spiritual uncompounded nature should be subject to corruptibility. Such as say the soul dies, I would demand of them wherein the soul of a man differs at death from the soul of a brute? By all which it appears that the soul of a believer after death goes immediately to God. 'This day shalt thou be with me in paradise' (Luke 23:43). That word 'with me' shows clearly that the thief on the cross was translated to heaven. For there Christ was (Ephesians 4:10). And the word 'this day' shows that the thief on the cross had an immediate passage from the cross to paradise, so that the souls of believers have a speedy vision of God after death. It is but winking, and they shall see God.

It is the sinner's misery that he shall not see God

See the misery of an impure sinner. He shall not be admitted to the sight of God. 'The pure in heart' only shall see God. Such as live in sin, whose souls are dyed black with the filth of hell, they shall never come where God is. They shall have an affrighting vision of God, but not a beatifical vision. They shall see the flaming sword and the burning lake, but not the mercy-seat. God in Scripture is sometimes called a 'consuming fire', sometimes the 'Father of lights'. The wicked shall feel the fire but not see the light. Impure souls shall be covered with shame and darkness as with a mantle, and shall never see the king's face. They who would not see God in his ordinances shall not see him in his glory.

We must labour to be rightly qualified for this vision

Is there such a blessed privilege after this life? Then let me persuade all who hear me this day:

1 To get into Christ. We cannot come to God but by Christ. Moses when he was in the rock saw God (Exodus 33:32). In this blessed rock, Christ, we shall see God.

2 To be purified persons. It is only the pure in heart who shall see God. It is only a clear eye can behold a bright transparent object. Those only

[1] Followers of a pagan writer of the 2nd century A.D.
[2] A French Calvinistic theologian (1540–1609) who finally settled at Leyden University.

who have their hearts cleansed from sin can have this blessed sight of God. Sin is such a cloud as, if it be not removed, will for ever hinder us from seeing the Sun of Righteousness. Christian, have you upon your heart 'holiness to the Lord'? Then you shall see God. There are many, says Augustine, could be content to go to heaven, but they are loath to take the way that leads thither. They would have the glorious vision but neglect the gracious union.

There are several sorts of eyes which shall never see God – the ignorant eye, the unchaste eye, the scornful eye, the malicious eye, the covetous eye. If you would see God when you die, you must be purified persons while you live: 'We shall see him as he is; and every man that hath this hope in him, purifieth himself' (1 John 3 : 2, 3).

A cordial for the pure in heart

Let me turn myself to the pure in heart.

1 Stand amazed at this privilege, that you who are worms crept out of the dust should be admitted to the blessed sight of God to all eternity. It was Moses' prayer, 'I beseech thee, show me thy glory' (Exodus 33 : 18). The saints shall behold God's glory. The pure in heart shall have the same blessedness that God himself has. For what is the blessedness of God but the contemplating his own infinite beauty!

2 Begin your sight of God here. Let the eye of your faith be still upon God. Moses by faith 'saw him who is invisible' (Hebrews 11 : 27). Often look upon him with believing eyes, whom you hope to see with glorified eyes. 'Mine eyes are ever towards the Lord' (Psalm 25 : 15). While others are looking towards the earth as if they would fetch all their comforts thence, let us look up to heaven. There is the best prospect. The sight of God by faith would let in much joy to the soul. 'Though now ye see him not, yet believing, ye rejoice with joy unspeakable' (1 Peter 1 : 8).

3 Let this be as cordial-water to revive the pure in heart. Be comforted with this, you shall shortly see God. The godly have many sights here that they would not see. They see a body of death; they see the sword unsheathed; they see rebellion wearing the mask of religion; they see the white devil. These sights occasion sorrow; but there is a blessed sight a-coming, 'They shall see God.' And in him are all sparkling beauties and ravishing joys to be found.

4 Be not discouraged at sufferings. All the hurt that affliction and death can do is to give you a sight of God. As one said to his fellow-martyr,

'One half hour in glory will make us forget our pain.' The sun arising, all the dark shadows of the night fly away. When the pleasant beams of God's countenance shall begin to shine upon the soul in heaven, then sorrows and sufferings shall be no more. 'The dark shadows of the night' shall fly away. The thoughts of this beatifical vision should carry a Christian full sail with joy through the waters of affliction. This made Job so willing to embrace death: 'I know that my redeemer liveth, and though worms destroy this body, yet in my flesh shall I see God' (Job 19:25, 26).

18 Concerning peaceableness

Blessed are the peace-makers.
MATTHEW 5:9

This is the seventh step of the golden ladder which leads to blessedness. The name of peace is sweet, and the work of peace is a blessed work. 'Blessed are the peace-makers.'

Observe the connection. The Scripture links these two together, pureness of heart and peaceableness of spirit. 'The wisdom from above is first pure, then peaceable' (James 3:17). 'Follow peace and holiness' (Hebrews 12:14). And here Christ joins them together – 'pure in heart' and 'peace-makers', as if there could be no purity where there is not a study of peace. That religion is suspicious which is full of faction and discord.

In the words there are three parts:

1. A duty implied, viz. peaceable-mindedness.
2. A duty expressed – to be peace-makers.
3. A title of honour bestowed – 'They shall be called the children of God.'

1 The duty implied, 'peaceable-mindedness'. For before men can make peace among others, they must be of peaceable spirits themselves. Before they can be promoters of peace, they must be lovers of peace.

Christians must be peaceable-minded. This peaceableness of spirit is the beauty of a saint. It is a jewel of great price: 'The ornament of a quiet spirit which is in the sight of God of great price' (1 Peter 3:4). The saints are Christ's sheep (John 10:27). The sheep is a peaceable creature. They are Christ's doves (Canticles 2:14), therefore they must be without gall. It becomes not Christians to be Ishmaels but Solomons. Though they must be lions for courage, yet lambs for peaceableness. God was not in the earthquake, nor in the fire, but in the 'still small voice' (1 Kings 19:12). God is not in the rough fiery spirit but in the peaceable spirit.

A four-fold peace

There is a four-fold peace that we must study and cherish.

(i) An Oeconomical [1] peace, peace in families. It is called 'the bond of peace' (Ephesians 4:3). Without this all drops in pieces. Peace is a girdle that ties together members in a family. It is a golden clasp that knits them together that they do not fall in pieces. We should endeavour that our houses should be 'houses of peace'. It is not fairness of rooms makes a house pleasant, but peaceableness of dispositions. There can be no comfortableness in our dwellings till peace be entertained as an inmate into our houses.

(ii) There is a parochial peace, when there is a sweet harmony, a tuning and chiming together of affections in a parish; when all draw one way and, as the apostle says, are 'perfectly joined together in the same mind' (1 Corinthians 1:10). One jarring string brings all the music out of tune. One bad member in a parish endangers the whole. 'Be at peace among yourselves' (1 Thessalonians 5:13). It is little comfort to have our houses joined together if our hearts be asunder. A geometrical union will do little good without a moral union.

(iii) There is a political peace, peace in city and country. This is the fairest flower of a prince's crown. Peace is the best blessing of a nation. It is well with bees when there is a noise; but it is best with Christians when (as in the building of the Temple) there is no noise of hammer heard. Peace brings plenty along with it. How many miles would some go on pilgrimage to purchase this peace! Therefore the Greeks made peace to be the nurse of Pluto, the god of wealth. Political plants thrive best in the sunshine of peace. 'He maketh peace in thy borders, and filleth thee with the finest of the wheat' (Psalm 147:14). 'Peace makes all things flourish.'

The ancients made the harp the emblem of peace. How sweet would the sounding of this harp be after the roaring of the cannon! All should study to promote this political peace. The godly man when he dies 'enters into peace' (Isaiah 57:2). But while he lives peace must enter into him.

(iv) There is an ecclesiastical peace, a church-peace, when there is unity and verity in the church of God. Never does religion flourish more than when her children spread themselves as olive-plants round about her table. Unity in faith and discipline is a mercy we cannot prize enough.

[1] A word formed from Greek 'oikos', a house.

This is that which God has promised (Jeremiah 32:39) and which we should pursue (Zechariah 8:18–23). Saint Ambrose says of Theodosius the Emperor,[1] that when he lay sick he took more care for the Church's peace than for his own recovery.

Two reasons for peaceable-mindedness

The reasons why we should be peaceable-minded are two:

First, we are called to peace (1 Corinthians 7:15). God never called any man to division. That is a reason why we should not be given to strife, because we have no call for it. But God has called us to peace.

Second, it is the nature of grace to change the heart and make it peaceable. By nature we are of a fierce cruel disposition. When God cursed the ground for man's sake, the curse was that it should bring forth 'thorns and thistles' (Genesis 3:18). The heart of man naturally lies under this curse. It brings forth nothing but the thistles of strife and contention. But when grace comes into the heart it makes it peaceable. It infuses a sweet, loving disposition. It smooths and polishes the most knotty piece. It files off the ruggedness in men's spirits. Grace turns the vulture into a dove, the briar into a myrtle tree (Isaiah 55:13), the lion-like fierceness into a lamb-like gentleness. 'The wolf also shall dwell with the lamb and the leopard shall lie down with the kid . . .' (Isaiah 11:6–9). It is spoken of the power which the gospel shall have upon men's hearts; it shall make such a metamorphosis that those who before were full of rage and antipathy shall now be made peaceable and gentle 'The leopard shall lie down with the kid.'

Peaceable-mindedness a saint's character

It shows us the character of a true saint. He is given to peace. He is the keeper of the peace. He is 'a son of peace'.

Caution: Not but that a man may be of a peaceable spirit, yet seek to recover that which is his due. If peace has been otherwise sought and cannot be attained, a man may go to law and yet be a peaceable man. It is with going to law as it is with going to war, when the rights of a nation are invaded (as 2 Chronicles 20:2, 3), and peace can be purchased by no other means than war; here it is lawful to beat the plough-share into a sword. So when there is no other way of recovering one's right but by going to law, a man may commence a suit in law yet be of a peaceable spirit. Going to law (in this case) is not so much striving

[1] See p. 163, fn 2.

with another as contending for a man's own. It is not to do another wrong, but to do himself right. It is a desire rather of equity than victory. I say as the apostle, 'the law is good if a man use it lawfully' (1 Timothy 1:8).

You may ask, Is all peace to be sought; how far is peace lawful? I answer, Peace with men must have this double limitation:

1 The peace a godly man seeks is not to have a league of amity with sinners. Though we are to be at peace with their persons, yet we are to have war with their sins. We are to have peace with their persons as they are made in God's image, but to have war with their sins as they have made themselves in the devil's image. David was for peace (Psalm 120:7), but he would not sit on the ale-bench with sinners (Psalm 26:4, 5). Grace teaches good nature. We are to be civil to the worst, but not twist into a cord of friendship. That were to be 'brethren in iniquity'. 'Have no fellowship with the unfruitful works of darkness' (Ephesians 5:11). Jehoshaphat (though a good man) was blamed for this: 'Shouldest thou help the ungodly and love them that hate the Lord?' (2 Chronicles 19:2). The fault was not that he entertained civil peace with Ahab, but that he had a league of friendship and was assistant to Ahab when he went contrary to God. 'Therefore was wrath upon Jehoshaphat from before the Lord' (verse 2). We must not so far have peace with others as to endanger ourselves. If a man has the plague, we will be helpful to him and send him our best recipes, but we are careful not to have too much of his company or suck in his infectious breath. So we may be peaceable towards all, nay helpful. Pray for them, counsel them, relieve them, but let us take heed of too much familiarity, lest we suck in their infection. In short we must so make peace with men that we do not break our peace with conscience. 'Follow peace and holiness' (Hebrews 12:14). We must not purchase peace with the loss of holiness.

2 We must not so seek peace with others as to wrong truth. 'Buy the truth and sell it not' (Proverbs 23:23). Peace must not be bought with the sale of truth. Truth is the ground of faith, the rule of manners. Truth is the most orient[1] gem of the churches' crown. Truth is a 'deposit' or charge that God has entrusted us with. We trust God with our souls. He trusts us with his truths. We must not let any of God's truths fall to the ground. Luther says, It is better that the heavens fall than that one crumb of truth perish. The least filings of this gold are

[1] See p. 40 fn.

precious. We must not so seek the flower of peace as to lose the pearl of truth.

Some say, let us unite, but we ought not to unite with error. 'What communion has light with darkness?' (2 Corinthians 6:14). There are many would have peace with the destroying of truth; peace with Arminian, Socinian, Anti-scripturist. This is a peace of the devil's making. Cursed be that peace which makes war with the Prince of peace. Though we must be peaceable, yet we are bid to 'contend for the faith' (Jude 3). We must not be so in love with the golden crown of peace as to pluck off the jewels of truth. Rather let peace go than truth. The martyrs would rather lose their lives than let go the truth.

A reproof for such as are unpeaceable

If Christians must be peaceable-minded, what shall we say to those who are given to strife and contention? to those who, like flax or gunpowder, if they be but touched, are all on fire? How far is this from the spirit of the gospel! It is made the note of the wicked. 'They are like the troubled sea' (Isaiah 57:20). There is no rest or quietness in their spirits, but they are continually casting forth the foam of passion and fury. We may with Strigelius [1] wish even to die to be freed from the bitter strifes which are among us. There are too many like the salamander who live in the fire of broils and contentions. 'If ye have bitter envying and strife, this wisdom descends not from above, but is devilish' (James 3:14, 15). The lustful man is brutish; the wrathful man is devilish. Everyone is afraid to dwell in an house which is haunted with evil spirits, yet how little afraid are men of their own hearts, which are haunted with the evil spirit of wrath and implacableness.

And then, which is much to be laid to heart, there are the divisions of God's people. God's own tribes go to war. In Tertullian's time it was said, See how the Christians love one another. But now it may be said, See how the Christians snarl one at another, 'They are comparable to ferocious bears.' Wicked men agree together, when those who pretend to be led by higher principles are full of animosities and heartburnings. Was it not sad to see Herod and Pilate uniting, and to see Paul and Barnabas falling out? (Acts 15:39). When the disciples called for fire from heaven, 'Ye know not (saith Christ) what manner of spirit ye are of' (Luke 9:55). As if the Lord had said, This fire you call for is not zeal, but is the wild-fire of your own passions. This spirit of yours

[1] A Lutheran theologian (1524–69).

does not suit with the Master you serve, the Prince of peace, nor with the work I am sending you about, which is an embassage of peace. It is Satan who kindles the fire of contention in men's hearts and then stands and warms himself at the fire. When boisterous winds are up, we are accustomed to talk of conjurors. Sure I am, when men's spirits begin to bluster and storm, the devil has conjured up these winds. Discords and animosities among Christians bring their godliness much into question, for 'the wisdom which is from above is peaceable, gentle, and easy to be entreated' (James 3 : 17).

An exhortation to peaceable-mindedness (under 11 heads)

Be of a peaceable disposition. 'If it be possible, as much as lieth in you, live peaceably with all men' (Romans 12 : 18). The curtains of the tabernacle were to be looped together (Exodus 26 : 3, 4). So should the hearts of Christians be looped together in peace and unity. That I may persuade to peaceable-mindedness, let me speak both to reason and conscience.

1 A peaceable spirit seems to be agreeable to the natural frame and constitution. Man by nature seems to be a peaceable creature, fitter to handle the plough than the sword. Other creatures are naturally armed with some kind of weapon wherewith they are able to revenge themselves. The lion has his paw, the boar his tusk, the bee his sting. Only man has none of these weapons. He comes naked and unarmed into the world as if God would have him a peaceable creature. 'White-robed peace is becoming to men, fierce anger is fitting for wild beasts.' Man has his reason given him that he should live amiably and peaceably.

2 A peaceable spirit is honourable. 'It is an honour for a man to cease from strife' (Proverbs 20 : 3). We think it a brave thing to give way to strife and let loose the reins to our passions. Oh no, 'it is an honour to cease from strife'. Noble spirits are such lovers of peace that they need not be bound to the peace. It is the bramble that rends and tears whatever is near it. The cedar and fig-tree, those more noble plants, grow pleasantly and peaceably. Peaceableness is the ensign and ornament of a noble mind.

3 To be of a peaceable spirit is highly prudential. 'The wisdom from above is peaceable' (James 3 : 17). A wise man will not meddle with strife. It is like putting one's finger into a hornets' nest; or to use Solomon's similitude, 'The beginning of strife is as when one letteth

out water' (Proverbs 17 : 14). To set out the folly of strife, it is as letting out of water in two respects:

(i) When water begins to be let out there is no end of it. So there is no end of strife when once begun.

(ii) The letting out of water is dangerous. If a man should break down a bank and let in an arm of the sea, the water might overflow his fields and drown him in the flood. So is he that intermeddles with strife. He may mischief himself and open such a sluice as may engulf and swallow him up. True wisdom espouses peace. A prudent man will keep off from the briars as much as he can.

4 To be of a peaceable spirit brings peace along with it. A contentious person vexes himself and eclipses his own comfort. He is like the bird that beats itself against the cage. 'He troubles his own flesh' (Proverbs 11 : 17). He is just like one that pares off the sweet of the apple and eats nothing but the core. So a quarrelsome man pares off all the comfort of his life and feeds only upon the bitter core of disquiet. He is a self-tormentor. The wicked are compared to a 'troubled sea' (Isaiah 57 : 20). And it follows 'there is no peace to the wicked' (verse 21). The Septuagint[1] renders it 'There is no joy to the wicked.' Froward spirits do not enjoy what they possess, but peaceableness of spirit brings the sweet music of peace along with it. It makes a calm and harmony in the soul. Therefore the psalmist says, it is not only good, but pleasant, to live together in unity (Psalm 133 : 1).

5 A peaceable disposition is a God-like disposition.

God the Father is called 'the God of peace' (Hebrews 13 : 20). Mercy and peace are about his throne. He signs the articles of peace and sends the ambassadors of peace to publish them (2 Corinthians 5 : 20).

God the Son is called 'the Prince of peace' (Isaiah 9 : 6). His name is Emmanuel, God with us, a name of peace. His office is to be a mediator of peace (1 Timothy 2 : 5). He came into the world with a song of peace; the angels sang it: 'Peace on earth' (Luke 2 : 14). He went out of the world with a legacy of peace: 'Peace I leave with you, my peace I give unto you' (John 14 : 27).

God the Holy Ghost is a Spirit of peace. He is the Comforter. He seals up peace (2 Corinthians 1 : 22). This blessed dove brings the olive-branch of peace in his mouth. Now a peaceable disposition evidences something of God in a man. Therefore God loves to dwell there. 'In

[1] The Version of the Seventy: the Old Testament translated into Greek in the 3rd century B.C.

Salem is God's tabernacle' (Psalm 76:2). Salem signifies 'peace'. God dwells in a peaceable spirit.

6 Christ's earnest prayer was for peace. He prayed that his people might be one (John 17:11, 21, 23), that they might be of one mind and heart. And observe the argument Christ uses in prayer [it is good to use arguments in prayer. They are as the feathers to the arrow, which make it fly swifter, and pierce deeper. Affections in prayer are as the fire in the gun; arguments in prayer are as the bullet]. The argument Christ urges to his Father is 'that they may be one, even as we are one' (verse 22). There was never any discord between the Father and Christ. Though God parted with Christ out of his bosom, yet not out of his heart. There was ever dearness and oneness between them. Now Christ prays that, as he and his Father were one, so his people might be all one in peace and concord. Did Christ pray so earnestly for peace, and shall not we endeavour what in us lies to fulfil Christ's prayer? How do we think Christ will hear our prayer if we cross his?

7 Christ not only prayed for peace, but bled for it. 'Having made peace through the blood of his cross' (Colossians 1:20). Peace of all kinds! He died not only to make peace between God and man, but between man and man. Christ suffered on the cross that he might cement Christians together with his blood. As he prayed for peace, so he paid for peace. Christ was himself bound to bring us into the 'bond of peace'.

8 Strife and contention hinder the growth of grace. Can good seed grow in a ground where there is nothing but thorns and briars to be seen? 'The thorns choked the seed' (Matthew 13:7). When the heart is, as it were, stuck with thorns and is ever tearing and rending, can the seed of grace ever grow there? Historians report of the Isle of Patmos that the natural soil of it is such that nothing will grow upon that earth. A froward heart is like the Isle of Patmos. Nothing of grace will grow there till God changes the soil and makes it peaceable. How can faith grow in an unpeaceable heart? For 'faith works by love'. Impossible it is that he should bring forth the sweet fruits of the Spirit who is 'in the gall of bitterness'. If a man has received poison into his body, the most excellent food will not nourish till he takes some antidote to expel that poison. Many come to the ordinances with seeming zeal, but being poisoned with wrath and animosity they receive no spiritual nourishment. Christ's body mystical 'edifieth itself in love' (Ephesians 4:16). There may be praying and hearing, but no spiritual concoction, no edifying of the body of Christ without love and peace.

9 Peaceableness among Christians is a powerful loadstone to draw the world to receive Christ. Not only gifts and miracles and preaching may persuade men to embrace the truth of the gospel, but peace and unity among the professors of it. When as there is one God and one faith, so there is one heart among Christians, this is as cummin seed, which makes the doves flock to the windows. The temple was adorned with 'goodly stones' (Luke 21:5). This makes Christ's spiritual temple look beautiful, and the stones of it appear goodly, when they are cemented together in peace and unity.

10 Unpeaceableness of spirit is to make Christians turn heathens. It is the sin of the heathens to be 'implacable' (Romans 1:31). They cannot be pacified. Their hearts are like adamant. No oil can supple them; no fire can melt them. It is a heathenish thing to be so fierce and violent, as if with Romulus [1] men had sucked the milk of wolves.

11 To add yet more weight to the exhortation, it is the mind of Christ that we should live in peace. 'Have peace one with another' (Mark 9:50). Shall we not be at peace for Christ's sake? If we ought to lay down our life for Christ's sake, shall we not lay down our strife for his sake?

To conclude: If we will neither be under counsels nor commands, but still feed the peccant humour, nourishing in ourselves a spirit of dissension and unpeaceableness, Jesus Christ will never come near us. The people of God are said to be his house: 'Whose house are we ...' (Hebrews 3:6). When the hearts of Christians are a spiritual house, adorned with the furniture of peace, then they are fit for the Prince of peace to inhabit. But when this pleasant furniture is wanting and instead of it nothing but strife and debate, Christ will not own it for his house, nor will he grace it with his presence. Who will dwell in an house which is smoky and all on fire?

Some helps to peaceable-mindedness

How shall we attain to peaceableness?

1 Take heed of those things which will hinder it. There are several impediments of peace which we must beware of, and they are either outward or inward.

(i) Outward: as whisperers (Romans 1:29). There are some who will

[1] Traditionally regarded as one of the founders of Rome: he is said to have been suckled by a wolf when a babe.

be buzzing things in our ears purposely to exasperate and provoke. Among these we may rank tale-bearers (Leviticus 19:16). The tale-bearer carries reports up and down. The devil sends his letters by this post. The tale-bearer is an incendiary. He blows the coals of contention. Do you hear (says he) what such an one says of you? Will you put up with such a wrong? Will you suffer yourself to be so abused? Thus does he, by throwing in his fireballs, foment differences and set men together by the ears. We are commanded indeed to provoke one another to love (Hebrews 10:24), but nowhere to provoke to anger. We should stop our ears to such persons as are known to come on the devil's errand.

2 Take heed of inward lets [1] to peace; for example:

(i) Self-love: 'Men shall be lovers of themselves' (2 Timothy 3:2). And it follows they shall be 'fierce' (verse 3). The setting up of this idol of self has caused so many law-suits, plunders, massacres in the world. 'All seek their own' (Philippians 2:21). Nay, it were well if they would seek but their own. Self-love angles away the estates of others either by force or fraud. Self-love sets up monopolies and enclosures. It is a bird of prey which lives upon rapine. Self-love cuts asunder the bond of peace. Lay aside self. The heathens could say 'We are not born for ourselves alone'.

(ii) Pride: 'He that is of a proud heart stirreth up strife' (Proverbs 28:25). Pride and contention, like Hippocrates' [2] twins, are both born at once. A proud man thinks himself better than others and will contend for superiority. 'Diotrephes, who loveth to have the pre-eminence' (3 John 9). A proud man would have all strike sail to him. Because Mordecai would not give Haman the cap and knee, he gets a bloody warrant signed for the death of all the Jews (Esther 3:9). What made all the strife between Pompey and Caesar but pride? Their spirits were too high to yield one to another. When this wind of pride gets into a man's heart, it causes sad earthquakes of division. The poets feign that when Pandora's [3] box was broken open it filled the world with diseases. When Adam's pride had broken the box of original righteousness it has ever since filled the world with debates and dissensions. Let us shake off this viper of pride. Humility solders Christians together in peace.

[1] Hindrances.
[2] Hippocrates the 'father of medicine' (born in Greece about 460 B.C.).
[3] Pandora (Greek: 'the All-gifted'), in Greek mythology, the first woman. Jupiter gave her a box which she was to present to the man who married her. When he opened it, all the evils flew forth.

(iii) Envy; envy stirreth up strife. The apostle has linked them together. 'Envy, strife' (1 Timothy 6:4). Envy cannot endure a superior. This made the plebeian faction so strong among the Romans; they envied their superiors. An envious man seeing another to have a fuller crop, a better trade, is ready to pick a quarrel with him. 'Who can stand before envy?' (Proverbs 27:4). Envy is a vermin that lives on blood. Take heed of it. Peace will not dwell with this inmate.

(iv) Credulity. 'The simple believeth every word' (Proverbs 14:15). A credulous man is akin to a fool. He believes all that is told him and this often creates differences. As it is a sin to be a tale-bearer, so it is a folly to be a tale-believer. A wise man will not take a report at the first bound, but will sift and examine it before he gives credit to it.

2 Let us labour for those things which will maintain and cherish peace.

(i) As faith; faith and peace keep house together. Faith believes the Word of God. The Word says, 'Live in peace' (2 Corinthians 13:11). And as soon as faith sees the king of heaven's warrant, it obeys. Faith persuades the soul that God is at peace, and it is impossible to believe this and live in variance. Nourish faith. Faith knits us to God in love and to our brethren in peace.

(ii) Christian communion. There should not be too much strangeness among Christians. The primitive saints had their 'agapai' that is, love-feasts. The apostle exhorting to peace brings this as an expedient: 'Be ye kind one to another' (Ephesians 4:32).

(iii) Do not look upon the failings of others, but upon their graces. There is no perfection here. We read of the 'spots of God's children' (Deuteronomy 32:5). The most golden Christians are some grains too light. Oh, let us not so quarrel with the infirmities of others as to pass by their virtues. If in some things they fail, in other things they excel. It is the manner of the world to look more upon the sun in an eclipse than when it shines in its full lustre.

(iv) Pray to God that he will send down the Spirit of peace into our hearts. We should not as vultures prey one upon another, but pray one for another. Pray that God will quench the fire of contention and kindle the fire of compassion in our hearts one to another. So much for the first thing in the text implied, that Christians should be peaceable-minded. I proceed to the second thing expressed, that they should be peace-makers.

All Christians must be peace-makers

All good Christians ought to be peace-makers; they should not only be peaceable themselves, but make others to be at peace. As in the body when a joint is out we set it again, so it should be in the body politic. When a garment is rent we sew it together again. When others are rent asunder in their affections we should with a spirit of meekness sew them together again. Had we this excellent skill we might glue and unite dissenting spirits. I confess it is often a thankless office to go about to reconcile differences (Acts 7:27). Handle a briar never so gently, it will go near to scratch. He that goes to interpose between two fencers many times receives the blow. But this duty, though it may lack success as from men, yet it shall not want a blessing from God. 'Blessed are the peace-makers.' O how happy were England if it had more peace-makers! Abraham was a peace-maker (Genesis 13:8). Moses was a peace-maker (Exodus 2:13), and that ever-to-be-honoured emperor Constantine, when he called the bishops together at that first Council of Nicaea [1] to end church controversies, they having instead of that prepared bitter invectives and accusations one against another, Constantine took their papers and rent them, gravely exhorting them to peace and unanimity.

It sharply reproves them that are so far from being peace-makers that they are peace-breakers. If 'blessed are the peace-makers', then cursed are the peace-breakers. If peace-makers are the children of God, then peace-breakers are the children of the devil. Heretics destroy the truth of the church by error, and schismatics destroy the peace of it by division. The apostle sets a brand upon such. 'Mark those which cause divisions and avoid them' (Romans 16:17). Have no more to do with them than with witches or murderers. The devil was the first peace-breaker. He divided man from God. He, like Phaeton,[2] set all on fire. There are too many make-bates in England whose sweetest music is in discord, who never unite but to divide. As it was said of one of the Arian emperors, he procured unity to prevent peace. How many in our days may be compared to Samson's fox-tails, which were tied together only to set the Philistines' corn on fire! (Judges 15:4, 5). Sec-

---

[1] A.D. 325.
[2] In classical mythology, the son of Phoebus (the Sun) who upset the sun-chariot and caused the Tropics to be unduly scorched with heat.

taries unite to set the church's peace on fire. These are the persons God's soul hates, 'Sowers of discord among brethren' (Proverbs 6:19). These are the children of a curse: 'Cursed be he that smiteth his neighbour secretly' (Deuteronomy 27:24), that is, who backbites and so sets one friend against another. If there be a devil in man's shape, it is the incendiary.

The text exhorts to two things:

1 Let us take up a bitter lamentation for the divisions of England. The wild beast has broken down the hedge of our peace. We are like a house falling to ruin, if the Lord does not mercifully under-prop and shore us up. None of the sons of England comfort her, but rather rake in her bowels. Will not an ingenuous [1] child grieve to see his mother rent and torn in pieces? It is reported of Cato [2] that from the time the civil wars began in Rome between Caesar and Pompey, he was never seen to laugh or shave his beard or cut his hair. That our hearts may be sadly affected with these our church and state divisions let us consider the mischief of divisions.

(i) They are a prognostic of much evil to a nation. Here that rule in philosophy holds true, 'All division tends to destruction.' When the veil of the temple was rent in pieces, it was a sad omen and fore-runner of the destruction of the temple. The rending the veil of the church's peace betokens the ruin of it. Josephus [3] observes that the city of Jerusalem when it was besieged by Titus Vespasian [4] had three great factions in it, which destroyed more than the enemy and was the occasion of the taking it. How fatal intestine divisions have been to this land! Camden [5] and other learned writers relate how our discerptions [6] and mutinies have been the scaling ladder by which the Romans and the Normans have formerly gotten into the nation. How is the bond of peace broken! We have so many schisms in the body and are run into so many particular churches that God may justly unchurch us, as he did Asia.

(ii) It may afflict us to see the garment of the church's peace rent, be-

---

[1] By an obvious mistake, the 1660 original reads 'ingenious'.
[2] A famous Stoic (1st century B.C.) noted for his truthfulness and self-discipline. He was the great-grandson of Cato the Censor (see p. 184 fn. 2).
[3] Jewish historian (c. A.D. 37–100).
[4] The Roman (son of the Emperor Vespasian) who destroyed Jerusalem in A.D. 70.
[5] William Camden, noted antiquary (d. 1623). His famous work is entitled 'Britannia'.
[6] Pullings apart, severances.

cause divisions bring an opprobrium and scandal upon religion. These make the ways of God evil spoken of, as if religion were the fomenter of strife and sedition. Julian,[1] in his invective against the Christians, said that they lived together as tigers rending and devouring one another. And shall we make good Julian's words? It is unseemly to see Christ's doves fighting; to see his lily become a bramble. Alexander Severus,[2] seeing two Christians contending, commanded them that they should not take the name of Christians any longer upon them, for (says he) you dishonour your Master Christ. Let men either lay down their contentions, or lay off the coat of their profession.

(iii) Divisions obstruct the progress of piety. The gospel seldom thrives where the apple of strife grows. The building of God's spiritual temple is hindered by the confusion of tongues. Division eats as a worm and destroys the 'peaceable fruits of righteousness' (Hebrews 12:11). In the Church of Corinth, when they began to divide into parties, one was for Paul, another for Apollos; there were but few for Christ. Confident I am that England's divisions have made many turn atheists.

2 Let us labour to heal differences and be repairers of breaches: 'Blessed are the peace-makers.' Jesus Christ was a great peace-maker. He took a long journey from heaven to earth to make peace. Peace and unity is a great means for the corroborating and strengthening the church of God. The saints are compared to living stones, built up for a spiritual house (1 Peter 2:5). You know the stones in an arch or fabric help to preserve and bear up one another. If the stones be loosened and drop out, all the fabric falls in pieces. When the Christians in the primitive church were of one heart (Acts 4:32) what a supporting was this! How did they counsel, comfort, build up one another in their holy faith! We see while the members of the body are united, so long they do adminster help and nourishment one to another; but if they be divided and broken off, they are no way useful, but the body languishes. Therefore let us endeavour to be peace-makers. The church's unity tends much to her stability.

Peace makes the church of God on earth in some measure like the church in heaven. The cherubims (representing the angels) are set out with their faces 'looking one upon another' to show their peace and unity. There are no jarrings or discords among the heavenly spirits. One angel is not of an opinion differing from another. Though they have different orders, they are not of different spirits. They are sera-

[1] Julian the Apostate (see p. 155 fn. 2).
[2] Better known as Marcus Aurelius (Roman Emperor of 3rd century).

phims, therefore burn, not in heat of contention, but love. The angels serve God not only with pure hearts, but united hearts. By an harmonious peace we might resemble the church triumphant.

He that sows peace shall reap peace. 'To the counsellors of peace is joy' (Proverbs 12:20). The peace-maker shall have peace with God, peace in his own bosom, and that is the sweetest music which is made in a man's own breast. He shall have peace with others. The hearts of all shall be united to him. All shall honour him. He shall be called 'the repairer of the breach' (Isaiah 58:12). To conclude, the peace-maker shall die in peace. He shall carry a good conscience with him and leave a good name behind him. So I have done with the first part of the text 'Blessed are the peace-makers'. I proceed to the next part.

19 *They shall be called the children of God*

They shall be called the children of God.
MATTHEW 5:9

In these words the glorious privilege of the saints is set down. Those who have made their peace with God and labour to make peace among brethren, this is the great honour conferred upon them, 'They shall be called the children of God.'

'They shall be (called)', that is, they shall be so reputed and esteemed of God. God never miscalls anything. He does not call them children which are no children. 'Thou shalt be called the prophet of the Highest' (Luke 1:76), that is, thou shalt be so. They shall be 'called the children of God', that is, they shall be accounted and admitted for children.

The proposition resulting is this: that peace-makers are the children of the most High. God is said in Scripture to have many children:

By *eternal generation*. So only Christ is the natural Son of his Father. 'Thou art my Son: this day have I begotten thee' (Psalm 2:7).

By *creation*. So the angels are the sons of God. 'When the morning stars sang together and all the sons of God shouted for joy' (Job 38:7).

By *participation of dignity*. So king and rulers are said to be children of the high God. 'I have said, ye are gods, and all of you are children of the most High' (Psalm 82:6).

By *visible profession*. So God has many children. Hypocrites forge a title of sonship. 'The sons of God saw the daughters of men that they were fair' (Genesis 6:2).

By *real sanctification*. So all the faithful are peculiarly and eminently the children of God.

That I may illustrate and amplify this, and that believers may suck much sweetness out of this gospel-flower, I shall discuss and demonstrate these seven particulars:

1 That naturally we are not the children of God.
2 What it is to be the children of God.
3 How we come to be made children.

4 The signs of God's children.
5 The love of God in making us children.
6 The honour of God's children.
7 The privileges of God's children.

By nature we are not children of God

Naturally we are not the children of God. As Jerome says, we are not born God's children but made so. By nature we are strangers to God, swine not sons (2 Peter 2:22). Will a man settle his estate upon his swine? He will give them his acorns, not his jewels. By nature we have the devil for our father: 'Ye are of your father the devil (John 8:44). A wicked man may search the records of hell for his pedigree.

Children of God are made such by adoption and infusion of grace

What it is to be the children of God. This childship consists in two things. Adoption; infusion of grace.

Childship consists in adoption: 'That we might receive the adoption of sons' (Galatians 4:5).

Wherein does the true nature of adoption consist?

In three things:

(i) A transition or translation from one family to another. He that is adopted is taken out of the old family of the devil and hell (Ephesians 2:2, 3) to which he was heir apparent, and is made of the family of heaven, of a noble family (Ephesians 2:19). God is his Father, Christ is his elder-brother, the saints co-heir, the angels fellow-servants in that family.

(ii) Adoption consists in an immunity and disobligement from all the laws of the former family. 'Forget also thy father's house' (Psalm 45:10). He who is spiritually adopted has now no more to do with sin. 'Ephraim shall say, what have I to do any more with idols?' (Hosea 14:8). A child of God has indeed to do with sin as with an enemy to which he gives battle, but not as with a lord to which he yields obedience. He is freed from sin (Romans 6:7). I do not say he is freed from duty. Was it ever heard that a child should be freed from duty to his parents? This is such a freedom as rebels take.

(iii) Adoption consists in a legal investiture into the rights and royalties of the family into which the person is to be adopted. These are chiefly two:

The first royalty is a new name. He who is divinely adopted assumes a new name; before, a slave; now, a son; of a sinner, a saint. This is a name of honour better than any title of prince or monarch. 'To him that overcometh I will give a white stone, and in the stone a new name written' (Revelation 2 : 17). The white stone signifies remission. The new name signifies adoption, and the new name is put in the white stone to show that our adoption is grounded upon our justification; and this new name is written to show that God has all the names of his children enrolled in the book of life.

The second royalty is a giving the party adopted an interest in the inheritance. The making one an heir implies a relation to an inheritance. A man does not adopt another to a title but to an estate. So God in adopting us for his children gives us a glorious inheritance : 'The inheritance of the saints in light' (Colossians 1 : 12).

It is pleasant; it is an inheritance in light.

It is safe; God keeps the inheritance for his children (1 Peter 1 : 4), and keeps them for the inheritance (1 Peter 1 : 5), so that they cannot be hindered from taking possession.

There is no disinheriting, for the saints are co-heirs with Christ (Romans 8 : 17). Nay, they are members of Christ (Colossians 1 : 18). The members cannot be disinherited but the head must.[1]

The heirs never die. Eternity is a jewel of their crown. 'They shall reign for ever and ever' (Revelation 22 : 5).

Before I pass to the next, here a question may arise. How do God's adopting and man's adopting differ?

1 Man adopts to supply a defect, because he has no children of his own, but God does not adopt upon this account. He had a Son of his own, the Lord Jesus. He was his natural Son and the Son of his love, testified by a voice from heaven, 'This is my beloved Son' (Matthew 3 : 17). Never was there any Son so like the Father. He was his exact effigy, 'the express image of his person' (Hebrews 1 : 3). He was such a Son as was worth more than all the angels in heaven : 'Being made so much better than the angels' (Hebrews 1 : 4); so that God adopts not out of necessity, but pity.

2 When a man adopts, he adopts but one heir, but God adopts many : 'In bringing many sons to glory' (Hebrews 2 : 10). Oh may a poor trembling Christian say, Why should I ever look for this privilege to be a child of God! It is true, if God did act as a man, if he adopted only one

[1] That is to say, if Christ's members were disinherited, Christ their Head would also be disinherited.

son, then you might despair. But he adopts millions. He brings 'many sons to glory'. Indeed this may be the reason why a man adopts but one, because he does not have enough estate for more. If he should adopt many his land would not hold out. But God has enough land to give to all his children. 'In my Father's house are many mansions' (John 14:2).

3 Man when he adopts does it with ease. It is but sealing a deed and the thing is done. But when God adopts, it puts him to a far greater expense. It sets his wisdom on work to find out a way to adopt us. It was no easy thing to reconcile hell and heaven, to make the children of wrath the children of the promise; and when God in his infinite wisdom had found out a way, it was no easy way. It cost God the death of his natural Son, to make us his adopted sons. When God was about to constitute us sons and heirs, he could not seal the deed but by the blood of his own Son. It did not cost God so much to make us creatures as to make us sons. To make us creatures cost but the speaking of a word. To make us sons cost the effusion of blood.

4 Man, when he adopts, settles but earthly privileges upon his heir, but God settles heavenly privileges – justification, glorification. Men but entail their land upon the persons they adopt. God does more. He not only entails his land upon his children, but he entails himself upon them. 'I will be their God' (Hebrews 8:10). Not only heaven is their portion, but God is their portion.

God's filiating or making of children is by infusion of grace. When God makes any his children he stamps his image upon them. This is more than any man living can do. He may adopt another, but he cannot alter his disposition. If he be of a morose rugged nature, he cannot alter it; but God in making of children fits them for sonship. He prepares and sanctifies them for this privilege. He changes their disposition. He files off the ruggedness of their nature. He makes them not only sons, but saints. They are of another spirit (Numbers 14:24). They become meek and humble. They are 'partakers of the divine nature' (2 Peter 1:4).

How we come to be children of God by faith

The third thing is how we come to be the children of God.

There is a double cause of our filiation or childship.

The impulsive cause is God's free grace. We were rebels and traitors, and what could move God to make sinners sons, but free grace? 'Having predestinated us unto the adoption of children according to the good pleasure of his will' (Ephesians 1:5). Free grace gave the casting voice. Adoption is a mercy spun out of the bowels of free grace. It were much for God to take a clod of earth and make it a star, but it is more for God to take a piece of clay and sin and instate it into the glorious privilege of sonship. How will the saints read over the lectures [1] of free grace in heaven!

The organical or instrumental cause of our sonship is faith. Baptism does not make us children. That is indeed a badge and livery and gives us right to many external privileges, but the thing which makes God take cognizance of us for children is faith. 'Ye are all the children of God by faith in Christ Jesus' (Galatians 3:26). Before faith be wrought we have nothing to do with God. We are (as the apostle speaks in another sense) bastards and not sons (Hebrews 12:8). An unbeliever may call God his Judge, but not his Father. Wicked men may draw near to God in ordinances, and hope that God will be their Father, but while they are unbelievers they are bastards, and God will not father them but will lay them at the devil's door. 'Ye are the children of God by faith.' Faith legitimates us. It confers upon us the title of sonship and gives us right to inherit.

How then should we labour for faith! Without faith we are creatures, not children. Without faith we are spiritually illegitimate. This word 'illegitimate' is a term of infamy. Such as are illegitimate are looked upon with disgrace. We call them base-born. You who ruffle [2] it in your silks and velvets, but are in the state of nature, you are illegitimate. God looks upon you with an eye of scorn and contempt. You are a vile person, a son of the earth, 'of the seed of the serpent'. The devil can show as good a coat of arms as you.

This word 'illegitimate' also imports infelicity and misery. Persons illegitimate cannot inherit legally. The land goes only to such as are lawful heirs. Till we are the children of God, we have no right to heaven, and there is no way to be children but by faith. 'Ye are the children of God by faith.'

Here two things are to be discussed:

1 What faith is.
2 Why faith makes us children.

1 What faith is. If faith instates us into sonship, it concerns us to know what faith is. There is a two-fold faith.

(i) A more lax general faith. When we believe the truth of all that is

[1] Used here with the sense of 'lections' or 'lessons'.　　　　[2] Behave proudly.

revealed in the Holy Scriptures, this is not the faith which privileges us in sonship. The devils believe all the articles in the creed. It is not the bare knowledge of a medicine or believing the sovereign virtue of it that will cure one that is ill. This general faith (so much cried up by some) will not save. This a man may have and not love God. He may believe that God will come to judge the quick and the dead, and hate him, as the prisoner believes the judge's coming to the assizes, and abhors the thoughts of him. Take heed of resting in a general faith. You may have this and be no better than devils.

(ii) There is a special faith, when we not only believe the report we hear of Christ, but rest upon him, embrace him, 'taking hold of the horns of this altar', resolving there to abide. In the body there are sucking veins, which draw the meat into the stomach and concoct[1] it there. So faith is the sucking vein which draws Christ into the heart and applies him there. This is the filiating faith. By this we are made the children of God, and wherever this faith is, it is not like physic in a dead man's mouth, but is exceedingly operative. It obliges to duty. It works by love (Galatians 5:6).

But why does faith makes us children? Why should not other graces, repentance, love etc., do so? I answer: Because faith is instituted of God and honoured to this work of making us children. God's institution gives faith its value and validity. It is the king's stamp makes the coin pass current. If he would put his stamp upon brass or leather, it would go as current as silver. The great God has authorized and put the stamp of his institution upon faith, and that makes it pass for current and gives it a privilege above all the graces to make us children.

Again, faith makes us children as it is the vital principle. 'The just shall live by faith' (Habakkuk 2:4). All God's children are living. None of them are still-born. Now 'by faith we live'. As the heart is the fountain of life in the body, so faith is the fountain of life in the soul.

Faith also makes us children as it is the uniting grace. It knits us to Christ. The other graces cannot do this. By faith we are one with Christ and so we are akin to God. Being united to the natural Son, we become adopted sons. The kindred comes in by faith. God is the Father of Christ. Faith makes us Christ's brethren (Hebrews 2:11), and so God comes to be our Father.

[1] Digest.

Nine signs of divine sonship

The fourth particular to be discussed is to show the signs of God's children. It concerns us to know whose children we are. Augustine says that all mankind are divided into two ranks; either they are the children of God or the children of the devil.

1 The first sign of our heavenly sonship is tenderness of heart: 'Because thy heart was tender' (2 Chronicles 34:27). A child-like heart is a tender heart. He who before had a flinty, has now a fleshy heart. A tender heart is like melting wax to God. He may set what seal he will upon it. This tenderness of heart shows itself three ways.

(i) A tender heart grieves for sin. A child weeps for offending his father. Peter showed a tender heart when Christ looked upon him and he remembered his sin, he wept as a child. Clement of Alexandria says, he never heard a cock crow but he wept. And some learned writers tell us that by much weeping there seemed to be as it were channels made in his blessed face. The least hair makes the eye weep. The least sin makes the heart smite. David's heart smote him when he cut off the lap of King Saul's garment! What would it have done if he had cut off his head?

(ii) A tender heart melts under mercy. Though when God thunders by affliction, the rain of tears falls from a gracious eye, yet the heart is never so kindly dissolved as under the sunbeams of God's mercy. See how David's heart was melted with God's kindness: 'Who am I, O Lord God, and what is my house, that thou hast brought me hitherto?' (2 Samuel 7:18). There was a gracious thaw upon his heart. So says a child of God, 'Lord, who am I (a piece of dust and sin kneaded together) that the orient[1] beams of free grace should shine upon me? Who am I, that thou shouldest pity me when I lay in my blood and spread the golden wings of mercy over me? The soul is overcome with God's goodness, the tears drop, the love flames; mercy has a melting influence upon the soul.

(iii) A tender heart trembles under God's threatenings. 'My flesh trembleth for fear of thee' (Psalm 119:120). 'Because thine heart was tender, and thou didst humble thyself before God, when thou heardest his words against this place, and didst rend thy clothes . . .' (2

[1] See p. 40 fn.

Chronicles 34:27). If the father be angry, the child trembles. When ministers denounce the menaces and threats of God against sin, tender souls sit in a trembling posture. This frame of heart God delights in. 'To this man will I look, even to him that trembleth at thy word' (Isaiah 66:2). A wicked man, like the Leviathan, 'is made without fear' (Job 41:33). He neither believes the promises nor dreads the threatenings. Let judgment be denounced against sin, 'he laughs at the shaking of a spear'. He thinks either that God is ignorant and does not see, or impotent and cannot punish. The mountains quake before the Lord, the hills melt, the rocks are thrown down by him (Nahum 1:5). But the hearts of sinners are more obdurate than the rocks. An hardened sinner like Nebuchadnezzar has 'the heart of a beast given to him' (Daniel 4:16). A child-like heart is a tender heart. The stone is taken away.

2 The second sign of sonship is assimilation. 'Ye have put on the new man which is renewed in knowledge after the image of him that created him' (Colossians 3:10). The child resembles the father. God's children are like their heavenly Father. They bear his very image and impress. Wicked men say they are the children of God, but there is too great a dissimilitude and unlikeness. The Jews bragged they were Abraham's children, but Christ disproves them by this argument, because they were not like him. 'Ye seek to kill me, a man that hath told you the truth, which I have heard of God; this did not Abraham' (John 8:40). You, Abraham's children, and go about to kill me! Abraham would not have murdered an innocent. You are more like Satan than Abraham. 'Ye are of your father the devil' (verse 44). Such as are proud, earthly, malicious may say, 'Our father which art in hell.' It is blasphemy to call God our Father and make the devil our pattern. God's children resemble him in meekness and holiness. They are his walking pictures. As the seal stamps its print and likeness upon the wax, so does God stamp the print and effigy of his own beauty upon his children.

3 The third sign of God's children is, they have the Spirit of God. It is called the Spirit of adoption; 'ye have received the Spirit of adoption . . .' (Romans 8:15).

How shall we know that we have received the Spirit of adoption, and so are in the state of adoption?

The Spirit of God has a three-fold work in them who are made children:

(i) A regenerating work.
(ii) A supplicating work.
(iii) A witnessing work.

(i) A regenerating work. Whomsoever the Spirit adopts, He regenerates. God's children are said to be 'born of the Spirit'. 'Except a man be born of water and of the Spirit, he cannot enter into the kingdom of God' (John 3:5). We must first be born of the Spirit before we are baptized with this new name of sons and daughters. We are not God's children by creation, but by renovation; not by our first birth, but by our new birth. This new birth produced by the Word as the material cause (James 1:18), and by the Spirit as the efficient cause, is nothing else but a change of nature (Romans 12:2), which though it be not a perfect change, yet is a thorough change (1 Thessalonians 5:23). This change of heart is as necessary as salvation.

How shall we know that we have this regenerating work of the Spirit?

Two ways: by the pangs; by the products.

By the pangs: there are spiritual pangs before the new birth, some bruisings of soul, some groanings and cryings out, some strugglings in the heart between flesh and Spirit. 'They were pricked at their heart' (Acts 2:37). The child has sharp throws before the birth; so it is in the new birth. I grant the new birth is marked by 'more and less'. All do not have the same pangs of humiliation, yet all have pangs; all feel the hammer of the law upon their heart, though some are more bruised with this hammer than others. God's Spirit is a Spirit of bondage before He is a Spirit of adoption (Romans 8:15). What then shall we say to those who are as ignorant about the new birth as Nicodemus: 'How can a man be born when he is old . . .?' (John 3:4). The new birth is 'a derision of the ungodly', though it be 'a great secret' to the godly. Some thank God they never had any trouble of spirit. They were always quiet. These bless God for the greatest curse. It is a sign they are not God's children. The child of grace is always born with pangs.

The new birth is known by the products, which are three:

Sensibility. The infant that is new-born is sensible of the least touch. If the Spirit has regenerated you, you are sensible of the ebullitions and first risings of sin which before you did not perceive. Paul cries out of the 'law in his members' (Romans 7:23). The new-born saint sees sin in the root.

Circumspection. He who is born of the Spirit is careful to preserve grace. He plies the breast of ordinances (1 Peter 2:1). He is fearful of that which may endanger his spiritual life (1 John 5:18). He lives by faith, yet passes the time of his sojourning in fear (1 Peter 1:17). This is the first work of the Spirit in them who are made children, a regenerating work.

(ii) The Spirit of God has a supplicating work in the heart. The Spirit of adoption is a Spirit of supplication. 'Ye have received the Spirit of adoption whereby we cry Abba, Father' (Romans 8:15). While the child is in the womb it cannot cry. While men lie in the womb of their natural estate, they cannot pray effectually, but when they are born of the Spirit, then they cry 'Abba, Father'. Prayer is nothing else but the soul's breathing itself into the bosom of its Father. It is a sweet and familiar intercourse with God. As soon as ever the Spirit of God comes into the heart, He sets it a-praying. No sooner was Paul converted but the next word is, 'Behold, he prayeth' (Acts 9:11). It is reported in the life of Luther that, when he prayed, it was with so much reverence as if he were praying to God, and with so much boldness, as if he had been speaking to his friend. And Eusebius reports of Constantine the Emperor that every day he used to shut up himself in some secret place in his palace, and there on bended knees make his devout prayers and soliloquies to God. God's Spirit tunes the strings of the affections, and then we make melody in prayer. For any to say, in derision, 'you pray by the Spirit', is a blasphemy against the Spirit. It is a main work of the Spirit of God in the hearts of his children to help them to pray: 'Because ye are sons, God has sent forth the Spirit of his Son into your hearts, crying, Abba, Father' (Galatians 4:6).

But many of the children of God do not have such abilities to express themselves in prayer. How then does the Spirit help their infirmities?

Though they do not have always the gifts of the Spirit in prayer, yet they have the groans of the Spirit (Romans 8:26). Gifts are the ornaments of prayer, but not the life of prayer. A carcase may be hung with jewels. Though the Spirit may deny fluency of speech, yet He gives fervency of desire, and such prayers are most prevalent. The prayers which the Spirit indites in the hearts of God's children have these three-fold qualifications.

The prayers of God's children are *believing* prayers. Prayer is the key. Faith is the hand that turns it. Faith feathers the arrow of prayer and makes it pierce the throne of grace. 'Whatsoever ye shall ask in prayer believing, ye shall receive' (Matthew 21:22). Whereupon, says Jerome, I would not presume to pray unless I bring faith along with me. To pray and not believe is (as one says) a kind of jeer offered to God, as if we thought either he did not hear or he would not grant.

That faith may be animated in prayer, we must bring Christ in our arms when we appear before God. 'And Samuel took a sucking lamb, and offered it for a burnt-offering; and Samuel cried unto the Lord for Israel, and the Lord heard him' (1 Samuel 7:9). This sucking lamb typified Christ. When we come to God in prayer we must bring the Lamb, Christ along with us. Themistocles [1] carried the king's son in his arms and so pacified the king when he was angry. The children of God present Christ in the arms of their faith.

The prayers of God's children indited by the Spirit are *ardent* prayers. 'Ye have received the Spirit, whereby we cry Abba, Father' (Romans 8:15). 'Father'; that implies faith. We cry; that implies fervency. The incense was to be laid upon burning coals (Leviticus 16:12). The incense was a type of prayer; the burning coals, of ardency in prayer. 'Elias prayed earnestly' (James 5:17). In the Greek it is 'in praying he prayed', that is, he did it with vehemency. In prayer the heart must boil over with heat of affection. Prayer is compared to groans unutterable (Romans 8:26). It alludes to a woman that is in pangs. We should be in pangs when we are travailing for mercy. Such prayer 'commands God himself' (Isaiah 45:11).

The prayers of God's children are *heart-cleansing* prayers. They purge out sin. Many pray against sin and sin against prayer. God's children not only pray against sin, but pray down sin.

(iii) The Spirit of God has a witnessing work in the heart. God's children have not only the influence of the Spirit, but the witness. 'The Spirit itself beareth witness with our spirit that we are the children of God' (Romans 8:16). There is a three-fold witness a child of God has – the witness of the Word, the witness of conscience, the witness of the Spirit. The Word makes the major proposition. He who is in such a manner qualified is a child of God. Conscience makes the minor proposition; but you are so divinely qualified. The Spirit makes the conclusion – therefore you are a child of God. The Spirit joins with the witness of conscience. 'The Spirit witnesseth with our spirits' (Romans 8:16). The Spirit teaches conscience to search the records of Scripture and

[1] Athenian statesman of the 5th century B.C. At one time, Themistocles, having angered the Athenians, fled for safety to Admetus, King of the Molossians (Epirus) although that king bore a grudge against him. To placate his enmity, and apparently with the help of the queen, Themistocles took the king's young son in his arms, and made supplication to the household gods of Admetus, whereupon the king's resentment gave place to friendship.

find its evidences for heaven. It helps conscience to spell out its name in a promise. It bears witness with our spirit.

But how shall I know the witness of the Spirit from a delusion?

The Spirit of God always witnesses according to the Word, as the echo answers the voice. Enthusiasts speak much of the Spirit, but they leave the Word. That inspiration which is either without the Word or against it, is an imposture. The Spirit of God indited the Word (2 Peter 1:21). Now if the Spirit should witness otherwise than according to the Word, the Spirit would be divided against Himself. He would be a spirit of contradiction, witnessing one thing for a truth in the Word and another thing different from it in a man's conscience.

4 The fourth sign of God's children is zeal for God. They are zealous for his day, his truth, his glory. They who are born of God are impatient of his dishonour. Moses was cool in his own cause, but hot in God's. When the people of Israel had wrought folly in the golden calf, he breaks the tables. When St. Paul saw the people of Athens given to idolatry 'his spirit was stirred in him' (Acts 17:16). In the Greek it is his spirit was 'embittered', or, as the word may signify, he was in a paroxysm or burning fit of zeal. He could not contain, but with this fire of zeal discharges against their sin. As we shall answer for idle words, so for sinful silence. It is dangerous in this sense to be possessed with a 'dumb devil'. David says, 'the zeal of God's house had eaten him up' (Psalm 69:9). Many Christians whose zeal once had almost eaten them up, now they have eaten up their zeal. They are grown tepid and neutral. The breath of preferment blowing upon them has cooled their heat. I can never believe that he has the heart of a child in him that can be patient when God's glory suffers. Can an ingenuous child endure to hear his father reproached? Though we should be silent under God's displeasure, yet not under his dishonour. When there is an holy fire kindled in the heart, it will break forth at the lips. Zeal tempered with holiness is the white and sanguine[1] which gives the soul its best complexion.

Of all others let ministers be impatient when God's glory is impeached and eclipsed. A minister without zeal is like 'salt that has lost its savour'. Zeal will make men take injuries done to God as done to themselves. It is reported of Chrysostom that he reproved any sin against God as if he himself had received a personal wrong. Let not ministers be either shaken with fear or seduced with flattery. God never made ministers to be as false glasses, to make bad faces look fair. For

[1] Blood-red.

want of this fire of zeal, they are in danger of another fire, even the 'burning lake' (Revelation 21 : 8), into which the fearful shall be cast.

5 Those who are God's children and are born of God are of a more noble and celestial spirit than men of the world. They mind 'things above' (Colossians 3 : 2). 'Whatsoever is born of God overcometh the world' (1 John 5 : 4). The children of God live in an higher region. They are compared to eagles (Isaiah 40 : 31), in regard of their sublimeness and heavenly-mindedness. Their souls are fled aloft. Christ is in their heart (Colossians 1 : 27) and the world is under their feet (Revelation 12 : 1). Men of the world are ever tumbling in thick clay. They are 'sons of earth'; not eagles, but earth-worms. The saints are of another spirit. They are born of God and walk with God as the child walks with the father. 'Noah walked with God' (Genesis 6 : 9). God's children show their high pedigree in their heavenly conversation (Philippians 3 : 20).

6 Another sign of adoption is love to them that are children. God's children are knit together with the bond of love, as all the members of the body are knit together by several nerves and ligaments. If we are born of God, then we 'love the brotherhood' (1 Peter 2 : 17); He that loves the person, loves the picture. The children of God are his walking pictures, and if we are of God, we love those who have his effigy and portraiture drawn upon their souls. If we are born of God, we love the saints notwithstanding their infirmities. Children love one another though they have some imperfections of nature, a squint-eye, or a crooked back. We love gold in the ore, though it has some drossiness in it. The best saints have their blemishes. We read of the 'spot of God's children' (Deuteronomy 32 : 5). A saint in this life is like a fair face with a scar in it. If we are born of God we love his children though they are poor. We love to see the image and picture of our Father, though hung in never so poor a frame. We love to see a rich Christ in a poor man.

And if we are children of the Highest, we show our love to God's children :

(i) By prizing their persons above others. He who is born of God 'honoureth them that fear the Lord' (Psalm 15 : 4). The saints are the 'dearly beloved of God's soul' (Jeremiah 12 : 7). They are his 'jewels' (Malachi 3 : 17). They are of the true blood-royal, and he who is divinely adopted sets an higher estimate upon these than upon others.

(ii) We show our love to the children of God by prizing their company above others. Children love to associate and be together. The communion of saints is precious. Christ's doves will flock together in company. 'Like associates with like.'[1] 'I am a companion of all them that fear thee' (Psalm 119:63). We read that 'Abraham bowed himself to the children of Heth' (Genesis 23:7). A child of God has a love of civility to all, but a love of complacency only to such as are fellow-heirs with him of the same inheritance.

By this persons may try their adoption. It appears plainly that they are not the children of God who hate those that are born of God. They soil and blacken the silver wings of Christ's doves by their aspersive reproaches. They cannot endure the society of the saints. As vultures hate sweet smells and are killed with them, so the wicked do not love to come near the godly. They cannot abide the precious perfume of their graces. They hate these sweet smells. It is a sign they are of the serpent's brood who hate the seed of the woman.

7 The seventh sign of God's children is to delight to be much in God's presence. Children love to be in the presence of their father. Where the king is, there is the court. Where the presence of God is, there is heaven. God is in a special manner present in his ordinances. They are the ark of his presence. Now if we are children, we love to be much in holy duties. In the use of ordinances we draw near to God. We come into our Father's presence. In prayer we have secret conference with God. In the Word we hear God speaking from heaven to us, and how does every child of God delight to hear his Father's voice! In the sacraments God kisses his children with the 'kisses of his lips'. He gives them a smile of his face and a privy-seal of his love. Oh it is 'good to draw near to God' (Psalm 73:28). It is sweet being in his presence. Every true child of God says, 'a day in thy courts is better than a thousand' (Psalm 84:10). Slighters of ordinances are none of God's children, because they care not to be in his presence. They love the tavern better than the temple. 'Cain went out from the presence of the Lord' (Genesis 4:16); not that he could go out of God's sight (Psalm 139:7), but the meaning is, Cain went from the church of God where the Lord gave the visible signs of his presence to his people.

8 The eighth sign is compliance with the will of our heavenly Father. A child-like heart answers to God's call as the echo answers to the voice. It is like the flower that opens and shuts with the sun. So it opens to God and shuts to temptation. This is the motto of a new-born saint – 'Speak, Lord, thy servant hears' (1 Samuel 3:9). When God bids his

[1] Quoted from Cicero's De Senectute iii. 7 (the Latin equivalent of 'Birds of a feather flock together').

children pray in their closets, mortify sin, suffer for his name, they are ambitious to obey. They will lay down their lives at their Father's call. Hypocrites court God and speak him fair, but refuse to go on his errand. They are not children but rebels.

9 The last sign is, He who is a child of God will labour to make others the children of God. The holy seed of grace propagates (Galatians 4:19; Philemon 10). He who is of the seed royal will be ambitiously desirous to bring others into the kindred. Are you divinely adopted? You will studiously endeavour to make your child a child of the most High.

How Christians should bring up their children

There are two reasons why a godly parent will endeavour to bring his child into the heavenly kindred:

(i) Out of conscience. A good parent sees the injury he has done to his child. He has conveyed the plague of sin to him, and in conscience he will endeavour to make some recompense. In the old law, he that had smitten and wounded another was bound to see him healed and pay for his cure. Parents have given their children a wound in their souls and therefore must do what in them lies by admonition, prayers, tears, to see the wound healed.

(ii) Out of flaming zeal to the honour of God. He who has tasted God's love in adoption looks upon himself as engaged to bring God all the glory he can. If he has a child or acquaintance that are strangers to God he would gladly promote the work of grace in their hearts. It is a glory to Christ when multitudes are born to him.

How far are they from being God's children who have no care to bring others into the family of God! To blame are those masters who mind more their servants' work than their souls. To blame are those parents who are regardless of their children. They do not drop in principles of knowledge into them, but suffer them to have their head. They will let them lie and swear, but not ask blessing; read play-books but not Scripture.

But, say some, to catechize and teach our children is to take God's name in vain.

Is the fulfilling God's command taking his name in vain? 'These words which I command thee this day, thou shalt teach them diligently to thy children' (Deuteronomy 6:6, 7). 'Train up a child in the way he should go, and when he is old he will not depart from it' (Proverbs

22 : 6). 'Ye fathers, provoke not your children to wrath, but bring them up in the nurture and admonition of the Lord' (Ephesians 6 : 4). This three-fold cord of Scripture is not easily broken.

The saints of old were continually grafting principles of holy knowledge in their children. 'I know that Abraham will command his children, and they shall keep the way of the Lord' (Genesis 18 : 19). 'And thou Solomon, my son, know thou the God of thy father and serve him with a perfect heart' (1 Chronicles 28 : 9). Sure Abraham and David did not take God's name in vain! What need is there of instilling holy instructions to over-top the poisonful weeds of sin that grow! As husbandmen, when they have planted young trees, they set stays to them to keep them from bending. Children are young plants. The heavenly precepts of their parents are like stays set about them, to keep them from bending to error and profaneness. When can there be a fitter season to disseminate and infuse knowledge into children than in their minority? Now is a time to give them the breast and let them suck in the 'sincere milk of the word' (1 Peter 2 : 2).

But some may object that it is to no purpose to teach our children the knowledge of God. They have no sense of spiritual things, nor are they the better for our instructions. I answer:

We read in Scripture of children who by virtue of instruction have had their tender years sanctified. Timothy's mother and grandmother taught him the Scriptures from his cradle: 'And that from a child thou hast known the holy Scriptures' (2 Timothy 3 : 15). Timothy sucked in religion as it were with his milk. We read of young children who cried 'Hosanna' to Christ and trumpeted forth his praises (Matthew 21 : 15). And sure those children of Tyre had some seeds of good wrought in them in that they showed their love to Paul and would help him on his way to the sea-shore. 'They all brought us on our way with wives and children' (Acts 21 : 5). Saint Paul had a convoy of young saints to bring him to take ship.

And again, suppose our counsel and instruction does not at present prevail with our children, it may afterwards take effect. The seed a man sows in his ground does not presently [1] spring up, but in its season it brings forth a crop. He that plants a wood does not see the full growth till many years after. If we must not instruct our children because at present they do not reap the benefit, by the same reason we should not baptize our children, because at present they do not have the sense of baptism. Nay, by the same reason ministers should not preach the Word, because at present many of their hearers have no benefit.

[1] Immediately.

Again, if our counsels and admonitions do not prevail with our children, yet 'we have delivered our own souls'. There is comfort in the discharge of conscience. We must let alone issues and events. Duty is our work; success is God's.

All which considered, should make parents whet holy instructions upon their children. They who are of the family of God and whom he has adopted for children, will endeavour that their children may be more God's children than theirs. They will 'travail in birth till Christ be formed in them'. A true saint is a loadstone that will be still drawing others to God. Let this suffice to have spoken of the signs of adoption. I proceed.

The love of God in making us his children

The fifth particular to be discussed is the love of God in making us children. 'Behold what manner of love the Father hath bestowed upon us, that we should be called the sons of God!' (1 John 3:1). God showed power in making us creatures, but love in making us sons. Plato gave God thanks that he had made him a man and not a beast, but what cause have they to adore God's love, who has made them children! The apostle puts a 'Behold' to it. That we may the better behold God's love in making us children, consider three things.

1 We were deformed. 'When I passed by thee and saw thee polluted in thine own blood, it was the time of love' (Ezekiel 16:6, 8). Mordecai adopted Esther because she was fair, but we were in our blood, and then God adopted us. He did not adopt us when we were clothed with the robe of innocency in paradise, when we were hung with the jewels of holiness and were white and ruddy; but when we were in our blood and had our leprous spots upon us. The time of our loathing was the time of God's loving.

2 As we did not deserve to be made children so neither did we desire it. No landed man will force another to become his heir against his will. If a king should go to adopt a beggar and make him heir of the crown, if the beggar should refuse the king's favour and say, 'I had rather be as I am, I would be a beggar still'; the king would take it in high contempt of his favour and would not adopt him against his will. Thus it was with us. We had no willingness to be made children. We would have been begging still, but God out of his infinite mercy and indul-

gence, not only offers to make us children, but makes us willing to embrace the offer (Psalm 110:3). 'Behold what manner of love' is this!

3 It is the wonder of love that God should adopt us for his children when we were enemies. If a man would make another heir of his land, he would adopt one that is near akin to him. No man would adopt an enemy. But that God should make us children when we were enemies; that he should make us heirs to the crown when we were traitors to the crown; oh amazing, astonishing love! 'Behold what manner of love' is this! We were not akin to God. We had by sin lost and forfeited our pedigree. We had done God all the injury and spite we could, defaced his image, violated his law, trampled upon his mercies, and when we had angered him, he adopted us. What stupendous love was this! Such love was never shown to the angels! When they fell (though they were of a more noble nature, and in probability might have done God more service than we can, yet) God never vouchsafed this privilege of adoption to them. He did not make them children, but prisoners. They were heirs only to 'the treasures of wrath' (Romans 2:5).

Let all who are thus nearly related to God, stand admiring his love. When they were like Saul, breathing forth enmity against God; when their hearts stood out as garrisons against him, the Lord conquered their stubbornness with kindness, and not only pardoned, but adopted them. It is hard to say which is greater, the mystery or the mercy. This is such amazing love as we shall be searching into and adoring to all eternity. The bottom of it cannot be fathomed by any angel in heaven. God's love in making us children is

A rich love. It is love in God to feed us, but it is rich love to adopt us. It is love to give us a crumb, but it is rich love to make us heirs to a crown.

It is *a distinguishing love* – that when God has passed by so many millions, he should cast a favourable aspect upon thee! Most are cut out for fuel, and are made vessels of wrath. And that God should say to thee, 'Thou art my son', here is the mirror of mercy, the meridian of love! Who, O who, can tread upon these hot coals, and his heart not burn in love to God?

The honour of God's children

The sixth particular is the honour and renown of God's children. For the illustration of this, observe two things:

1. God makes a precious account of them.
2. He looks upon them as persons of honour.

1 God makes a precious account of them. 'Since thou wast precious in my sight . . .' (Isaiah 43:4). A father prizes his child above his estate. How dearly did Jacob prize Benjamin! His 'life was bound up in the life of the lad' (Genesis 44:30). God makes a precious valuation of his children. The wicked are of no account with God. They are vile persons. 'I will make thy grave for thou art vile' (Nahum 1:14). Therefore the wicked are compared to chaff (Psalm 1:4), to dross (Psalm 119:119). There is little use of a wicked man while he lives and no loss of him when he dies. There is only a little chaff blown away, which may well be spared. But God's children are precious in his sight. They are his jewels (Malachi 3:17). The wicked are but lumber which serves only to 'cumber the ground'. But God's children are his jewels locked up in the cabinet of his decree from all eternity. God's children are 'the apple of his eye' (Zechariah 2:8), very dear and very tender to him, and the eyelid of his special providence covers them. The Lord accounts every thing of his children precious.

Their *name* is precious. The wicked leave their name for a curse (Isaiah 65:15). The names of God's children are embalmed (Isaiah 60:15). So precious are their names that God enters them in the book of life and Christ carries them on his breast. How precious must their name needs be, who have God's own name written upon them! 'Him that overcometh, I will write upon him the name of my God' (Revelation 3:12).

Their *prayers* are precious. 'O my dove, in the clefts of the rock, let me hear thy voice, for sweet is thy voice' (Canticles 2:14). Every child of God is this dove. Prayer is the voice of the dove, and 'sweet is this voice'. The prayer of God's children is as sweet to him as music. A wicked man's prayer is as the 'howling' of a dog (Hosea 7:14). The prayer of the saints is as the singing of the bird. The finger of God's Spirit touching the lute-strings of their hearts, they make melody to the Lord. 'Their sacrifices shall be accepted upon mine altar' (Isaiah 56:7).

Their *tears* are precious. They drop as pearls from their eyes. 'I have seen thy tears' (Isaiah 38:5). The tears of God's children drop as precious wine into God's bottle. 'Put thou my tears into thy bottle' (Psalm 56:8). A tear from a broken heart is a present for the king of heaven.

Their *blood* is precious. 'Precious in the sight of the Lord is the death of his saints' (Psalm 116:15). This is the blood God will chiefly make inquisition for. Athaliah shed the blood of the king's children (2 Kings 11:1). The saints are the children of the most High, and such as shed

[237]

their blood shall pay dear for it. 'Thou hast given them blood to drink for they are worthy' (Revelation 16:6).

2 God looks upon his children as persons of honour. 'Since thou wast precious in my sight, thou hast been honourable . . .' (Isaiah 43:4).

God esteems them honourable. He calls them a crown and a royal diadem (Isaiah 62:3). He calls them his glory: 'Israel my glory (Isaiah 46:13).

God makes them honourable. As a king creates dukes, marquesses, earls, barons etc., so God installs his children into honour. He creates them noble persons, persons of renown. David thought it no small honour to be the king's son-in-law. 'Who am I that I should be son-in-law to the king?' (1 Samuel 18:18). What an infinite honour is it to be the children of the High God, to be of the blood-royal of heaven! The saints are of an ancient family. They are sprung from 'the Ancient of days' (Daniel 7:9). That is the best pedigree which is fetched from heaven. Here the youngest child is an heir, a co-heir with Christ who is heir of all (Hebrews 1:2; Romans 8:17). Consider the honour of God's children positively and comparatively.

Positively: They have titles of honour. They are called 'kings' (Revelation 1:6); 'the excellent of the earth' (Psalm 16:3); 'vessels of honour' (2 Timothy 2:21).

They have their scutcheon. You may see the saints' scutcheon or coat-armour. The Scripture has set forth their heraldry. Sometimes they give the lion in regard of their courage (Proverbs 28:1). Sometimes they give the eagle in regard of their sublimeness. They are ever flying up to heaven upon the two wings of faith and love. 'They shall mount up with wings as eagles' (Isaiah 40:31). Sometimes they give the dove in regard of their meekness and innocency (Canticles 2:14). This shows the children of God to be persons of renown.

Consider the honour of God's children *comparatively*; and this comparison is double. Compare the children of God with Adam; with the angels.

Compare the children of God with Adam in a state of innocency. Adam was a person of honour. He was the sole monarch of the world. All the creatures vailed [1] to him as their sovereign. He was placed in the garden of Eden which was a paradise of pleasure. He was crowned with all the contentments of the earth. Nay more, Adam was God's lively picture. He was made in the likeness of God himself. Yet the state of the meanest of God's children by adoption is far more excellent and

[1] To lower or doff one's plumes, as a mark of honour and respect to a superior.

honourable than the state of Adam was, when he wore the robe of innocency, for Adam's condition, though it was glorious yet it was mutable, and was soon lost; Adam was a bright star, yet a falling star. But God's children by adoption are in a state unalterable. Adam had a 'posse non peccare',[1] a possibility of standing, but believers have a 'non posse peccare',[2] an impossibility of falling; once adopted, and ever adopted. As Isaac said, when he had given the blessing to Jacob, 'I have blessed him and he shall be blessed' (Genesis 27 : 33). So may we say of all God's children, they are adopted, and they shall be adopted; so that God's children are in a better and more glorious condition now than Adam was in all his regal honour and majesty.

Let us ascend as high as heaven and compare God's children with the glorious and blessed angels. God's children are equal to the angels, in some sense above them, so that they must be persons of honour.

God's children are equal to the angels. This is acknowledged by some of the angels themselves. 'I am thy fellow-servant' (Revelation 19 : 10). Here is a parallel made between John the Divine and the angel. The angel says to John, 'I am thy fellow-servant.'

The children of God by adoption are in some sense above the angels, and that two ways.

The angels are servants to God's children (Hebrews 1 : 14). Though they are 'glorious spirits', yet they are 'ministering spirits'. The angels are the saints' servitors. We have examples in Scripture of angels attending the persons of God's children. We read of angels waiting upon Abraham, Moses, Daniel, the Virgin Mary etc. Nor do the angels only render service to God's children while they live, but at their death too. Lazarus had a convoy of angels to carry him into the paradise of God. Thus we see the children of God have a pre-eminence and dignity above the angels. The angels are their servants both living and dying; and this is more to be observed, because it is never said in Scripture that the children of God are servants to the angels.

God's children are above the angels, because Christ by taking their nature has ennobled and honoured it above the angelical. 'He in no wise took the nature of angels' (Hebrews 2 : 16). God by uniting us to Christ has made us nearer to himself than the angels. The children of God are members of Christ (Ephesians 5 : 30). This was never said of the angels. How can they be members of Christ, who are of a different nature from him? Indeed metaphorically and improperly Christ may be called the

[1] 'to be able not to sin'.
[2] 'not to be able to sin' (the expression is used here with the meaning of 'inability to perish').

head of the angels, as they are subject to him (1 Peter 3:22). But that Christ is head of the angels in that near and sweet conjunction, as he is head of the believers, we nowhere find in Scripture. In this respect therefore I may clearly assert that the children of God have a superiority and honour even above the angels. Though by creation they are 'a little lower than the angels', yet by adoption and mystical union they are above the angels.

How may this comfort a child of God in the midst either of calumny or penury! He is a person of honour. He is above the angels. A gentleman that is fallen to decay will sometimes boast of his parentage and noble blood; so a Christian who is poor in the world, yet by virtue of his adoption he is of the family of God. He has the true blood-royal running in his veins. He has a fairer coat of arms to show than the angels themselves.

Twelve high privileges of God's children

The seventh particular to be explained is to show the glorious privileges of God's children; and what I shall say now belongs not to the wicked. It is 'children's bread'. The fruit of paradise was to be kept with a flaming sword. So these sweet and heart-ravishing privileges are to be kept with a flaming sword, that impure sensual persons may not touch them. There are twelve rare privileges which belong to the children of God.

God's love towards them

1 If we are children, then God will be full of tender love and affection towards us. A father compassionates his child. 'Like as a father pitieth his children, so the Lord pitieth them that fear him' (Psalm 103:13). Oh the yearning of God's bowels to his children! 'Is Ephraim my dear son? Is he a pleasant child? My bowels are troubled for him, I will surely have mercy upon him, saith the Lord' (Jeremiah 31:20). Towards the wicked God's wrath is kindled (Psalm 2:12). Towards them that are children, God's repentings are kindled (Hosea 11:8). Mercy and pity as naturally flow from our heavenly Father as light from the sun.

Some may object: But God is angry and writes bitter things. How does this stand with love?

God's love and his anger towards his children are not in opposition but 'showing a difference'. They may stand together. He is angry in love. 'As many as I love I rebuke and chasten' (Revelation 3:19). We have as much need of afflictions as ordinances. A bitter pill may be as needful for preserving health as a julep or cordial. God afflicts with the same love as he adopts. God is most angry when he is not angry. His hand is heaviest when it is lightest (Hosea 14:4). Affliction is an argument of son-ship. 'If ye endure chastening, God dealeth with you as with sons' (Hebrews 12:7).

Oh, says one, surely God does not love me. I am none of his child, because he does not follow me with such sore afflictions. Why, it is a sign of childship to be sometimes under the rod. God had one son without sin, but no son without stripes. God puts his children to the school of the cross, and there they learn best. God speaks to us in the Word – children, do not be proud, do not love the world; 'Walk circumspectly' (Ephesians 5:15). But, we are 'dull of hearing'; nay we 'stop the ear'. 'I spake to thee in thy prosperity, but thou saidst, I will not hear' (Jeremiah 22:21). Now, says God, I shall lose my child if I do not correct him. Then God in love smites that he may save. Aristotle [1] speaks of a bird that lives among thorns, yet sings sweetly. God's children make the best melody in their heart, when God 'hedgeth their way with thorns' (Hosea 2:6). Afflictions are refining. 'The fining pot is for silver, and the furnace for gold' (Proverbs 17:3). Fiery trials make golden Christians. Afflictions are purifying. 'Many shall be tried and made white' (Daniel 12:10). We think God is going to destroy us, but he only lays us a-whitening. Some birds will not hatch but in time of thunder. Christians are commonly best in affliction. God will make his children at last bless him for sufferings. The eyes that sin shuts affliction opens. When Manasseh was in chains, 'then he knew the Lord was God' (2 Chronicles 33:13). Afflictions fit for heaven. First the stones of Solomon's temple were hewn and polished and then set up into a building. First the saints (who are called 'living stones') must be hewn and carved by sufferings as the corner stone was, and so made meet for the celestial building (Colossians 1:12). And is there not love in all God's Fatherly castigations?

But there may be another objection, that sometimes God's children are under the black clouds of desertion. Is not this far from love?

Concerning desertion, I must needs say that this is the saddest condition that can betide God's children. When the sun is gone, the dew falls. When the sunlight of God's countenance is removed, then the dew of tears falls from the eyes of the saints. In desertion God rains hell out of heaven (to use Calvin's expression). 'The arrows of the Almighty are within me, the poison whereof drinketh up my spirit' (Job

[1] Greek philosopher and scientist, 4th century B.C.

6 : 4). This is the poisoned arrow that wounds to the heart. Desertion is a taste of the torments of the damned. God says, 'In a little wrath I hid my face from thee' (Isaiah 54 : 8). I may here gloss with Saint Bernard, 'Lord, dost thou call that a little wrath when thou hidest thy face? Is it but a little? What can be more bitter to me than the eclipsing of thy face?' God is in the Scripture called a light and a fire. The deserted soul feels the fire but does not see the light. But yet you who are adopted may spell love in all this. They say of Hercules' club that it was made of wood of olive. The olive is an emblem of peace. So God's club, whereby he beats down the soul in desertion, has something of the olive. There is peace and mercy in it. I shall hold forth a spiritual rainbow wherein the children of God may see the love of their Father in the midst of the clouds of desertion.

Therefore I answer:

(i) In time of desertion God leaves in his children a seed of comfort. 'His seed remaineth in him' (1 John 3 : 9). This seed of God is a seed of comfort. Though God's children in desertion lack the seal of the Spirit, yet they have the unction of the Spirit (1 John 2 : 27). Though they lack the sun, yet they have a day-star in their hearts. As the tree in winter, though it has lost its leaves and fruit, yet there is sap in the root; so in the winter of desertion there is the sap of grace in the root of the heart. As it is with the sun masking itself with a cloud when it denies light to the earth, yet it gives forth its influence; so though God's dear adopted ones may lose sight of his countenance, yet they have the influence of his grace.

What grace appears in the time of desertion? I answer:

An *high prizing of God's love*. If God should say to the deserted soul, What wilt thou and it shall be granted to half of the kingdom?, he would reply, Lord that I might see thee 'as I was wont to see thee in the sanctuary'; that I may have one golden beam of thy love. The deserted soul slights all other things in comparison. It is not gardens or orchards, or the most delicious objects that can give him contentment. They are like music to a sad heart. He desires, as Absalom, 'to see the king's face'.

A *lamenting after the Lord*. It is the saddest day for him when the sun of righteousness is eclipsed. A child of God can better bear the world's stroke than God's absence. He is even melted into tears; the clouds of desertion produce spiritual rain, and whence is this weeping but from love?

Willingness to suffer anything so he may have sight of God. A child of God could be content with Simon of Cyrene to carry the cross if he were sure Christ were upon it. He could willingly die, if with Simeon he might die with Christ in his arms. Behold here, 'the seed of God' in a believer, the work of sanctification, when he lacks the wine of consolation.

(ii) I answer, God has a design of mercy in hiding his face from his adopted ones.

First, it is for the trial of grace, and there are two graces brought to trial in time of desertion, faith and love.

Faith: When we can believe against sense and feeling; when we are without experience, yet can trust to a promise; when we do not have the 'kisses of God's mouth', yet can cleave to 'the word of his mouth'; this is faith indeed. Here is the sparkling of the diamond.

Love: When God smiles upon us, it is not much to love him, but when he seems to put us away in anger (Psalm 27:9), now to love him and be as the lime – the more water is thrown upon it the hotter it burns – this is love indeed. That love sure is 'strong as death' (Canticles 8:6) which the waters of desertion cannot quench.

Secondly, it is for the exercise of grace. We are all for comfort. If it be put to our choice, we would be ever upon Mount Pisgah,[1] looking into Canaan. We are loath to be in trials, agonies, desertions, as if God could not love us except he had us in his arms. It is hard to lie long in the lap of spiritual joy and not fall asleep. Too much sunshine causes a drought in our graces. Oftentimes when God lets down comfort into the heart, we begin to let down care. As it is with musicians, before they have money they will play you many a sweet lesson, but as soon as you throw them down money they are gone. You hear no more of them. Before joy and assurance, O the sweet music of prayer and repentance! But when God throws down the comforts of his Spirit, we either leave off duty or at least slacken the strings of our viol and grow remiss in it. You are taken with the money, but God is taken with the music. Grace is better than comfort. Rachel is more fair, but Leah is more fruitful. Comfort is fair to look upon, but grace has the fruitful womb. Now the only way to exercise grace and make it more vigorous and lively is sometimes to 'walk in darkness and have no light' (Isaiah 50:10). Faith is a star that shines brightest in the night of desertion. 'I said, I am cast out of thy sight; yet will I look again toward thy holy temple' (Jonah 2:4). Grace usually puts forth its most heroical acts at such a time.

(iii) I answer: God may forsake his children in regard of vision, but not

[1] The 1660 volume reads 'Tabor', but this is obviously a mistake.

in regard of union. Thus it was with Jesus Christ when he cried out, 'my God, my God'. There was not a separation of the union between him and his Father, only a suspension of the vision. God's love through the interposition of our sins may be darkened and eclipsed, but still he is a Father. The sun may be hid in a cloud, but it is not out of the firmament. The promises in time of desertion may be, as it were, sequestered. We do not have the comfort from them as formerly, but still the believer's title holds good in law.

(iv) I answer: when God hides his face from his child, his heart may be towards him. As Joseph, when he spake roughly to his brethren and made them believe he would take them for spies, still his heart was towards them and he was as full of love as ever he could hold. He was fain to go aside and weep. So God is full of love to his children even when he seems to look strange. And as Moses' mother when she put her child into the ark of bulrushes and went away a little from it, yet still her eye was toward it. 'The babe wept'; aye, and the mother wept too. So God, when he goes aside as if he had forsaken his children, yet he is full of sympathy and love towards them. God may change his countenance but not break his covenant. It is one thing for God to desert, another thing to disinherit. 'How shall I give thee up, Ephraim ...' (Hosea 11: 8). It is a metaphor taken from a father going to disinherit his son, and while he is setting his hand to the deed, his bowels begin to melt and to yearn over him and he thinks thus within himself, Though he be a prodigal child, yet he is a child; I will not cut off the entail. So says God, 'How shall I give thee up?' Though Ephraim has been a rebellious son, yet he is a son, I will not disinherit him. God's thoughts may be full of love when there is a veil upon his face. The Lord may change his dispensation towards his children, but not his disposition. He may have the look of an enemy, but the heart of a Father. So that the believer may say, I am adopted; let God do what he will with me; let him take the rod or the staff; it is all one; He loves me.

God bears with their infirmities

2 The second adoptional privilege is this – if we are children then God will bear with many infirmities. A father bears much with a child he loves. 'I will spare them, as a man spareth his own son that serveth him' (Malachi 3: 17). We often grieve the Spirit, abuse kindness. God will pass by much in his children. 'He hath not seen iniquity in Jacob' (Numbers 23: 21). His love does not make him blind. He sees sin in his people but not with an eye of revenge, but pity. He sees sin in his chil-

dren as a physician does a disease in his patient. He has not seen iniquity in Jacob so as to destroy him. God may use the rod (2 Samuel 7:14), not the scorpion. O how much is God willing to pass by in his children, because they are children! God takes notice of the good that is in his children, and passes by the infirmity. God does quite contrary to us. We often take notice of the evil that is in others and overlook the good. Our eye is upon the flaw in the diamond, but we do not observe its sparkling. But God takes notice of the good that is in his children. God sees their faith and winks at their failings (1 Peter 3:6). Even as 'Sarah obeyed Abraham, calling him lord'; the Holy Ghost does not mention her unbelief and laughing at the promise, but takes notice of the good in her, namely, her obedience to her husband. 'She obeyed Abraham, calling him lord.' God puts his finger upon the scars and infirmities of his children. How much did God wink at in Israel his firstborn! Israel often provoked him with their murmurings (Deuteronomy 1:27), but God answered their murmurings with mercies. He spared them as a father spares his son.

God accepts of their imperfect services

3 The third privilege is this – if we are children then God will accept of our imperfect services. A parent takes anything in good part from his child. God accepts of the will for the deed (2 Corinthians 8:12). Oftentimes we come with broken prayers, but if we are children, God spells out our meaning and will take our prayers as a grateful present. A father loves to hear his child speak, though he but lisps and stammers. Like a 'crane, so did I chatter' (Isaiah 38:14). Good Hezekiah looked upon his praying as chattering, yet that prayer was heard (verse 5). A sigh and groan from an humble heart goes up as the smoke of incense. 'My groaning is not hid from thee' (Psalm 38:9). When all the glistering shows of hypocrites evaporate and come to nothing, a little that a child of God does in sincerity is crowned with acceptance. A father is glad of a letter from his son though there are blots in the letter, though there are false spellings and broken English. O what blottings are there in our holy things! What broken English sometimes! Yet coming from broken hearts it is accepted. Though there be weakness in duty, yet if there be willingness, the Lord is much taken with it. Says God, it is my child and he would do better. 'He hath accepted us in the beloved' (Ephesians 1:6).

God provides for them

4 If we are children then God will provide for us. A father will take care

for his children. He gives them allowance and lays up a portion (2 Corinthians 12 : 14). So does our heavenly Father.

He gives us our allowance: 'The God which fed me all my life long unto this day' (Genesis 48 : 15). Whence is our daily bread, but from his daily care? God will not let his children starve, though our unbelief is ready sometimes to question his goodness and say, 'Can God prepare a table?' See what arguments Christ brings to prove God's paternal care for his children. 'Behold the fowls of the air, they sow not, neither do they reap, yet your heavenly Father feedeth them' (Matthew 6 : 26). Does a man feed his bird, and will he not feed his child? 'Consider the lilies how they grow; they toil not, they spin not; if then, God so clothe the grass . . .' (Luke 12 : 27). Does God clothe the lilies and will he not clothe his lambs? 'The Lord careth for you' (1 Peter 5 : 7). As long as his heart is full of love, so long his head will be full of care. This should be as physic to kill the worm of unbelief.

As God gives his children a 'viaticum' or bait[1] by the way, so he lays up a portion for them. 'It is your Father's good pleasure to give you the kingdom' (Luke 12 : 32). Our Father keeps the purse and will give us enough to bear our charges here, and when at death we take shipping and shall be set upon the shore of eternity, then will our heavenly Father bestow upon us a kingdom immutable and immarcescible.[2] Lo, here is a portion which can never be summed up.

God shields off dangers from them

5 If we are children then God will shield off dangers from us. A father will protect his child from injuries. God ever lies sentinel to keep off evil from his children – temporal evil; spiritual evil.

(i) God screens off temporal evil. There are many casualties and contingencies which are incident to life. God mercifully prevents them. He keeps watch and ward for his children. 'My defence is of God' (Psalm 7 : 10). 'He that keeps Israel shall neither slumber nor sleep' (Psalm 121 :4). The eye of providence is ever awake. God gives his angels change over his children (Psalm 91 : 11). A believer has a guard of angels for his life-guard. We read of the wings of God in Scripture. As the breast of his mercy feeds his children, so the wings of his power cover them. How miraculously did God preserve Israel his first-born! He with his wings sometimes covered, sometimes carried them. 'He bare you as upon eagles' wings' (Exodus 19 :4), an emblem of God's providential care. The eagle fears no bird from above to hurt her

[1] A bite.   [2] See p. 50 fn.

young, only the arrow from beneath. Therefore she carries them upon her wings that the arrow must first hit her before it can come at her young ones. Thus God carries his children upon the wings of providence, and they are such that there is no clipping these wings, nor can any arrow hurt them.

(ii) God shields off spiritual evils from his children. 'There shall no evil befall thee' (Psalm 91:10). God does not say no afflictions shall befall us, but no evil.

But some may say, that sometimes evil in this sense befalls the godly. They spot themselves with sin. I answer:

But that evil shall not be mortal. As quicksilver is in itself dangerous, but by ointments it is so tempered that it is killed, so sin is in itself deadly but being tempered with repentance and mixed with the sacred ointment of Christ's blood, the venomous damning nature of it is taken away.

God reveals to them the great things of his law

6 If we are children then God will reveal to us the great and wonderful things of his law. 'I thank thee, O Father, Lord of heaven and earth, because thou hast hid these things from the wise and prudent and hast revealed them unto babes' (Matthew 11:25). A father will teach his children. The child goes to his father, saying, 'Father, teach me my lesson.' So David goes to God: 'Teach me to do thy will, for thou art my God' (Psalm 143:10). The Lord glories in this title, 'I am the Lord thy God which teacheth thee to profit' (Isaiah 48:17). God's children have that anointing which teaches them all things necessary to salvation. They see those mysteries which are veiled over to carnal eyes, as Elisha saw those horses and chariots of fire which his servant did not see (2 Kings 6:17). The adopted see their own sins, Satan's snares, and Christ's beauty which they whom the god of the world has blinded cannot discern. Whence was it that David understood more than the ancients (Psalm 119:100)? He had a Father to teach him. God was his instructor. 'O God, thou hast taught me from my youth' (Psalm 71:17). Many a child of God complains of ignorance and dullness. Remember this – your Father will be your tutor. He has promised to give 'his Spirit to lead thee into all truth' (John 16:13). And God not only informs the understanding, but inclines the will. He not only teaches us what we should do but enables us to do it. 'I will cause you to walk in my statutes' (Ezekiel 36:27). What a glorious privilege is this, to have the star of the Word pointing us to Christ, and the loadstone of the Spirit drawing!

God gives them boldness in prayer

7 If we are children this gives us boldness in prayer. The child goes with confidence to his father, and he cannot find in his heart to deny him: 'How much more shall your heavenly Father give his Holy Spirit to them that ask him!' (Luke 11:13). All the father has is for his child. If he comes for money, who is it for but his child? If you come to God for pardon, for brokenness of heart, God cannot deny his child. Whom does he keep his mercies in store for, but his children?

And that which may give God's children holy boldness in prayer is this; when they consider God not only in the relation of a father, but as having the disposition of a father. Some parents are of a morose, rugged nature, but God is the 'Father of mercies' (2 Corinthians 1:3). He begets all the bowels in the world. In prayer we should look upon God under this notion, 'a Father of mercy', sitting upon a 'throne of grace'. We should run to this heavenly Father in all conditions.

In our sins, as that sick child who 'said unto his father, my head, my head!' (2 Kings 4:19). As soon as he found himself not well, he ran to his father to succour him. So in case of sin, run to God: 'My heart, my heart! O this dead heart, Father, quicken it; this hard heart, Father, soften it; Father, my heart, my heart!'

In our temptations: A child, when another strikes him, runs to his father and complains. So when the devil strikes us by his temptations, let us run to our Father: 'Father, Satan assaults and hurls in his fiery darts. He would not only wound my peace, but thy glory. Father, take off the tempter. It is your child that is worried by this "red dragon". Father, will you not "bruise Satan" under my feet?' What a sweet privilege is this! When any burden lies upon our spirits, we may go to our Father and unload all our cares and griefs into his bosom!

God brings them into a state of freedom

8 If we are children, then we are in a state of freedom. Claudius Lysias valued his freedom of Rome at an high rate (Acts 22:28). A state of sonship is a state of freedom. This is not to be understood in an Antinomian sense, that the children of God are freed from the rule of the moral law. This is such a freedom as rebels take. Was it ever heard that a child should be freed from duty to his parents? But the freedom which God's children have is an holy freedom. They are freed from 'the law of sin' (Romans 8:2).

It is the sad misery of an unregenerate person that he is in a state of vassalage. He is under the tyranny of sin. Justin Martyr [1] used to say, It

[1] An eminent Christian of the 1st century.

is the greatest slavery in the world for a man to be subject to his own passions. A wicked man is as very a slave as he that works in the galley. Look into his heart and there are legions of lusts ruling him. He must do what sin will have him. A slave is at the service of an usurping tyrant. If he bid him dig in the mine, hew in the quarries, tug at the oar, he must do it. Thus every wicked man must do what corrupt nature inspired by the devil bids him. If sin bids him be drunk, be unchaste, he is at the command of sin, as the ass is at the command of the driver. Sin first enslaves and then damns.

But the children of God, though they are not free from the in-being of sin, yet they are freed from the law of sin. All sin's commands are like laws repealed which are not in force. Though sin live in a child of God it does not reign. 'Sin shall not have dominion over you' (Romans 6:14). Sin does not have a coercive power over a child of God. There is a principle of grace in his heart which gives check to corruption. This is a believer's comfort – though sin be not removed, yet it is subdued; and though he cannot keep sin out, yet he keeps sin under. The saints of God are said to 'crucify the flesh' (Galatians 5:24). Crucifying was a lingering death. First one member died, then another. Every child of God crucifies sin. Some limb of the old man is ever and anon dropping off. Though sin does not die perfectly, it dies daily. This is the blessed freedom of God's children, they are freed from the law of sin. They are led by the Spirit of God (Roman 8:14). This Spirit makes them free and cheerful in obedience. 'Where the Spirit of the Lord is, there is liberty' (2 Corinthians 3:17).

God makes them heirs apparent to the promises

9 If we are children then we are heirs apparent to all the promises. The promises are called precious (2 Peter 2:4). The promises are a cabinet of jewels. They are breasts full of the milk of the gospel. The promises are enriched with variety and are suited to a Christian's present condition. Does he want pardoning grace? There is a promise carries forgiveness in it (Jeremiah 31:34). Does he want sanctifying grace? There is a promise of healing (Hosea 14:4). Does he want corroborating grace? There is a promise of strength (Isaiah 41:10). And these promises are the children's bread. The saints are called 'heirs of the promise' (Hebrews 6:17). There is Christ and heaven in a promise; and there is never a promise in the Bible but an adopted person may lay a legal claim to it and say, 'This is mine.' The natural man who remains still in the old family has nothing to do with these promises. He may read over the promises (as one may read over another man's will

or inventory) but has no right to them. The promises are like a garden of flowers, paled in and enclosed, which no stranger may gather, only the children of the family. Ishmael was the son of the bond-woman. He had no right to the family. 'Cast out the bond-woman and her son,' as Sarah once said to Abraham (Genesis 21:10). So the unbeliever is not adopted, he is none of the household, and God will say at the day of judgment, 'Cast out this son of the bond-woman into utter darkness', where is weeping and gnashing of teeth.

God gives them his blessing

10 If we are children, then we shall have our Father's blessing. 'They are the seed which the Lord has blessed' (Isaiah 61:9). We read that Isaac blessed his son Jacob: 'God give thee of the dew of heaven' (Genesis 27:28), which was not only a prayer for Jacob, but (as Luther says) a prophecy of that happiness and blessing which should come upon him and his posterity. Thus every adopted child has his heavenly Father's benediction. There is a special blessing distilled into all that he possesses. 'The Lord will bless his people with peace' (Exodus 23:25; Psalm 29:11). He will not only give them peace, but they shall have it with a blessing. The wicked have the things they enjoy with God's leave, but the adopted have them with God's love. The wicked have them by providence; the saints by promise. Isaac had but one blessing to bestow. 'Hast thou but one blessing, my father?' (Genesis 27:38). But God has more blessings than one for his children. He blesses them in their souls, bodies, names, estate, posterity. He blesses them with the upper-springs and the nether springs. He multiplies to bless them and his blessing cannot be reversed. As Isaac said concerning Jacob, 'I have blessed him, yea and he shall be blessed' (Genesis 27:33), so God blesses his children and they shall be blessed.

God works all things for their good

11 If we are children, then all things that fall out shall turn to our good. 'All things work together for good to them that love God' (Romans 8:28): good things; evil things.

(i) Good things work for good to God's children. Mercies shall do them good. The mercies of God shall soften them. David's heart was overcome with God's mercy. 'Who am I, and what is my house . . .?' (2 Samuel 7:18). I who was of a mean family, I who held the shepherd's staff, that now I should hold the royal sceptre! Nay, Thou hast spoken of thy servant's house for a great while to come. Thou hast made a promise that my children shall sit upon the throne; yea, that the blessed

Messiah shall come of my line and race. And is this the manner of man, O Lord God! As if he had said, 'Do men show such kindness undeserved? See how this good man's heart was dissolved and softened by mercy! The flint is soonest broken upon a soft pillow.

Mercies make the children of God more fruitful. The ground bears the better crop for the cost that is laid upon it. God gives his children health and they spend and are spent for Christ. He gives them estates and they honour the Lord with their substance. The backs and bellies of the poor are the field where they sow the precious seed of their charity. A child of God makes his estate a golden clasp to bind his heart faster to God, a footstool to raise him up higher towards heaven.

Ordinances shall work for good to God's children. The word preached shall do them good; it is a savour of life; it is a lamp to the feet and a laver to their hearts. The word preached is a means of health, a chariot of salvation. It is an ingrafting and a transforming word; it is a word with unction, anointing their eyes to see that light. The preaching of the Word is that lattice where Christ looks forth and shows himself to his saints. This golden pipe of the sanctuary conveys the water of life. To the wicked the word preached works for evil; even the word of life becomes a savour of death. The same cause may have divers, nay, contrary effects. The sun dissolves the ice but hardens the clay. To the unregenerate and profane, the Word is not humbling but hardening. Jesus Christ, the best of preachers, was to some a rock of offence. The Jews sucked death from his sweet lips. It is sad that the breast should kill any. The wicked suck poison from that breast of ordnances where the children of God suck milk and are nourished unto salvation.

The sacrament works for good to the children of God. In the Word preached the saints hear Christ's voice; in the sacrament they have his kiss. The Lord's Supper is to the saints 'a feast of fat things'. It is an healing and a sealing ordinance. In this charger, or rather chalice, a bleeding Saviour is brought in to revive drooping spirits. The sacrament has glorious effects in the hearts of God's children. It quickens their affections, strengthens their faith, mortifies their sin, revives their hopes, increases their joy. It gives a pre-libation and foretaste of heaven.

(ii) Evil things work for good to God's children. 'Unto the upright ariseth light in the darkness' (Psalm 112:4).

Poverty works for good to God's children. It starves their lusts. It increases their graces. 'Poor in the world, rich in faith' (James 2:5). Poverty tends to prayer. When God has clipped his children's wings by poverty, they fly swiftest to the throne of grace.

Sickness works for their good. It shall bring the body of death into a consumption. 'Though our outward man perish, yet the inward man is renewed day by day' (2 Corinthians 4:16). Like those two laurels at Rome, when the one withered the other flourished.[1] When the body withers the soul of a Christian flourishes. How often have we seen a lively faith in a languishing body! Hezekiah was better on his sick bed than upon his throne. When he was upon his sick-bed he humbles himself and weeps. When he was on his throne he grew proud (Isaiah 39:2). God's children recover by sickness. In this sense, 'out of weakness they are made strong' (Hebrews 11:34).

Reproach works for good to God's children; it increases their grace and their glory.

Disgrace increases their grace. The husbandman by dunging his ground makes the soil more rich and fertile. God lets the wicked dung his people with reproaches and calumnies, that their hearts may be a richer soil for grace to grow in.

Reproach increases their glory. He that unjustly takes from a saint's credit shall add to his crown. The sun shines brighter after an eclipse. The more a child of God is eclipsed by reproaches the brighter he shall shine in the kingdom of heaven.

Persecution to God's children works for good. The godly may be compared to that plant which Gregory Nazianzen speaks of. It lives by dying and grows by cutting. The zeal and love of the saints is blown up by sufferings. Their joy flourishes. Tertullian says the primitive Christians rejoiced more in their persecutions than in their deliverances.

Death works for good to the children of God. It is like the whirlwind to the prophet Elijah, which blew off his mantle, but carried him up to heaven. So death to a child of God is like a boisterous whirlwind which blows off the mantle of his flesh (for the body is but the mantle the soul is wrapped in), but it carries up the soul to God. This is the glorious privilege of the sons of God. Everything that falls out shall do them good. The children of God, when they come to heaven (as Chrysostom speaks), shall bless God for all cross providences.

God keeps them from perishing

12 And lastly, if we are children we shall never finally perish (John 5:24; 10:28). Those who are adopted are out of the power of damnation. 'There is no condemnation to them that are in Christ' (Romans 8:1). Will a father condemn his own son? God will never disinherit any of his children. Fathers may disinherit for some fault. Reuben for

[1] In the classical world, the laurel was linked with the 'spirit of prophecy'.

incest lost the prerogative of his birthright (Genesis 49:4). What is the reason parents disinherit their children? Surely this, because they can make them no better. They cannot make them fit for the inheritance. But when we are bad our heavenly Father knows how to make us better. He can make us fit to inherit. 'Giving thanks to the Father who hath made us meet for the inheritance' (Colossians 1:12). Therefore it being in his power to make us better and to work in us an idoneity[1] and meetness for the inheritance, certainly he will never finally disinherit.

Because this is so sweet a privilege, and the life of a Christian's comfort lies in it, therefore I shall clear it by arguments that the children of God cannot finally perish. The entail of hell and damnation is cut off. Not but that the best of God's children have that guilt which deserves hell, but Christ is the friend at court which has begged their pardon. Therefore the damning power of sin is taken away, which I prove thus:

The children of God cannot finally perish, because God's justice is satisfied for their sins. The blood of Christ is the price paid not only meritoriously, but efficaciously for all them that believe. This being the 'blood of God' (Acts 20:28), justice is fully satisfied and does not meddle to condemn those for whom this blood was shed and to whom it is applied. Jesus Christ was a sponsor. He stood bound for every child of God as a surety. He said to justice, 'Have patience with them and I will pay thee all', so that the believer cannot be liable to wrath. God will not require the debt twice, both of the surety and the debtor (Romans 3:24–26). God is not only merciful in pardoning his children, but 'righteous' 'He is just to forgive' (1 John 1:9). It is an act of God's equity and justice to spare the sinner when he has been satisfied in the surety.

A damnatory sentence cannot pass upon the children of God, because they are so God's children, as withal they are Christ's spouse (Canticles 4:11). There is a marriage union between Christ and the saints. Every child of God is a part of Christ. He is 'Christ mystical'. Now, shall a member of Christ perish? A child of God cannot perish but Christ must perish. Jesus Christ who is the Husband, is the Judge, and will he condemn his own spouse?

Every child of God is transformed into the likeness of Christ. He has the same Spirit, the same judgment, the same will. He is a lively picture of Christ. As Christ bears the saints' names upon his breast, so they bear his image upon their hearts (Galatians 4:19). Will Christ suffer his own image to be destroyed? Theodosius[2] counted them traitors who defaced his image. Christ will not let his image in believers be defaced and rent. He will not endure to see his own picture take fire. The sea

[1] Fitness, aptitude.   [2] Roman Emperor (see p. 163 fn. 2).

has not only stinking carrion, but jewels thrown into it, but none of God's jewels shall ever be thrown into the dread sea of hell.

If God's children could be capable of final perishing then pardon of sin were no privilege. The Scripture says, 'Blessed is he whose transgression is forgiven' (Psalm 32:1). But what blessedness were there in having sin forgiven, if afterwards a final and damnatory sentence should pass upon the heirs of promise? What were a man the better for the king's pardon if he were condemned after he were pardoned?

If the children of God should be finally disinherited then the Scripture could not be fulfilled which tells us of glorious rewards. 'Verily there is a reward for the righteous' (Psalm 58:11). God sweetens his commands with promises. He ties duty and reward together. As in the body the veins carry the blood and the arteries carry the spirits, so one part of the Word carries duty in it, and another part of the Word carries reward. Now if the adopted of God should eternally miscarry, what reward were there for the righteous? And Moses did indiscreetly in looking to the 'recompense of the reward' (Hebrews 11:26). And so by consequence there would be a door opened to despair.

By all which it appears that the children of God cannot be disinherited or reprobated. If they should lose happiness Christ should lose his purchase and should die in vain.

Thus we have seen the glorious privileges of the children of God. What an encouragement is here to religion! How may this tempt men to turn godly! Can the world vie with a child of God? Can the world give such privileges as these? As Saul said, 'Will the son of Jesse give everyone of you fields and vineyards, and make you all captains of thousands?' (1 Samuel 22:7). Can the world do that for you which God does for his children? Can it give you pardon of sin or eternal life? 'Are not the gleanings of Ephraim better than the vintage of Abiezer?' (Judges 8:2). Is not godliness gain? What is there in sin that men should love it? The work of sin is drudgery and the wages death. They who see more in sin than in the privileges of adoption, let them go on and have their ears bored to the devil's service.

20 *Exhortations to Christians as they are children of God*

1 There is a bill of indictment against those who declare to the world they are not the children of God: all *profane persons*. These have damnation written upon their forehead.

Scoffers at religion. It were blasphemy to call these the children of God. Will a true child jeer at his Father's picture?

Drunkards, who drown reason and stupefy conscience. These declare their sin as Sodom. They are children indeed, but 'cursed children' (2 Peter 2: 14).

2 Exhortation, which consists of two branches.

(i) Let us prove ourselves to be the children of God.
(ii) Let us carry ourselves as the children of God.

Let us prove ourselves to be the children of God

(i) Let us prove ourselves to be the children of God. There are many false and unscriptural evidences.

Says one, The gravest divines in the country think me to be godly, and can they be mistaken? Are the seers blind?

Others can but see the outward carriage and deportment. If that be fair, they may by the rule of charity judge well of thee. But what say God and conscience? Are these your compurgators?[1] Are you a saint in God's calendar? It is a poor thing to have an applauding world and an accusing conscience.

Oh but, says another, I hope I am a child of God; I love my heavenly Father.

Why do you love God? Perhaps because God gives you corn and wine. This is a mercenary love, a love to yourself more than to God. You may lead a sheep all the field over with a bottle[2] of hay in your

---

[1] Vindicators.   [2] Bundle.

hand, but throw away the hay, now the sheep will follow you no longer. So the squint-eyed hypocrite loves God only for the provender. When this fails, his affection fails too.

But leaving these vain and false evidences of adoption, let us enquire for a sound evidence. The main evidence of adoption is sanctification. Search, O Christian, whether the work of sanctification has passed upon your soul! Is your understanding sanctified to discern the things which are excellent? Is your will sanctified to embrace heavenly objects? Do you love where God loves and hate where God hates? Are you a consecrated person? This argues the heart of a child. God will never reject those who have his image and superscription upon them.

Let us carry ourselves as becomes the children of God

(ii) Let us carry ourselves as becomes the children of God, and let us deport ourselves as the children of the High God.

In *obedience*: 'As obedient children' (1 Peter 1:14). If a stranger bid a child to do a thing, he regards him not. But if his father command, he presently [1] obeys. Obey God out of love, obey him readily, obey every command. If he bid you part with your bosom-sin, leave and loathe it. 'I set before the sons of the house of the Rechabites pots full of wine, and cups, and I said unto them, Drink ye wine; but they said, we will drink no wine, for Jonadab, the son of Rechab our father, commanded us saying, Ye shall drink no wine, neither ye nor your sons for ever' (Jeremiah 35:5, 6). Thus when Satan and your own heart would be tempting you to a sin and set cups of wine before you, refuse to drink. Say, 'My heavenly Father has commanded me not to drink.' Hypocrites will obey God in some things which are consistent either with their credit or profit, but in other things they desire to be excused. Like Esau who obeyed his father in bringing him venison, because probably he liked the sport of hunting, but refused to obey him in a business of greater importance, namely, in the choice of his wife.

Let us carry ourselves as God's children in *humility*. 'Be ye clothed with humility' (1 Peter 5:5). It is a becoming garment. Let a child of God look at his face every morning in the glass of God's Word and see his sinful spots. This will make him walk humbly all the day after. God cannot endure to see his children grow proud. He suffers them to fall into sin, as he did Peter, that their plumes may fall, and that they may learn to go on lower ground.

Let us walk as the children of God in *sobriety*. 'But let us who are

[1] Immediately.

of the day be sober' (1 Thessalonians 5:8). God's children must not do as others. They must be sober.

In their *speeches*; not rash, not unseemly. 'Let your speech be seasoned with salt' (Colossians 4:6). Grace must be the salt which seasons our words and makes them savoury. Our words must be solid and weighty, not feathery. God's children must speak the language of Canaan. Many pretend to be God's children, but their speech betrays them. Their lips do not drop as an honey-comb, but are like the sink, where all the filth of the house is carried out.

The children of God must be sober in their *opinions*; hold nothing but what a sober man would hold. Error, as Saint Basil says, is a spiritual intoxication, a kind of frenzy. If Christ were upon the earth again, he might have patients enough. There are abundance of spiritual lunatics among us which need healing.

The children of God must be sober in their *attire*. 'Whose adorning, let it not be that outward adorning of plaiting the hair and of wearing of gold . . . but let it be the hidden man of the heart' (1 Peter 3:3). God's children must not be conformed to the world (Romans 12:2). It is not for God's children to do as others, taking up every fashion. What is a naked breast but a glass in which you may see a vain heart? What is spotting of faces, but learning the black art? God may turn these black spots into blue. Walk soberly.

Let us carry ourselves as the children of God in *sedulity*. We must be diligent in our calling. Religion does not seal warrants to idleness. It was Jerome's advice to his friend to be always well employed. 'Six days shalt thou labour.' God sets all his children to work. They must not be like the 'lilies which toil not, neither do they spin'. Heaven indeed is a place of rest. 'They rest from their labours' (Revelation 14:13). There the saints shall lay aside all their working tools, and take the harp and viol, but while we are here, we must labour in a calling. God will bless our diligence, not our laziness.

Let us carry ourselves as the children of God in *magnanimity* and heroicalness. The saints are high-born. They are of the true blood-royal, born of God. They must do nothing sneakingly or sordidly. They must not fear the faces of men. As said that brave-spirited Nehemiah, 'Shall such a man as I flee?' (Nehemiah 6:11) so should a child of God say, Shall I be afraid to do my duty? Shall I unworthily comply and prostitute myself to the lusts and humours of men? The children of the most High should do nothing to stain or dishonour their noble birth. A king's son scorns to do anything that is below him.

Let us carry ourselves as the children of God in *sanctity* (1 Peter

[257]

1 : 16). Holiness is the diadem of beauty. In this let us imitate our heavenly Father. A debauched child is a disgrace to his father. There is nothing more casts a reflection on our heavenly Father than the irregular actings of such as profess themselves his children. What will others say? Are these the children of the Most High? Is God their Father? 'The Name of God is blasphemed through you Gentiles' (Romans 2 : 24). Oh let us do nothing unworthy of our heavenly Father.

Let us carry ourselves as the children of God in *cheerfulness*. It was the speech of Jonadab to Amnon, 'Why art thou, being the king's son, lean?' (2 Samuel 13 : 4). Why do the children of God walk so pensively? Are they not 'heirs of heaven'? Perhaps they may meet with hard usage in the world, but let them remember they are the seed-royal, and are of the family of God. Suppose a man were in a strange land, and should meet there with unkind usage, yet he rejoices that he is son and heir, and has a great estate in his own country; so should the children of God comfort themselves with this, though they are now in a strange country, yet they have a title to the Jerusalem above, and though sin at present hangs about them (for they still have some relics of their disease) yet shortly they shall get rid of it. At death they shall shake off this viper.

And lastly, let us carry ourselves as the children of God in *holy longings and expectations*. Children are always longing to be at home. 'We groan earnestly ...' (2 Corinthians 5 : 2). There is bread enough in our Father's house. How should we long for home! Death carries a child of God to his Father's house. Saint Paul therefore desired to be dissolved. It is comfortable dying when by faith we can resign up our souls into our Father's hands. 'Father, into thy hands I commend my spirit' (Luke 23 : 46).

21 *Concerning persecution*

Blessed are they which are persecuted for righteousness' sake for theirs is the kingdom of heaven.

MATTHEW 5 : 10

We are now come to the last beatitude: 'Blessed are they which are persecuted ...' Our Lord Christ would have us reckon the cost. 'Which of you intending to build a tower sitteth not down first and counteth the cost, whether he have enough to finish it?' (Luke 14:28). Religion will cost us the tears of repentance and the blood of persecution. But we see here a great encouragement that may keep us from fainting in the day of adversity. For the present, blessed; for the future, crowned.

The words fall into two general parts.

1 The condition of the godly in this life: 'They are persecuted.'

2 Their reward after this life: 'Theirs is the kingdom of heaven.'

Observations on persecution

I shall speak chiefly of the first, and wind in the other in the applicatory.

The observation is that true godliness is usually attended with persecution. 'We must through much tribulation enter into the kingdom of God' (Acts 14:22). 'The Jews stirred up the chief men of the city and raised persecution against Paul ...' (Acts 13:50). Luther makes it the very definition of a Christian, 'Christianus quasi crucianus.'[1] Though Christ died to take away the curse from us, yet not to take away the cross from us. Those stones which are cut out for a building are first under the saw and hammer to be hewed and squared. The godly are called 'living stones' (1 Peter 2:5). And they must be hewn and polished by the persecutor's hand that they may be fit for the heavenly building. The saints have no charter of exemption from trials. Though they be never so meek, merciful, pure in heart, their piety will not shield them from sufferings. They must hang their harp on the willows and take the cross. The way to heaven is by way of thorns and blood.

[1] Christians, as if (the word meant) crucified ones.

Though it be full of roses in regard of the comforts of the Holy Ghost, yet it is full of thorns in regard of persecutions. Before Israel got to Canaan, a land flowing with milk and honey, they must go through a wilderness of serpents and a Red Sea. So the children of God in their passage to the holy land must meet with fiery serpents and a red sea of persecution. It is a saying of Ambrose, 'There is no Abel but has his Cain.' St Paul fought with beasts at Ephesus (1 Corinthians 15 : 32). Set it down as a maxim, if you will follow Christ, you must see the swords and staves. Put the cross in your creed. For the amplification of this, there are several things we are to take cognizance of.

1 What is meant by persecution.
2 The several kinds of persecution.
3 Why there must be persecution.
4 The chief persecutions are raised against the ministers of Christ.
5 What that persecution is which makes a man blessed.

What is meant by persecution?

What is meant by persecution? The Greek word 'to persecute', signifies 'to vex and molest', sometimes 'to prosecute another', to 'arraign him at the bar', and 'to pursue him to the death'. A persecutor is a 'pricking briar' (Ezekiel 28 : 24); therefore the church is described to be a 'lily among thorns' (Canticles 2 : 2).

Various kinds of persecution

What are the several kinds of persecution? There is a two-fold persecution; a persecution of the hand; a persecution of the tongue.

1 A persecution of the hand. 'Which of the prophets have not your fathers persecuted?' (Acts 7 : 52). 'For thy sake we are killed all the day long' (Romans 8 : 36; Galatians 4 : 29). This I call a bloody persecution, when the people of God are persecuted with fire and sword. So we read of the ten persecutions in the time of Nero, Domitian, Trajan [1] etc.; and of the Marian persecution.[2] England for five years drank a cup of blood and lately Piedmont [3] and the confines of Bohemia [4] have been

---

[1] Roman emperors : A.D. 54–69; A.D. 81–96; A.D. 98–117, respectively.
[2] 1553–58.   [3] See p. 69 fn. 3.
[4] This seems to refer to the awful devastation caused by the Thirty Years' War ending in 1648.

scourged to death with the rod of the persecutor. God's Church has always, like Abraham's ram, been tied in a bush of thorns.

2 The persecution of the tongue, which is two-fold.

(i) Reviling. This few think of or lay to heart, but it is called in the text, persecution. 'When men shall revile you and persecute you.' This is tongue persecution. 'His words were drawn swords' (Psalm 55:21). You may kill a man as well in his name as in his person. A good name is as 'precious ointment' (Ecclesiastes 7:1). A good conscience and a good name is like a gold ring set with a rich diamond. Now to smite another by his name is by our Saviour called persecution. Thus the primitive Christians endured the persecution of the tongue. 'They had trial of cruel mockings' (Hebrews 11: 36). David was 'the song of the drunkards' (Psalm 69: 12). They would sit on their ale-bench and jeer at him. How frequently do the wicked cast out the squibs of reproach at God's children: 'These are the holy ones!' Little do they think what they do. They are now doing Cain's work and Julian's.[1] They are persecuting.

(ii) Slandering. So it is in the text: 'When they shall persecute you and say all manner of evil against you falsely.' Slandering is tongue persecution. Thus Saint Paul was slandered in his doctrine. Report had it that he preached, 'Men might do evil that good might come of it' (Romans 3:8). Thus Christ who cast out devils was charged to have a devil (John 8:48). The primitive Christians were falsely accused for killing their children and for incest. 'They laid to my charge things that I knew not' (Psalm 35:11).

Let us take heed of becoming persecutors. Some think there is no persecution but fire and sword. Yes, there is persecution of the tongue. There are many of these persecutors nowadays who by a devilish chemistry can turn gold into dung, the precious names of God's saints into reproach and disgrace. There have been many punished for clipping of coin. Of how much sorer punishment shall they be thought worthy, who clip the names of God's people to make them weigh lighter!

The causes of persecution

Why there must be persecution. I answer for two reasons.

1 In regard of God: his decree and his design.

God's *Decree*: 'We are appointed thereunto' (1 Thessalonians 3:3).

[1] Julian the Apostate (see p. 155 fn. 2).

Whoever brings the suffering, God sends it. God bade Shimei curse. Shimei's tongue was the arrow, but it was God that shot it.

God's *Design*. God has a two-fold design in the persecutions of his children.

(i) *Trials*. 'Many shall be tried' (Daniel 12:10). Persecution is the touchstone of sincerity. It discovers[1] true saints from hypocrites. Unsound hearts pretend fair in prosperity, but in time of persecution fall away (Matthew 13:20, 21). Hypocrites cannot sail in stormy weather. They will follow Christ to Mount Olivet, but not to Mount Calvary. Like green timber they shrink in the scorching sun of persecution. If trouble arises, hypocrites will rather make Demas their choice than Moses their choice. They will prefer thirty pieces of silver before Christ. God will have persecutions in the world to make a discovery of men. Suffering times are sifting times. 'When I am tried I shall come forth as gold' (Job 23:10). Job had a furnace-faith. A Christian of right breed (who is born of God), whatever he loses, will 'hold fast his integrity' (Job 2:3). Christ's true disciples will follow him upon the water.

(ii) *Purity*. God lets his children be in the furnace that they may be 'partakers of his holiness' (Hebrews 12:10). The cross is physic. It purges out pride, impatience, love of the world. God washes his people in bloody waters to get out their spots and make them look white (Daniel 12:10). 'I am black, but comely' (Canticles 1:5). The torrid zone of persecution made the spouse's skin black, but her soul fair. See how differently afflictions work upon the wicked and godly. They make the one worse, the other better. Take a cloth that is rotten. If you scour and rub it, it frets and tears; but if you scour a piece of plate, it looks brighter. When afflictions are upon the wicked, they fret against God and tear themselves in impatience, but when the godly are scoured by these, they look brighter.

There will be persecutions in regard of the enemies of the church. These vultures prey upon God's turtles. The church has two sorts of enemies.

Open enemies. The wicked hate the godly. There is 'enmity between the seed of the woman and the seed of the serpent' (Genesis 3:15). As in nature there is an antipathy between the vine and the bay-tree, the elephant and the dragon; and as vultures have an antipathy against sweet smells; so in the wicked there is an antipathy against the people of God. They hate the sweet perfumes of their graces. It is true the saints have their infirmities, but the wicked do not hate them for these,

[1] Distinguishes.

[262]

but for their holiness, and from this hatred arises open violence. The thief hates the light, therefore would blow it out.

Secret enemies, who pretend friendship but secretly raise persecutions against the godly. Such are hypocrites and heretics. Saint Paul calls them 'false brethren' (2 Corinthians 11 : 26). The church complains that her own sons had vexed her (Canticles 1 : 6). That is, those who had been bred up in her bosom and pretended religion and sympathy, these false friends vexed her. The church's enemies are them 'of her own house'. Such as are open pretenders but secret opposers of the faith are ever worst. A wen seems to be a part of the body, but is indeed an enemy to it. It disfigures and endangers it. They are the vilest and basest of men who hang forth Christ's colours, yet fight against him.

The persecution of ministers

The fourth particular is that the chief persecutions are raised against the ministers. Our Lord Christ turns himself directly to the apostles whom he was ready to commission and send abroad to preach: 'Blessed are ye when men shall persecute you' (verse 11). 'So persecuted they the prophets before you' (verse 12). 'Take, my brethren, the prophets for an example of suffering affliction' (James 5 : 10). No sooner is any man a minister, but he is a piece of a martyr. The ministers of Christ are his chosen vessels. Now as the best vessel of gold and silver passes through the fire, so God's chosen vessels pass often through the fire of persecution. All times are not like the silver age wherein Constantine lived. He was an honourer of the ministry. He would not sit down in the Council of Nicaea till the bishops who were convened there came and besought him. He would say, if he saw an infirmity in the clergy, that his royal purple would cover it. Ministers must not always look for such shines of the prince's favour. They must expect an alarum. Peter, a famous preacher, knew how 'to cast the net on the right side of the ship', and at one sermon he converted three thousand souls. Yet neither the divinity of his doctrine nor the sanctity of his life could exempt him from persecution. 'When thou shalt be old, another shall gird thee, and carry thee whither thou wouldest not.' It alludes to his suffering death for Christ. He was (says Eusebius) bound with chains and afterwards crucified at Jerusalem with his head downwards. Saint Paul, a holy man, who is steeled with courage, and fired with zeal, as soon as he entered into the ministry 'bonds and persecutions did abide him' (Acts 9 : 16; 20 : 23). He was made up of sufferings. 'I am ready to be offered up' (2 Timothy 4:6). He alludes to the drink offerings wherein the wine or blood used in sacrifice was poured out, thereby intimating by what manner of death he should glorify God; not by being sacrificed in the fire, but by pouring out his blood, which was when he was beheaded. And that it might seem no strange thing for God's ministers to be under the heat and rage of persecution, Stephen puts the question, 'Which of the prophets have not your fathers persecuted?' (Acts 7 : 52). Ignatius [1] was torn with wild beasts. Cyprian,[2] Polycarp [3] martyred. Maximus,[4] the emperor (as Eusebius relates), gave charge to his officers to put none to death but the governors and pastors of the Church.

The reasons why the storm of persecution has chiefly fallen upon the ministers are:

1 They have their corruptions as well as others, and lest they should be lifted up 'through the abundance of revelation', God lets loose some 'messenger of Satan' to vex and persecute them. God sees they have need of the flail to thresh off their husks. The fire God puts them into is not to consume but to refine them.

2 The ministers are Christ's ensign-bearers to carry his colours. They are the captains of the Lord's host, therefore they are the most shot at. 'I am set for the defence of the gospel' (Philippians 1 : 17). The Greek word here used alludes to a soldier that is set in the forefront of the battle and has all the missiles flying about his ears. The minister's work is to preach against men's sins which are as dear to them as their right eye, and they cannot endure this. Every man's sin is his king to which he yields love and subjection. Now as Pilate said, 'Shall I crucify your king?' Men will not endure to have their king-sin crucified. This then being the work of the ministry, to divide between men and their lusts, to part these two old friends, no wonder it meets with so much opposition. When Paul preached against Diana, all the city was in an uproar. We preach against men's Dianas, those sins which bring them in pleasure and profit. This causes an uproar.

3 From the malice of Satan. The ministers of Christ come to destroy his kingdom, therefore the old serpent will spit all his venom at them. If we tread upon the devil's head, he will bite us by the heel. The devil sets up several forts and garrisons in men's hearts — pride, ignorance, unbelief. Now the weapons of the ministry beat down these strongholds (2

1 Bishop of Antioch (martyred in 107).
2 Bishop of Carthage (martyred, 258).
3 Bishop of Smyrna (martyred, 155).
4 Roman Emperor, 286–305, 308–9).

Corinthians 10:4). Therefore Satan raises his militia, all the force and power of hell against the ministry. The kingdom of Satan is a 'kingdom of darkness' (Acts 26:18; Revelation 16:10), and God's ministers are called the 'light of the world' (Matthew 5:14). They come to enlighten those that sit in darkness. This enrages Satan. Therefore he labours to eclipse the lights, to pull down the stars, that his kingdom of darkness may prevail. The devil is called a lion (1 Peter 5:8). The souls of people are the lion's prey. The ministers' work is to take away this prey from this lion. Therefore how will he roar upon them, and seek to destroy them!

(i) It shows us what a work the ministry is; though full of dignity, yet full of danger. The persecution of the tongue is the most gentle persecution can be expected. It is not possible (says Luther) to be a faithful preacher and not to meet with trials and oppositions.

(ii) It shows the corruption of men's nature since the fall. They are their own enemies. They persecute those who come to do them most good. What is the work of the ministry but to save men's souls? to pull them as 'brands out of the fire'. Yet they are angry at this. We do not hate the physician who brings such physic as makes us sick, because it is to make us well; nor the surgeon who lances the flesh, because it is in order to a cure. Why then should we quarrel with the minister? What is our work but to bring men to heaven? 'We are ambassadors for Christ . . .' (2 Corinthians 5:20). We would have a peace made up between you and God; yet this is the folly of depraved nature, to requite evil for good. Aristoxenus [1] used to moisten his flowers with wine, honey, and perfumes that they might not only smell more fragrantly but put forth more vigorously. So should we do with our ministers. Give them wine and honey. Encourage them in their work that they might act more vigorously. But instead of this we give them gall and vinegar to drink. We hate and persecute them. Most deal with their ministers as Israel did with Moses. He prayed for them and wrought miracles for them, yet they were continually quarrelling with him and sometimes ready to take away his life.

(iii) If the fury of the world be against the ministers, then you that fear God had need pray much for them. 'Pray for us, that the Word of the Lord may have free course, and that we may be delivered from unreasonable and wicked men.' (2 Thessalonians 3:1, 2). People should pray for their ministers that God would give them the 'wisdom of the

---

[1] A Greek philosopher of the 4th century B.C.

serpent', that they may not betray themselves to danger by indiscretion; and the boldness of the lion, that they may not betray the truth by fear.

The persecution that makes one blessed

The next thing to be explained is what that suffering persecution is which makes a man blessed.

1 I shall show what that suffering is which will not make us blessed.

(i) That suffering is not reckoned for martyrdom, when we pull a cross upon ourselves. There is little comfort in such suffering. Augustine speaks of some in his time who were called Circumcellions,[1] who out of an itch rather than zeal of martyrdom, would run themselves into sufferings. These were accessory to their own death, like King Saul who fell upon his own sword. We are bound by all lawful means to preserve our own lives. Jesus Christ did not suffer till he was called to it. Suspect that to be a temptation which bids us cast ourselves down into sufferings. When men through precipitancy and rashness run themselves into trouble, it is a cross of their own making and not of God's laying upon them.

(ii) That is not to be accounted martyrdom when we suffer for our offences. 'Let none of you suffer as an evil-doer' (1 Peter 4:15). 'We indeed suffer justly' (Luke 23:41). I am not of Cyprian's mind that the thief on the cross suffered as a martyr. No, he suffered as an evil-doer! Christ indeed took pity on him and saved him. He died a saint, but not a martyr. When men suffer by the hand of the magistrate for their uncleanness, blasphemies etc., these do not suffer persecution, but execution. They die not as martyrs, but as malefactors. They suffer evil for being evil.

(iii) That suffering will not make men blessed, when they suffer, out of sinister respects, to be cried up as head of a party, or to keep up a faction. The apostle implies that a man may give his body to be burned, yet go to hell (1 Corinthians 13:3). Ambitious men may sacrifice their lives to purchase fame. These are the devil's martyrs.

2 What that suffering persecution is which will make us blessed, and shall wear the crown of martyrdom.

(i) When we suffer in a good cause. So it is in the text. 'Blessed are they which suffer for righteousness' sake.' It is the cause that makes a mar-

[1](Christian) fanatics of the 4th century who roved about from house to house.

tyr. When we suffer for the truth and espouse the quarrel of religion, this is to suffer for righteousness' sake. 'For the hope of Israel I am bound with this chain' (Acts 28:20).

(ii) When we suffer with a good conscience. A man may have a good cause and a bad conscience. He may suffer for 'righteousness' sake', yet he himself be unrighteous. Saint Paul, as he had a just cause, so he had a pure conscience. 'I have lived in all good conscience to this day' (Acts 23:1). Paul kept a good conscience to his dying day. It has made the saints go as cheerfully to the stake as if they had been going to a crown. Look to it that there be no flaw in conscience. A ship that is to sail upon the waters must be preserved from leaking. When Christians are to sail on the waters of persecution, let them take heed there be no leak of guilt in their conscience. He who suffers (though it be in God's own cause) with a bad conscience, suffers two hells; a hell of persecution, and an hell of damnation.

(iii) When we have a good call. 'Ye shall be brought before kings . . .' (Matthew 10:18). There is no question but a man may so far consult for his safety that if God by his providence open a door, he may fly in time of persecution (Matthew 10:23). But when he is brought before kings, and the case is such that either he must suffer or the truth must suffer, here is a clear call to suffering, and this is reckoned for martyrdom.

(iv) When we have good ends in our suffering, namely, that we may glorify God, set a seal to the truth, and show our love to Christ. 'Ye shall be brought before kings for my sake' (Matthew 10:18). The primitive Christians burned more in love than in fire. When we look at God in our sufferings and are willing to make his crown flourish, though it be in our ashes, this is that suffering which carries away the garland of glory.

(v) When we suffer as Christians. 'If any man suffer as a Christian, let him not be ashamed' (1 Peter 4:16). To suffer as a Christian is to suffer with such a spirit as becomes a Christian, which is:

When we suffer with *patience*. 'Take, my brethren, the prophets for an example of suffering affliction and of patience' (James 5:10). A Christian must not repine but say, 'Shall I not drink the cup' of martyrdom which my Father has given me? There should be such a spirit of meekness in a Christian's suffering that it should be hard to say which is greater, his persecution or his patience. When Job had lost all, he kept the breast-plate of innocency and the shield of patience. An impatient martyr is a solecism.

To suffer as Christians is when we suffer with *courage*. Courage is a Christian's armour of proof. It steels and animates him. The three children or rather the three champions were of brave heroic spirits. They do not say to the king, 'We ought not to serve your gods', but 'We will not' (Daniel 3:18). Neither Nebuchadnezzar's music nor his furnace could alter their resolution. Tertullian was called an adamant for his invincible courage. Holy courage makes us (as one of the fathers says) 'have such faces of brass that we are not ashamed of the cross'. This is to suffer as Christians, when we are meek yet resolute. The more the fire is blown the more it flames. So it is with a brave-spirited Christian. The more opposition he meets with the more zeal and courage flames forth. What a spirit of gallantry was in Luther who said, writing to Melanchthon, 'If it be not the cause of God we are embarked in, let us desert it! If it be his cause and will bear us out, why do we not stand to it?'

To suffer as Christians is to suffer with *cheerfulness*. Patience is a bearing the cross; cheerfulness is a taking up the cross. Christ suffered for us cheerfully. His death was a free-will offering (Luke 12:50). He thirsted to drink of that cup of blood. Such must our sufferings be for Christ. Cheerfulness perfumes martyrdom and makes it the sacrifice of a sweet-smelling savour to God. Thus Moses suffered cheerfully. 'Moses, when he was come to years, chose rather to suffer affliction with the people of God than to enjoy the pleasures of sin for a season' (Hebrews 11:24, 25). Observe: 'When he was come to years': It was no childish act. It was not in his nonage, but when he was of years of discretion. 'He chose to suffer affliction': Suffering was not so much his task as his choice. The cross was not so much imposed as embraced. This is to suffer as Christians, when we are volunteers; we take up the cross cheerfully, nay, joyfully. 'They departed from the presence of the council rejoicing that they were counted worthy to suffer shame for his name' (Acts 5:41). Or as it is more emphatic in the original, 'They rejoiced that they were so far graced as to be disgraced for the name of Christ.' Tertullian says of the primitive Christians, that they took more comfort in their sufferings than in their deliverance. And indeed well may a Christian be joyful in suffering because it is a great favour when God honours a man to be a witness to the truth. Christ's marks in Saint Paul's body were prints of glory. The saints have worn their sufferings as ornaments. Ignatius' chains were his jewels. Never have any princes been so famous for their victories as the martyrs for their sufferings.

We suger as Christians when we suffer and *pray*. 'Pray for them which despitefully use you' (Luke 6:28).

There are two reasons why we should pray for our persecutors.

Because our prayers may be a means to convert them. Stephen prayed for his persecutors: 'Lord, lay not this sin to their charge' (Acts 7:60). And this prayer was effectual to some of their conversions. Augustine says that the church of God was beholden to Stephen's prayer for all that benefit which was reaped by Paul's ministry.

We should pray for our persecutors because they do us good, though against their will. They shall increase our reward. Every reproach shall add to our glory. Every injury shall serve to make our crown heavier. As Gregory Nazianzen speaks in one of his orations, Every stone which was thrown at Stephen was a precious stone which enriched him and made him shine brighter in the kingdom of heaven. Thus have I shown what that suffering is which makes us blessed, and shall wear the crown of martyrdom.

Lessons to be learned from persecution

1 It shows us what the nature of Christianity is, namely, sanctity joined with suffering. A true saint carries Christ in his heart and the cross on his shoulders. 'All that will live godly in Christ Jesus shall suffer persecution' (2 Timothy 3:12). Christ and his cross are never parted. It is too much for a Christian to have two heavens, one here and another hereafter. Christ's kingdom on earth is the kingdom of the cross. What is the meaning of the shield of faith, the helmet of hope, the breast-plate of patience, but to imply that we must encounter sufferings? It is one of the titles given to the church, 'afflicted' (Isaiah 54:11). Persecution is the legacy bequeathed by Christ to his people. 'In the world ye shall have tribulation' (John 16:33). Christ's spouse is a lily among thorns. Christ's sheep must expect to lose their golden fleece. This the flesh does not like to hear of. Therefore Christ calls persecution 'the cross' (Matthew 16:24). It is cross to flesh and blood; we are all for reigning. 'When wilt thou restore the kingdom again to Israel?' (Acts 1:6). But the apostle tells of suffering before reigning. 'If we suffer, we shall also reign with him' (2 Timothy 2:12). How loath is corrupt flesh to put its neck under Christ's yoke, or stretch itself upon the cross! But religion gives no charter of exemption from suffering. To have two heavens is more than Christ had. Was the head crowned with thorns and do we think to be crowned with roses? 'Think it not strange concerning the fiery trial' (1 Peter 4:12). If we are God's gold, it is not strange to be cast into the fire. Some there are that picture Erasmus half in heaven and half out. Methinks it represents a Christian in this life. In regard of his

inward consolation he is half in heaven. In regard of his outward persecution he is half in hell.

2 See hence that persecutions are not signs of God's anger or fruits of the curse, for 'blessed are they that are persecuted'. If they are blessed who die in the Lord, are they not blessed who die for the Lord? We are very apt to judge them hated and forsaken of God who are in a suffering condition. 'If thou be the Son of God, come down from the cross' (Matthew 27:40).The Jews made a question of it. They could hardly believe Christ was the Son of God when he hung upon the cross. Would God let him be reproached and forsaken if he were the Son of God? When the barbarians saw the viper on Paul's hand, they thought he was a great sinner. 'No doubt this man is a murderer' (Acts 28:4). So when we see the people of God afflicted and the viper of persecution fastens upon them, we are apt to say, These are greater sinners than others, and God does not love them. This is for want of judgment. 'Blessed are they who are persecuted.' Persecutions are pledges of God's love, badges of honour (Hebrews 12:7). In the sharpest trial there is the sweetest comfort. God's fanning his wheat is but to make it purer.

Two sharp reproofs

1 It reproves such as would be thought good Christians but will not suffer persecution for Christ's sake. Their care is not to take up the cross, but to avoid the cross. 'When persecution arises because of the word, by and by he is offended' (Matthew 13:21). There are many professors who speak Christ fair, but will suffer nothing for him. These may be compared to the crystal which looks like pearl till it comes to the hammering, then it breaks. Many, when they see the palm-branches and garments spread, cry 'Hosanna' to Christ, but if the swords and staves appear, then they slink away. Beza[1] urged King Henry the Fourth (of France), then of Navarre, to engage himself in the Protestant religion, but he told him he would not launch out too far into the deep, so that, if a storm should arise, he might retreat back to the shore. It is to be feared there are some among us, who, if persecutions should come, would rather make Demas his choice than Moses his choice, and would study rather to keep their skin whole than their conscience pure. Erasmus highly extolled Luther's doctrine, but when the Emperor threatened all that should favour Luther's cause, he unworthily deserted it. Hypocrites will sooner renounce their baptism than take up

[1] Successor of John Calvin at Geneva (d. 1605).

the cross. If ever we should show ourselves Christians to purpose, we must with Peter throw ourselves upon the water to come to Christ. He that refuses to suffer, let him read over that sad scripture, 'Whosoever shall deny me before men, him will I also deny before my Father which is in heaven' (Matthew 10:33).

2 It reproves them who are the opposers and persecutors of the saints. How great is their sin! They resist the Holy Ghost. 'Ye do always resist the Holy Ghost; which of the prophets have not your fathers persecuted?' (Acts 7:51, 52). Persecutors offer affront to Christ in heaven. They tread his jewels in the dust, touch the apple of his eye, pierce his sides. 'Saul, Saul, why persecutest thou me?' (Acts 9:4). When the foot was trodden on, the head cried out. As the sin is great, so the punishment shall be proportionable. 'They have shed the blood of saints and prophets, and thou hast given them blood to drink, for they are worthy' (Revelation 16:6). Will not Christ avenge those who die in this quarrel? What is the end of persecutors? Diocletian [1] proclaimed that the Christian churches and temples should be razed down, their Bibles burned. He would not permit any man that was a Christian to hold an office. Some of the Christians he cast alive into boiling lead. Others had their hands and lips cut off; only they had their eyes left that they might behold the tragedy of their own miseries. What was the end of this man? He ran mad and poisoned himself. Felix, captain to Emperor Charles the Fifth,[2] being at supper at Augsburg, vowed he would ride up to the spurs in the blood of the Lutherans. A flux of blood came up that night into his throat wherewith he was choked. It were easy to tell how God's hand has so visibly gone out against persecutors that they might read their sin in their punishment.

Christians should possess themselves beforehand with thoughts of sufferings
1 Let it exhort Christians to think beforehand and make account of sufferings. This reckoning beforehand can do us no hurt; it may do us much good.

(i) The fore-thoughts of suffering will make a Christian very serious. The heart is apt to be feathery and frothy. The thoughts of suffering persecution would consolidate it. Why am I thus light? Is this a posture fit for persecution? Christians grow serious in the casting up their spiritual accounts. They reckon what religion must cost them and may cost

---

[1] Roman Emperor, A.D. 284–305. He instigated the last Great Persecution of the Christian Church in 303.   [2] 'Holy Roman Emperor', 1519–55.

them. It must cost them the blood of their sins. It may cost them the blood of their lives.

(ii) The fore-thoughts of persecution will be as sauce to season our delights, that we do not surfeit upon them. How soon may there be an alarum sounded? How soon may the clouds drop blood? The thoughts of this would take off the heart from the immoderate love of the creature. Our Saviour at a great feast breaks out into mention of his death. 'She hath prepared this against my burial' (Mark 14:8). So the fore-thoughts of a change would be an excellent antidote against a surfeit.

(iii) The fore-thoughts of sufferings would make them lighter when they come. The suddenness of an evil adds to the sadness. This was ill news to the fool in the gospel (who reckoned without his host). 'This night shall thy soul be required of thee' (Luke 12:20). This will be an aggravation of Babylon's miseries: 'Her plagues shall come in one day' (Revelation 18:8). Not that antichrist shall be destroyed in a day, but ('in a day') that is, suddenly. The blow shall come unawares, when he does not think of it. The reckoning beforehand of suffering alleviates and shakes off the edge of it when it comes. Therefore Christ, to lighten the cross, still fore-warns his disciples of sufferings that they might not come unlooked for (John 16.33; Acts 1:7).

(iv) Fore-thoughts of persecution would put us in mind of getting our armour ready. It is dangerous as well as imprudent to have all to seek when the trial comes, as if a soldier should have his weapons to get when the enemy is in the field. Caesar, seeing a soldier whetting his sword when he was just going to fight, cashiered him. He that reckons upon persecution will be in a ready posture for it. He will have the shield of faith and the sword of the Spirit ready, that he may not be surprised unawares.

Let us prepare for persecution. A wise pilot in a calm will prepare for a storm. God knows how soon persecution may come. There seems to be a cloud of blood hanging over the nation.

Christians must arm themselves for suffering

How shall we prepare for sufferings? Do three things.

1 Be persons rightly qualified for suffering.
2 Avoid those things which will hinder suffering.
3 Promote all helps to suffering.

Labour to get rightly qualified for suffering

1 Labour to be persons rightly qualified for suffering. Be righteous persons. That man who would suffer 'for righteousness' sake' must himself be righteous. I mean evangelically righteous. In particular I call him righteous:

(i) who breathes after sanctity (Psalm 119:5). Though sin cleaves to his heart yet his heart does not cleave to sin. Though sin has an alliance, yet no allowance. 'What I do I allow not!' (Romans 7:15). A good man hates the sin to which Satan most tempts and his heart most inclines (Psalm 119:128).

(ii) A righteous person is one who makes God's grace his centre. The glory of God is more worth than the salvation of all men's souls. He who is divinely qualified is so zealously ambitious of God's glory that he does not care what he loses, so God may be a gainer. He prefers the glory of God before credit, estate, relations. It was the speech of Kiliaz,[1] that blessed martyr, 'Had I all the gold in the world to dispose of, I would give it to live with my relations (though in prison), yet Jesus Christ is dearer to me than all.'

(iii) A righteous person is one who values the jewel of a good conscience at an high rate. Good conscience is a saint's festival, his music, his paradise, and he will rather hazard anything than violate his conscience. They say of the Irish, if they have a good scimitar, a warlike weapon, they had rather take a blow on their arm than their scimitar should be hurt. To this I may compare a good conscience. A good man had rather sustain hurt in his body or estate than his conscience should be hurt. He had rather die than violate the virginity of his conscience. Such a man as this is evangelically righteous, and if God call him to it he is fit to suffer.

Avoid things which will hinder suffering

2 Avoid those things which will hinder suffering.

(i) The love of the world. God allows us the use of the world (1 Timothy 6:7, 8). But take heed of the love of it. He that is in love with the world will be out of love with the cross. 'Demas hath forsaken me, having loved this present world' (2 Timothy 4:10). He not only forsook Paul's company but his doctrine. The love of the world chokes our

[1] The reference seems to be to Kilian (or Kyllena), an Irishman of the 7th century who, with twelve companions, preached the Word in Thuringia (Central Germany). They were 'rewarded with the crown of martyrdom'.

zeal. A man wedded to the world will for thirty pieces of silver betray Christ and a good cause. Let the world be as a loose garment that you may throw off at pleasure. Before a man can die for Christ he must be dead to the world. Paul was crucified to the world (Galatians 6:14). It will be an easy thing to die when we are dead before in our affections.

(ii) Carnal fear. There is a two-fold fear:

A *filial* fear, when a man fears to displease God. When he fears he should not hold out, this is a good fear. 'Blessed is he that feareth always.' If Peter had feared his own heart better, and said, 'Lord Jesus, I fear I shall forsake thee; Lord strengthen me'; doubtless Christ would have kept him from falling.

There is a *cowardly* fear, when a man fears danger more than sin, when he is afraid to be good; this fear is an enemy to suffering. God proclaimed that those who were fearful should not go to the wars (Deuteronomy 20:8). The fearful are unfit to fight in Christ's wars. A man possessed with fear does not consult what is best, but what is safest. If he may save his estate, he will snare his conscience. 'In the fear of man there is a snare' (Proverbs 29:25). Fear made Peter deny Christ, Abraham equivocate, David fain himself to be mad. Fear will put men upon indirect courses, making them study rather compliance than conscience. Fear makes sin appear little and suffering great. The fearful man sees double. He looks upon the cross through his perspective twice as big as it is. Fear argues sordidness of spirit. It will put one upon things most ignoble and unworthy. A fearful man will vote against his conscience. Fear enfeebles. It is like the cutting off Samson's locks. Fear melts away the courage. 'Their hearts melt because of you' (Joshua 2:9). And when a man's strength is gone he is very unfit to carry Christ's cross. Fear is the root of apostasy. Spira's[1] fear made him abjure and recant his religion. Fear hurts one more than the adversary. It is not so much an enemy without the castle as a traitor within endangers it. It is not so much sufferings without as traitorous fear within which undoes a man. A fearful man is versed in no posture so much as in retreating. Oh take heed of this! Be afraid of this fear. 'Fear not them that can kill the body' (Luke 12:4). Persecutors can but kill the body which must shortly die. The fearful are set in the forefront of them that shall go to hell (Revelation 21:8). Let us get the fear of God into our hearts. As one wedge drives out another, so the fear of God will drive out all other base fear.

[1] See p. 293 fn. 1.

(iii) Take heed of a facile spirit. A facile-spirited man will be turned any way with a word. He will be wrought as wax. He is so tame that you may lead him whither you will. 'With fair speeches they deceive the hearts of the simple' (Romans 16 : 18). A facile Christian is malleable to anything. He is like wool that will take any dye. He is a weak reed that will be blown any way with the breath of men. One day you may persuade him to engage in a good cause, the next day to desert it. He is not made of oak but of willow. He will bend every way. Oh take heed of a facile spirit! It is not ingenuity but folly to suffer one's self to be abused. A good Christian is like Mount Sion that cannot be moved (Psalm 125 : 1). He is like Fabricius [1] of whom it was said, a man might as well alter the course of the sun as turn him aside from doing justice. A good Christian must be firm to his resolution. If he be not a fixed, he will be a falling star.

(iv) Take heed of listening to the voice of the flesh. St Paul 'conferred not with flesh and blood' (Galatians 1 : 16). The flesh will give bad counsel. First King Saul consulted with the flesh and afterwards he consulted with the devil. He sends to the witch of Endor. Oh, says the flesh, the cross of Christ is heavy! There is a nail in the yoke which will tear, and fetch blood. Be as a deaf adder stopping your ears to the charmings of the flesh.

Promote those things which will help you to suffer

3 Promote those things which will help to suffer.

(i) Inure yourselves to suffering. 'As a good soldier of Christ endure hardship' (2 Timothy 2 : 3). Jacob made the stone his pillow (Genesis 28 : 18). 'It is good for a man that he bear the yoke in his youth' (Lamentations 3 : 27). The bearing of a lighter cross will fit for the bearing of an heavier. Learn to bear a reproach with patience and then you will be fitter to bear an iron chain. Saint Paul died daily. He began with lesser sufferings and so by degrees learned to be a martyr. As it is in sin, a wicked man learns to be expert in sin by degrees. First he commits a lesser sin, then a greater, then he arrives at custom in sin, then he grows impudent in sin, then he glories in sin (Philippians 3 : 19); so it is in suffering. First a Christian takes up the chips of the cross, a disgrace, a prison, and then he carries the cross itself.

Alas how far are they from suffering who indulge the flesh : '. . . that lie upon beds of ivory and stretch themselves upon their couches' (Amos

[1] A Roman consul and general, noted for his incorruptibility (3rd century B.C.)

6:4); a very unfit posture for suffering. That soldier is like to make but poor work of it who is stretching himself upon his bed when he should be in the field exercising his arms. What shall I say, says Jerome, to those Christians who make it all their care to perfume their clothes, to crisp their hair, to sparkle their diamonds, but if sufferings come, and the way to heaven has any water in it, they will not endure to set their feet upon it! Most people are too effeminate. They use themselves too nicely and tenderly. Those 'silken Christians' (as Tertullian calls them) that pamper the flesh, are unfit for the school of the cross. The naked breast and bare shoulder is too soft and tender to carry Christ's cross. Inure yourselves to hardship. Do not make your pillow too easy.

(ii) Be well skilled in the knowledge of Christ. A man can never die for him he does not know. 'For which cause I suffer those things; for I know whom I have believed' (2 Timothy 1:12). Blind men are always fearful. A blind Christian will be fearful of the cross. Enrich yourselves with knowledge. Know Christ in his virtues, offices, privileges. See the preciousness in Christ. 'To you that believe he is precious' (1 Peter 2:7). His name is precious; it is as ointment poured forth. His blood is precious; it is as balm poured forth. His love is precious; it is as wine poured forth. Jesus Christ is made up of all sweets and delights. He himself is all that is desirable. He is light to the eye, honey to the taste, joy to the heart. Get but the knowledge of Christ and you will part with all for him. You will embrace him though it be in the fire. An ignorant man can never be a martyr. He may set up an altar, but he will never die for an unknown God.

(iii) Prize every truth of God. The filings of gold are precious. The least ray of truth is glorious. 'Buy the truth and sell it not' (Proverbs 23:23). Truth is the object of faith (2 Thessalonians 2:13), the seed of regeneration (James 1:18), the spring of joy (1 Corinthians 13:6). Truth crowns us with salvation (1 Timothy 2:4). If ever you would suffer for the truth, prize it above all things. He that does not prize truth above life will never lay down his life for the truth. The blessed martyrs sealed to the truth with their blood. There are two things God counts most dear to him, his glory and his truth. 'I will', says Bishop Jewel [1], 'deny my bishopric; I will deny my name and credit, but the truths of Christ I cannot deny.'

(iv) Keep a good conscience. If there be any sin allowed in the soul, it

[1] Bishop of Salisbury 1560–71; he is famous as the author of the 'Apology for the Church of England'.

will unfit for suffering. A man that has a bile[1] upon his shoulders cannot carry a heavy burden. Guilt of conscience is like a bile. He that has this can never carry the cross of Christ. If a ship be sound and well-rigged, it will sail upon the water, but if it be full of holes and leaks, it will sink in the water. If conscience be full of guilt (which is like a leak in the ship), it will not sail in the bloody waters of persecution. An house will not stand in a storm, the pillars of it being rotten. If a man's heart be rotten, he will never stand in a storm of tribulation. How can a guilty person suffer when for ought he knows he is like to go from the fire at the stake to hell-fire! Let conscience be pure. 'Holding the mystery of the faith in a pure conscience' (1 Timothy 3:9). A good conscience will abide the fiery trial. This made the martyrs' flames beds of roses. Good conscience is a wall of brass. With the Leviathan, 'it laughs at the shaking of a spear' (Job 41:29). Let one be in prison, good conscience is a bird that can sing in this cage. Augustine calls it 'the paradise of a good conscience'.

(v) Make the Scripture familiar to you (Psalm 119:50). The Scripture well digested by meditation will fit for suffering. The Scripture is a Christian's palladium, his magazine and fort-royal. It may be compared to the 'tower of David on which there hang a thousand bucklers' (Canticles 4:4). From these breasts of Scripture divine strength flows into the soul. 'Let the word of Christ dwell in you richly' (Colossians 3:16). Jerome speaks of one who by frequent studying the Scripture made his breast 'the library of Christ'. The blessed Scripture as it is an honeycomb for comfort, so an armoury for strength. First, the martyrs' 'hearts did burn within them' (Luke 24:32) by reading the Scripture, and then their bodies were fit to burn. The Scripture arms a Christian both against temptation and persecution.

Against *temptation*: Christ himself, when he was tempted by the devil ran to Scripture for armour: 'It is written.' Three times he wounds the old serpent with his sword. Jerome says of Saint Paul, he could never have gone through so many temptations but for his Scripture-armour. Christians, are you tempted? Go to Scripture; gather a stone hence to fling in the face of a Goliath-temptation. Are you tempted to pride? Read that scripture, 'God resisteth the proud' (1 Peter 5:5). Are you tempted to lust? Read James 1:15, 'When lust hath conceived, it bringeth forth sin; and sin when it is finished, bringeth forth death.'

Against *persecution*: When the flesh draws back the Scripture will recruit us. It will put armour upon us and courage into us. 'Fear none

[1] Boil, tumour.

of those things which thou shalt suffer. Behold the devil shall cast some of you into prison that you may be tried and you shall have tribulation ten days. Be thou faithful unto death and I will give thee a crown of life' (Revelation 2:10). O, says the Christian, I am not afraid to suffer. 'Fear none of those things thou shalt suffer.' But why should I suffer? I love God and is not this sufficient? Nay, but God will try your love. It is 'that ye may be tried'. God's gold is best tried in the furnace. But this persecution is so long! No, it is but for 'ten days'. It may be lasting but not everlasting. What are ten days put in balance with eternity? But what am I the better if I suffer? What comes of it? 'I will (says God) give thee a crown of life.' Though your body be martyred your soul shall be crowned. But I shall faint when trials come! 'My grace shall be sufficient' (2 Corinthians 12:9). The weak Christian has omnipotency to underprop him.

(vi) Get a suffering frame of heart.

What is that? you say. I answer: A self-denying frame. 'If any man will come after me let him deny himself and take up his cross' (Matthew 16:24). Self-denial is the foundation of godliness, and if this be not well-laid, the whole building will fall. If there be any lust in our souls which we cannot deny, it will turn at length either to scandal or apostasy. Self-denial is the thread which must run along through the whole work of religion. The self-denying Christian will be the suffering Christian. 'Let him deny himself and take up his cross.'

For the further explication of this, I shall do two things.

1 Show what is meant by this word *deny*.

2 What is meant by *self*.

1 What is meant by *deny*? The word 'to deny' signifies to lay aside, to put off, to annihilate oneself. Beza renders it 'let him renounce himself'.

2 What is meant by *self*? Self is taken four ways:

Worldly self,
Relative self,
Natural self,
Carnal self.

A man must deny *worldly self*, that is, his estate. 'Behold we have forsaken all and followed thee' (Matthew 19:27). The gold of Ophir must be denied for the pearl of price. Let their money perish with them (said that noble Marquess of Vico) who esteem all the gold and silver in the world worth one hour's communion with Christ.

A man must deny *relative self*, that is, his dearest relations, if God calls. If our nearest alliance, father or mother, stand in our way and would hinder us from doing our duty, we must either leap over them or tread upon them. 'If any man come to me and hate not father and mother and wife and children, etc., he cannot be my disciple' (Luke 14 : 26). Relations must not weigh heavier than Christ.

A man must deny *natural self*. He must be willing to become a sacrifice and make Christ's crown flourish, though it be in his ashes. 'They loved not their lives unto the death' (Luke 14 : 26); (Revelation 12 : 11). Jesus Christ was dearer to them than their own heart's blood.

A man must deny *self self*. This I take to be the chief sense of the text. He must deny carnal ease. The flesh cries out for ease. It is loath to put its neck under Christ's yoke or stretch itself upon the cross. The flesh cries out, 'There is a lion in the way' (Proverbs 22 : 13). We must deny our self-ease. They that lean on the soft pillow of sloth will hardly take up the cross. 'Thou as a good soldier of Christ endure hardness' (2 Timothy 2 : 3). We must force a way to heaven through sweat and blood. Caesar's soldiers fought with hunger and cold.

A man must deny self-opinion. Every man by nature has an high opinion of himself. He is drunk with spiritual pride, and a proud man is unfit for suffering. He thinks himself too good to suffer. What (says he) I that am of such a noble descent, such high parts, such repute and credit in the world, shall I suffer? A proud man disdains the cross. Oh deny self-opinion! How did Christ come to suffer? 'He humbled himself and became obedient unto death' (Philippians 2 : 8). Let the plumes of pride fall.

A man must deny self-confidence. Peter's confidence undid him. 'Though all men shall be offended because of thee, yet will I never be offended; though I should die with thee, yet will I not deny thee' (Matthew 26 : 33, 35). How did this man presume upon his own strength, as if he had more grace than all the apostles besides! His denying Christ was for want of denying himself. Oh deny your own strength! Samson's strength was in his locks. A Christian's strength lies in Christ. He who trusts to himself shall be left to himself. He who goes out in his own strength comes off to his own shame.

A man must deny self-wisdom. We read of the 'wisdom of the flesh' (2 Corinthians 1 : 12). Self-wisdom is carnal policy. It is wisdom (says the flesh) to keep out of suffering. It is wisdom not to declare against sin. It is wisdom to find out subtle distinctions to avoid the cross. The wisdom of the flesh is to save the flesh. Indeed there is a Christian prudence to be used. The serpent's eye must be in the dove's head. Wisdom and innocency do well, but it is dangerous to separate them. Cursed be that policy which teaches to avoid duty. This wisdom is not from above but is devilish (James 3:15). It is learned from the old serpent. This wisdom will turn to folly at last. It is like a man who to save his gold throws himself overboard into the water. So the politician to save his skin will damn his soul.

A man must deny self-will. Saint Gregory calls the will the commander-in-chief of all the faculties of the soul. Indeed, in innocency, Adam had rectitude of mind and conformity of will. The will was like an instrument in tune. It was full of harmony and tuned sweetly to God's will, but now the will is corrupt and like a strong tide carries us violently to evil. The will has not only an indisposition to good, but an opposition. 'Ye have always resisted the Holy Ghost' (Acts 7:51. There is not a greater enemy than the will. It is up in arms against God (2 Peter 2:10). The will loves sin and hates the cross. Now if ever we suffer for God we must cross our own will. The will must be martyred. A Christian must say, Not my will but thy will be done.

A man must deny self-reasonings. The fleshy part will be reasoning and disputing against sufferings. 'Why reason you these things in your hearts?' (Mark 2:8). Such reasonings as these will begin to arise in our hearts:

1 Persecution is bitter.

Oh but it is blessed! 'Blessed is he that endureth temptation . . .' (James 1:12). The cross is heavy, but the sharper the cross, the brighter the crown.

2 But it is sad to part with estate and relations.

But Christ is better than all. He is manna to strengthen; he is wine to comfort; he is salvation to crown.

3 But liberty is sweet.

This restraint makes way for enlargement. 'Thou hast enlarged me in distress' (Psalm 4:1). When the feet are bound with irons, the heart may be sweetly dilated and enlarged.

Thus should we put to silence those self-reasonings which are apt to arise in the heart against sufferings.

This self-denying frame of heart is very hard. This is 'to pluck out the right eye'. One says, a man has not so much to do in overcoming men and devils as in overcoming himself. 'Stronger is he who conquers himself than he who conquers the strongest walled city.' Self is the idol, and how hard it is to sacrifice this idol and to turn self-seeking into self-denial! But though it be difficult it is essential to suffering. A Christian must first lay down self before he can take up the cross.

Alas! how far are they then from suffering that cannot deny themselves in the least things; who in their diet or apparel, instead of martyring the flesh, pamper the flesh! Instead of taking up the cross take up their cups! Is this self-denial, to let loose the reins to the flesh? It is sure that they who cannot deny themselves, if sufferings come, will deny Christ. Oh Christians, as ever you would be able to carry Christ's cross, begin to deny yourselves. Consider:

Whatever you deny for Christ, you shall find again in Christ. 'Every one that hath forsaken houses or brethren or sisters or father or mother or wife or children or lands for my name's sake shall receive an hundredfold, and shall inherit everlasting life' (Matthew 19:29). Here is a very saving bargain. Is it not gain enough to have ten in the hundred, nay above an hundred for one?

It is but equity that you should deny yourselves for Christ. Did not Jesus Christ deny himself for you? He denied his joy; he left his Father's house; he denied his honour; he endured the shame (Hebrews 12:2); he denied his life; he poured out his blood as a sacrifice upon the altar of the cross (Colossians 1:20). Did Christ deny himself for you, and will not you deny yourselves for him?

Self-denial is the highest sign of a thorough-paced Christian. Hypocrites may have great knowledge and make large profession, but it is only the true-hearted saint that can deny himself for Christ. I have read of an holy man who was once tempted by Satan, to whom Satan said, Why do you take all these pains? You watch and fast and abstain from sin. O man, what do you more than I? Are you no drunkard, no adulterer? No more am I. Do you watch? Let me tell you, I never slept. Do you fast? I never eat. What do you more than I? Why, says the good man, I will tell thee, Satan; I pray; I serve the Lord; nay, more than all, I deny myself. Nay, then, says Satan, you go beyond me for I exalt myself. And so he vanished. Self-denial is the best touchstone of sincerity. By this you go beyond hypocrites.

To deny yourselves is but what others have done before you. Moses was a self-denier. He denied the honours and profits of the court (Hebrews 11:24–26). Abraham denied his own country at God's call (Hebrews 11:8). Marcus Arethusus[1] who lived in the time of Julian

[1]Marcus, a 4th-century Bishop of Arethusa (Syria). His sufferings are narrated in Foxe's Book of Martyrs, Vol. I, 287 (8-vol. edition pub. by R.T.S.).

the Emperor endured great torments for religion. If he would but have given an half-penny towards the rebuilding of the idol's temple, he might have been released, but he would not do it, though the giving of an half-penny might have saved his life. Here was a self-denying saint.

There is a time shortly coming, that if you do not deny the world for Christ, the world will deny you. The world now denies satisfaction, and ere long it will deny house-room. It will not suffer you so much as to breathe in it. It will turn you out of possession; and, which is worse, not only the world will deny you, but Christ will deny you. 'Whosoever shall deny me before men, him will I also deny before my Father which is heaven' (Matthew 10:33).

Get suffering graces: faith, love, patience

(vii) Get suffering graces; these three in particular:
Faith; Love; Patience.

1 *Suffering grace is faith.* 'Above all, taking the shield of faith' (Ephesians 6:16). The pretence of faith is one thing, the use of faith another. The hypocrite makes faith a cloak, the martyr makes it a shield. A shield is useful in time of danger; it defends the head; it guards the vitals. Such a shield is faith. Faith is a furnace grace. 'Though it be tried with fire, it is found unto praise and honour' (1 Peter 1:7). Faith, like Hercules' club, beats down all oppositions. By faith we resist the devil (1 Peter 5:9). By faith we resist unto blood (Hebrews 11:34). Faith is a victorious grace. The believer will make Christ's crown flourish, though it be in his own ashes. An unbeliever is like Reuben: 'Unstable as water he shall not excel' (Genesis 49:4). A believer is like Joseph, who, though the archers shot at him, 'his bow abode in strength.' Cast a believer upon the waters of affliction, he can follow Christ upon the water, and not sink. Cast him into the fire, his zeal burns hotter than the flame. Cast him into prison, he is enlarged in spirit. Paul and Silas had their prison songs. 'Thou shalt tread upon the lion and adder' (Psalm 91:13). A Christian, armed with faith as a coat of mail, can tread upon those persecutions which are fierce as the lion and sting as the adder. Get faith.

But how comes faith to be such armour of proof? I answer,
Six manner of ways.

(1) Faith unites the soul to Christ, and that blessed Head sends forth spirits into the members. 'I can do all things through Christ . . .' (Philippians 4:13). Faith is a grace that lives all upon the borrow. As when
[282]

we want water, we go to the well and fetch it; when we want gold, we go to the mine; so faith goes to Christ and fetches his strength into the soul, whereby it is enabled both to do and suffer. Hence it is that faith is such a wonder-working grace.

(2) Faith works in the heart a contempt of the world. Faith gives a true map of the world (Ecclesiastes 2 : 11). Faith shows the world in its night-dress, having all its jewels pulled off. Faith makes the world appear in an eclipse. The believer sees more eclipses than the astronomer. Faith shows the soul better things than the world. It gives a sight of Christ and glory. It gives a prospect of heaven. As the mariner in a dark night climbs up to the top of the mast and cries out, 'I see a star', so faith climbs up above sense and reason into heaven and sees Christ, that bright and morning star; and the soul, having once viewed his super-lative excellencies, becomes crucified to the world. Oh, says the Christian, shall not I suffer the loss of all these things that I may enjoy Jesus Christ!

(3) Faith gets strength from the promise. Faith lives in a promise. Take the fish out of the water and it dies. Take faith out of a promise and it cannot live. The promises are breasts of consolation. The child by suck-ing the breast gets strength; so does faith by sucking the breast of a promise. When a garrison is besieged and is ready almost to yield to the enemy, auxiliary forces are sent in to relieve it. So when faith begins to be weak and is ready to faint in the day of battle, then the promises muster their forces together, and all come in for faith's relief and now it is able to hold out in the fiery trial.

(4) Faith gives the soul a right notion of suffering. Faith draws the true picture of sufferings. What is suffering? Faith says, it is but the suffer-ing of the body, that body which must shortly by the course of nature drop into the dust. Persecution can but take away my life. An ague or fever may do as much. Now faith giving the soul a right notion of sufferings and taking (as it were) a just measure of them, enables a Christian to prostrate his life at the feet of Christ.

(5) Faith reconciles providences and promises. As it was on St Paul's voyage, providence seemed to be against him. There was a crosswind arose called Euroclydon (Acts 27 : 14), but God had given him a promise that he would save his life, and the lives of all that sailed with him in the ship (verse 24). Therefore when the wind blew never so contrary, Paul believed it would at last blow him to the haven. So when sense says, Here is a cross providence, sufferings come, I shall be undone, then

faith says 'all things shall work for good to them that love God' (Romans 8:28). This providence, though bloody, shall fulfil the promise. Affliction shall work for my good. It shall heal my corruption and save my soul. Thus faith, making the wind and tide go together, the wind of a providence with the tide of the promise, enables a Christian to suffer persecution.

(6) Faith picks sweetness out of the cross. Faith shows the soul God reconciled and sin pardoned; and then how sweet is every suffering! The bee gathers the sweetest honey from the bitterest herb. 'A bitter medicine often gives strength to the weary.' So faith from the sharpest trials gathers the sweetest comforts. Faith looks upon suffering as God's love-token. Afflictions (says Nazianzen[1]) are sharp arrows, but they are shot from the hand of a loving Father. Faith can taste honey at the end of the rod. Faith fetches joy out of suffering (John 16:20). Faith gets an honey-comb in the belly of the lion; it finds a jewel under the cross; and thus you see how faith comes to be such armour of proof. 'Above all, taking the shield of faith.' A believer having cast his anchor in heaven cannot sink in the waters of persecution.

2 *Suffering grace is love.* Get hearts fired with love to the Lord Jesus. Love is a grace both active and passive.

(1) Love is active. It lays a law of constraint upon the soul; 'The love of Christ constrains us' (2 Corinthians 5:14). Love is the wing of the soul that sets it flying and the weight of the soul that sets it going. Love never thinks it can do enough for Christ. As he who loves the world never thinks he can take enough pains for it, love is never weary. It is not tired unless with its own slowness.

(2) Love is passive; it enables to suffer. A man that loves his friend will suffer anything for him rather than he shall be wronged. The Curtii[2] laid down their lives for the Romans because they loved them. Love made our dear Lord suffer for us. As the pelican out of her love to her young ones, when they are bitten with serpents, feeds them with her own blood to recover them again, so when we had been bitten by the old serpent, that Christ might recover us he fed us with his own blood. Jacob's love to Rachel made him almost hazard his life for her. 'Many

[1] Gregory of Nazianzus (see p. 159 fn. 1).
[2] According to Roman tradition a young knight named M. Curtius, in obedience to an oracle, leapt armed and on horseback into a chasm which had opened in the Forum at Rome, and thereby saved his country. Watson is in error in speaking of more than one such person.

waters cannot quench love' (Canticles 8:7). No, not the waters of persecution. 'Love is strong as death' (Canticles 8:6). Death makes its way
through the greatest oppositions. So love will make its way to Christ
through the prison and the furnace.

But all pretend love to Christ. How shall we know that we have
such a love to him as will make us suffer? I answer: True love is *a
love of friendship*, which is genuine and ingenuous when we love
Christ for himself. There is a mercenary and meretricious [1] love, when
we love divine objects for something else. A man may love the queen
of truth for the jewel at her ear, because she brings preferment. A man
may love Christ for his 'head of gold' (Canticles 5:11), because he
enriches with glory. But true love is when we love Christ for his love-
liness, namely, that infinite and superlative beauty which shines in him,
as Augustine says, 'We love Jesus on account of Jesus'; that is, as a
man loves sweet wine for itself.

True love is *a love of desire*, when we desire to be united to Christ
as the fountain of happiness. Love desires union. The soul that loves
Christ is ambitious of death because this dissolution tends to union.
Death slips one knot and ties another.

True love is *a love of benevolence*, when so far as we are able we
endeavour to lift up Christ's name in the world. As the wise men
brought him 'gold and frankincense' (Matthew 2:11), so we bring him
our tribute of service and are willing that he should rise though it be
by our fall. In short, that love which is kindled from heaven makes us
give Christ the pre-eminence of our affection. 'I would cause thee to
drink of spiced wine of the juice of my pomegranate' (Canticles 8:2).
If the spouse has a cup which is more juicy and spiced Christ shall
drink off that. Indeed we can never love Christ too much. We may
love gold in the excess, but not Christ. The angels do not love Christ
to his worth. Now when love is boiled up to this height, it will enable
us to suffer. 'Love is strong as death.' The martyrs first burned in love,
and then in fire.

3 The third suffering grace is patience. Patience is a grace made and
cut out for suffering. Patience is a sweet submission to the will of God,
whereby we are content to bear anything that he is pleased to lay upon
us. Patience makes a Christian invincible. It is like the anvil that bears
all strokes. We cannot be men without patience. Passion unmans a
man. It puts him beside the use of reason. We cannot be martyrs without patience. Patience makes us endure (James 5:10). We read of a

[1] Befitting a harlot.

beast 'like unto a leopard and his feet were as the feet of a bear and the dragon gave him his power . . .' (Revelation 13:2). This beast is to be understood of the antichristian power. Antichrist may be compared to a leopard for subtlety and fierceness, and on his head was the name of blaspheming (verse 1), which agrees with that description of the man of sin, 'He sitteth in the temple of God showing himself that he is God' (2 Thessalonians 2:4); and the 'dragon gave him power' (verse 2), that is the devil, and 'it was given to him to make war with the saints' (Revelation 13:7). Well, how come the saints to bear the heat of this fiery trial? (verse 10): 'Here is the patience of the saints.' Patience overcomes by suffering. A Christian without patience is like a soldier without arms. Faith keeps the heart up from sinking. Patience keeps the heart down from murmuring. Patience is not provoked by injuries. It is sensible but not peevish. Patience looks to the end of sufferings. This is the motto: 'God will guarantee the end also.' As the watchman waits for the dawning of the morning, so the patient Christian suffers and waits till the day of glory begins to dawn upon him. Faith says, God will come, and patience says, I will stay his leisure. These are those suffering graces which are a Christian's armour of proof.

Treasure up suffering promises

(viii) Treasure up suffering promises. The promises are faith's bladders to keep it from sinking. They are the breast-milk a Christian lives on in time of sufferings. They are honey at the end of the rod. Hoard up the promises.

God has made promises of *direction* that he will give us a spirit of wisdom in that hour, teaching us what to say. 'I will give you a mouth and wisdom which all your adversaries shall not be able to gainsay nor resist' (Luke 21:15). You shall not need study. God will put an answer into your mouth. This many of God's sufferers can set their seal to. The Lord has on a sudden darted such words into their mouths as their enemies could easier censure than contradict.

God has made promises of *protection*. 'No man shall set on thee to hurt thee' (Acts 18:10). How safe was Paul when he had omnipotency itself to screen off danger! And 'there shall not an hair of your head perish' (Luke 21:18). Persecutors are lions, but chained lions.

God has made promises of his *special presence* with his saints in suffering. 'I will be with him in trouble' (Psalm 91:15). If we have such a friend to visit us in prison, we shall do well enough. Though we change our place we shall not change our keeper. 'I will be with him.' God will hold our head and heart when we are fainting! What if we have more afflictions than others, if we have more of God's company! God's honour is dear to him. It would not be for his honour to bring his children into sufferings and leave them there. He will be with them to animate and support them, yea, when new troubles arise; 'He shall deliver thee in six troubles' (Job 5 : 19).

The Lord has made promises of *deliverance*. 'I will deliver him and honour him' (Psalm 91 : 15). God will open a back door for his people to escape out of sufferings. 'He will with the temptation make a way to escape' (1 Corinthians 10 : 13). Thus he did to Peter (Acts 12 : 7–10). Peter's prayers had opened heaven, and God's angel opens the prison. God can either prevent a snare or break it. 'To God the Lord belong the issues from death' (Psalm 68 : 20). He who can strengthen our faith can break our fetters. The Lord sometimes makes enemies the instruments of breaking those snares which themselves have laid (Esther 8 : 8).

In the case of martyrdom God has made promises of *consolation*. 'Your sorrow shall be turned into joy' (John 16 : 20). There is the water turned into wine. 'Be of good cheer, Paul' (Acts 23 : 11). In time of persecution God broaches the wine of consolation. Cordials are kept for fainting. Philip the Landgrave of Hesse,[1] professed that he himself experienced the divine consolations of the martyrs. Stephen 'saw the heavens opened' (Acts 7 : 56). Glover,[2] that blessed martyr, cried out at the stake in an holy rapture, 'He is come, He is come', meaning the Comforter.

Promises of *compensation*. God will abundantly recompense all our sufferings, 'in this life an hundredfold' and in the world to come 'life everlasting' (Matthew 19 : 29). Augustine calls this the best and greatest usury. Our losses for Christ are gainful. 'He that loseth his life for my sake shall find it' (Matthew 10 : 39).

Keep in view examples of suffering

(ix) Set before your eyes suffering examples. Look upon others as patterns to imitate. 'Take my brethren the prophets for an example of suffering affliction' (James 5 : 10). Examples have more influence upon us than precepts. The one instruct, the other animate. As they show elephants the blood of grapes and mulberries to make them fight the bet-

---

[1] One of the most prominent of German Lutheran princes in the Reformation period. He was imprisoned by the Emperor Charles V from 1547 to 1552.
[2] Robert Glover, burned at Coventry, September, 1555 (Foxe's Book of Martyrs, Vol. VII, pp. 384–99).

ter, so the Holy Ghost shows us the blood of saints and martyrs to infuse a spirit of zeal and courage into us. Micaiah was in the prison; Jeremiah in the dungeon; Isaiah was sawn asunder. The primitive Christians, though their flesh boiled, roasted, dismembered, yet like the adamant they remained invincible. Such was their zeal and patience in suffering that their persecutors stood amazed and were more weary in tormenting than they were in enduring. When John Huss[1] was brought to be burned, they put upon his head a triple crown of paper printed with red devils, which when he saw, says he, 'My Lord Jesus Christ wore a crown of thorns for me, why then shall I not wear this crown, how ignominious soever?' Polycarp,[2] Bishop of Smyrna, when he came before the proconsul was bidden to deny Christ and swear by the Emperor; he replied: 'I have served Christ these eighty-six years and he has not once hurt me, and shall I deny him now?' Saunders[3] that blessed martyr, said, 'Welcome the cross of Christ; my Saviour began to me[4] in a bitter cup and shall not I pledge him? You Baynham, you papist that look for miracles, I feel no more pain in the fire than if I were in a bed of down.[5] Another of the martyrs said, 'The ringing of my chain has been sweet music in my ears. O what a comforter (says he) is a good conscience!' Another martyr, kissing the stake, said, 'I shall not lose my life but change it for a better. Instead of coals I shall have pearls!' Another, when the chain was fastening to him, said, 'Blessed be God for this wedding girdle!' These suffering examples we should lay up. God is still the same God. He has as much love in his heart to pity us and as much strength in his arm to help us. Let us think with ourselves what courage the very heathens have shown in their sufferings. Julius Caesar was a man of an heroic spirit. When he was foretold of a conspiracy against him in the senate-house, he answered he had rather die than fear. Mutius Scaevola[6] having his hand held over the fire till the flesh fried and his sinews began to shrink, yet he bore it with an un-

[1] Reformer of Bohemia: martyred at Constance, 1415.
[2] Burned to death about A.D. 155 (see p. 186 fn. 3).
[3] Laurence Saunders, burned at Coventry, February, 1555.
[4] A long-disused idiom meaning 'pledged himself to'.
[5] The reference is to James Bainham of Gloucestershire and London who was burned at Smithfield, April 1532. The record in Foxe's Book of Martyrs reads: '"O ye papists, behold, ye look for miracles, and here now ye may see a miracle; for in this fire I feel no more pain than if I were in a bed of down; but it is to me as sweet as a bed of roses." These words spake he in the midst of the flaming fire when his legs and arms were half consumed.' (IV, p. 705).
[6] A Roman tortured by the Tuscan king Porsenna at the time of the war in which (Macaulay's) Horatius played a conspicuous part.

daunted spirit. Quintus Curtius[1] reports of Lysimachus,[2] a brave captain, that being adjudged to be cast naked to a lion, when the lion came roaring upon him, Lysimachus wrapped his shirt about his arm and thrust it into the lion's mouth and taking hold of his tongue killed the lion. Did nature infuse such a spirit of courage and gallantry into heathens! How should grace much more into Christians! Let us be of St Paul's mind: 'Not counting my life dear, so that I might finish my course with joy' (Acts 20 : 24).

Nine considerations

(x) Let us lay in suffering considerations. A wise Christian is considerative.

Consider whom we suffer for. It is for Christ, and we cannot suffer for a better friend. There is many a man will suffer shame and death for his lusts. He will suffer disgrace for a drunken lust. He will suffer death for a revengeful lust. Shall others die for their lusts and shall not we die for Christ? Will a man suffer for that lust which damns him, and shall not we suffer for that Christ which saves us? Oh remember we espouse God's own quarrel and he will not suffer us to be losers. If no man shall 'kindle a fire on God's altar for nought' (Malachi 1 : 10), then surely no man shall sacrifice himself for God in the fire for nought.

It is a great honour to suffer persecution. Ambrose, speaking in the encomium of his sister said, 'I will say this of her, she was a martyr.' It is a great honour to be singled out to bear witness to the truth. 'They departed from the council rejoicing that they were counted worthy to suffer shame for his name' (Acts 5 : 41). It is a title that has been given to kings, 'Defender of the faith.' A martyr is in a special manner, a 'defender of the faith'. Kings are defenders of the faith by their swords, martyrs by their blood. Gregory Nazianzen calls Athanasius[3] the bulwark of truth.' It is a credit to appear for God. Martyrs are not only Christ's followers, but his ensign-bearers. The Romans had their Camilli and Fabricii,[4] brave warriors which graced the field. God calls out none but his champions to fight his battles. We read that Abraham called forth his trained soldiers (Genesis 14 : 14), such as were more expert and valiant. What an honour is it to be one of Christ's trained

---

[1] A Roman historian of the 1st century A.D.
[2] One of the generals of Alexander the Great. Having offended his king, he was thrown into a lion's den. His courage and skill in killing the lion caused Alexander to pardon him and to esteem him highly.
[3] Bishop of Alexandria (d. 373) and the chief opponent of the Arian heresy.
[4] Families which specially distinguished themselves for military prowess.

band! The disciples dreamed of a temporal reign (Acts 1:6). Christ tells them (verse 8), 'Ye shall be witnesses unto me in Jerusalem . . .' To bear witness by their sufferings to the truth of Christ's divinity and passion was a greater honour to the disciples than to have had a temporal reign upon earth. A bloody cross is more honourable than a purple robe. Persecution is called the 'fiery trial' (1 Peter 4:12). God has two fires, one where he puts his gold, and another where he puts his dross. The fire where he puts his dross is hell-fire. The fire where he puts his gold is the fire of persecution. God honours his gold when he puts it into the fire. 'A spirit of glory rests upon you' (1 Peter 1:7; 1 Peter 4:14). Persecution, as it is a badge of our Order, so an ensign of our glory. What greater honour can be put upon a mortal man than to stand up in the cause of God? And not only to die in the Lord but to die for the Lord? Ignatius called his fetters his spiritual pearls. St Paul gloried more in his iron chain than if it had been a gold chain (Acts 28:20).

Consider what Jesus Christ endured for us. Calvin says that Christ's whole life was a series of sufferings. Christian, what is your suffering? Are you poor? So was Christ. 'Foxes have holes and the birds of the air have nests, but the Son of Man hath not where to lay his head' (Matthew 8:20). Are you surrounded with enemies? So was Christ. 'Against thy holy child Jesus whom thou hast anointed, both Herod and Pontius Pilate with the Gentiles . . . were gathered together' (Acts 4:27). Do our enemies lay claim to religion? So did his. 'The chief priests took the silver pieces and said, It is not lawful to put them into the treasury because it is the price of blood' (Matthew 27:6). Godly persecutors! Are you reproached? So was Christ. 'They bowed the knee before him, and mocked him, saying, Hail, King of the Jews' (Matthew 27:29). Are you slandered? So was Christ. 'He casteth out devils through the prince of devils' (Matthew 9:34). Are you ignominiously used? So was Christ. 'Some began to spit upon him' (Mark 14:65). Are you betrayed by friends? So was Christ. 'Judas, betrayest thou the Son of Man with a kiss?' (Luke 22:48). Is your estate sequestered? And do the wicked cast lots for it? So Christ was dealt with. 'They parted his garments, casting lots' (Matthew 27:35). Do we suffer unjustly? So did Christ. His very judge acquitted him. 'Then said Pilate to the chief priests and to the people, I find no fault in this man' (Luke 23:4). Are you barbarously dragged and haled away to suffering? So was Christ. 'When they had bound him (though he came to loose them) they led him away' (Matthew 27:2). Do you suffer death? So did Christ. 'When they were come to Calvary, there they crucified him' (Luke 23:33). They gave him gall and vinegar to drink, the one deciphering the bitterness, the other the sharpness of his death. Christ underwent not only the blood of the cross but the curse of the cross (Galatians 3:13). He had an agony in his soul. 'My soul is exceeding sorrowful unto death' (Matthew 26:38). The soul of Christ was overcast with a cloud of God's displeasure. The Greek Church speaking of the sufferings of Christ, calls them 'unknown sufferings'. Did the Lord Jesus endure all this for us, and shall not we suffer persecution for his name? Say, as holy Ignatius, 'I am willing to die for Christ, for Christ my love was crucified.' Our cup is nothing to the cup which Christ drank. His cup was mixed with the wrath of God, and if he bore God's wrath for us, well may we bear man's wrath of him.

Great is the honour we bring to Christ and the gospel by suffering. It was an honour to Caesar that he had such soldiers as were able to fight with hunger and cold and endure hardship in their marches. It is an honour to Christ that he has such listed under him as will leave all for him. It proclaims him to be a good Master when his servants will wear his livery though it be sullied with disgrace and lined with blood. Paul's iron chain made the gospel wear a golden chain. Tertullian says of the saints in his time that they took their sufferings more kindly than if they had had deliverance. Oh, what a glory was this to the truth, when they durst embrace it in the flame! And as the saints' sufferings adorn the gospel, so they propagate it. Basil says, the zeal and constancy of the martyrs in the primitive times made some of the heathens to be Christianized. 'The Church is founded in blood and by blood it increases.' The showers of blood have ever made the church fruitful. Paul's being bound made the truth more enlarged (Philippians 1:13). The gospel has always flourished in the ashes of martyrs.

Consider who it is that we have engaged ourselves to in baptism. There we took our press-money. We solemnly vowed that we would be true to Christ's interest and fight it out under his banner to the death. And how often have we in the blessed supper taken the oath of allegiance to Jesus Christ that we would be his liege-servants and that death should not part us! Now if when being called to it, we refuse to suffer persecution for his name, Christ will bring our baptism as an indictment against us. Christ is called 'the Captain of our salvation' (Hebrews 2:10). We have listed ourselves by name under this Captain. Now if, for fear, we shall fly from our colours, it is perjury in the highest degree, and how shall we be able to look Christ in the face another day? That oath which is not kept inviolably shall be punished infallibly. Where does the 'flying roll' of curses light, but in the house of him that 'sweareth falsely' (Zechariah 5:4)?

Our sufferings are light. This 'light affliction . . .' (2 Corinthians 4:17)! It is heavy to flesh and blood, but it is light to faith. Affliction is light in a three-fold respect:

1 It is light in comparison of sin. He that feels sin heavy feels suffering light. Sin made Paul cry out, 'O wretched man that I am!' (Romans 7:24). He does not cry out of his iron chain but of his sin. The greater noise drowns the lesser. When the sea roars the rivers are silent. He that is taken up about his sins, and sees how he has provoked God, thinks the yoke of affliction light (Micah 7:9).

2 Affliction is light in comparison of hell. What is persecution to damnation? What is the fire of martyrdom to the fire of the damned? It is no more than the pricking of a pin to a death's wound. 'Who knoweth the power of thine anger' (Psalm 90:11)? Christ himself could not have borne that anger had he not been more than a man.

3 Affliction is light in comparison of glory. The weight of glory makes persecution light. If, says Chrysostom,[1] the torments of all the men in the world could be laid upon one man, it were not worth one hour's being in heaven. And if persecution be light we should in a manner set light by it. Let us neither faint through unbelief, nor fret through impatience.

Our sufferings are short: 'After ye have suffered awhile' (1 Peter 5:10); or as it is in the Greek, 'a little'. Our sufferings may be lasting, not everlasting. Affliction is compared to a 'cup' (Lamentations 4:21). The wicked drink of a sea of wrath which has no bottom. It will never be emptied. But it is only a cup of martyrdom, and God will say, 'Let this cup pass away.' 'The rod of the wicked shall not rest upon the lot of the righteous' (Psalm 125:3). The rod may be there, it shall not rest. Christ calls his sufferings 'an hour' (Luke 22:53). Can we not suffer one hour? Persecution is sharp, but short. Though it has a sting to torment, yet it has a wing to fly. 'Sorrow shall fly away' (Isaiah 35:10). It is but awhile when the saints shall have a writ of ease granted them. They shall weep no more, suffer no more. They shall be taken off the torturing wrack and laid in Christ's bosom. The people of God shall not always be in the iron furnace; a year of Jubilee will come. The water of persecution like a land-flood will soon be dried up.

While we suffer for Christ we suffer with Christ: 'If we suffer with him . . .' (Romans 8:17). Jesus Christ bears part of the suffering with us. Oh, says the Christian, I shall never be able to hold out. But remember you suffer with Christ. He helps you to suffer. As our blest Saviour said : 'I am not alone; the Father is with me' (John 16 : 32); so a believer may say, 'I am not alone, my Christ is with me.' He bears the heaviest end of the cross. 'My grace is sufficient for thee' (2 Corinthians 12 : 9). 'Underneath are the everlasting arms' (Deuteronomy 33 : 27). If Christ put the yoke of persecution over us, he will put his arms under us. The Lord Jesus will not only crown us when we conquer, but he will enable us to conquer. When the dragon fights against the godly, Christ is that Michael which stands up for them and helps them to overcome (Daniel 12 : 1).

He that refuses to suffer persecution shall never be free from suffering:

Internal sufferings. He that will not suffer for conscience shall suffer in conscience. Thus Francis Spira,[1] after he had for fear abjured that doctrine which once he professed, was in great terror of mind and became a very anatomy.[2] He professed he felt the very pains of the damned in his soul. He who was afraid of the stake was set upon the wrack of conscience.

External sufferings : Pendleton[3] refused to suffer for Christ; not long after, his house was on fire and he was burned in it. He who would not burn for Christ was afterwards made to burn for his sins.

Eternal sufferings : 'Suffering the vengeance of eternal fire' (Jude 7).

These present sufferings cannot hinder a man from being blessed. 'Blessed are they that are persecuted . . .' We think, 'Blessed are they that are rich; nay, but Blessed are they that are persecuted. 'Blessed is the man that endures temptation . . .' (James 1 : 12). 'If ye suffer for righteousness' sake, happy are ye' (1 Peter 3 : 14).

Persecution cannot hinder us from being blessed, I shall prove this by four demonstrations :

They are blessed who have God for their God. 'Happy is that people whose God is the Lord' (Psalm 144 : 15). But persecution cannot hinder us from having God for our God. 'Our God is able to deliver us' (Daniel

---

[1] A lawyer of great repute in Italy in the mid-16th century. He professed gospel principles, but afterwards relapsed into Romanism and became a victim of black despair. Readers of John Bunyan's writings will have noted how much their author was impressed by the narrative entitled 'The Fearful Estate of Francis Spira.' See Grace Abounding, Section 163. The man in the iron cage, at the Interpreter's House (Pilgrim's Progress) probably represents Spira.

[2] Emaciated creature.

[3] Dr. Henry Pendleton, a zealous Protestant under Edward VI and a zealous Romanist under Mary.

3:17). Though persecuted, yet they could say, 'our God'. Therefore persecution cannot hinder us from being blessed.

They are blessed whom God loves, but persecution cannot hinder the love of God. 'Who shall separate us from the love of Christ? Shall persecution?' (Romans 8:35). The goldsmith loves his gold as well when it is in the fire as when it is in his bag. God loves his children as well in adversity, as in prosperity. 'As many as I love I rebuke' (Revelation 3:19). God visits his children in prison. 'Be of good cheer, Paul' (Acts 23:11). God sweetens their sufferings. 'As the sufferings of Christ abound in us, so our consolation also aboundeth' (2 Corinthians 1:5). As the mother, having given her child a bitter pill, gives it afterwards a lump of sugar; persecution is a bitter pill but God gives the comforts of his Spirit to sweeten it. If persecution cannot hinder God's love, then it cannot hinder us from being blessed.

They are blessed for whom Christ prays; but such as are persecuted have Christ praying for them. 'Keep through thine own name those whom thou hast given me' (John 17:11); which prayer, though made for all believers, yet especially for his apostles which he foretold should be martyrs (John 16:2). Now if persecution cannot hinder Christ's prayer for us, then it cannot impede or obstruct our blessedness.

They are blessed that have sin purged out; but persecution purges out sin (Isaiah 27:9; Hebrews 12:11). Persecution is a corrosive to eat out the proud flesh. It is a fan to winnow us, a fire to refine us. Persecution is the physic God applies to his children to carry away their ill humours. That surely which purges out sin cannot hinder blessedness.

(xi) *The great suffering consideration is the glorious reward which follows sufferings:* 'Theirs is the kingdom of heaven.' The hope of reward, says Saint Basil, is very powerful and moving. Moses had an eye at the 'recompence of reward' (Hebrews 11:26), yea, Christ himself (Hebrews 12:2). Many have done great things for hope of a temporal reward. Camillus [1] when his country was oppressed by the Gauls, ventured his life for his country, to purchase fame and honour. If men will hazard their lives for a little temporal honour, what should we do for the reward of glory? A merchant, says Chrysostom, does not mind a few storms at sea, but he thinks of the emolument and gain when the ship comes fraught home. So a Christian should not be over-solicitous about his present sufferings, but think of the rich reward when he shall arrive at the heavenly port. 'Great is your reward in heaven' (verse 12).

[1] Appointed as dictator (4th century B.C.) in order to drive the Gauls from Rome (cf. p. 289 fn. 4).

The cross is a golden ladder by which we climb up to heaven. A Christian may lose his life, but not his reward. He may lose his head, but not his crown. If he that gives 'a cup of cold water' shall not lose his reward, then much less he that gives a draught of warm blood. The rewards of glory may sweeten all the waters of Marah. It should be a spur to martyrdom.

Not that we can merit this reward by our sufferings. 'I will give thee a crown of life' (Revelation 2:10). The reward is the legacy which free grace bequeathes. Alas, what proportion is there between a drop of blood and a weight of glory? Christ himself, as he was man only (setting aside his Godhead), did not merit by his sufferings, for Christ, as he was man only, was a creature. Now a creature cannot merit from the Creator. Christ's sufferings, as he was man only, were finite, therefore could not merit infinite glory. Indeed, as he was God, his sufferings were meritorious; but consider him purely as man, they were not. This I urge against the Papists. If Christ's sufferings, as he was man only (though as man he was above the angels), could not merit, then what man upon earth, what prophet or martyr is able to merit anything by his sufferings?

But though we have no reward 'ex merito', by merit, we shall have it 'ex gratia', by grace. So it is in the text, 'Great is your reward in heaven.' The thoughts of this reward should animate Christians. Look upon the crown, and faint if you can. The reward is as far above your thoughts as it is beyond your deserts. A man that is to wade through a deep water, fixes his eyes upon the firm land before him. While Christians are wading through the deep waters of persecution they should fix the eyes of their faith on the land of promise. 'Great is your reward in heaven.' They that bear the cross patiently shall wear the crown triumphantly.

Christ's suffering saints shall have greater degrees in glory (Matthew 19:28). God has his highest seats, yea, his thrones for his martyrs. It is true, he that has the least degree of glory, a door-keeper in heaven, will have enough; but as Joseph gave to Benjamin a double mess above the rest of his brethren, so God will give to his sufferers a double portion of glory. Some orbs in heaven are higher, some stars brighter. God's martyrs shall shine brighter in the heavenly horizon.

Oh, often look upon 'the recompence of the reward'. Not all the silks of Persia, the spices of Arabia, the gold of Ophir, can be compared to this glorious reward. How should the thoughts of this whet and steel us with courage in our sufferings! When they threatened Basil with banishment, he comforted himself with this, that he should be either under heaven or in heaven. It was the hope of this reward which so animated those primitive martyrs, who, when there was incense put into their hands and there was no more required of them for the saving of their lives but to sprinkle a little of that incense upon the altar in honour of the idol, they would rather die than do it. This glorious reward in heaven is called a reigning with Christ. 'If we suffer, we shall also reign with him': first martyrs, then kings. Julian [1] honoured all those who were slain in his battles. So does the Lord Jesus. After the saints' crucifixion, follows their coronation. 'They shall reign.' The wicked first reign and then suffer. The godly first suffer and then reign. The saints shall have a happy reign. It shall be both peaceable and durable. Who would not swim through blood to this crown? Who would not suffer joyfully? Christ says, 'Be exceeding glad' (verse 12). The Greek word signifies 'to leap for joy'. Christians should have their spirits elevated and exhilarated when they contemplate the weight of glory.

If you would be able to suffer, pray much. Beg of God to clothe you with a spirit of zeal and magnanimity. 'To you it is given in the behalf of Christ, not only to believe on him, but also to suffer for his sake' (Philippians 1:29). It is a gift of God to be able to suffer. Pray for this gift. Do not think you can be able of yourselves to lay down life and liberty for Christ. Peter was over-confident of himself. 'I will lay down my life for thy sake' (John 13:37). But Peter's strength undid him. Peter had habitual grace, but he lacked auxiliary grace. Christians need fresh gales from heaven. Pray for the Spirit to animate you in your sufferings. As the fire hardens the potter's vessel which is at first weak and limber,[2] so the fire of the Spirit hardens men against sufferings. Pray that God will make you like the anvil that you may bear the strokes of persecutors with invincible patience.

[1] Julian the Apostate (Roman Emperor). See p. 155, fn. 2.
[2] Flexible.

22 *An appendix to the beatitudes*

His commandments are not grievous
I JOHN 5 : 3

You have seen what Christ calls for – poverty of spirit, pureness of heart, meekness, mercifulness, cheerfulness in suffering persecution, etc. Now that none may hesitate or be troubled at these commands of Christ, I thought good (as a closure to the former discourse) to take off the surmises and prejudices in men's spirits by this sweet, mollifying Scripture, 'His commandments are not grievous.'

The Lord's commandments are not grievous

The censuring world objects against religion that it is difficult and irksome. 'Behold what a weariness is it!' (Malachi 1:13). Therefore the Lord, that he may invite and encourage us to obedience, draws religion in its fair colours and represents it to us as beautiful and pleasant, in these words: 'His commandments are not grievous.' This may well be called a sweetening ingredient put into religion and may serve to take off that asperity and harshness which the carnal world would put upon the ways of God.

For the clearing of the terms, let us consider:

1. What is meant here by commandments?

By this word, commandments, I understand gospel-precepts; faith, repentance, self-denial etc.

2. What is meant by 'not grievous?'

The Greek word signifies they are not tedious or heavy to be borne. There is a meiosis [1] in the words. 'His commands are not grievous', that is, they are easy, sweet, excellent.

Hence observe that none of God's commandments are grievous, when he calls us to be meek, merciful, pure in heart. These commandments

[1] The stressing of a quality by the denial of its contrary. It is more commonly known as 'litotes' and is frequent in the Acts of the Apostles.

are not grievous. 'My burden is light' (Matthew 11:30). The Greek word there for 'burden,' signifies properly 'the ballast of a ship' which glides through the waves as swiftly and easily as if the ship had no weight or pressure in it. Christ's commandments are like the ballast of a ship, useful, but not troublesome. All his precepts are sweet and facile, therefore called 'pleasantness' (Proverbs 3:17).

To illustrate and amplify this, consider two things:

1. Why Christ lays commands upon his people.
2. That these commands are not grievous.

1 Why Christ lays commands upon his people. There are two reasons.

(i) In regard of Christ, it is suitable to his dignity and state. He is Lord paramount. This name is written on his thigh and vesture, 'King of kings' (Revelation 19:16). And shall not a king appoint laws to his subjects? It is one of the regal rights, the flowers of the crown, to enact laws and statutes. What is a king without his laws? And shall not Christ (by whom 'kings reign', Proverbs 8:15) put forth his royal edicts by which the world shall be governed?

(ii) In regard of the saints, it is well for the people of God that they have laws to bind and check the exorbitancies of their unruly hearts. How far would the vine spread its luxuriant branches were it not pruned and tied? The heart would be ready to run wild in sin if it did not have affliction to prune it and the laws of Christ to bind it. The precepts of Christ are called 'a yoke' (Matthew 11:30). The yoke is useful. It keeps the oxen in from straggling and running out. So the precepts of Christ as a yoke keep the godly from straggling into sin. Whither should we not run, into what damnable opinions and practices, did not Christ's laws lay a check and restraint upon us? Blessed be God for precepts! That is a blessed yoke which yokes our corruptions. We should run to hell were it not for this yoke. The laws of Christ are a spiritual hedge which keeps the people of God within the pastures of ordinances. Some that have broken this hedge and have straggled are now in the devil's pound. Thus we see what need the saints have of the royal law.

2 The second thing I am to demonstrate is that Christ's commands are not grievous. I confess they are grievous to the unregenerate man. To mourn for sin, to be pure in heart, to suffer persecution for righteousness' sake, is a hard word, grievous to flesh and blood. Therefore Christ's commands are compared to bands and cords, because carnal men look upon them so. God's commands restrain men from their excess and bind them to their good behaviour. Therefore, they hate these

bonds and instead of breaking off sin, say, 'Let us break their bands asunder and cast away their cords from us' (Psalm 2 : 3). A carnal man is like an untamed heifer which will not endure the yoke, but kicks and flings, or like a 'wild bull in a net' (Isaiah 51 : 20). Thus to a person in the state of nature Christ's commands are grievous.

Nay, to a child of God, so far as corruption prevails (for he is but in part regenerate), Christ's laws seem irksome. The flesh cries out that it cannot pray or suffer. 'The law in the members' rebels against Christ's law. Only the spiritual part prevails and makes the flesh stoop to Christ's injunctions. A regenerate person, so far as he is regenerate, does not count God's commandments grievous. They are not a burden, but a delight.

Eight particulars showing that God's commands are not grievous

Divine commands are not grievous if we consider them first positively in these eight particulars :

(1) A Christian consents to God's commands, therefore they are not grievous. 'I consent to the law that it is good' (Romans 7 : 16). What is done with consent is easy. If the virgin gives her consent, the match goes on cheerfully. A godly man in his judgment approves of Christ's laws, and in his will consents to them. Therefore they are not grievous. A wicked man is under a force; terror of conscience hales him to duty. He is like a slave that is chained to the galley. He must work whether he will or no. He is forced to pull the rope, tug at the oar. But a godly man is like a free subject that consents to his prince's laws and obeys out of choice as seeing the equity and rationality of them. Thus a gracious heart sees a beauty and equity in the commands of heaven that draws forth consent, and this consent makes them that they are not grievous.

(2) They are *Christ*'s commands, therefore not grievous. 'Take my yoke' (Matthew 11 : 29). Gospel commands are not the laws of a tyrant, but of a Saviour. The husband's commands are not grievous to the wife. It is her ambition to obey. This is enough to animate and excite obedience, *Christ*'s commands. As Peter said in another sense, 'Lord if it be thou, bid me come unto thee upon the water' (Matthew 14 : 28), so says a gracious soul; 'Lord, if it be thou that wouldest have me mourn for sin and breathe after heart purity; if it be thou (dear Saviour) that biddest me do these things, I will cheerfully obey. Thy commandments are not grievous.' A soldier at the word of his general makes a brave onset.

(3) Christians obey out of a principle of love, and then God's commandments are not grievous. Therefore in Scripture serving and loving of God are put together. 'The sons of the strangers that join themselves to the Lord, to serve him and to love the name of the Lord ...' (Isaiah 56:6). Nothing is grievous to him that loves. Love lightens a burden; it adds wings to obedience. An heart that loves God counts nothing tedious but its own dullness and slowness of motion. Love makes sin heavy and Christ's burden light.

(4) A Christian is carried on by the help of the Spirit, and the Spirit makes every duty easy. 'The Spirit helpeth our infirmities' (Romans 8:26). The Spirit works in us 'both to will and to do' (Philippians 2:13). When God enables us to do what he commands then 'his commandments are not grievous'. If two carry a burden it is easy. The Spirit of God helps us to do duties, to bear burdens. He draws as it were in the yoke with us. If the scrivener[1] guides the child's hand and helps it to frame its letter, now it is not hard for the child to write. If the loadstone draw the iron, it is not hard for the iron to move. If the Spirit of God as a divine loadstone draw and move the heart, now it is not hard to obey. When the bird has wings given it, it can fly. Though the soul of itself be unable to do that which is good, yet having two wings given it (like that woman in the Revelation, Revelation 12:14), the wing of faith and the wing of the Spirit, now it flies swiftly in obedience. 'The Spirit lifted me up' (Ezekiel 11:1). The heart is heavenly in prayer when the Spirit lifts it up. The sails of a mill cannot move of themselves, but when the wind blows then they turn round. When a gale of the Spirit blows upon the soul, now the sails of the affections move swiftly in duty.

(5) All Christ's commands are beneficial, not grievous. 'And now, O Israel, what doth the Lord thy God require of thee, but to fear the Lord thy God, to love him, to keep his statutes which I command thee this day for thy good' (Deuteronomy 10:12, 13). Christ's commands carry meat in the mouth of them, and then surely they are not grievous. Salvation runs along in every precept. To obey Christ's laws is not so much of duty as our privilege. All Christ's commands centre in blessedness. Physic is in itself very unpleasant, yet because it tends to health no man refuses it. Divine precepts are to the fleshy part irksome, yet, having such excellent operation as to make us both holy and happy, they are not to be accounted grievous. The apprentice is content to go through hard service, because it makes way for his freedom. The scholar will-

[1] Writer (skilled).

ingly wrestles with the knotty difficulties of arts and sciences because they serve both to ennoble and advance him. How cheerfully does a believer obey those laws which reveal Christ's love! That suffering is not grievous which leads to a crown. This made Saint Paul say, 'I take pleasure in infirmities, in persecutions' (2 Corinthians 12:10).

(6) It is honourable to be under Christ's commands. Therefore they are not grievous. The precepts of Christ do not burden us but adorn us. It is an honour to be employed in Christ's service. How cheerfully did the rowers row the barge that carried Caesar! The honour makes the precept easy. A crown of gold is in itself heavy, but the honour of the crown makes it light and easy to be worn. I may say of every command of Christ, as Solomon speaks of wisdom, 'She shall give to thine head an ornament of grace: a crown of glory shall she deliver to thee' (Proverbs 4:9). It is honourable working at court. The honour of Christ's yoke makes it easy and eligible.[1]

(7) Christ's commands are sweetened with joy and then they are not grievous. Cicero[2] questions whether that can properly be called a burden which is carried with joy and pleasure? When the wheels of a chariot are oiled they run swiftly. When God pours in the oil of gladness, how fast does the soul run in the ways of his commandments! Joy strengthens for duty. 'The joy of the Lord is your strength' (Nehemiah 7:10); and the more strength, the less weariness. God sometimes drops down comfort and then a Christian can run in the yoke.

(8) Gospel commands are finite, therefore not grievous. Christ will not always be laying his commands upon us. Christ will shortly take off the yoke from our neck and set a crown upon our head. There is a time coming when we shall not only be free from our sins, but our duties too. Prayer and fasting are irksome to the flesh. In heaven there will be no need of prayer or repentance. Duties shall cease there. Indeed in heaven the saints shall love God, but love is no burden. God will shine forth in his beauty, and to fall in love with beauty is not grievous. In heaven the saints shall praise God, but their praising of him shall be so sweetened with delight that it will not be a duty any more, but part of their reward. It is the angels' heaven to praise God. This then makes Christ's commands not grievous; though they are spiritual, yet they are temporary; it is but a while and duties shall be

---

[1] Desirable.
[2] One of the greatest of Roman orators, philosophers and statesmen (died 43 B.C.), also known as Tully.

no more. The saints shall not so much be under commands as embraces. Wait but a while and you shall put off your armour and end your weary marches. Thus we have seen that Christ's commands considered in themselves are not grievous.

Christ's commands compared with :

Let us consider Christ's commands comparatively, and we shall see they are not grievous. Let us make a four-fold comparison. Compare Gospel commands :

1 With the severity of the moral law,
2 With the commands of sin,
3 With the torments of the damned,
4 With the glory of heaven

The law

1 Christ's commands in the gospel are not grievous compared with the severity of the moral law. The moral law was such a burden as neither we nor our fathers could bear. 'Cursed is every one that continueth not in all things which are written in the book of the law to do them'(Galatians 3 : 10). Impossible it is that any Christian should come up to the strictness of this. The golden mandates of the gospel comparatively are easy. For :

(1) In the gospel, if there be a desire to keep God's commandments, it is accepted. 'If there be first a willing mind it is accepted' (Nehemiah 1 : 11; 2 Corinthians 8 : 12). Though a man had had never so good a mind to have fulfilled the moral law, it would not have been accepted. He must 'de facto' (in actual deed) have obeyed (Galatians 3 : 12). But in the gospel God crowns the desire. If a Christian says in humility, 'Lord, I desire to obey thee, I would be more holy' (Isaiah 26 : 8), this desire springing from love passes for current.

(2) In the gospel a surety is admitted in the court. The law would not admit of a surety. It required personal obedience. But now, God so far indulges us that, what we cannot of ourselves do, we may do by a proxy. Christ is called 'a surety of a better testament' (Hebrews 7 : 22). We cannot walk so exactly. We tread awry and fall short in everything, but God looks upon us in our surety, and Christ 'having fulfilled all righteousness' (Matthew 3 : 15), it is all one as if we had fulfilled the law in our own persons.

(3) The law commanded and threatened, but gave no strength to

perform. It Egyptianized, requiring the full tale of brick, but gave no straw. But now God with his commands gives power. Gospel-precepts are sweetened with promises. God commands, 'Make you a new heart' (Ezekiel 18:31). Lord, may the soul say, I make a new heart? I can as well make a new world. But see Ezekiel 36:26, 'A new heart also will I give you.' God commands us to cleanse ourselves: 'Wash you, make you clean ' (Isaiah 1:16). Lord, where should I have power to cleanse myself? 'Who can bring a clean thing out of an unclean?' (Job 14:4). See the precept turned into a promise: 'From all your filthiness and from your idols will I cleanse you' (Ezekiel 36:25). If, when the child cannot go, the father takes it by the hand and leads it, now it is not hard for the child to go. When we cannot go, God takes us by the hand, 'I taught Ephraim also to go, taking them by their arms' (Hosea 11:3).

(4) In the gospel God winks at infirmities where the heart is right. The law called for perfect obedience. It was death to have shot but an hairbreadth short of the mark. It were sad if the same rigour should continue upon us. Woe to the holiest man that lives (says Augustine) if God comes to weigh him in the balance of his justice. It is with our best duties as with gold. Put the gold in the fire and you will see dross come out. What drossiness in our holy things! But in the gospel, though God will not endure haltings, yet he will pass by failings. Thus Christ's commands in the gospel are not grievous compared with the severity of the moral law.

The commands of sin

2 Christ's commands are not grievous compared with the commands of sin. Sin lays an heavy yoke upon men. Sin is compared to a talent of lead (Zechariah 5:7) to show the weightiness of it. The commands of sin are burdensome. Let a man be under the power and rage of any lust (whether it be covetousness or ambition), how he tires and excruciates himself! What hazards does he run, even to the endangering of his health and soul, that he may satisfy his lust! 'They weary themselves to commit iniquity' (Jeremiah 9:5). And are not Christ's precepts easy and sweet in comparison of sin's austere and inexorable commands? Therefore Chrysostom says well that virtue is easier than vice. Temperance is less burdensome than drunkenness. Doing justice is less burdensome than violence. There is more difficulty and perplexity in the contrivement (Micah 2:1) and pursuit of wicked ends than in obeying the sweet and gentle precepts of Christ. Hence it is that a wicked man is said to 'travail with iniquity' (Psalm 7:14), to show what anxious pain and trouble he has in bringing about his wickedness. What

[303]

tedious and hazardous journeys did Antiochus Epiphanes[1] take in persecuting the people of the Jews! Many have gone with more pain to hell than others have to heaven.

The torments of the damned

3 Christ's commands are not grievous compared with the grievous torments of the damned. The rich man cries out 'I am tormented in this flame' (Luke 16:24). Hell fire is so inconceivably torturing that the wicked do not know either how to bear or to avoid it. The torment of the damned may be compared to a yoke and it differs from other yokes. Usually the yoke is laid but upon the neck of the beast, but the hell-yoke is laid upon every part of the sinner. His eyes shall behold nothing but bloody tragedies. His ears shall hear the groans and shrieks of blaspheming spirits. He shall suffer in every member of his body and faculty of his soul, and this agony though violent yet perpetual. The yoke of the damned shall never be taken off. 'The footprints show no return'[2] Sinners might break the golden chain of God's commands, but they cannot break the iron chain of his punishments. It is as impossible for them to file this chain as to scale heaven.

And are not gospel-commands easy in comparison of hell-torments? What does Christ command? He bids you repent. Is it not better to weep for sin than bleed for it? Christ bids you pray in your families and closets. Is it not better praying than roaring? He bids you sanctify the Sabbath. Is it not better to keep an holy rest to the Lord than to be for ever without rest? Hell is a restless place. There is no intermission of torment for one minute of an hour. I appeal to the consciences of men. Are not Christ's commands sweet and facile in comparison of the insupportable pains of reprobates? Is not obeying better than damning? Are not the cords of love better than the chains of darkness?

The glory of heaven

4 Gospel commands are not grievous compared with the glory of heaven. What an infinite disproportion is there between service and reward! What are all the saints' labours and travails in religion compared with the crown of recompence? The weight of glory makes duty light.

Behold here an encouraging argument to religion. How may this

---

[1] King of Syria, 175–163 B.C. His title of 'Epiphanes' denotes his claim to Deity.
[2] Horace: Epistles I. i. 74–75. Watson calls to mind the reply of a wary fox to a sick lion, 'The footprints frighten me, since they all point toward your den, and none of them shows a return from it.'

make us in love with the ways of God! 'His commandments are not grievous.' Believers are not now under the thundering curses of the law, no, nor under the ceremonies of it, which were both numerous and burdensome. The ways of God are equal, his statutes eligible.[1] He bids us mourn that we may be comforted. He bids us be poor in spirit that he may settle a kingdom upon us. God is no hard Master. 'His commandments are not grievous.' O Christian, serve God out of choice (Psalm 119:3). Think of the joy, the honour, the reward of godliness. Never more grudge God your service. Whatever he prescribes, let your hearts subscribe.

Various reproofs

It reproves them that refuse to obey these sweet and gentle commands of Christ. 'Israel would none of me' (Psalm 81:11). We may cry out with Augustine that the generality of men choose rather to put their neck in the devil's yoke than to submit to the sweet and easy yoke of Christ. What should be the reason that, when God's 'commandments are not grievous', his ways pleasantness, his service perfect freedom, yet men should not vail [2] to Christ's sceptre nor stoop to his laws?

Surely the cause may be that inbred hatred which is naturally in men's hearts against Christ. Sinners are called 'God-haters' (Romans 1:30). Sin begets not only a dislike of the ways of God, but hatred; and from disaffection flows disloyalty. 'His citizens hated him and sent a message after him, saying, We will not have this man to reign over us' (Luke 19:14).

Besides this inbred hatred against Christ, the devil labours to blow the coals and increase this odium and antipathy. He raises an evil report upon religion as those spies did on Canaan. 'They brought up an evil report of the land' (Numbers 13:32). Satan is implacably malicious, and as he sometimes accuses us to God, so he accuses God to us, and says, He is an hard Master and his commandments are grievous. It is the devil's design to do as the sons of Eli, 'who made the offering of God to be abhorred' (1 Samuel 2:17). If there be any hatred and prejudice in the heart against religion, 'an enemy hath done this' (Matthew 13:28, 38). The devil raises in the hearts of men a twofold prejudice against Christ and his ways:

(1) The paucity of them that embrace religion. The way of Christ is but a pathway (Psalm 119:35), whereas the way of pleasure and vanity

---

[1] Desirable.   [2] Yield to; uncover as a token of respect.

is the roadway. Many ignorantly conclude that must needs be the best way which most go. I answer: There are but few that are saved, and will not you be saved because so few are saved? A man does not argue thus in other things: there are but few rich, therefore I will not be rich; nay, therefore, he the rather strives to be rich. Why should not we argue thus wisely about our souls? There are but few that go to heaven, therefore we will labour the more to be of the number of that few.

What a weak argument is this: there are but few that embrace religion, therefore you will not! Those things which are more excellent are more rare. There are but few pearls and diamonds; in Rome, few senators. The fewness of them that embrace religion argues the way of religion excellent. 'It is not every man than can get to Corinth.'[1]

We are warned not to sail with the multitude (Exodus 23:2). Most fish goes to the Devil's net.

(2) The ways of religion are rendered deformed and unlovely by the scandals of professors.

I answer: I acknowledge the lustre of religion has been much eclipsed and sullied by the scandals of men. This is an age of scandals. Many have made the pretence of religion a key to open the door to all ungodliness. Never was God's name more taken in vain. This is that our Saviour has foretold. 'It must needs be that offences come' (Matthew 18:7). But to take off this prejudice, consider: scandals are not from religion, but for want of religion. Religion is not the worse, though some abuse it. To dislike religion because some of the professors of it are scandalous is as if one should say, Because the servant is dishonest, therefore he will not have a good opinion of his master. Is Christ the less glorious because some that wear his livery are scandalous? Is religion the worse because some of her followers are bad? Is wine the worse because some are intemperate? Shall a woman dislike chastity because some of her neighbours are unchaste? Let us argue soberly. 'Judge not according to the appearance, but judge righteous judgment' (John 7:24).

God sometimes permits scandals to fall out in the church out of a design:

(1) As a just judgment upon hypocrites. These squint-eyed devotionists who serve God for their own ends, the Lord in justice suffers them to fall into horrid debauched practices that he may lay open their baseness to the world and that all may see they were but piebald Chris-

[1] Horace Epistles I. xvii, 36; a proverbial Latin saying of any difficult attainment.

tians, painted devils; Judas, first a sly hypocrite, afterwards a visible traitor.

(2) Scandals are for hardening of the profane. Some desperate sinners who would never give God a good word, they would not be won by religion, they shall be wounded by it. God lets scandals be to be a break-neck to men and to engulf them more in sin. Jesus Christ ('God blessed for ever') is to some a 'rock of offence' (Romans 9:33). His blood, which is to some balm, is to others poison. If the beauty of religion does not allure, the scandals of some of its followers shall precipitate men to hell.

(3) Scandals in the church are for the caution of the godly. The Lord would have his people walk tremblingly. 'Be not high-minded, but fear' (Romans 11:20). When cedars fall, let the 'bruised reed' tremble. The scandals of professors are not to discourage us but to warn us. Let us tread more warily. The scandals of others are sea-marks for the saints to avoid. And let all this serve to take off these prejudices from religion. Though Satan may endeavour by false disguises to render the gospel odious, yet there is a beauty and a glory in it. God's 'commandments are not grievous'.

Let me persuade all men cordially to embrace the ways of God. 'His commandments are not grievous.' God never burdens us but that he may unburden us of our sins. His commands are our privileges. There is joy in the way of duty (Psalm 19:11), and heaven at the end.